750 German Verbs
and Their Uses

Jan R. Zamir, Ph.D.
Rolf Neumeier, StD

New York • Chichester • Brisbane • Toronto • Singapore

Published by John Wiley & Sons, Inc.

Library of Congress Cataloging-in-Publication Data

Zamir, Jan R., 1941–
    750 German verbs and their uses / by Jan R. Zamir and Rolf Neumeier.
      p. cm.
    Includes index.
    ISBN 0-471-54026-9 (pbk. : alk. paper)
    1. German language–Verb.   2. German language–Textbooks for
foreign speakers–English.   I. Neumeier, Rolf. II. Title.
III. Title: Seven hundred fifty German verbs and their uses.
PF3271.Z27   1992
438.2'421–dc20   91-14754

Printed in the United States of America

10 9 8 7 6 5 4 3 2 1

We wish to thank Sonia Nelson Zamir
for her valuable advice
and editorial suggestions.

Preface

This book is a usage guide to German verbs and their respective prepositions and can be used at all levels of competency.

We have made several critical decisions in the format of this book that, we believe, make it uniquely valuable. First, based upon our pedagogical experience, we have varied the number of examples for each entry depending upon the level of difficulty posed by the verb to an English-speaking person. Hence, the more unusual expressions are treated more extensively. Second, the examples attempt to give as wide a range as possible for the semantic domain of each entry. Third, every attempt is made to present the examples in a structurally diversified manner so as to show various tenses. Further, at least one example of the first or second person singular pronoun has been given for each reflexive verb so that the distinction between the accusative and dative is clearly demonstrated.

In representing the verbs with their prepositions, we distinguish between two types of verbal expressions. First, the verbs and the prepositions that form phrasal verbs; these verbs are predominantly fixed to their prepositions and often their collocations represent a meaning distinct from that of the main verb. For example, in English we would have such phrasal verbs as "hold up," "hold out," "hold on," "hold back," "hold down," "hold in," "hold off," "hold with," and so on. The main emphasis of this book is on verbal phrases of this nature in German. We have represented these, together with their object(s), which are given in angled brackets after each entry.

In addition to the phrasal verbs, we have also included many common verbs that are not linguistically collocated with any fixed preposition, but which are prevalently found with certain prepositions in a specific context(s). We have represented this unbound and less rigid relationship of the verb and the preposition by having the (+ prep) convention following the verb entry. For example, in English the use of "to speak" with the prepositions "up" or "out" is bound and constitutes a phrasal verb; however, we find it rather useful for the reader to also be aware of the association of "to speak" with other commonly used prepositions as in the phrases "to speak on (the phone)" or "to speak over (the loudspeaker)," "to speak under (his breath)," "to speak in (a whisper)," etc. Thus, under the convention (+ prep) we have included adverbial and prepositional phrases that are commonly associated with the verbs. On rare occasions, we also felt obliged to include verbs in the subentries as specifically *not* taking prepositional objects (without prep). We felt that the inclusion of these instances is helpful and may help the reader avoid wrong conclusions.

In addition to the obvious use of this book as a reference guide, we would also recommend its use in essay writing or whenever writing is required.

Preface

Vorwort

Dieses Buch gibt einen Überblick über den Gebrauch deutscher Verben und der mit ihnen verbundenen Präpositionen. Es kann auf allen Ebenen der Sprachkompetenz benutzt werden.

Wir haben die Eintragungen so gestaltet, daß sie leicht zugänglich und durch ihren hohen Informationsgehalt in einzigartiger Weise wertvoll für den Nachschlagenden sind. Dabei haben wir folgende Entscheidungen getroffen: *Erstens* variiert die Anzahl der Beispiele für den Gebrauch jedes Verbs, und zwar abhängig davon, wie schwierig es uns—basierend auf unseren pädagogischen Erfahrungen—für Menschen mit Englisch als Muttersprache erscheint. So werden oft weniger häufige Ausdrücke stärker berücksichtigt. *Zweitens* versuchen wir mit den Beispielen, die semantische Bandbreite der Verben soweit wie möglich abzudecken. *Drittens* bemühen wir uns intensiv, die Verben in unterschiedlich strukturierten Sätzen zu präsentieren, so daß auch der Gebrauch der Zeiten im Zusammenhang mit diesen Verben deutlich wird. *Schließlich* haben wir besonders darauf geachtet, bei reflexiven Verben mindestens ein Beispiel in der ersten oder zweiten Person Singular anzubieten, so daß der Unterschied zwischen dativischem und akkusativischem Gebrauch durch die Beispiele einsichtig wird.

Bei der Präsentation der Verben mit ihren Präpositionen unterscheiden wir zwei Arten verbaler Ausdrücke. *Zunächst* sind da die Verben, die mit ihren Präpositionen eine feste semantische Verbindung eingehen. Die Kollokation aus Verb und Präposition hat so oft eine ganz eigene Bedeutung, die sich von der des Ausgangsverbs unterscheidet. Beispiele: sich täuschen in, sich tragen mit, trinken auf, übergehen auf.

Diese Verb/Präpositions-Kollokationen bilden den Schwerpunkt unseres Buches. Lexikographischen Gewohnheiten folgend, geben wir sie zusammen mit ihren Objekten (in spitzen Klammern direkt nach jedem Stichwort) an.

Zusätzlich zu diesen „phrasal verbs" erfaßt das Buch viele gewöhnliche Verben, die keine feste Kollokation mit einer Präposition bilden, die aber vorwiegend mit spezifischen Präpositionen in bestimmten Zusammenhängen vorkommen, z. B. teilnehmen an, telefonieren mit, träumen von. Diese weniger feste Verbindung machen wir durch die Eintragung (+ prep) nach dem Stichwort deutlich. Die Information über möglichst viele häufig mit dem Verb zusammen erscheinende Präpositionen scheint uns eine große Hilfe für den täglichen Gebrauch (innerhalb und außerhalb des Klassenzimmers).

Die Beispiele unter den mit (+ prep) gekennzeichneten Stichwörtern liefern also adverbiale und präpositionale Objekte, die häufig mit dem Verb zusammen benutzt werden.

Nur gelegentlich fühlten wir uns verpflichtet, bei den Unterstichworten auch Verwendungen der Verben zu berücksichtigen, bei denen kein präpositionales Objekt folgt. Die Kennzeichnung hier ist (without prep). Wir möchten mit der Aufnahme dieser Stichworte falsche Schlußfolgerungen aus den gegebenenen Beispielen vermeiden helfen.

Abbreviations
Used in This Book

English	Abb.	German
accusative	A	Akkusativ
biblical	Bibl	biblisch
dative	D	Dativ
et cetera	etc.	et cetera, und so weiter
something	etw	etwas
figurative	fig	figurativ, übertragen
	formal	förmlich
genitive	G	Genitiv
humorous	hum	scherzhaft
	idiom	Idiom
informal	inf	umgangssprachlich
infinitive	infin	Infinitiv
	ironic	ironisch
someone, someone's	jd, jds, jdm, jdn	jemand, jemandes
to someone, someone		jemandem, jemanden
literal	lit	wörtlich
literary	liter	literarisch
military	mil	militärisch
nominative	N	Nominativ
	or	oder
oneself	o.s.	sich
part participle	pp	Partizip Perfekt
preposition	prep	Präposition
preterite	pret	Präteritum, Imperfekt
proverb	prov	Sprichwort
	rare	selten
reflexive	s.	Reflexiv
slang	sl	Slang
somebody	sb	jemand
something	sth	etwas

Contents

abbiegen (+ prep)   to turn

- An der Kreuzung mußt du nach links (/nach rechts/nach Norden/in einen Seitenweg/von der Straße) abbiegen.
  At the intersection you must turn left (/right/north/on the side street/from the street).
- Der Bus (/Die Straße) bog nach rechts (/in den Wald/in die Berge) ab.
  The bus turned (/The street curved to the) right (/into the forest/into the mountains).

abbringen von + D ⟨jdn von etw a.⟩   to dissuade (sb) from (sth); persuade (sb) not to do (sth)

- Deine Einwände können mich nicht davon abbringen, Franz zu heiraten.
  Your objections cannot dissuade me from marrying Franz.
- Ich bin überzeugt, daß die Bekanntschaft mit diesen Jugendlichen ihn vom rechten Weg abbringen wird.
  I am convinced that the company of those adolescents will lead him astray.
- Er ließ sich nicht von seinem Ziel abbringen.
  He let nothing divert him from his goal.

s. abfinden mit + D ⟨sich mit jdm/etw a.⟩   to come to terms with (sb); to resign *or* reconcile oneself with (sth); to put up with (sth)

- Zuerst war die Schülerin von ihrer Gastfamilie enttäuscht; aber nach ein paar Monaten hat sie sich mit ihr abgefunden.
  At first the student was disappointed in her host family; but, after a few months, she came to terms with them.
- Wie soll ich mich damit abfinden, daß . . . ?
  How am I supposed to put up with the fact that . . . ?

abgeben (+ prep)   to hand *or* give in; to leave; to deposit

- Das Kind gibt seinem Freund von den Bonbons ein paar ab.
  The child is giving his friend some of his candies.
- Hast du dein Gepäck (an der Gepäckaufbewahrung) abgegeben?
  Did you check in your luggage (with the luggage attendant)?

s. abgeben mit + D ⟨**sich mit jdm/etw a.**⟩   to bother *or* concern oneself with (sb/sth)

■   Gib dich damit (/mit seinem Vorschlag) nicht ab!
Don't bother about it (/with his proposal)!

■   Ich kann mich nicht dauernd mit deinen Problemen abgeben.
I can't be bothered with your problems all the time.

■   Mit diesem Jungen will sich der Lehrer gar nicht abgeben.
The teacher doesn't want to be bothered with this boy.

(s.) abgrenzen gegen + A ⟨**etw gegen etw a.**⟩   to demarcate (sth) against (sth); to mark off (sth) against (sth)

■   Viele Tiere grenzen ihre Reviere gegeneinander ab.
Many animals mark off their territory (from one another).

■   Diese beiden Einflußbereiche (/Begriffe/Kompetenzen) lassen sich nur schwer gegeneinander abgrenzen.
It is hard to distinguish between these two influences (/concepts/jurisdictions).

■   Mit einer kleinen Bar wurde die Küche gegen das Wohnzimmer abgegrenzt.
The kitchen was separated from the living room by a small bar.

■   Die CDU bemüht sich sehr, ihre Politik gegen die der FDP abzugrenzen.
The CDU has been trying hard to delineate its political position from that of the FDP.

abgucken bei/von + D ⟨**von jdm a., bei jdm/etw a.**⟩   (*school*) to cheat *or* copy (sth) from (sb)

■   Peter hat von (*or* bei) Carola abgeguckt.
Peter copied (cheated) from Carola.

■   Der faule Schüler guckte bei der Klassenarbeit ab.
The lazy student cheated on the exam.

■   Dieses Jahr haben die Pariser die Sommermode von (*or* bei) den New Yorkern abgeguckt.
This year the Parisians have copied summer fashions from the New Yorkers.

abhängen von + D ⟨**von jdm/etw a.**⟩   to depend on (sb/sth)

■   Das hängt von Ihnen ab.
That's up to you/That depends on you.

■   Es hängt ganz davon ab, wieviel Geld sie haben.
It all depends on how much money they have.

■   Die Stimmung meiner Mutter hängt vom Wetter ab.
My mother's mood depends on the weather.

■ Der Student hängt finanziell von seinem Vater (/mir) ab.
The student depends financially on his father (/me).

■ Von diesem Krieg hatte die Zukunft unseres Landes abgehangen.
The future of our country had depended on this war.

■ Es hängt viel für mich davon ab, ob ich den Job bekomme.
It is very important for me whether I get the job (or not).

abhängig sein von + D ⟨von jdm/etw a. sein⟩   to be dependent on (sb/sth)

■ Seine Ankunftszeit ist vom Wetter (/von den Umständen) abhängig.
His arrival time depends on the weather (/circumstances).

■ Sein Sohn ist von Heroin (/Alkohol) abhängig.
His son is dependent on heroin (/alcohol).

abholen (+ prep)   to pick up; to collect

■ Hast du ihn schon am Flughafen (/vom Flughafen/an der Haltestelle) abgeholt?
Did you already pick him up at the airport (/from the airport/at the bus stop)?

■ Er holte es beim Lebensmittelgeschäft (/auf der Post) ab.
He picked it up at the grocery store (/at the post office).

■ Mein Freund will mich heute zu einem Spaziergang abholen.
My friend is going to pick me up to go for a walk today.

ableiten aus/von + D ⟨etw aus/von etw a.⟩   to be derived from (sth)

■ Das Wort „hungrig" ist von „Hunger" abgeleitet.
The word "hungrig" is derived from "Hunger."

■ Das Wort „Pyjama" leitet man vom Persischen ab.
The word "pajamas" comes from (or goes back to) Persian.

■ Diese Annahme leitet sich aus Chomskys Theorie der Sprache ab.
This assumption stems from Chomsky's theory of language.

■ Das Wort leitet sich aus dem Griechischen (/Persischen/Sanskrit/Lateinischen) ab.
The word stems from Greek (/Persian/Sanskrit/Latin).

ablenken von + D ⟨jdn von etw a.⟩   to distract (sb) from (sth); to deflect (sth) from (sb); to turn away (sth) from (sb)

■ Die laute Musik lenkte sie dauernd von der Arbeit (/vom Studium/von ihrem Ziel) ab.
The loud music constantly distracted her from her work (/studies/goal).

■ Seine Frau versuchte, den Verdacht von ihm abzulenken.
His wife attempted to deflect the suspicion from him.

■ Eine Reise (/Ein gutes Buch) lenkt von Sorgen ab.
A trip (/good book) takes one's mind off things.

ablesen aus + D ⟨etw aus etw a.⟩ to read from (sth)

■ Aus den Protesten und Demonstrationen war die Stimmung im Volke deutlich abzulesen.
The mood of the people could be clearly gauged from the protests and demonstrations.

■ Die Stimmung der Abgeordneten kann man daraus ablesen, daß....
One can tell the mood of the representatives from the fact that....

ablesen von + D ⟨etw von etw a.⟩   to read from (sth); to anticipate (sth)

■ Die Temperatur kannst du vom Thermometer ablesen.
You can read the temperature from the thermometer.

■ Er hat seiner Frau alle Wünsche von den Augen abgelesen.
He saw all his wife's wishes in her eyes.

■ Die Furcht vorm Fliegen konnte man ihm vom Gesicht (*or* von den Augen) ablesen.
One could see his fear of flying in his face (or eyes).

■ Sie las ihm von den Lippen ab.
She read his lips.

abraten von + D ⟨jdm von etw a.⟩   to warn (sb) against (sth); to advise (sb) against (sth)

■ Der Anwalt riet mir davon ab, mit ihm zu sprechen.
The attorney advised me against speaking to him.

■ Warum rätst du ihm von der langen Reise ab?
Why are you advising him against taking the long trip?

abrechnen mit + D ⟨mit jdm a.⟩ to settle up with (sb)

■ Wir sollten mit ihm über die Ausgaben abrechnen.
We ought to settle up with him about the expenditures.

■ Al Capone rechnete kaltblütig mit seinen Gegnern ab.
Al Capone settled up with his opponents in cold blood.

abschließen mit + D ⟨mit etw a.⟩   to end *or* finish (sth)

■ Er schließt mit allem (/dem Leben/der Vergangenheit) ab.
He is finishing with everything (/is ending his life/is breaking with the past).

■ Das Jahr schloß mit einem Feuerwerk (/schrecklichen Unwetter) ab.
The year ended with fireworks (/a horrible thunderstorm).

■ Wir haben das Mittagessen mit einem Espresso (/einem leckeren Nachtisch) abgeschlossen.
We ended lunch with an expresso (/a delicious dessert).

⟨**etw mit jdm abschließen**⟩   to conclude (sth) with (sb); to take out (insurance)

■ Nach dem Ende des Studiums mußt du mit einer anderen Gesellschaft eine Versicherung abschließen.
When you have finished your studies, you will have to get insurance from a different company.

s. abschließen von + D ⟨sich von etw a.⟩   to cut oneself off from (sth)

■ Du mußt dich nicht von der Außenwelt abschließen.
You must not shut yourself off from the outside world.

abschreiben von/bei + D ⟨von/bei jdm a.⟩   to copy *or* cheat from (sb)

■ Kann ich das Rezept bei (*or* von) dir abschreiben?
May I copy the recipe from you?

■ Lehrer: Du hast wieder bei (*or* von) deinem Nachbarn abgeschrieben!
Teacher: You have copied (or cheated) from your neighbor (classmate) again!

⟨**von/bei jdm etw abschreiben**⟩   to copy *or* cheat from (sb/sth)

■ Schreibt jetzt bitte die Regeln von der Tafel ab!
Please copy the rules from the blackboard now.

■ Es ist verboten, bei einer Klassenarbeit vom Nachbarn abzuschreiben!
It is forbidden to copy from a neighbor during a test!

s. absprechen mit + D ⟨sich mit jdm a.⟩   to make an arrangement with (sb)

■ Die beiden Frauen hatten sich vor der Konferenz abgesprochen.
Both women had agreed (on what to do/say, etc.) before the meeting.

■ Wann sprichst du dich mit ihnen (über die Reisepläne) ab?
   When will you arrange things (the details of the trip) with them?

s. absprechen über + A ⟨sich über jdn/etw a.⟩   to agree upon (sb/sth)

■ Die OPEC-Länder sprachen sich über die Höhe der Ölpreise ab.
   The OPEC countries came to an agreement on the oil prices.

abstimmen auf + A ⟨etw auf etw a.⟩   to adjust to (sth); tune in (sth: *radio, circuit, etc*); to adjust (sth); to suit (sth); to coordinate with (sth)

■ In der Konferenz haben die Lehrer ihre Pläne für das neue Schuljahr (aufeinander) abgestimmt.
   In the faculty meeting the teachers coordinated their plans for the next school year.

■ Ich habe mein Radio auf NDR 2 abgestimmt.
   I tuned my radio in to NDR 2.

s. abstimmen mit + D ⟨sich mit jdm a.⟩   to come to an agreement with (sb); to coordinate (sth) with (sb)

■ Ich stimmte mich mit meinen Kollegen ab.
   I came to an agreement with my co-workers.

■ Ihr müßt euch miteinander abstimmen.
   You will have to come to an agreement with one another.

abstimmen über + A ⟨über jdn/etw a.⟩   to vote *or* take a vote on (sb/sth)

■ Der Ausschuß stimmt über das Projekt durch Handaufheben ab.
   The committee is voting on the project by a show of hands.

■ Sie haben über den Präsidenten geheim (/offen) abgestimmt.
   They took a secret (/open) ballot for the president.

■ Der Bundestag hat über den Antrag ohne Aussprache abgestimmt.
   Parliament voted on the motion without discussion.

aufeinander abgestimmt sein   to be in tune with (each other)

■ Die Spieler der Fußballmannschaft von Bayern München sind gut aufeinander abgestimmt.
   The Bayern München soccer team players are well-matched.

- Im Kollegium sollten alle aufeinander abgestimmt sein.
  The faculty of a school should be well-matched (to one another).
- Ihre Ideen (/Persönlichkeiten) sind gut aufeinander abgestimmt.
  Their ideas (/personalities) are well–matched.

abtun mit + D ⟨etw mit etw a.⟩   to shrug (sth) off with (sth); to dismiss (sth)

- Er tat meinen Vorschlag mit der Bemerkung „unmöglich" ab.
  He dismissed my proposal with the remark "impossible."
- Der Vorsitzende hat meine Einwände mit einem arroganten Lachen (/einem Achselzucken/einer Handbewegung) abgetan.
  The chairman dismissed my objections with an arrogant laugh (/shrug/a wave of his hand).

s. abwechseln mit + D ⟨sich mit jdm a⟩   to take turns with (sb)

- Sie haben sich miteinander (bei der Arbeit) abgewechselt.
  They took turns or alternated with each other (at work).
- Ich werde mich mit ihm am Lenkrad abwechseln.
  I'll take turns at the wheel with him/We'll alternate the driving.

abweichen von + D ⟨von etw a.⟩   to deviate from (sth)

- Er wich vom Thema (/von der Frage) ab.
  He digressed from the point (/question).
- Mein Vorschlag weicht deutlich von deinen Vorstellungen ab.
  My suggestion deviates significantly from your ideas.
- Das Schiff (/Das Flugzeug/Der Pilot) wich vom Kurs ab.
  The ship (/airplane/pilot) deviated from its (/his) course.

abzielen auf + A ⟨auf jdn/etw a.⟩   to aim at (sb/sth)

- Er hat seine Einwände auf den Vorsitzenden (/die Partei) abgezielt.
  He aimed his objections at the chairman (/the party).
- Worauf zielst du ab?
  What are you driving at?
- Das war auf ihn abgezielt.
  That was aimed at (or meant for) him.

achten auf + A ⟨auf jdn/etw a.⟩   to be careful about (sb/sth); to pay attention to (sb/sth)

- Er hat auf die richtige Reihenfolge nicht geachtet.
  He didn't pay attention to the right order (or sequence).

- Bitte achte auf die Kinder! Sie achten nicht auf den Autoverkehr, wenn sie über die Straße laufen.
  Please keep an eye on the children. They don't pay attention to the traffic when they walk across the street.

- Der Schulleiter achtet genau auf Pünktlichkeit der Lehrer.
  The principal pays close attention to the teachers' punctuality.

- Normalerweise achte ich nicht auf das Wetter.
  Normally, I don't pay any attention to the weather.

s. amüsieren bei + D ⟨sich bei etw a.⟩   to have a good time at (sth)

- Letztes Jahr haben wir uns köstlich beim Karneval in Köln (/bei Peters Geburtstagsfeier) amüsiert.
  Last year we had a very good time during the carnival in Cologne (/at Peter's birthday party).

s. amüsieren mit + D ⟨sich mit jdm/etw a.⟩   to amuse oneself with (sth); to have a good time with (sb)

- Paul ist immer so lustig; mit ihm (/mit seinen Witzen) amüsieren wir uns immer gut.
  Paul is such a funny guy; we always have a good time with him (/listening to his jokes).

s. amüsieren über + A ⟨sich über jdn/etw a.⟩   to laugh at (sb/sth); to make fun of (sb/sth)

- Ich habe mich über den Clown (/die Scherze des Clowns/seine ungeschickten Bewegungen) amüsiert.
  I laughed at the clown (/the clown's jokes/his clumsy movements).

- Als er auf der Bananenschale ausrutschte, amüsierten sich alle (auch noch) über ihn.
  When he slipped on the banana skin, everybody made fun of him (to boot).

angestellt sein bei + D ⟨bei etw (Firma, *etc.*)/jdm a. sein⟩   to be employed at (sth) (company, *etc.*)/with (sb)

- Ich bin bei der Reederei angestellt.
  I am employed at the shipping company.

- Bei wem waren Sie früher angestellt?
  At whose place were you employed earlier?

angewiesen sein auf + A ⟨auf jdn/etw a. sein⟩   to be dependent on (sb/sth)

- Er war auf seine Familie (/seine Frau/andere) angewiesen.
  He was dependent on his family (/his wife/others).
- Ich bin auf den Stadtplan angewiesen. Ohne ihn finde ich mich nicht zurecht.
  I am dependent on the city map. Without it I can't find my way around.
- Der Arme war auf Sozialhilfe angewiesen.
  The poor man depended on welfare.

Angst haben um + A ⟨um jdn/etw A. haben⟩   to be anxious *or* worried about (sb/sth)

- Meine Mutter hat Angst um mich.
  My mother is worried about me.
- Sie hat Angst um die Kinder, die an dieser gefährlichen Stelle die Straße überqueren.
  She worries about the children who cross the street at this dangerous place.

Angst haben vor + D ⟨vor etw A. haben⟩   to be afraid of (sb/sth)

- Die Kinder haben Angst vor dem bösen Wolf (/den Spinnen).
  The children are afraid of the mean wolf (/spiders).
- Ich habe vor meinem Chef (/vorm Fliegen) Angst.
  I am afraid of my boss (/flying).
- Wovor hattest du Angst? —Vor dem bissigen Hund.
  What were you afraid of? —Of being bitten by the dog.

anklagen wegen + G ⟨jdn wegen etw a.⟩   to charge (sb) with (sth); to accuse (sb) of (sth)

- Der Staatsanwalt hat ihn wegen Diebstahls angeklagt.
  The district attorney charged him with theft.
- Man klagte ihn (vor Gericht) wegen eines Verbrechens an.
  They accused him (in front of the court) of a crime.

ankleben an + A/D ⟨an etw a.⟩ to stick on (sth)

- Die Lehrerin hat den Zettel an die (*or* an der) Tür angeklebt.
  The teacher stuck the piece of paper on the door.

anklopfen an + A/D ⟨an etw a.⟩ to knock at/on (sth)

- Der Detektiv klopfte an die (*or* an der) Tür an.
  The detective knocked on the door.

ankommen (+ prep) to arrive

- Der Zug kam pünktlich in der Stadt (/in Berlin) an.
  The train arrived in the city (/in Berlin) on time.

ankommen auf + A ⟨es kommt auf jdn/etw an⟩ to depend on (sb/sth)

- Das kommt auf die Umstände (/die Stimmen) an.
  That depends on the circumstances (/votes).
- Es kommt darauf an, wie die Kinder sich benehmen.
  It depends on how the children behave themselves.
- Es kommt mir (/meiner Mutter) sehr darauf an, erfolgreich zu sein.
  It is very important to me (/to my mother) to be succesful.
- Auf den Preis (/das Geld/die Zeit) kommt es nicht an.
  The price (/money/time) is no object.
- Worauf es ankommt, ist, daß er die Arbeit rechtzeitig tut.
  What matters is that he does the work in time.

ankommen bei + D ⟨bei jdm/etw a.⟩ to be successful with; to go down well with (sb/sth)

- Mit deiner Schleimerei kommst du bei dem Lehrer nicht an!
  You won't get anywhere with that teacher with your brown nosing!
- Weißt du, wie dieser Lehrer bei den Schülern ankommt?
  Do you know how this teacher's rapport is with the students?
- Peter hat eine prima Persönlichkeit. Er kommt bei Mädchen (/allen) an.
  Peter has a great personality. He is a great success with the girls (/everybody).

ankommen gegen + A ⟨gegen etw a.⟩   to be able to fight (sth)

- Kaum eine Autofirma kann gegen die japanische Konkurrenz ankommen.
  Hardly any car company can fight the Japanese competition.
- Dieser Boxer ist zu stark, sein Gegner kommt gegen ihn nicht an.
  This boxer is too strong; his opponent is no match for him.
- Es wird immer schwerer für uns, gegen unseren Jungen anzukommen.
  It's becoming more and more difficult to cope (or deal) with our boy.

anlachen (without prep) ⟨jdn a.⟩   to smile at (sb); (stronger) to laugh (happily) at (sb)

- Das Mädchen lachte ihn charmant an.
  The girl smiled charmingly at him.

s. anlachen ⟨sich jdn a.⟩   to pick (sb) up

- Ich habe mir auf dem Schultanz ein Mädchen angelacht.
  I picked up a girl at the school dance.

anlegen (+ prep)   to put up against; to be based

- Ulrich hat die Leiter an das Haus (/den Baum) angelegt.
  Ulrich put up the ladder against the house (/tree).
- Sie legte den Zollstock an das Fenster an und maß die Breite.
  She put the yardstick against the window and measured its width.

anlegen auf + A ⟨auf jdn/etw a.⟩   to aim at (sb/sth)

- Der Polizist hat (mit dem Gewehr) auf den Verbrecher angelegt.
  The policeman aimed (the gun) at the criminal.

  ⟨es auf jdn/etw anlegen⟩   to be determined at/with (sb/sth)

  - Jens hat es wohl darauf angelegt, mich zu ärgern (/seine Arbeit schneller als alle anderen zu schaffen)!
    Jens is determined to make me angry (/to finish his work before everybody else).
  - Das Mädchen hat es auf ihn (/Peter) angelegt.
    The girl has an eye on him (/Peter).

s. anlegen mit + D ⟨**sich mit jdm a.**⟩   to pick an argument *or* quarrel *or* fight with (sb)

■ Du bist ärgerlich, und ich will mich nicht mit dir anlegen.
   You are angry, and I don't want to quarrel with you!

⟨**auf etwas angelegt sein**⟩   to be based on (sth)

■ Ihre Ehe ist auf Vertrauen (/Betrug) angelegt.
   Their marriage is based on trust (/deception).

(s.) anlehnen an + A ⟨**sich/etw an etw a.**⟩   to lean *or* rest against (sth)

■ Ich habe mich (mit der Schulter) an die Tür angelehnt.
   I leaned (with my shoulder) against the door.
■ Der Zimmerman lehnte das Brett an die Wand an.
   The carpenter rested the board against the wall.

s. anlehnen an + A ⟨**sich an etw a.**⟩   (*fig*) to follow (sth)

■ Mit seinem neuen Buch lehnt der Professor sich stark an Arbeiten griechischer Philosophen an.
   In his new book the professor closely follows the works of Greek philosophers.

anleiten zu + D ⟨**jdn zu etw a.**⟩   to teach (sb) (sth)

■ Der Lehrer wollte ihn zu selbständigem Denken anleiten.
   The teacher wanted to teach him to think for himself.
■ Die Mutter leitete ihre Kinder zu Sauberkeit (/Ehrlichkeit/Ordnung) an.
   The mother taught her children to be clean (/honest/orderly).

(s.) anmelden bei + D ⟨**(sich) bei jdm/etw a.**⟩   to enroll at (sth); to tell (sb) that (sb) is coming

■ Er meldet sich morgen bei der Schule (/dem Kurs/dem Professor) an.
   He'll enroll at the school (/in the course/with the professor) tomorrow.
■ Jeder muß sich polizeilich anmelden.
   Everyone has to register with the police.
■ Ich muß mich beim Arzt anmelden.
   I must make an appointment at the doctor's (or with the doctor).

■   Die Sekretärin hat die Besucher beim Chef angemeldet.
    *The secretary announced the visitors to the boss (i.e., she went to the office to
    tell him they were there).*

annehmen von + D ⟨**von jdm etw a.**⟩   to expect (sth) of (sb)

■   Niemand konnte ernstlich von ihr annehmen, daß sie Opfer der Drogen werden
    würde.
    Nobody could seriouly expect her to become a victim of drugs.

■   Wie konntest du das tun? Das hätte ich nie von dir angenommen!
    How could you do that? I would never have expected that of you!

s. anpassen an + A ⟨**sich an etw a.**⟩   to adjust *or* adapt to (sb/sth); to conform to
(sb/sth)

■   Er paßt sich leicht an verschiedene Verhältnisse an.
    He adapts easily to various circumstances.

■   Als Martin neu in die Klasse kam, war er fleißig, aber bald paßte er sich an die
    Faulheit der anderen an.
    *When Martin was new in the class, he was very diligent, but soon he conformed
    to match the laziness of the others.*

■   Du mußt dich (ihren Erwartungen *or* an ihre Erwartungen) anpassen.
    You must conform (to their expectations).

anpassen (without prep)   to try on; to fit (on); to adapt

■   Du mußt die Schuhe anpassen, um zu sehen, ob sie groß genug sind.
    You must try on the shoes to find out if they are big enough.

■   Der Schneider paßt dem Bräutigam den neuen Anzug an.
    The tailor is fitting the groom's new suit.

anreden mit + D ⟨**jdn mit etw a.**⟩   to address (sb) with (sth)

■   Wir reden einander mit „du" an.
    We use the "du" form (of address) to each other.

■   Warum redetest du ihn mit seinem Titel (/mit „Herr Doktor") an?
    Why did you address him by his title (/as "doctor")?

anreizen zu + D ⟨**jdn zu etw a.**⟩   to encourage (sb) to (sth); to induce

■   Die Anzeige hat ihn zum Kauf des Autos angereizt.
    The advertisement induced him to buy the car.

■ Die Aussicht, viel Geld verdienen zu können, reizte sie zu großen Leistungen an.
The prospect of being able to earn a lot of money encouraged her to perform great feats.

anrufen (+ prep)   to call; to phone

■ Ich soll von hier bei meiner Frau anrufen.
I should call my wife (on the phone) from here.

■ Frau Schmidt will nach Deutschland (/in die Schweiz/ins Ausland) anrufen.
Mrs. Schmidt wants to phone Germany (/Switzerland/abroad).

■ Ich rufe dich heute (um drei Uhr) an.
I'll call you today (at three o'clock).

anschließen an + A ⟨etw an etw a.⟩   to fasten (with a lock); to connect

■ Ich habe mein Fahrrad an den Zaun angeschlossen.
I fastened my bike to the fence.

■ Die Spülmaschine muß noch an das Wasser (/an die Elektrizität) angeschlossen werden.
The dishwasher still has to be connected to the water (/the electricity).

■ Unser Haus ist an das Fernsehkabel (/ans Stromnetz/an die Wasserleitung) angeschlossen.
Our house is connected to the TV cable (/main or electricity/water).

⟨**s. einer Sache (D)** *or* **an etw. (A) auschließen.**⟩   to follow (sth)

■ An die Rede schloß sich eine Diskussion an.
The speech was followed by a discussion.

s. anschließen an + A ⟨sich an jdn/etw a.⟩   to make friends with (sb/sth); to join (sb/sth)

■ Der neue Schüler schloß sich leicht an andere an.
The new student made friends easily.

s. anschmiegen an + A ⟨sich an jdn/etw a.⟩   to snuggle up to *or* against (sb/sth); to cling to (sb/sth)

■ Im Kino schmiegte er sich eng an seine Freundin an.
He cuddled up to his girlfriend in the cinema.

■ Die Kleidung (/Bluse/Der Rock) schmiegt sich an ihren Körper an.
   The dress (/blouse/skirt) outlines her shape (or clings to her body).

(s.) ansehen (+ prep)   to look at; to (have a) look at

■ Er sieht sie (/von der Seite/freundlich) an.
   He's looking at her (/from the side/in a friendly way).

■ Ich will mir den Film in einem großen Kino ansehen.
   I want to watch the film in a big theater.

ansetzen an + D ⟨etw an etw a.⟩   to attach to (sth); to place in position at (sth)

■ Setze die Leiter weiter oben an der Wand an!
   Put the ladder further up against the wall.

■ Du solltest den Wagenheber an dieser Stelle ansetzen.
   You ought to put the jack in this spot.

ansetzen auf + A ⟨jdn auf jdn/etw a.⟩   to put (sb) on(to) (sb/sth)

■ Man hat vier Arbeiter auf das neue Projekt angesetzt.
   They put four workers on the new project.

■ Die Polizei setzte die Hunde auf seine Spur an.
   The police put the dogs onto his trail.

ansetzen zu + D ⟨zu etw a.⟩   to begin (sth)

■ Das Flugzeug setzt jetzt zur Landung an.
   The plane is getting ready to land.

■ Alle setzten zum Trinken (/Sprechen/Essen) an.
   Everyone started to drink (/speak/eat).

■ Andreas hat zum Sprung angesetzt.
   Andreas prepared (or got ready) to jump.

anspielen auf + A ⟨auf jdn/etw a.⟩   to allude to (sb/sth)

■ Worauf spielst du an?—Ich spiele auf seine rücksichtslosen Bemerkungen an.
   What are you insinuating (or alluding to)?—I'm alluding to his inconsiderate remarks.

■ Er spielte in seinem Buch auf den Präsidenten (/auf Watergate) an.
He alluded to the president (/Watergate) in his book.

■ Das (/Seine sarkastische Bemerkung) spielte auf mich an.
That (/His sarcastic remark) was meant for me.

ansprechen auf + A ⟨**jdn auf etw a.**⟩   to ask *or* approach (sb) about/for (sth)

■ Er sprach das Ehepaar auf diese Angelegenheit an.
He approached the married couple about this matter.

ansprechen (without prep)   to speak to

■ Er sprach die Demonstranten vor dem Theater (/auf der Straße) an.
He spoke to the demonstrators in front of the theater (/on the street).

■ Ich lasse mich nicht von solchen Menschen ansprechen.
I won't allow myself to be spoken to by such people.

■ Wie sprichst du ihn an?—Ich spreche ihn mit seinem Titel (/Vornamen) an.
How do you address him?—I address him by his title (/first name).

(s.) anstecken (+ prep)   to catch; to infect (sb)

■ Das Kind hat mich (mit der Grippe) angesteckt.
The child gave it (the flu) to me; he infected me with the flu.

■ Ich will dich nicht (mit meiner Erkältung) anstecken.
I don't want to give (my cold) to you.

■ Ich habe mich bei meinem Bruder (/bei der Arbeit) angesteckt.
I caught it from my brother (/at work).

anstoßen (+ prep)   to bump; to knock

■ Paß' auf, daß du nicht an den Tisch anstößt!
Be careful that you don't bump into the table.

■ Er ist mit dem Kopf an die (*or* au der) Lampe angestoßen.
He bumped (or knocked) his head on the lamp.

■ Viele Leute stoßen mit der Zunge an, wenn sie jünger sind. (*idiom*)
Many people lisp when they are younger.

■ Er stieß mich mit dem Ellbogen an.
He nudged me with his elbow.

anstoßen auf + A ⟨**auf jdn/etw a.**⟩   to drink to (sb/sth)

■ Die Gäste stießen mit einem Glas Sekt auf ihre Silberne Hochzeit (/die Jubilare) an.
The guests drank to their 25th anniversary (/the couple celebrating it) with a glass of champagne.

anstoßen bei + D ⟨**bei jdm a.**⟩   to offend (sb)

■ Der Vater ist mit seinem Einwand beim Schulleiter angestoßen.
The father offended the principal with his objection.

s. anstrengen (+ prep)   to strain; to exert

■ Du mußt dich in der Schule mehr anstrengen.
You must exert yourself more in school.

■ Der alte Mann hat sich zu sehr bei der Wanderung angestrengt.
The old man exerted himself too much during the hike.

antworten auf + A ⟨**jdm auf etw a.**⟩   to answer *or* reply to (sb/sth); to respond to (sb/sth)

■ Sie antwortete ihrem Lehrer auf die Frage.
She answered her teacher's question.

■ Worauf antwortest du?—Auf einen Liebesbrief.
What are you replying to?—To a love letter.

■ Der Politiker hat auf meinen Brief geantwortet. (*or* Der Politiker hat meinen Brief beantwortet.)
The politician answered my letter.

■ Mit der Lohnerhöhung antwortete die Firma auf den Druck der Angestellten.
The company responded to the pressure of the employees with (by granting) the pay hike.

anwenden auf + A ⟨**etw auf jdn/etw a.**⟩   to apply to (sb/sth)

■ Man wendet die Prinzipien der Linguistik auf die Soziologie an.
They apply the principles of linguistics to sociology.

■ Normale Maßstäbe lassen sich auf diese Person nicht anwenden.
Ordinary standards cannot be applied to this person.

■ Man kann die Regeln auf die Wirtschaft (/diesen Fall) anwenden.
One can apply the rules to economics (/this case).

appellieren an + A ⟨**an jnd/etw a.**⟩   to appeal to (sb/sth)

■ Ich appelliere an deine Vernunft (/deinen Intellekt).
I appeal to your reason (/your intellect).

■ Viele haben an den Bürgermeister appelliert, das Schauspielhaus zu renovieren.
Many people appealed to the mayor to renovate the city theater.

■ Der Papst appellierte an alle Christen.
The Pope made an appeal to all Christians.

arbeiten (+ prep)   to work

■ Ich arbeite am Schreibtisch (/beim Fleischer/als Elektriker/auf dem Bau/in der Fabrik/bei meinem Onkel).
I work at the desk (/at the butcher's/as an electrician/in construction work/in the factory/at my uncle's house).

■ Er hat nur für (*or* gegen) gute Bezahlung gearbeitet.
He only worked for good pay.

■ Sie arbeiteten in zwei Schichten.
They worked in two shifts.

arbeiten an + D ⟨**an etw a.**⟩   to work on (sth)

■ Er arbeitet an seinem nächsten Buch.
He's working on his next book.

■ Mein Sohn arbeitet an seinem Auto, weil es wieder kaputt ist.
My son is working on his car because it has broken down again.

■ Sie arbeitet im Akkord an der Nähmaschine.
She is working on the sewing machine doing piecework.

arbeiten für/gegen + A ⟨**für/gegen etw a.**⟩   to work for/against (sth)

■ Der Spion arbeitete für (/gegen) sein Land.
The spy worked for (/against) his country.

■ Wir müssen für eine bessere Zukunft (/gegen die Verschmutzung der Welt/für den Frieden) arbeiten.
We must work for a better future (/against world pollution/for peace).

arbeiten über + A ⟨**über jdn/etw a.**⟩   to work *or* do research on (sb/sth)

■ Er arbeitet über ägyptische Mumien (/englische Geschichte/Goethe).
He's working on (a project on) Egyptian mummies (/English history/Goethe).

arbeiten zu + D ⟨zu etw a.⟩   to work toward (sth)

■ Martin Luther King arbeitete zum Wohle der Schwarzen in der USA.
Martin Luther King worked for the (welfare of) blacks in the USA.

s. ärgern über + A ⟨sich über jdn/etw ä.⟩   to get angry with (sb/sth); blow up over (sb/sth)

■ Warum ärgerten Sie sich über diese Frau?
Why were you angry with this woman?

■ Ich habe mich krank (/zu Tode) über dich (/darüber) geärgert.
I was furious with you (/about that).

■ Jens ärgerte sich über das langweilige Fernsehprogramm.
The boring TV program aggravated Jens.

s. arrangieren mit + D ⟨sich mit jdm/etw a.⟩   to come to an agreement with (sb); to come to terms with (sth)

■ Du mußt dich mit deinem neuen Mitarbeiter (/den schlechten klimatischen Bedingungen) arrangieren.
You must come to an agreement with your new colleague (/come to terms with the unpleasant climatic conditions).

aufbauen (+ prep)   to put up; to fix up; to set *or* lay out

■ Seine Eltern bauten alle Geschenke auf dem Weihnachtstisch auf.
His parents set out all the gifts on the Christmas table.

aufbauen auf + A/D ⟨etw auf etw a.⟩   to base *or* found (sth) on (sth)

■ Meine Behauptung baut auf diese (*or* auf dieser) Beobachtung auf.
My contention is based on this observation.

■ Sein Verdacht baute auf die (*or* auf der) Tatsache auf, daß. . . .
His suspicion was based on the fact that. . . .

aufbauen zu + D ⟨jnd/etw zu etw a.⟩   to build (sb/sth) up into (sth)

■ In drei Jahren baute er seinen Verlag zum größten in Deutschland auf.
Within three years he built his publishing house up into the biggest in Germany.

■ Der erfolgreiche Produzent hat eine unbekannte Sängerin in kurzer Zeit zu einem Popstar aufgebaut.
The successful producer built the unknown singer up to being a popstar in a short period of time.

auffallen (+ prep)   to stand out; to attract attention

- Das Kind fiel durch seine gelbe Hose auf.
  The child's yellow pants made him stand out.

- Was mir an diesem Buch auffällt, ist. . . .
  What strikes me about this book is. . . .

- Der Star verließ das Cafe durch die Hintertür. Sonst wäre er aufgefallen.
  The star left the cafe through the backdoor; otherwise he would have attracted attention.

- Gestern fiel mir zum ersten Mal auf, daß du einen Leberfleck hinter dem Ohr hast.
  Yesterday I noticed for the first time that you have a mole behind your ear.   .

auffordern zu + D ⟨jdn zu etw a.⟩   to ask (sb) to (sth)

- Markus forderte seine Kusine zum Tanzen (/Essen/Singen) auf.
  Markus asked his cousin to dance (/eat/sing).

- Ich fordere Sie jetzt zum letzten Mal auf, Ihre Rechnung zu bezahlen.
  I am calling on you one last time to pay your bill.

- Der Trainer hat seine Spieler immer zu Bestleistungen aufgefordert.
  The coach always asked his players to do their best.

(s.) aufhalten (+ prep)   to be; to spend time

- Ich habe mich am Bahnhof (/im Ausland/zu Hause/bei meinem Onkel) aufgehalten.
  I was at the train station (/abroad/at home/at my uncle's house).

- Wo hat sie sich zur Zeit des Mordes aufgehalten?
  Where was she at the time of the murder?

- Ich möchte mich mehr im Freien aufhalten.
  I would like to spend more time outdoors.

- Sechs Stunden lang wurden wir durch ein Unwetter aufgehalten.
  We were delayed by a thunderstorm for six hours.

s. aufhalten bei/mit + D ⟨sich bei/mit etw a.⟩   to dwell on (sth); to spend too much time on (sth)

- Du kannst dich nicht bei (*or* mit) Kleinigkeiten aufhalten.
  You cannot dwell on (or linger over) small details.

- Der Lehrer kann sich nicht stundenlang mit nur einem Schüler aufhalten.
  The teacher cannot spend hours dealing with one student.

■ Ich halte mich mit deinem Vorschlag schon zulange auf.
I have already spent too long on (dealing with) your suggestion.

s. aufhalten über + A ⟨**sich über etw a.**⟩   to find fault with (sth); to criticize (sth)

■ Du sollst dich nicht immer über die schlechten Gewohnheiten deines Sohnes aufhalten.
You shouldn't always criticize the bad habits of your son.

aufhetzen zu + D ⟨**jdn zu etw a.**⟩   to incite (sb) to (do) sth

■ Der Diktator hetzte die Bevölkerung zum Krieg auf.
The dictator incited the population to go to war.

■ Die Russen wurden von Lenin zum Aufstand (/zur Revolution) aufgesetzt.
The Russians were incited by Lenin to revolt.

aufhören mit + D ⟨**mit etw a.**⟩   to stop (sth)

■ Sie haben mit der Arbeit (/dem Streik) aufgehört.
They stopped working (/striking).

■ Das Kind hörte endlich mit dem Spielen (/dem Geschrei/dem Weinen) auf.
The child finally stopped playing (/screaming/crying).

■ Hört damit auf!
Stop it! (Cut it out!)

■ Er hörte endlich mit dem Gemecker auf.
He finally stopped his belly-aching (grumbling).

aufklären über + A ⟨**jdn über etw a.**⟩   to inform (sb) about (sth)

■ Die Regierung muß die Bürger über die Gefahr des DDT erklären.
The government must inform the public about the danger of DDT.

■ Die Schule muß das Kind über die sexuellen Sachen aufklären.
The school must inform the child about sexual matters.

■ Der Lehrer klärte den Jungen über seine Fehler auf.
The teacher informed the boy of his mistakes.

aufkommen für + A ⟨**für jdn/etw a.**⟩   to pay for (sb/sth)

■ Mein Vater kam für meine Schwester (/die Kosten/die Unkosten) auf.
My father paid my sister's way (i.e., she has no income of her own, or The father compensates for the damage done/expenditure she has made) (/My father paid for the cost/My father paid the expenses).

■ Die Versicherungsgesellschaft ist für das Unglück (/den Schaden) aufgekommen.
The insurance company paid for the accident (/damage).

aufkommen gegen + A ⟨gegen jdn/etw a.⟩ to prevail against (sb/sth)

■ Hoffentlich kommst du gegen ihn (/seinen Vorschlag) auf.
Hopefully you'll prevail against him (/his proposal).

■ Die demokratischen Parteien konnten nicht gegen den Diktator aufkommen.
The democratic parties could not prevail against the dictator.

(s.) auflösen in + D ⟨sich/etw in etw a.⟩ to dissolve in (sth)

■ Salz löst sich in Wasser auf.
Salt dissolves in water.

■ Du kannst die Tabletten in Wasser auflösen.
You can dissolve the pills in water.

■ Alle meine Pläne haben sich leider in nichts aufgelöst. (*fig*)
Unfortunately all my plans have dissolved into thin air (or have disappeared).

■ Sie war über den Tod ihres Kindes in Tränen aufgelöst. (*fig*)
She was drowned in tears over the death of her child.

aufmerksam machen auf + A ⟨jdn auf jdn/etw a. machen⟩ to draw (sb)'s attention to (sb/sth)

■ Die Frau hat ihren Mann auf die Sache aufmerksam gemacht.
The wife drew her husband's attention to the matter.

■ Mein Nachbar machte mich daurauf aufmerksam, daß die Fahrpreise erhöht worden waren.
*My neighbor drew my attention to the fact that the (*bus, train, etc.*) fares had been raised.*

■ Der Lehrer hat die Schüler auf die Klassenarbeit in der nächsten Woche aufmerksam gemacht.
The teacher brought next week's test to the attention of the students.

aufnehmen in + A ⟨in etw a.⟩ to admit to (sth); to accept (sth); to include in (sth)

■ Der Junge konnte nicht ins Gymnasium (/in den Sportverein) aufgenommen werden.
The boy could not be admitted to the "Gymnasium" (/the sports club).

■ Wir können Sie in unsere Adressenliste aufnehmen.
We can include you on our mailing list.

- Diese Frage ist in die Tagesordnung aufgenommen worden.
  This question has been included on the agenda.
- Dieses Wort ist in das Wörterbuch aufgenommen worden.
  This word has been included in the dictionary.

aufnehmen mit + D ⟨es mit jdm/etw a.⟩   to be a match for (sb/sth)

- Keiner konnte es an Dummheit mit ihm aufnehmen.
  No one could match his stupidity.
- Mit Ali konnte es kein anderer Boxer aufnehmen.
  No other boxer was a match for Ali.

aufpassen auf + A ⟨auf jdn/etw a.⟩   to watch (out for) (sb/sth)

- Sie hat auf die Suppe aufgepaßt, damit sie nicht überkochte.
  She watched the soup so that it wouldn't boil over.
- Wenn die Eltern spazierengehen, muß Elke auf das Baby aufpassen.
  When the parents go out walking, Elke must watch the baby.
- Wie lange soll ich auf den Kuchen (/den Puter) im Ofen aufpassen?
  How long do you want me to watch the cake (/turkey) in the oven?

s. aufregen über + A ⟨sich über jdn/etw a.⟩   to be indignant at/about (sb/sth); to get worked up about (sb/sth)

- Ich rege mich über meine Nachbarn (/seine dummen Witze) auf.
  My neighbors (/His dumb jokes) get on my nerves.
- Sie hat sich über jede Kleinigkeit (/die Verspätung der U-Bahn) aufgeregt.
  She got mad about any insignificant matter (/the delay of the subway).
- Rege dich nicht darüber auf!
  Don't get worked up about it!

auftragen auf + A ⟨etw auf etw a.⟩   to put (sth) on (sth); to apply (sth) to (sth)

- Jetzt tragen wir die Farben dick auf die Wände auf.
  Now we will put a thick coat on the walls.
- Sie trug ihr Make-up auf die Wangen immer zu dick auf.
  She always put makeup on her cheeks too thickly.
- Du sollst Salbe auf die Brandblasen (/Wunde) auftragen.
  You should put ointment on the blisters (/wound).

ausbrechen in ⟨in etw a.⟩ to break into (sth)

■ Als Peter die Nachricht bekam, brach er in Jubel (/in Schweiß/in Zorn/in Gelächter/in Tränen) aus.
When Peter got the news, he was overjoyed (/broke out in sweat/exploded in rage/burst into laughter/burst into tears).

s. ausbreiten über + A ⟨sich über etw a.⟩ to spread on (sth); (*fig*) to dwell on (sth)

■ Ich will mich nicht in allen Einzelheiten über das Thema (/meine Zukunftpläne) ausbreiten.
I don't want to go into great detail concerning that subject (/my future plans).

■ Darüber will mein Mann sich jetzt nicht ausbreiten.
My husband would rather not go into that now.

■ Das Feuer (/das Gerücht/Der Klatsch) hat sich schnell über die ganze Stadt ausgebreitet.
The fire (/rumor/gossip) quickly spread over the whole town.

s. ausdehnen auf/über + A ⟨sich auf/über etw a.⟩ to spread over (sth)

■ Sein Einfluß (/Die Hitze) dehnte sich auf das ganze Land aus.
His influence (/The heat) spread over the whole country.

■ Der Streik hat sich schnell auf viele Fabriken ausgedehnt.
The strike spread quickly to many factories.

■ Die Konferenz dehnte sich über Tage aus.
The conference was drawn out over (or went on for) days.

s. auseinandersetzen mit + D ⟨sich mit jdm a.⟩ to argue *or* quarrel with (sb); to discuss with (sb)

■ Ich setzte mich immer mit meiner Mutter über die Erziehung unserer Kinder auseinander.
I always discussed the education of our children with my mother.

■ Du solltest dich häufiger mit ihm auseinandersetzen.
You ought to discuss things more thoroughly with him.

> **⟨sich mit etw auseinandersetzen⟩** to have a good look at (sth); to argue a thing (*to the advisability of . . .*); to examine *or* consider (*in detail*); to tackle (sth); to deal with (sth)
>
> ■ Immer mehr Parteien setzen sich mit Umweltproblemen auseinander.
> *More and more political parties tackle environmental problems.*
>
> ■ Er setzte sich ernsthaft mit den Einwänden seiner Gegner auseinander.
> *He seriously considered (or examined) the objections of his opponents.*

■ Wir müssen uns ehrlich mit unseren Schwierigkeiten auseinandersetzen.
We have to deal with (or address or face up to) our difficulties honestly.

■ Du solltest dich auch mit anderen Meinungen (/Lehren) auseinandersetzen.
You ought to also consider other opinions (/doctrines).

s. ausgeben als ⟨sich als jd/etw a.⟩   to pass off as (sb/sth); to pass oneself off as (sb/sth)

■ Er gibt sich als Amerikaner aus (, ist es aber nicht).
He passes himself off as an American (but he is not).

■ Schäm dich! Du darfst dich nicht als Neffe Rockefellers ausgeben.
Shame on you! You mustn't pass yourself off as Rockefeller's nephew.

■ Sie wollten das Pferd als reinrassig ausgeben (, obwohl es es nicht ist).
They wanted to pass off the horse as a thoroughbred (although it is not).

ausgeben für + A ⟨(Geld) für etw a.⟩   to spend (money) on/for (sth)

■ Seine Frau gibt für Schmuck viel Geld aus.
His wife spends so much money for (or on) jewelry.

■ Er hat all sein Erbe für ein teueres Auto ausgegeben.
He spent all of his inheritance (or inherited money) on an expensive car.

■ Sie gaben all ihr Geld für ihre Ferien aus.
They spent all of their money on their vacation.

■ Wofür gabst du so viel Geld aus? Das war es nicht wert.
What did you spend so much money for? It wasn't worth it.

ausgehen auf + A ⟨auf etw a.⟩   to be intent on (sth)

■ Jens geht nur auf Spaß (/Abenteuer) aus.
Jens is always intent on having fun (/adventure).

■ Sie ist nur auf ihren Vorteil ausgegangen.
She only thought of herself (her own advantage).

■ Ich gehe nur darauf aus, mein Studium so bald wie möglich zu beenden.
I am intent on completing my studies as soon as possible.

ausgehen von + D ⟨von etw a.⟩   to start out on (sth); to base (sth) on (sth)

■ Die Revolution ist von dieser Stadt ausgegangen.
The revolution started in this town.

- Wir sind von diesem Punkt ausgegangen.
  We started from this point.
- Wir gehen von der Tatsache (/Annahme) aus, daß. . . .
  We begin with the fact (/assumption) that. . . .
- Er ging bei seiner These davon aus, daß. . . .
  He based his thesis on the fact that. . . .

aushalten (+ prep)   to bear; to stand; to endure

- Das ist einfach nicht auszuhalten *or* zum Aushalten (mit ihm).
  It's simply unbearable (/He is simply unbearable).
- Wie kann man es in dieser Stadt (/in diesem Büro/bei dieser Arbeit) bloß aushalten?
  How can anyone stand working in this city (/office/on this job)?
- Können Sie es noch bis zum Abendbrot (/nächsten Bahnhof) aushalten?
  Can you hold out until supper (/the next train station)?
- Mit David ist es am Tisch nicht mehr auszuhalten.
  David has become quite unbearable at the table.

aushalten mit + D ⟨etw mit etw a.⟩   to bear comparison with (sth)

- Die deutsche Autoindustrie hält den Vergleich mit der japanischen aus.
  The German car industry bears comparison with the Japanese.

s. aushalten von + D ⟨sich von jdm a. lassen⟩   to be kept by (sb)

- Jahrelang wurde sie von ihrem reichen Freund ausgehalten.
  For years she was kept as a mistress by her rich boyfriend.
- Der Gigolo läßt sich (von ihr) aushalten.
  The gigolo lives off her.

auskommen mit + D ⟨mit jdm a.⟩   to get along with (sb)

- Wir sind gut miteinander ausgekommen.
  We got along well together.
- Die Frau bemüht sich sehr, mit ihrem Mann auszukommen.
  The wife is trying hard to get along with her husband.
- Der Schüler kam nicht gut mit seinem neuen Lehrer aus.
  The student didn't get along with his new teacher.

⟨**mit etw auskommen**⟩ to get by on/with (sth); to manage on/with (sth)

- Wie kommt dein Sohn mit seinem Geld aus? —Er kommt gut damit aus.
  How does your son manage his money? —He manages it well.
- Mit der Milch müßten wir bis Sonntag auskommen.
  We should get by till Sunday with the milk (we have).

auslassen an + D ⟨**etw an jdm a.**⟩ to vent (sth) on (sb)

- Er hat seine Gefühle (/seinen Frust) an ihr ausgelassen.
  He vented his feelings (/frustration) on her.
- Mein Partner ließ seinen Zorn (/seine schlechte Laune) an mir aus.
  My partner vented his anger (/his bad mood) on me.

s. auslassen über + A ⟨**sich über jdn/etw a.**⟩ to go on about (sb/sth); to air one's opinion (disparagingly) about (sb/sth)

- Ich habe mich nicht weiter über meine Privatangelegenheiten ausgelassen.
  I didn't say any more about my private affairs.
- Die Polizistin hat sich lang und breit über den Vorfall (/Unfall) ausgelassen.
  The policewoman went on and on about the incident (/accident).
- Der Chef hat sich sehr negativ über den neuen Mitarbeiter ausgelassen.
  The boss aired a very negative opinion about the new employee.

ausreichen (+ prep) to be sufficient *or* enough

- Das Brot reicht für uns alle aus.
  There is enough bread for all of us.
- Das Geld reicht (für mich/für das Kleid) nicht aus.
  There is not enough money (for me/for the dress).
- Die Zeit reichte für die Planung (/für mich) aus.
  There was enough time for planning (/for me).

ausreichen mit + D ⟨**mit etw a.**⟩ to manage on (sth)

- Wir werden mit dieser Geldsumme (/mit deinem Gehalt allein) ausreichen (*or more commonly:* Diese Geldsumme/Dein Gehalt allein wird ausreichen).
  We'll manage on this fund (/your salary alone).
- Ich weiß nicht, ob ich damit (/mit diesem Betrag) ausreiche (*or more commonly:* Ich weiß nicht, ob das/dieser Betrag ausreicht).
  I don't know if I can manage on that (/this amount).

ausrüsten mit + D ⟨jdn/etw mit etw a.⟩ to fit out (sb/sth) with (sth)

- Wenn ein Mechaniker das Auto mit einem Sicherheitsgurt ausrüstet,. . . .
  When a mechanic fits the car with a seat belt,.. . .
- Unsere Firma rüstet Schiffe mit Proviant und Wasser aus.
  Our company supplies ships with food and water.

ausgerüstet sein mit + D ⟨mit etw a. sein⟩ to come with (sth); to be equipped with (sth)

- Dieses Auto ist mit Nebelscheinwerfern ausgerüstet.
  This car comes with fog lights.
- Das Hospital war mit den modernsten Instrumenten ausgerüstet.
  The hospital was equipped with the most modern instruments.
- Die Kinder sind gut mit wetterfester Kleidung ausgerüstet.
  The children are well-equipped with weatherproof clothing.

aussagen für/gegen + A ⟨für/gegen jdn a.⟩ to testify for/against (sb)

- Der Zeuge hat gegen (/für) den Angeklagten ausgesagt.
  The witness testified against (/for) the accused.

aussagen über + A ⟨über jdn/etw a.⟩ to give evidence about (sb/sth); to say (sth) about

- Leider kann ich nichts über den Unfall (/ihn) aussagen.
  Unfortunately, I can't give evidence about the accident (/him).
- Über seinen neuen Plan kann ich noch nichts aussagen; ich habe ihn noch nicht gesehen.
  I cannot say anything about his new plan yet; I haven't seen it yet.

aussehen nach + D ⟨nach etw a.⟩ to look like (sb/sth)

- Es sieht nach Regen (/Schnee/Gewitter) aus.
  It looks like there's going to be rain (/snow/a storm).
- Mit nur drei Rosen sieht der Blumenstrauß nach nichts aus.
  With only three roses the bouquet doesn't look like much of anything.
- Das sieht nach Täuschung (/Manipulation/Liebe) aus.
  It looks like deception (/manipulation/love).
- Es sieht danach (*or* so) aus, als ob er gewinnen sollte.
  It looks as if he should win.

- Seh' ich so (*or* danach) aus?
  What do you take me for/Do I look like that?

(s.) äußern (+ prep)   to say

- Ich äußere mich zu deinen Vorwürfen nicht.
  I am not going to counter your reproaches.
- Bitte äußere dich dazu!
  Please give your opinion on that.
- Er äußerte sein Bedauern (/seine Gefühle/seine Meinung) über ihr Verhalten.
  He expressed his regret (/feelings/opinion) about her behavior.
- Er äußerte sich dahingehend, daß er uns nicht besuchen wollte.
  He made a comment to the effect that he didn't want to visit us.

s. äußern über + A ⟨sich über jdn/etw ä.⟩   to express *or* voice (sth) about (sb/sth)

- Ein paar Männer äußerten sich negativ über die Vorstellung.
  A few men expressed negative feelings about the performance.
- Ich äußere mich lieber nicht über dein Kleid...!
  I'd rather not say anything about your dress...!
- In der Diktatur wagen die Menschen nicht, sich abfällig über die Politik der Regierenden zu äußeren.
  In a dictatorship people do not dare to talk disparagingly about the policies of the ruling class.

aussetzen an + D ⟨etw an jdm/etw a.; *or* an jdm/etw etw auszusetzen haben⟩   to find fault with (sb/sth)

- Was hast du daran auszusetzen?
  What don't you like about it?
- An ihrer Theorie (/Handarbeit) ist nichts auszusetzen.
  Her theory (/handicraft) cannot be faulted.
- Er hat an allem etwas auszusetzen, aber nichts an sich selbst.
  He finds fault with everything except himself.
- Ich habe an ihm auszusetzen, daß er nicht immer pünktlich ist.
  What I don't like about him is that he is not always punctual.

aussöhnen mit + D ⟨jdn mit jdm a.⟩   to reconcile (sb) with (sb)

- Der Eheberater hat die Frau mit ihrem Mann ausgesöhnt.
  The marriage counselor reconciled the woman with her husband.

⟨**sich mit jdm/etw aussöhnen**⟩   to become reconciled with/to (sb /sth)

■ Ich habe mich mit meiner Frau ausgesöhnt.
I reconciled myself (or became reconciled) with my wife.

■ Er hat sich mit seinem Schicksal ausgesöhnt.
He reconciled himself (or has become reconciled) to his fate.

ausspielen gegen + A ⟨**jdn gegen jdn a.**⟩   to play (sb) off against (sb)

■ Die Opposition versucht, den Regierungschef gegen den Parteivorsitzenden auszuspielen.
The opposition tries to play the head of the government off against the party chairman.

s. aussprechen für/gegen + A ⟨**sich für/gegen jdn/etw a.**⟩   to declare *or* pronounce oneself in favor of/against (sb/sth); to come out in favor of/against (sb/sth)

■ Wir müssen uns gegen/für Atomkraftwerke aussprechen.
We must come out against/for nuclear power plants.

■ Ich werde mich für/gegen seine Wiederwahl (/ihn) aussprechen.
I'll pronounce myself in favor of /against his re-election (/him).

s. aussprechen über + A ⟨**sich über jdn/etw a.**⟩   to speak of (sb/sth); to discuss things

■ Die Kollegen sprachen sich lobend über diesen Lehrer aus.
The colleagues spoke highly of this teacher.

■ Wir müssen uns einmal über die Atmosphäre in der Belegschaft aussprechen.
We will have to discuss the atmosphere among the staff.

ausstatten mit + D ⟨**jdn/etw mit etw a.**⟩   to equip (sb/sth) with (sth); to furnish *or* provide (sb/sth) with (sth)

■ Die Natur hat sie mit Schönheit (/Humor/Intelligenz) ausgestattet.
She was born with beauty (/a sense of humor/intelligence).

■ Die Eltern werden sie mit allem Notwendigen ausstatten.
Her parents will furnish her with all the necessities.

ausgestattet sein mit + D ⟨**mit etw a. sein**⟩   to come *or* be equipped with (sth); to be authorized (to do sth); to be endowed with (sth)

■ Das Mädchen ist mit einem guten Sinn für Humor ausgestattet.
The girl has a good sense of humor.

- Der Präsident ist mit einer Vollmacht ausgestattet. . . .
  The president is empowered (or authorized) with/to. . . .
- Dieses Auto ist mit Nebelscheinwerfern ausgestattet.
  This car comes with fog lights.
- Der Raum ist mit einer Klimaanlage ausgestattet.
  The room is equipped with air conditioning.

aussteigen aus + D ⟨aus etw a.⟩   to get out of (sth); to get off (sth: *bus, train, etc*)

- Er ist aus dem Bus (/der Straßenbahn/dem Zug) ausgestiegen.
  He got off the bus (/the streetcar/the train).

  ⟨**aus etw aussteigen**⟩   *(fig)* to give up *or* withdraw from (sth) (*e.g. sports*)

  - Peter (/Mein Partner) will aus dem Unternehmen aussteigen.
    Peter (/My partner) wants to get out of the business.
  - Er ist aus der Konkurrenz (/dem Autorennen/dem Tennisturnier) ausgestiegen.
    He withdrew from the competition (/car race/tennis tournament).

austauschen gegen + A ⟨jdn/etw gegen jdn/etw a.⟩   to exchange (sb/sth) for (sb/sth) else

- Die politischen Gefangenen werden gegeneinander ausgetauscht.
  The political prisoners are being exchanged for one another.
- Der Mechaniker hat das defekte Getriebe gegen ein neues ausgetauscht.
  The mechanic exchanged the defective transmission with a new one.
- Der Tennisspieler hat seinen Trainer gegen einen noch vielseitigeren Trainer ausgetauscht.
  The tennis player exchanged his coach for a more all-around coach.

ausüben auf + A ⟨auf jdn etw a.⟩   to exert on (sb/sth); to have an effect on (sb/sth)

- Die Regierung übte Druck (/ihren Einfluß) auf die Terroristen aus, die Geiseln freizulassen.
  The government put pressure (/exerted its influence) on the terrorists to let the hostages go free.
- Sein Aussehen übt eine starke Anziehungskraft auf Frauen aus.
  His looks have a strong attractive power on women.
- Der Politiker übt einen Reiz auf die Wähler aus.
  The politician has a charming attraction for the voters.

s. auswachsen zu + D ⟨sich zu etw a.⟩   to turn into (sth)

- Der Aufstand wuchs sich zu einer Gefahr für das Land aus.
  The uprising turned into a danger for the country.

- Die scheinbar unbedeutende Affäre hat sich zu einem handfesten Skandal ausgewachsen.
  The seemingly insignificant affair has developed into a full-blown scandal.

- Karl, du hast dich zu einem großen (/gutaussehenden/wohlerzogenen/gut angepaß-
  ten) jungen Mann ausgewachsen!
  *Carl, you have turned into a tall (/handsome/well-behaved/well-adjusted) young
  man!*

auswandern (+ prep)   to emigrate

- Er wanderte nach Australien (/in die Vereinigten Staaten/nach Berlin/nach Kanada
  /in den Iran) aus.
  He emigrated to Australia (/the United States/Berlin/Canada/Iran).

- Meine Großeltern sind aus Schweden ausgewandert.
  My grandparents emigrated from Sweden.

B

bangen um + A ⟨**um jdn/etw b.**⟩   to fear for (sb/sth); to worry about (sb/sth)

- Unser Arzt hatte um das Leben meines Vaters gebangt.
  Our doctor had feared for the life of my father.
- Ich bange um sein Leben (/meine Stellung/meinen heranwachsenden Sohn).
  I fear for his life (/my job; i.e., I may lose my job/(the safety of) my adolescent son).

bangen vor + D ⟨**jdm bangt vor jdm/etw**⟩   to be afraid of (sb/sth)

- Es bangt mir davor (/vor dem Tode/vor ihm).
  I'm afraid of that (/death/him).
- Es bangte ihr vor der Zukunft (/einem Atomkrieg).
  She was afraid of the future (/a nuclear war).

basieren auf + D ⟨**auf etw b.**⟩   to be based on (sth)

- Die Geschichte basiert auf einem authentischen Gerichtsfall.
  The story is based on a true court case.
- Die Ehe basierte auf falschen Vorstellungen (/der Hoffnung, daß sie trotz unterschiedlicher Interessen gut miteinander auskommen würden).
  The marriage was based on misconceptions (/on the hope that they would get along well in spite of their different interests).
- Worauf basiert dieses Argument?
  What is this argument based on?

bauen an + D ⟨**an etw b.**⟩   to be working on (sth); to be building (sth)

- Sie bauten viele Jahre an dieser Kirche (/dem Kölner Dom).
  They were working many years on this church (/the Cologne cathedral).
- Es wird noch an diesem Haus gebaut.
  They are still building this house (i.e., it has not been finished).

bauen auf + A ⟨**auf jdn/etw b.**⟩   to build on (sth); to rely on (sb/sth)

- Labov baute seine Theorie auf soziolinguistischen Beobachtungen auf.
  Labov based his theory on sociolinguistic observations.

■ Sie baute ihre Hoffnungen auf ihren Mann.
She built her hopes on her husband.

■ Er hat immer auf sein Geld (/sein Aussehen/seinen Charme) gebaut.
He always relied on his money (/his looks/his charm).

■ Wir können nicht auf diesen Mechaniker (/sein Geschick) bauen.
We cannot rely on this mechanic (/on his skill).

■ Die Müllers haben auf Föhr gebaut.
The Muellers built a house on (the island of) Föhr.

beantragen (+ prep)   to apply

■ Sabina hat einen Paß (/ein Visum) bei der Behörde beantragt.
Sabina applied to the authorities for a passport (/a visa).

■ Sie beantragte, in der (*or* zur) Universität aufgenommen zu werden.
She applied for admission to the university.

■ Der Staatsanwalt beantragte bei dem Gericht die Todesstrafe.
The district attorney asked the court for the death sentence.

s. bedanken bei/für + D/A ⟨sich bei jdm b. für etw⟩   to thank (sb) for (sth)

■ Ich bedankte mich bei seiner Frau für die Hilfe.
I thanked his wife for the help.

■ Dafür bedanke ich mich. (*ironic*)
No, thank you! (Thank you for nothing!/None of that!)

■ Bei wem hast du dich dafür bedankt?
Whom did you thank for it?

■ Er soll die ganze Arbeit machen? Dafür wird er sich schön bedanken. (*ironic*)
He is to do all the work? He'll love that.

s. befassen mit + D ⟨sich mit jdm/etw b.⟩   to be concerned with (sb/sth); to attend to (sb/sth); to work on (sth)

■ Warum hast du dich so lange mit persischen Dialekten befaßt?
Why did you devote so much time to Persian dialects?

■ Wer sich gründlicher mit einem Problem befassen will, sollte Spezialwerke zur Hand nehmen.
Whoever wants to examine a problem more thoroughly ought to consult special reference books.

■ Ich will mich im Moment nicht damit (/mit dieser Angelegenheit) befassen.
I don't want to be concerned with (or worried about) that right now.

s. befinden (+ prep)   to be; to be situated

- Die Chefin befindet sich oft auf Reisen (/im Ausland).
  The boss often travels (/travels out of the country).
- Ich befinde mich in guter Laune (/im Irrtum/in Verwirrung).
  I am in a good mood (/mistaken/confused).
- Unser Büro befindet sich im 2. Stock.
  Our office is on the third floor.

befinden für/als + A ⟨jdn/etw für/als etw b.⟩   to find (sb/sth) (to be) as (sth); to deem

- Das Gericht befand den Verräter für (*or* als) schuldig.
  The court found the traitor guilty.
- Wir befinden seine Unterstützung für (*or* als) nötig.
  We find his support essential.
- Sie haben es für (*or* als) angemessen befunden.
  They deemed (or found) it to be appropriate.

befinden über + A ⟨über jdn/etw b.⟩   to decide about (sb/sth)

- Der Arzt hat darüber zu befinden, welche Medizin du nehmen mußt.
  It is for the doctor to decide what medicine you must take.
- Über die Höhe der Beiträge wird der Ausschuß befinden.
  The committee will decide (or It is up to the committee to decide) about the fees.

(s.) befreien aus + D ⟨sich/jdn aus etw b.⟩   to liberate (o.s./sb) from (sth)

- Das Mädchen konnte aus den Händen der Entführer befreit werden.
  The girl could be freed from the hands of the kidnappers.
- Ich habe mich aus einer schwierigen Lage befreit.
  I rescued myself (or liberated myself) from a tricky situation.

(s.) befreien von + D ⟨sich/jdn/etw von etw b.⟩   to free *or* liberate (sb/sth) from (sth); to rid (sb/sth) from (sth)

- Houdini konnte sich (/Ich konnte mich) schnell von seinen (/meinen) Ketten befreien.
  Houdini was able to rid himself of his chains (/I was able to rid myself of my chains).

- Die Medizin befreite sie von ihrem Leiden.
  The medicine freed her from her suffering.

- Die Amerikaner befreiten das Land von der Fremdherrschaft.
  The Americans liberated the country from foreign domination.

- Die Aussage des Zeugen befreite ihn von dem Verdacht, am Mord teilgenommen zu haben.
  The witness's testimony exonerated him from the charge of having participated in the murder.

- Manche Menschen sind (*or* werden) von den Steuern (/vom Wehrdienst) befreit.
  Some people are exempt from taxes (/military service).

- Die Frauen sind dabei, sich von der Doppelbelastung durch Beruf und Familie zu befreien.
  Women are in the process of emancipating themselves from the double burden of job and family.

s. befreunden mit + D ⟨**sich mit jdm/etw b.**⟩   to make friends with (sb); to get used to (sb/sth); to warm to (sth)

- Ich habe mich schnell mit dem Austauschschüler befreundet.
  I quickly made friends with the exchange student/The exchange student and I quickly became friends.

- Im Urlaub befreundeten wir uns mit einem Ehepaar aus Chikago.
  On our vacation we became friends with a couple from Chicago.

- Ich kann mich nicht mit dem Gedanken befreunden, noch 30 Aufsätze korrigieren zu müssen.
  I cannot get used to (or warm to) the idea of still having to grade 30 compositions.

s. begeben (+ prep)   to betake oneself; to go (*liter*)

- Ich begebe mich nach Hause (*or* auf den Heimweg/auf eine Reise).
  I'll make my way home (/undertake a trip).

- Wann hast du dich in ärztliche Behandlung begeben?
  When did you get (or start getting) medical treatment?

- Er begab sich zu Bett (/zur Ruhe).
  He repaired to his bed (/retired).

- Sie hat sich in den Garten (/auf die Toilette) begeben.
  She went in the garden (/to the bathroom).

s. begeben an + A ⟨**sich an etw b.**⟩   to start doing (sth)

- Nach dem Streik begaben sich die Arbeiter wieder an die Arbeit.
  After the strike the workers took up work again (or started working again).

- Wann werden sie sich an den Bau der neuen Autobahn begeben?
  When will they start working on the new expressway?

s. begeistern für + A ⟨sich für jdn/etw⟩   to be *or* get enthusiastic about (sb/sth)

■ Ich begeistere mich für griechische Kultur (/das neue Auto/Musik).
   I am (or get) enthusiastic about Greek culture (/the new car/music).

■ Ich kann mich nicht für den Rockmusiker begeistern.
   I cannot get enthusiastic about the rock musician.

begeistert sein von + D ⟨von etw b. sein⟩   to go for (sth); to be enthusiastic about (sth)

■ Ich bin von seinem neuen Auto (/Haus) ganz begeistert.
   I really go for his new car (/house).

■ Sind Sie von der Olympiade begeistert?
   Are you enthusiastic about the Olympics?

beginnen mit + D ⟨mit etw b.⟩   to begin with (sth)

■ Hast du mit der dritten Lektion begonnen?
   Did you begin (with) the third lesson?

■ Die Aufführung beginnt mit einem Prolog.
   The performance begins with a prologue.

beglückwünschen zu + D ⟨jdn zu etw b.⟩   to congratulate (sb) on (sth)

■ Ich beglückwünsche dich zur Geburt deines Sohnes (/zu deiner neuen Arbeit).
   I congratulate you on the birth of your son (/your new job).

■ Hast du sie zu ihrer Schwangerschaft beglückwünscht?
   Did you congratulate her on her pregnancy?

s. begnügen mit + D ⟨sich mit etw b.⟩   to be happy *or* content with (sth); to content oneself with (sth); to put up with (sth)

■ Nils begnügt sich mit dem Wenigen, was er hat.
   Nils is content with what little he's got.

■ Warum begnügst du dich mit diesem schlechten Auto?
   Why are you happy with this bad car?

■ Menschen in Entwicklungsländern müssen sich oft mit dem Existenzminimun begnügen.
   People in developing countries often have to content themselves with a minimal existence.

beharren auf + D ⟨auf etw b.⟩   to insist on (sth); to persist in (sth)

- Nils beharrt eigensinnig auf der Entscheidung, keine psychologische Hilfe anzunehmen.
  Nils obstinately insists on his decision not to accept psychological help.
- Er beharrte auf seinem Standpunkt (/Vorsatz/Entschluß/Willen).
  He insisted on his point of view (/intention/decision/will).
- Sie hat auf ihrer Meinung beharrt, daß Deutschland zweigeteilt bleiben sollte.
  She persisted in her opinion that Germany should remain divided.

beitragen zu + D ⟨zu etw b.⟩   to contribute to (sth)

- Alle trugen zum Gelingen des Festes bei.
  Everyone contributed to the success of the party.
- Er hat sehr zu unserer Unterhaltung beigetragen.
  He contributed a lot to our entertainment.
- Du mußt auch deinen Teil dazu beitragen.
  You must also contribute your share to that.
- Die Vermittlung durch die Vereinten Nationen trug dazu bei, die Lage zu verbessern.
  The mediation of the United Nations served to make the situation better.

bekanntmachen mit + D ⟨jdn mit jdm/etw b.⟩   to show (sb) how to do (sth); to introduce (sb) to (sb)

- Der Meister macht den Lehrling mit der Arbeit bekannt.
  The supervisor is showing the apprentice how to do the work.
- Die Lehrerin machte die Schüler mit den Regeln für den Gebrauch des Adverbs bekannt.
  The teacher informed the students of the rules governing the usage of adverbs.
- Ich werde dich mit ihr bekanntmachen.
  I will introduce you to her.

bekannt sein/werden mit + D ⟨mit jdm/etw b. sein/werden⟩   to be/become acquainted with (sb/sth); to know (sb/sth)

- Ich bin mit der Angelegenheit seit langem bekannt.
  I've known about the matter for a long time.
- Du brauchst sie einander nicht vorzustellen; sie sind schon miteinander bekannt.
  You don't need to introduce them to each other; they already know each other.

s. beklagen über + A ⟨sich über jdn/etw, wegen etw b.⟩   to complain about (sb/sth) because of (sth)

- Ich wollte mich nicht wieder bei dem Gastwirt über das schlechte Essen beklagen.
  I didn't want to complain again about the bad food to the owner of the restaurant.
- Er hat sich bei mir über die (/wegen der) Ungerechtigkeit beklagt.
  He complained to me about the injustice.

s. beklagen (without prep)   to complain

- Wie gefällt es Ihnen bei uns im Hotel? —Oh, wir können uns nicht beklagen.
  How do you like it in our hotel? —Oh, we have nothing to complain about.

s. belaufen auf + A ⟨sich auf etw b.⟩   (*bill, etc*) to come to *or* amount to (sth)

- Die Rechnung beläuft sich auf 100 Mark.
  The bill amounts to 100 marks.
- Die Vertragsfrist belief sich auf 10 Jahre.
  The time span of the treaty came to 10 years.
- Die Anzahl der Spieler beim Fußball beläuft sich auf 11 pro Mannschaft.
  Each soccer team consists of 11 players.

s. bemühen um + A ⟨sich um jdn/etw b.⟩   to strive for (sb/sth); to endeavor to do (sth); to trouble over *or* bother about (sb/sth)

- Ich bemühte mich um eine gute Stelle (/gute Beziehungen zu unseren Nachbarn).
  I tried to get a good job (/good relations with our neighbors).
- Er bemüht sich immer um das Wohl (/das Vertrauen/die Gunst) seines Freundes.
  He always troubles himself over the welfare (/to win the trust/goodwill) of his friend.
- Hast du dich um eine Verbesserung der Lage bemüht?
  Did you try to improve the situation?
- Meine Frau und ich bemühen uns um meinen alten Opa (/unser krankes Kind).
  My wife and I are looking after my old grandfather (/our sick child).
- Er hat sich um die Wohnung bemüht, um näher zu seinem Arbeitsplatz zu wohnen.
  He strove to get the apartment in order to live closer to his work place.
- Ich bemühe mich darum, dich zu verstehen.
  I am trying to understand you.
- Wir bemühten uns um die drogensüchtigen Menschen.
  We tried to help the drug addicts.

beneiden um/wegen + A/G ⟨**jdn um jdn/etw, wegen etw b.**⟩   to envy (sb/sth) for/because of (sth)

■ Ich beneide dich um dein schönes Kleid (*or* wegen deines schönen Kleides).
I envy you your beautiful dress.

■ Inge beneidete ihn um seine Kinder (/um seinen Reichtum/um sein Glück/um seine *or* wegen seiner Fähigkeiten).
Inge envied him his children (/his fortune/his luck/his ability).

■ Ich beneide ihn um seine (*or* wegen seiner) Ruhe (/Energie /Fähigkeiten).
I envy him his calm (/energy/ability).

beneiden (without prep)   to envy

■ Du bist nicht zu beneiden.
I don't envy you.

benutzen als + A ⟨**jdn/etw als etw b.**⟩   to use (sb/sth) as (sth)

■ Ich benutze das Stück der Berliner Mauer als Briefbeschwerer.
I use the piece of the Berlin wall as a paperweight.

■ Natürlich wollen sie sich nicht als billige Arbeitskraft benutzen lassen.
They do not want of course to be used as cheap labor.

■ Sie benutzten die leichte Krankheit ihrer Tochter als Vorwand, die Einladung an die Schwiegermutter abzusagen.
They used their daughter's minor illness as an excuse to cancel the invitation to the mother-in-law.

berichten über/von + A/D ⟨**über jdn/etw, von jdm/etw b.**⟩   to report on (sb/sth); to talk about (sb/sth)

■ Dieser Autor berichtet über das (*or* vom) Verhalten der Tiere.
This author is talking about the behavior of animals.

■ Sie berichtete von ihrer alten (*or* über ihre alte) Tante.
*She reported on (*or* talked about) her old aunt.*

■ Die Professorin berichtete über ihre (*or* von ihren) Erfahrungen mit Schimpansen im Urwald.
The professor gave a report on her experiences with chimpanzees in the jungle.

■ Die Zeitungen haben über diese (*or* von dieser) Gerichtsverhandlung berichtet.
The newspapers reported about these legal proceedings.

berufen (+ prep)   to appoint (*chairmanship, etc.*)

■ Der Professor wurde auf einen Lehrstuhl an die Universität Hamburg berufen.
The professor was appointed to a chair at the University of Hamburg.

■ Die Frau da wurde ins Kabinett berufen.
That woman was appointed to the cabinet.

beruhen auf + D ⟨auf etw b.⟩   to be based on (sth); to be founded on (sth)

■ Der Bericht beruht auf einem Irrtum (/auf der Wahrheit).
The report is based on a mistake (/based on the truth).

■ Die Geschichte beruht auf einer wahren Begebenheit (/auf Tatsachen).
The story is based on a true incident (/on facts).

■ Unsere Zuneigung beruht auf Gegenseitigkeit.
Our affection is mutual.

■ Er ist schon genug bestraft worden. Lassen wir die Sache auf sich beruhen.
He has already been punished sufficiently. Let's leave it at that.

s. berufen auf + A ⟨sich auf jdn/etw b.⟩   to appeal to (sb/sth); to refer to (sb/sth)

■ Das Unfallopfer berief sich auf den Polizisten als Zeugen.
The victim referred to the policeman as a witness.

■ Ich habe mich auf das Urteil des Sachverständigen berufen.
I referred to the opinion of the expert.

■ Der Polizist berief sich auf das neue Gesetz, als er den Autofahrer anhielt.
The policeman referred to (or based his action on) the new law when he stopped the driver.

beschäftigen (without prep)   to employ; to occupy

■ Diese Sache beschäftigt meinen Vater sehr.
This thing keeps my father occupied a great deal.

■ Die Firma beschäftigt 45 Angestellte. Er beschäftigt in seiner Firma 45 Angestellte.
The company has (or provides jobs for) 45 employees. He employs 45 workers in his company.

(s.) beschäftigen mit + D ⟨sich mit jdm/etw b.⟩   to occupy with (sb/sth); to be occupied with (sb/sth); to busy *or* be busy with (sb/sth)

■ Der Vater beschäftigte sich viel mit den Kindern (/sinnlosen Aufgaben/seinen Gedanken/einem Problem).
The father was so occupied with the children (/senseless tasks/his thoughts/a problem).

■ Der Professor beschäftigt sich schon lange mit der Literatur (/mit diesem Phänomen).
The professor has devoted himself to (the study of) literature (/this phenomenon) for a long time.

■ Ich beschäftige mich mit dem neuen Lehrplan (/Fall/Vorschlag).
I am occupying myself with (or studying) the new curriculum (/case/proposal).

■ Ihr neues Buch beschäftigt sich mit der Interpretation von Gedichten.
Her new book deals with the interpretation of poetry.

beschäftigt sein bei + D ⟨bei etw (Arbeit) b. sein⟩   to be employed by *or* work for (sth) (*firm, etc.*)

■ Mein Freund ist bei dieser Firma beschäftigt.
My friend is employed by this firm.

■ Sie ist bei dieser Schule (/bei McDonald) beschäftigt gewesen.
She was employed by this school (/by McDonald's).

beschäftigt sein mit + D ⟨mit jdm/etw b. sein⟩   to be busy with (sth); to be occupied with (sth)

■ Die Mutter war mit dem neugeborenen Baby so sehr beschäftigt, daß sie den Kuchen im Ofen vergaß.
The mother was so busy with the newborn baby that she forgot about the cake in the oven.

■ Sie ist mit ihrer neuen Arbeit (/mit sich selbst) sehr beschäftigt.
She is busy with her new job (preoccupied with herself).

(s.) beschränken auf + A ⟨sich auf jdn/etw b.⟩   to confine *or* be confined to (sb/sth); to limit *or* be limited to (sb/sth)

■ Ich kann jetzt nicht die ganze Geschichte erzählen; ich beschränke mich auf das Wesentliche (/das Wichtigste).
I cannot tell you the whole story; I'll limit myself to the essential points (/most important matters).

■ Die Feuerwehr versuchte, das Feuer auf den Brandherd (/die Küche) zu beschränken.
The fire department attempted to confine the fire to its source (/the kitchen).

■ Wir sollten uns auf fünf Mitglieder für den Ausschuß beschränken.
We should limit ourselves to having five members on the committee.

- Die Wirkung dieser Medizin beschränkt sich darauf, daß Sie ruhiger schlafen können.
  The sole effect of this medicine is that you will be able to sleep more calmly.

s. beschweren über + A ⟨**sich über jdn/etw, wegen einer Sache b.**⟩   to complain about (sb/sth) because of a thing

- Ich finde, Anne hat sich zu Recht über ihn (/über sein Verhalten/wegen der Vernachlässigung) beschwert.
  I think Anne was justified in complaining about him (/about his behavior/because of his neglect).
- Ich beschwerte mich über die schlechte Bedienung (/das schlechte Essen).
  I complained about the bad service (/bad food).
- Warum haben Sie sich nicht beim Vermieter über Ihren lauten Nachbarn beschwert?
  Why didn't you complain about your noisy neighbor to your landlord?

s. beschweren (without prep)   to complain

- Wie geht es dir? —Ich kann mich nicht beschweren.
  How are you doing? —I can't complain.

besorgt sein über + A ⟨**über etw b. sein**⟩   to be worried about (sth)

- Der Schüler ist über seine schlechten Leistungen besorgt.
  The student is worried about his bad performance (in class).

besorgt sein um + A ⟨**um jdn/etw b. sein**⟩   to be concerned about (sb/sth)

- Ich bin um meinen kranken Opa (/das Glück meines Sohnes) besorgt.
  I am worried about my sick grandfather (/the luck of my son).
- An dieser gefährlichen Kreuzung muß man um die Sicherheit der Kinder besorgt sein.
  At this dangerous intersection one must be concerned about the safety of the children.

besorgt sein (without prep)   to be concerned

- Ich war sehr besorgt, weil sie nicht kam.
  I was worried because she didn't come.

bestätigen in + D ⟨jdn in/als etw b.⟩   to acknowledge (sb/sth); to confirm (sb/sth); to recognize (sb/sth)

■ Das Parlament hat ihn im Amt (/als Bundeskanzler) bestätigt.
Parliament confirmed his appointment (/him as chancellor).

■ Ich hatte angenommen, daß er sehr klug war und fand mich darin durch seine Tests bestätigt.
I had assumed that he was very intelligent, and my assumption was confirmed by his tests.

bestehen auf + D ⟨auf etw b.⟩   to insist on (sth)

■ Ich bestand auf Pünktlichkeit (/meinem Recht).
I insisted on punctuality (/my rights).

■ Ich bestehe darauf (/auf meinem Standpunkt).
I insist (/on my point of view).

■ Sie besteht darauf, daß die Kinder pünktlich nach Hause kommen.
She insists that the children come home on time.

bestehen aus + D ⟨aus etw b.⟩   to consist of (sth)

■ Die Postsendung besteht aus drei Paketen.
The mail consists of three packages.

■ Die Torte bestand aus vielen exotischen Zutaten.
The cake contained many exotic ingredients.

■ Die Stöcke bestehen aus leichtem Metall.
The sticks are made from a light metal.

bestehen gegen + A ⟨gegen jdn b.⟩   to hold up against (sb)

■ Frazier konnte gegen Ali nicht bestehen.
Frazier was no match for Ali.

bestehen in + D ⟨in etw b.⟩   to consist *or* exist in (sth)

■ Seine einzige Chance besteht darin, im Lotto zu gewinnen.
His only chance is to win the lottery.

■ Die Schwierigkeit (/Das Problem) besteht darin, daß wir zu wenige qualifizierte Leute haben.
The difficulty (/problem) lies in the fact that we have too few qualified people.

■ Das Leben Schweitzers bestand in Hilfe für andere.
Schweitzer's life consisted of helping others.

bestehen neben + D ⟨neben etw b.⟩   to hold up *or* stand up against (sth); to compare with (sth)

■ Die Produkte aus den östlichen Giebieten Deutschlands können bisher nicht neben denen aus den westlichen bestehen.
So far East German products cannot compare to those manufactured in the West.

bestehen vor + D ⟨vor jdm/etw b.⟩   to stand up to/against (sb/sth)

■ Kann er mit dem, was er tut, vor seinem Gewissen bestehen?
Can he live with what he is doing?

■ Dieses Buch wird vor jeder Kritik bestehen.
This book will stand up to any criticism.

■ Wir müssen alle einmal vor Gott bestehen.
We will all have to face up to God sometime.

bestehen (without prep)   to be in existence; to exist; to remain

■ Die Universität besteht seit hundert Jahren.
The university has been in existence for a hundred years.

■ Es besteht die Hoffnung (/die Aussicht/der Verdacht/die Gefahr), daß die USA die einzige Supermacht sein werden.
There is (the) hope (/the prospect/the suspicion/the danger) that the USA will be the only remaining superpower.

bestellen (+ prep)   to have an appointment

■ Ich bin auf (für, um) 5 Uhr (zu Ihnen) bestellt.
I have an appointment for (or at) 5 o'clock (with you).

■ Die Sprechstundenhilfe hat mich für Freitag bestellt.
The doctor's receptionist gave me an appointment for Friday.

bestellen (+ prep) ⟨jdn b.⟩   to ask (sb) to come; to summon (sb)

■ Ich bestellte ihn in das Restaurant.
I asked him to meet me at the restaurant.

- Ich habe sie zu mir bestellt.
  I asked her to come (to see me).
- Der Leiter des Krankenhauses hat den Arzt in sein Büro bestellt.
  The director of the hospital summoned the doctor to his office.

  ⟨es ist um jdm/etw, mit jdm/etw gut/schlecht bestellt⟩   to be good/bad

  - Es ist schlecht (/gut) um ihn (/mit seinen Finanzen) bestellt.
    He is (/His finances are) in a bad (/good) way.
  - Um seine Gesundheit (/Mit ihm) ist es schlecht (/gut) bestellt.
    His health is bad (/good).

bestellen als + N ⟨jdn als etw b.⟩   to appoint (sb) as (sth)

- Er wurde vom Gericht als Gutachter bestellt.
  He was called in as an expert witness by the court.

bestellen zu + D ⟨jdn zu etw b.⟩   to appoint (sb) (sth)

- Der ältere Sohn wurde zu seinem Nachfolger (Vertreter) bestellt.
  The older son was appointed his successor (/as his representative).
- Sie haben sie zur Richterin (/Schulleiterin) bestellt.
  They have appointed her judge (/principal).

bestellen (without prep)   to order; to reserve; to have an appointment

- Ich habe mir ein neues Hemd beim Otto-Versand bestellt.
  I have ordered a new shirt from Otto mail-order.
- Hast du schon (/ein Bier/ein Taxi) bestellt?
  Did you already order (/a beer/a taxi)?
- Ich bestellte (beim Reisebüro) ein Hotelzimmer (/eine Theaterkarte).
  I reserved a hotel room (/a theater ticket) (at the travel agency).
- Sind Sie bestellt?
  Do you have an appointment?
- Er kam wie bestellt.
  He came as if it had been arranged (for him to come).
- Bitte bestell' deinen Eltern (/Peter/ihm) einen schönen Gruß von uns.
  Please give our greetings to your parents (/Peter/him).
- Ich soll Ihnen bestellen, daß meine Tochter heute nicht zur Schule kommen kann.
  I was asked to inform you that my daughter cannot come to school today.

bestimmen für/zu + A/D ⟨jdn/etw für/zu etw b.⟩   to intend *or* to mean (sb/sth) for (sth); to choose *or* to designate (sb) as (sth)

■ Wieviel Geld ist für Anschaffungen (/zum Bau der Autobahn) bestimmt?
How much money has been earmarked for purchases (/for the construction of the highway)?

■ Die beiden waren für einander bestimmt.
Those two were meant for each other.

■ Ich glaube, euer Sohn ist für eine große Zukunft bestimmt.
I think your son is destined for higher things.

■ Die Tochter wurde zur Nachfolgerin der Königin bestimmt.
The daughter was named the successor of the queen.

bestimmen über + A ⟨über jdn/etw b.⟩   to decide on (sb/sth)

■ Du kannst über deine Zukunft allein bestimmen.
It is up to you what you do with your future.

■ Du kannst nicht über ihn (/seine Zeit/sein Geld) bestimmen.
It's not up to you to decide what he's going to do (/how his time is to be spent/how he spends his money).

■ Sie allein bestimmt über die Verwendung des Geldes.
She alone decides about the use of the money.

bestrafen für + A ⟨jdn für etw b.⟩   to punish (sb) for (sth)

■ Er ist genug für seine Verbrechen bestraft worden.
He's been punished enough for his crimes.

■ Der Junge wurde für seinen Übermut (/das Abgucken) bestraft.
The boy was punished for his recklessness (/cheating).

bestrafen mit + D ⟨jdn/etw mit etw b.⟩   to sentence (sb) to (sth)

■ Der Mörder wird mit lebenslänglicher Haft bestraft.
The murderer is sentenced to life imprisonment.

■ Der Richter bestrafte ihn mit zwei Jahren Gefängnis.
The judge sentenced him to two years in jail.

■ Der Schiedsrichter bestrafte das Foul mit zwei Schüssen.
The referee awarded (or gave) two shots for the foul.

s. betätigen (+ prep)   to work; to be active; to busy o.s.

- Herr Schmidt betätigt sich am Wochenende oft als Hobbygärtner.
  On weekends Mr. Schmidt often works in his garden as a hobby.
- Wenn du dich als Babysitter betätigst, kannst du ein bißchen Geld verdienen.
  When you work as a babysitter, you can earn a little money.
- Ich betätige mich politisch bei einer großen Partei.
  I am politically active in a big party.

s. beteiligen an + D ⟨sich an etw b.⟩   to take part in (sth); to participate in (sth); (*finance*) to give (sb) a share in (sth)

- Ich wollte mich an dem nutzlosen Gespräch (/Diskussionen über dieses Thema) nicht beteiligen.
  I didn't want to take part in the pointless conversation (/discussions of this topic).
- Werdet ihr euch auch an den Unkosten (/dem Geschenk) beteiligen?
  Are you going to contribute to the costs (/the gift), too ?
- Ich beteiligte mich an der Aufführung (/dem Brettspiel).
  I participated in the performance (/the board game).
- Die Bank hat sich mit einer halben Million Dollar an dem Unternehmen beteiligt.
  The bank bought a share of the company worth half a million dollars.

beteiligt sein/werden an + D   to be/become involved in (sth); to have a part in (sth); to have an interest *or* a share in (sth); to be/become interested in (*a business*)

- Er soll an einem Skandal (/einem Einbruch) beteiligt gewesen sein.
  He is said to have been involved in a scandal (/burglary).
- Er war an der Entdeckung der Bakterien maßgeblich beteiligt.
  He made a major contribution to the discovery of the bacteria.
- Meine Kusine ist an der Erbschaft (/der Unternehmung) beteiligt.
  My cousin has a share in the inheritance (/the endeavour).
- Jutta ist mit 40% an dem Geschäft beteiligt.
  Jutta has a 40% share in the business.

beten (+ prep)   to pray

- Er betete zu Gott.
  He prayed to god.
- Laßt uns für den Frieden beten!
  Let's pray for peace.

■ Die Bauern haben um (*or* für) eine gute Ernte gebetet.
The farmers prayed for a good crop.

■ Herr und Frau Rose beten immer bei Tisch.
Mr. and Mrs. Rose always say grace.

betroffen sein über + A ⟨**über etw b. sein**⟩   to be dismayed by (sth)

■ Viele Menschen waren sehr betroffen über das schwere Unglück.
Many people were very dismayed by the serious accident.

betroffen sein von + D ⟨**von etw b. sein**⟩   to be affected by (sth); to be hit by (sth); to be dismayed at (sth)

■ Die Rentner sind von der Steuererhöhung nicht betroffen.
Pensioners are not affected by the tax hike.

■ Die alten Häuser waren am stärksten von dem Feuer betroffen.
The old houses were hit the worst by the fire.

■ Viele Menschen waren von dem schweren Unglück betroffen.
A lot of people were affected by the serious accident.

bewahren vor + D ⟨**jdn vor etw b.**⟩   to keep *or* prevent (sb) from (doing) (sth)

■ Der liebe Gott bewahre meinen Sohn davor, so etwas zu tun!
*May God keep (*or *prevent) my son from doing something like this!*

■ Dieser Entschluß sollte uns vor Verlusten (/Enttäuschungen/Abhängigkeit) bewahren.
This decision should save us from losses (/disappointments/dependence).

■ Vitamin C soll uns vor Krankheit (/vor Erkältung) bewahren.
Vitamin C should protect us from getting sick (/catching cold).

■ Ich wollte dich nur vor einer Dummheit bewahren.
I only wanted to stop you from doing something stupid.

bewegen zu + D ⟨**jdn zu etwas b.**⟩   to induce *or* persuade (sb) to do (sth)

■ Was hat dich zu diesem Schritt bewogen?
What made you take this step?

■ Kann ich dich dazu bewegen, mit mir ins Kino zu gehen?
Can I persuade you to go to the movies with me?

■ Er bewog mich zu einem Kinobesuch.
*He persuaded me to take in (*or *go to) a movie.*

■ Der Eheberater bewog ihn (dazu), sich mit seiner Exfrau zu versöhnen.
   The marriage counselor persuaded him to make his peace with his ex-wife.

   ⟨sich zu etw bewegen lassen⟩   to be persuaded to do (sth)

   ■ Ich ließ mich dazu bewegen, den Abgabetermin für die Hausaufgaben
      zu verschieben.
      *I allowed myself to be persuaded to put off the deadline for the home-
      work.*

s. bewerben um + A ⟨sich um etw (bei einer Firma, etc) b.⟩   to apply for (sth) (to
or at a firm for a job)

■ Ich bewerbe mich morgen um die Stelle (bei der Versicherung).
   I'll apply for the job tomorrow (at the insurance company).

■ Er bewarb sich um eine Professur (/einen Studienplatz in Medizin).
   He applied for a (professorship) chair (/a place to study medicine).

■ Die Firma hat sich erfolgreich um den Auftrag beworben.
   The company put in a successful bid for the contract.

bewerten mit + D ⟨jdn/etw mit etw b.⟩   to judge (sb/sth); to value *or* to put a value
on (sb/sth); to assess (sb/sth)

■ Der Lehrer hat den Schüler in Englisch (/die Arbeit des Schülers) mit (der Note)
   „sehr gut" bewertet.
   The teacher gave the student the grade "very good" in English (on his test).

■ Der Kampfrichter bewertete ihre Kür (Leistung) nur mit der Note 4,9.
   The referee gave her only 4.9 points for her free section (performance).

■ Der Versicherungsexperte bewertete den Verlust (/Schaden) mit 2000 DM.
   The insurance expert assessed the loss (/damage) at 2000 marks.

bezahlen (+ prep)   to pay

■ Er bezahlt in bar (/in ausländischer Währung/in Dollar/in italienischen Lire/mit
   einem Scheck).
   He pays in cash (/in foreign currency/in dollars/in Italian lira/with a check).

■ Er wird seinen Mangel an Vorsicht mit seinem Leben bezahlen müssen.
   He'll have to pay with his life for his lack of care (or attention).

■ Ich bezahlte 15 DM für den Hut (/dafür).
   I paid 15 marks for the hat (/it).

■ Die Arbeiter werden nach (/über/unter) Tarif bezahlt.
The workers are paid according to (/above/below) the (union) rate.

(s.) bezeichnen als + A ⟨sich/jdn/etw als etw b.⟩   to describe (o.s./sb/sth) as (sth)

■ Sie bezeichnet sich (/ihn) gern als Künstler.
She likes to call herself (/him) an artist.

■ Die Polizei hat ihn als Betrüger (/hat es als Betrug) bezeichnet.
The police called him a swindler (/it a swindle).

bezeichnen mit + D ⟨jdn/etw mit etw b.⟩   to describe *or* signify (sb/sth) with (sth)

■ Mit dem Wort „Anorak" bezeichnet man. . . .
The word "Anorak" describes (or signifies). . . .

s. beziehen auf + A ⟨sich auf jdn/etw b.⟩   to refer to (sb/sth)

■ In meinem letzten Brief bezog ich mich auf Ihr Angebot vom. . . .
In my last letter I referred to your offer of. . . .

■ Wir beziehen uns auf Ihr Schreiben vom 13.11 (/auf unser Ferngespräch vom *or* am Donnerstag) und teilen Ihnen mit. . .
We are referring to your letter of November 11 (/to our telephone conversation on Thursday) and share with you. . . .

■ Mit seiner Meinung bezieht er sich auf George Bush, der sagte. . . .
In his opinion he refers to George Bush who said. . . .

■ Die Zeitung bezieht sich auf den Watergateskandal (/Nixon).
The newspaper refers to the Watergate scandal (/Nixon).

■ Diese Kritik bezog sich nicht auf dich (/auf deine Arbeit).
This criticism was not directed at you (/your work).

■ Warum bezieht er (bloß) immer alles auf sich?
Why does he always take everything personally?

beziehen aus + D ⟨aus etw b.⟩   to draw from (sth)

■ Er bezieht sein Wissen ausschließlich aus Büchern.
He draws his knowledge exclusively from books.

■ Entwicklungsländer beziehen fast alle Industrieprodukte aus dem Ausland (/den Industrieländern).
Developing countries obtain almost all their industrial goods from foreign countries (/industrialized countries).

s. binden an + A ⟨**sich an jdn b.**⟩   to tie (up) to; to commit *or* bind oneself to (sb)

■ Wer sich für immer an jemanden bindet, muß sich die Sache vorher gut überlegen.
Whoever is going to seriously commit himself to someone must reflect well on the matter.

■ Ich habe mich zu früh an das Mädchen gebunden.
I got tied up too quickly with that girl.

■ Buchhändler in Deutschland sind an feste Preise (/vorgeschriebene Ladenschlußzeiten) gebunden.
Booksellers in Germany have fixed prices (/must conform to prescribed hours of business).

binden zu/in + D/A ⟨**etw zu /in etw b.**⟩   to tie *or* bind (sth) into (sth)

■ Er hat die Blumen zu einem Strauß (/Kranz) gebunden.
He arranged the flowers in a bouquet (/wreath).

■ Der Weizen (/Das Korn) wurde in (*or* zu) Garben gebunden.
The wheat (/grain) was bound into sheaves.

bitten um + A ⟨**jdn um etw b.**⟩   to ask (sb) for (sth)

■ Ich werde sie um Geld (/eine Unterredung/einen Gefallen/den nächsten Tanz) bitten.
I'll ask her for money (/an appointment/a favor/the next dance).

■ Ich bat ums Wort.
I asked for the floor.

■ Du hast mich nicht um Erlaubnis gebeten.
You didn't ask me for permission.

blättern in + D ⟨**in etw b.**⟩   to leaf through (sth) (*a book*); to flip through (sth)

■ Er blätterte in einem Album (/in einer Zeitschrift/in den Akten).
He leafed through an album (/a magazine/the files).

bleiben (+ prep)   to stay, to remain

■ Die Kranke mußte ein paar Tage im Bett bleiben.
The sick woman had to stay in bed a few days.

■ Sie wollten über Nacht (/über Weihnachten/unter der Decke) bleiben.
They wanted to stay overnight (/over Christmas/under cover).

■ Bleibt ihr heute bei uns zum Essen?
Are you going to stay (at our house) for dinner?

■ Er ist zu Hause (/an der Macht) geblieben.
He stayed at home (/in power).

■ Er ist auf der Couch sitzen geblieben.
He remained sitting on the couch.

bleiben bei + D ⟨**bei jdm/etw b.**⟩   (*fig*) to keep *or* stick to (sb/sth)

■ Ihm fällt es sehr schwer, lange bei einer Sache zu bleiben.
He finds it very hard to concentrate on one thing for a long time.

■ Er blieb bei der Aussage, daß er das Opfer noch nie gesehen hatte.
He insisted that he had never seen the victim.

■ Trotz vieler Angriffe ist er bei seiner Meinung geblieben.
Despite many attacks he stuck to his guns.

■ Auch wenn es nicht angenehm ist, mußt du bei der Wahrheit bleiben.
You have to stick to the truth even if it may not be pleasant.

■ Sie blieb bei ihm, obwohl sie ihn nicht mehr liebte.
She stayed with him although she did not love him anymore.

blicken (+ prep)   to look, to glance

■ Der Junge blickt flüchtig auf die Uhr.
The boy is glancing at (or looking briefly) at his watch.

■ Vom Fernsehturm kann man auf die ganze Stadt blicken.
One can see the entire city from the television tower.

■ Das Mädchen blickte geradeaus (/zur Seite/hin und her/nach unten).
The girl glanced straight ahead (/to the side/back and forth/down).

■ Er blickte durch den Türspalt (/ins Zimmer/in das Magazin/um sich/ zur Seite/zu Boden).
He glanced through the crack of the door (/into the room/at the magazine/around himself/to the side/at the floor).

■ Der Mond blickte durch die Wolken.
The moon peeked through the clouds.

(s.) borgen von/bei + D ⟨**(sich) etw von** *or* **bei jdm b.**⟩   to borrow (sth) from (sb)

■ Ich habe mir die Dylan-Platte von (*or* bei) Rolf geborgt.
I borrowed the Dylan record from Rolf.

■ Fast alle originellen Gedanken für sein neues Buch hat er bei (*or* von) anderen Autoren geborgt.
He borrowed almost all his original ideas from other authors.

■ Er borgte das Geld für ein neues Auto von (*or* bei) seinen Eltern.
He borrowed the money for a new car from his parents.

brauchen für + A ⟨jdn/etw für jdn/etw b.⟩   to need (sb/sth) for (sb/sth)

■ Er braucht das Geld für ein neues Auto (/das Studium seines Sohnes).
He needs the money for a new car (/his son's studies).

■ Ich brauche diese Batterien für mein Radio.
I need these batteries for my radio.

■ Wir brauchen mindestens fünf Leute für diese Arbeit (/für den Umzug).
We need at least five people for this job (/for the move).

■ Für den Grenzübertritt nach Polen brauchte man Paß und Visum.
In order to cross the border into Poland, one needed a passport and a visa.

■ Der Mechaniker hat für die Reparatur vier Stunden gebraucht.
The mechanic needed four hours for the repair job.

brauchen für/zu + A/D ⟨jdn/etw für/zu etw b.⟩   to need (sb/sth) for (sth)

■ Er braucht das Geld zur (*or* für die) Tilgung seiner Schulden (/Abzahlung seiner Hypothek).
He needs the money for the repayment of his debt (/the payment of his mortgage).

■ Brauchen Sie all das Material zum (*or* für den) Bau ihrer Garage?
Do you need all this material for the construction of your garage?

■ Zur (*or* Für die) Reparatur des Kühlschranks brauchen wir einen Techniker (/besondere Teile).
For the repair of the refrigerator we need a technician (/special parts).

brauchen zu   (with infinitive/nominal forms) to need for

■ Die Studentin braucht zum Schreiben einen Füller (/völlige Ruhe).
The student needs a pen (/absolute silence) for writing.

■ Ich brauchte heute nicht zu arbeiten (/zu kochen/zu kommen).
I didn't need to work (/to cook/to come) today.

(s.) brennen (+ prep)   to burn oneself

■ Die neue Mückensalbe brennt auf der Haut.
The new mosquito repellent burns (causes the skin to burn).

- Diese Kontaktlinse (/Kontaktlinsenflüssigkeit) brennt im Auge.
  This contact lens (/contact solution) burns (or stings) my eye.

- Ihm brennen die Füße vom vielen Gehen (/Fußballspielen).
  His feet are burning from walking (/playing soccer) so much.

- Das Essen (/Der Pfeffer) brennt mir auf der Zunge.
  The food (/pepper) is burning my tongue.

- Ich habe mich am Herd (/Kühler) gebrannt.
  I burned myself at the stove (/radiator).

brennen auf + A ⟨**auf etw b.**⟩   to die *or* itch for (sth) *(fig)*

- Die Großmutter brennt darauf, den neuen Jungen zu sehen.
  The grandmother is dying to see the new boy.

- Er brannte auf Vergeltung (/Rache).
  He was dying to retaliate (/take revenge).

brennen in + A ⟨**in etw b.**⟩   to burn (sth) *(a sign, etc)* in(to) *or* on(to) (sth)

- Er brannte ein Zeichen in die Haut (/auf das Fell) des Tieres.
  He burned the ranch's brand into the hide of the animal.

- Ein Blumenmuster ist in das Porzellan (/die Vase) gebrannt.
  The flower pattern is baked into the china (/vase).

brennen vor + D ⟨**vor etw brennen**⟩   to be impatient with (sth)

- Er brennt vor Ungeduld (/Neugier/Ehrgeiz).
  He is burning with impatience (/curiosity/ambition).

bringen (+ prep)   to bring

- Ich brachte ihn an die Bahn (/zum Flughafen/ins Krankenhaus).
  I brought (or took) him to the train station (/to the airport/to the hospital).

- Peter hat seine Freundin nach Hause gebracht.
  Peter saw his girlfrend home.

- Die Mutter brachte das Kind ins (or zu) Bett.
  The mother put the child to bed.

- Sie konnte das (/ihren Einwand) nicht über die Lippen bringen.
  She could not bring it (/her objection) to her lips.

bringen auf + A ⟨es auf etw b.⟩   to bring to (sth); to attain *or* to achieve (sth)

- Er hat es beim Kartenspiel auf 25 Punkte gebracht.
  He got (or received) 25 points in the card game.
- Der Motor hat es auf 200.000 Kilometer gebracht.
  The engine kept going for 200,000 kilometers.
- Sie haben den Satelliten auf eine Umlaufbahn um die Erde gebracht.
  They got the satellite to rotate around the earth.
- Der Vorsitzende brachte das Gespräch auf ein anderes Thema.
  The chairman brought the conversation around to another subject.
- Mein Großvater hat es auf 80 Jahre gebracht.
  My grandfather reached the age of 80.

> ⟨jdn auf etw bringen⟩   to suggest (sth) to (sb); to lead (sb) astray; to bring
> (sb) back to the straight and narrow
>
> - Was du sagst, bringt mich auf eine gute Idee (/auf andere Gedanken).
>   Wir können eine Nacht in New York verbringen.
>   *What you say gives me a good idea (/other thoughts). We could spend
>   a night in New York.*
> - Seine Bemerkungen brachten mich auf die richtige Spur.
>   *His remarks put me on the right track.*
> - Die Jungen brachten ihn auf die schiefe Bahn (/auf den rechten Weg).
>   *The boys led him astray (/got him back on the straight and narrow).*

bringen um + A ⟨jdn um etw b.⟩   to make (sb) lose (sth), to do (sb) out of (sth)

- Die niedrigen Weizenpreise haben den Bauern um sein ganzes Vermögen (/seine
  gesamten Ersparnisse) gebracht.
  The low price of wheat made the farmer lose his entire fortune (/his entire savings).
- Man hat ihn um den verdienten Lohn (/seine Ehre/die Erbschaft) gebracht.
  They did him out of his earned salary (/honor/inheritance).
- Der Schiedsrichter in Wimbledon hat durch seine Fehlentscheidung den Tennis-
  spieler um den Sieg gebracht.
  *Through his mistake, the referee at Wimbledon cheated the tennis player out of
  the victory.*
- Er tut das doch nur, um mich um den Verstand zu bringen.
  He only does that to drive me mad.
- Die Kuckucksuhr hat mich um den Schlaf gebracht.
  The cuckoo clock kept me from getting any sleep.
- Er hat sie (/den Mann/die Frau) ums Leben gebracht.
  He killed them (/the man/the woman).

■ Er brachte sich ums Leben.
He killed himself (He committed suicide).

bringen zu + D ⟨**es zu etw b.**⟩   to get (sth) (*somewhere/nowhere*), to achieve (*something/nothing*)

■ Hans hat es in kurzer Zeit zum Direktor (/zum Manager) gebracht.
Hans became a director (/manager) in a short time.

■ Ihr Sohn hat es schon zu manchem schönen Erfolg gebracht.
Her son attained great success.

■ Mein Vater hat das Auto gerade noch zum Stehen gebracht.
My father barely managed to bring the car to a stop.

⟨**jdn zu etw bringen**⟩   (with infinitive/nominal complements) to make (sb) act, behave, move, etc

■ Der Schauspieler hat uns zum Lachen (/Weinen) gebracht.
The actor made us laugh (/cry).

■ Der Staatsanwalt versuchte den Zeugen zum Reden zu bringen.
The prosecuting attorney attempted to make the witness talk.

■ Man brachte ihn schließlich dazu, sein Amt niederzulegen.
They finally made him retire from his office.

■ Barbara brachte mich zur Verzweiflung (/zur Vernunft).
Barbara drove me to despair (/brought me to my senses).

buchen (+ prep)   to book; to reserve

■ Udo buchte einen Platz im Flugzeug (/auf dem Schiff/nach Chikago).
Udo booked a place on the plane (/on the ship/to Chicago).

bummeln (+ prep)   to stroll; to dawdle; to hang about; to idle; to bum around; to take it easy

■ Wir sind durch die Straßen (/über den Piccadilly/durch den Supermarkt) gebummelt.
We strolled through the streets (/across Piccadilly/through the supermarket).

■ Das Liebespaar ging am Strand (/im Park) bummeln.
The lovers went for (or took) a stroll on the beach (/in the park).

■ Er bummelte im Büro (/im zweiten Semester/bei der Arbeit).
He loafed in the office (/in the second semester/on the job).

büßen für + A ⟨für etw b.⟩   to pay for (sth); to atone for (sth); to pay the penalty for (sth); to suffer for (sth)

■   Er mußte für seine Dummheit (/Unachtsamkeit) schwer büßen.
He had to pay dearly for his stupidity (/lack of attention).

■   Der Student wird dafür büßen, daß er während seines Studiums nicht hart genug arbeitete.
The student will pay for the fact that he did not work hard enough at the university.

büßen mit + D ⟨mit etw b.⟩   to pay for (sth) with (sth)

■   Er mußte den Fehler mit seinem Leben büßen.
He had to pay for his mistake with his life.

D

danken für + A ⟨jdm für etw d.⟩   to thank (sb) for (sth)

■ Ich möchte Ihnen (/allen meinen Freunden) für die Geschenke danken.
  I'd like to thank you (/all my friends) for the gifts.

davonkommen mit + D ⟨mit etw d.⟩   to escape with (sth); to get off with (sth)

■ Er ist mit dem Schrecken (/knapper Not/einer Bewährungsstrafe) davongekommen.
  He escaped with no more than a scare (/He had a narrow escape/got off with a probation period).

■ Das Auto überschlug sich dreimal. Aber der Fahrer kam mit dem Leben (/einem gebrochenen Bein) davon.
  The car turned over three times. But the driver escaped with his life (/with only a broken leg).

■ Allein auf den gefährlichen Berg zu klettern, war eine Dummheit von dir. Zum Glück bist du mit einem blauen Auge davongekommen.
  To climb the dangerous mountain alone was really stupid of you. Fortunately, you got off easy.

decken für + A ⟨etw für jdn d.⟩   to set (sth) for (sb)

■ Seine Mutter deckte eine Tafel für acht Personen.
  His mother set the table for eight people.

■ Der Tisch ist für vier Personen (/zum Frühstück) gedeckt.
  The table is set for four people (/for breakfast).

decken mit + D ⟨etw mit etw d.⟩   to cover (sth) with (sth)

■ Sie haben das Dach mit Ziegeln (/Stroh) gedeckt.
  They roofed the building with tiles (/thatched the roof with straw).

■ Ich muß den Fehlbetrag (/die Kosten) mit einem Scheck decken.
  I'll have to cover the remaining balance (/expenses) with a check.

■ Ihr müßt den gegnerischen Linksaußen mit eurem besten Verteidiger decken; sonst verliert ihr.
  You ought to cover the opposing left forward with your best defender; otherwise, you'll lose.

s. decken mit + D ⟨sich mit etw d.⟩   to coincide *or* agree (sth) with (sth)

- Deine Behauptung deckt sich nicht mit den Tatsachen.
  Your statement does not square (or agree) with the facts.
- Meine Ansichten (/Interessen/Pläne) decken sich mit denen meiner Freunde.
  My views (/interests/plans) coincide with my friends'.

decken über + A ⟨etw über etw d.⟩   to spread (sth) over (sth)

- Kannst du mir helfen, die Tischdecke über den Tisch zu decken?
  Can you help me spread the tablecloth over the table?
- Laß uns den Mantel des Schweigens über deine Verfehlungen decken.
  Let's not talk about your misdeeds any more.

degradieren zu + D ⟨jdn/etw zu etw d.⟩   to demote (sb/sth) to (sth)

- Der Offizier wurde zu einem niedrigeren Rang degradiert.
  The officer was demoted to a lower rank.
- Der General degradierte den Hauptmann wegen Feigheit zum Leutnant.
  The general demoted the captain for cowardice to (the rank of) lieutenant.
- Die Schulaufsicht degradierte den Schulleiter zum einfachen Lehrer.
  The board of education demoted the principal to the position of classroom teacher.

demonstrieren für/gegen + A ⟨für/gegen jdn/etw d.⟩   to demonstrate in support of/against (sb/sth)

- Sie demonstrierten gegen den Diktator (/für den beliebten Präsidenten/für den Frieden/gegen politische Korruption).
  They demonstrated against the dictator (/in support of the popular president/for peace/against political corruption).

denken an + A ⟨an jdn/etw d.⟩   to think of (sb/sth); to have (sb/sth) in mind; to think back on (sb/sth)

- Die werdende Mutter denkt oft an ihre Jugendzeit (/tote Oma).
  The expectant mother often thinks of her youth (/dead grandmother).
- Ich denke an dich (/das neue Buch/die schöne Zeit in Hamburg).
  I'm thinking of you (/the new book/the great time in Hamburg).
- An meinen Vorteil (/mein Studium) habe ich gar nicht gedacht.
  I didn't have my own advantage (/my studies) in mind.
- Paul ist ein Egoist. Er denkt nur an sich (/an seinen Vorteil).
  Paul is an egotist. He only thinks of himself (/of his advantage).

■ Bei dieser Aufgabe haben wir an Hartmut gedacht.
We think that Hartmut is the right person to do this job.

s. denken bei + D ⟨sich etw bei etw d.⟩   to mean (sth) by (sth)

■ Ich habe ihn zufällig gestoßen, aber ich habe mir nichts Böses dabei gedacht.
I accidentally pushed him, but I didn't mean any harm (in it).

■ Was hast du dir bei dieser Dummheit bloß gedacht?
What were you thinking of when you did this stupid thing?

■ Er raucht Marihuana gern und denkt sich nichts dabei.
He enjoys smoking marijuana and doesn't think anything of it.

denken in + D ⟨in etw d.⟩   to think in (sth)

■ Er spricht Englisch aber denkt in seiner eigenen Sprache (/in Deutsch).
He speaks English but thinks in his own language (/in German).

■ Sonia hält nichts vom Feminismus. In dieser Hinsicht (/in diesem Punkt/in dieser Frage) denke ich ganz anders als sie.
Sonia doesn't think much of feminism. In this regard (/on this point/with regard to this question) I am of a totally different opinion.

■ Die Amerikaner denken in anderen Kategorien (/Begriffen/Größenordnungen/ Dimensionen) als die Deutschen.
Americans think in different categories (/concepts/sizes/dimensions) than the Germans.

denken über/von + A/D ⟨über etw, *rarely* von etw d.⟩   to think about/of (sb/sth)

■ Wie denkst du über die Abtreibungsfrage ?
What do you think about the abortion question?

■ Ich denke über die Verhältnisse in Kuwait (/darüber) ganz anders als du.
I think differently about the situation in Kuwait (/it) than you.

denken von/über + D/A ⟨etw von jdm, *rarely* über jdn d.⟩   to think (sth) of (sb)

■ Meine Mutter denkt immer gleich das Schlimmste von meinem (*or* über meinen) Bruder.
My mother always thinks the worst of my brother.

■ Wie niedrig Sie von Menschenwürde denken! (Schiller)
How lowly you consider the worthiness of man!

■ Ich denke gerade im Moment schöne Sachen über dich.
I'm thinking nice things about you right at this moment.

(nicht) denken von + D ⟨etw von jdm (nicht) denken⟩   (not) to think of (sb) (in reference to an act perceived as implausible for (sb/sth))

- Er hat seine Kinder erschossen. Wer hätte das von ihm gedacht?
  He shot his children. Who would have expected that from him?
- Niemand hätte das von ihr gedacht.
  No one would have thought that of her.

desinteressiert sein an + D ⟨an etw d. sein⟩   to be uninterested in (sth)

- Er ist an Politik (/Philosophie/Linguistik) desinteressiert.
  He is uninterested in politics (/philosophy/linguistics).
- Sie ist an einer Gehaltserhöhung nicht desinteressiert.
  She is not uninterested in a raise.

deuten auf + A ⟨auf jdn/etw d.⟩   to point at (sb/sth); to indicate to (sb/sth)

- Der Zeuge deutete (mit dem Finger) auf den Verbrecher und sagte . . . .
  The witness pointed to the criminal and said . . . .
- Alles deutet auf eine Inflation (/höhere Preise) hin.
  Everything points to (or indicates) inflation (/higher prices).
- Seine Ansichten deuten darauf hin, daß . . . .
  His views point to the fact that . . . .
- Die Wolken deuten auf eine Wetteränderung (/Regen) hin.
  The clouds indicate that there is going to be a change of weather (/it is going to rain).
- Das Kind deutet auf das Gebäude (/das Bild/den doofen Jungen).
  The child is pointing to the building (/the picture/the dumb boy).

deuten in/nach + A/D ⟨in/nach etw d.⟩   to point to (sth)

- Die Wetterfahne deutete nach Süden (/Norden).
  The weather vane pointed to the south (/north).
- Er deutet in die andere Richtung.
  He's pointing in the other direction.

dienen (+ prep)   to serve

- Ich habe keinen Schreiber. Kannst du mir mit einem Kuli dienen?
  I have no writing utensil. Can you help me out with a ballpoint pen?

■ Er diente als Hauptmann (/als Buchhalter) in der Bundeswehr.
He served as a captain (/a bookkeeper) in the West German army.

■ Mein Onkel hat bei der Artillerie (/bei der Luftwaffe) gedient.
My uncle served in the artillery (/in the air force).

■ Er diente unter General Eisenhower.
He served under General Eisenhower.

dienen als/zu + N/D ⟨als etw/zu etw d.⟩   to serve as (sth)

■ Dieses Schloß dient heute als beliebtes Ausflugsziel.
This castle serves today as a popular tourist destination.

■ Wozu sollen diese Vitamintabletten dienen?—Sie dienen zur Verhinderung von Krankheiten.
What are these vitamin tablets good for?—They serve as a prevention against illnesses.

■ Zu welchem Zweck dient dieser Hebel?
What purpose does this lever serve?

⟨**jdm als/zu etw d.**⟩   to serve (for) (sb) as (sth)

■ Seine Aussage (/Das) möge (*or* soll) dir zur Warnung dienen.
His statement (/That) may (or should) serve you as a warning.

■ Er hatte dem Senator nur als Assistent (/Unterhändler) gedient.
He had only served the senator as a page-boy (/a negotiator).

differieren von + D ⟨von jdm/etw (um etw) d.⟩   to differ from (sb/sth)

■ Meine Meinung differiert oft von der meines Vaters (/von seiner).
My opinion often differs from my father's (/from his).

■ Das Wahlergebnis der Labor Party differiert um 15% von dem Ergebnis der letzten Wahlen vor fünf Jahren.
The election result of the Labor Party differs by 15% from that of the last elections five years ago.

diskutieren über + A ⟨mit jdm über etw d.⟩   to discuss (sth) with (sb)

■ Wir möchten über den Umweltschutz (/das Wetter) diskutieren.
We would like to discuss conservation (/the weather).

■ In der Konferenz diskutierten die Lehrer lange mit dem Schulleiter über das Rauchen in der Schule.
At the faculty meeting the teachers discussed smoking on the school grounds for a long time with the principal.

disponieren über + A ⟨**über jdn/etw d.**⟩   to command (sb's) services/to do as one wishes *or* likes with (sth)

■ Ich kann nicht über alle meine Mitarbeiter disponieren.
I can't tell all my co-workers what to do.

■ Herr Schmidt kann über das Auto nicht disponieren. Es gehört nicht ihm, sondern der Firma, für die er arbeitet.
Herr Schmidt cannot do as he wishes with the car. He does not own it, but the company he works for does.

■ Ich kann nach Belieben über meine Zeit (/mein Geld) disponieren.
I can do what I feel like with my time (/money).

disponiert sein für/zu + A/D ⟨**zu/für etw d. sein**⟩   (*medical*) to be prone to (sth)

■ Er war von Geburt an zu (*or* für) Diabetes disponiert.
From birth he was prone to diabetes.

■ Heute bin ich überhaupt nicht dazu disponiert, soviel auf einmal zu entscheiden.
Today I am not in the mood at all to decide so many things at once.

(s.) distanzieren von + D ⟨**sich von jdm/etw d.**⟩   to dissociate (o.s.) from (sb/sth); (*sport*) to outdistance

■ Ich habe mich von dieser Resolution distanziert.
I dissociated myself from this resolution.

■ Der Politiker distanzierte sich von diesem Gesetzentwurf (/seinen Kollegen).
The poltician dissasociated himself from this bill (/his collegues).

■ In der dritten Runde konnte sich der führende Läufer vom Feld distanzieren.
In the third lap the leading runner managed to outdistance the pack.

(s.) drängen (+ prep)   to push, to press

■ Tausende drängten sich vor den Eingängen zum Stadion.
Thousands of people were pushing and shoving in front of the entrances to the stadium.

■ Er drängte ihn zur Seite (/in die Ecke/nach vorn/ durch die Menge/zur Kasse).
He pushed him to the side (/into the corner/towards the front/through the crowd/to the box office).

■ In der Pause drängten die Kinder den kleinen Jens in eine Ecke.
During the break the children pushed little Jens into a corner.

■ Ich lasse mich nicht von dem neuen Abteilungsleiter drängen!
I don't let myself be pushed around by the new department head (i.e., pushed into doing something I don't really want to do).

drängen auf + A ⟨**auf etw d.**⟩   to press for (sth)

- Der Ausschuß drängte auf eine Antwort (/auf eine Lösung der Probleme).
  The committee pressed for an answer (/for a solution to the problems).

- Seine Frau hatte auf eine Entscheidung gedrängt, weil sie wissen wollte, ob er geht oder bleibt.
  His wife pressed for a decision because she wanted to know whether he would stay or go.

drängen zu + D ⟨**jdn zu etw d.**⟩   to press to/towards (movement *or* action); to urge (sb) to do (sth)

- Die Menge drängte zum Ausgang des Stadions.
  The crowd pressed towards the exit of the stadium.

- Die Bank drängte ihn, seine Schulden zu bezahlen.
  The bank pressed him to pay his debts.

- Die militärische Provokation drängt (den General) zur unmittelbaren Entscheidung.
  The military provocation calls for an immediate decision (forces the general to make an immediate decision).

(s.) drehen (+ prep)   to turn

- Der Verschluß läßt sich nicht (/nach links) drehen.
  The lock can't be turned (/to the left).

- Die Schlittschuhläuferin drehte sich im Kreis.
  The skater turned round and round.

- Drehen Sie die Flamme hoch (/auf klein).
  Turn the flame up (/down low).

s. drehen (+ prep)   to turn

- Die Turnerin drehte sich seitwärts (/nach links/zur anderen Seite).
  The gymnast turned sideways (/to the left/to the other side).

drehen an + D ⟨**an etw d.**⟩   to turn (sth)

- Er drehte am Radio (/am Lenkrad/an der Kurbel).
  He turned a knob on the radio (/the steering wheel/the crank).

- Er drehte an dem Knopf und stellte lauter.
  He turned the knob and raised the volume.

■ Das Kind drehte an einem Knopf im Auto, und plötzlich ging das Radio an.
The child turned a button in the car and suddenly the radio came on.

s. drehen um + A ⟨sich um jdn/etw d.⟩   to revolve around (sb/sth); to hinge on
(sb/sth)

■ Die Erde dreht sich (/um die Sonne).
The earth revolves (/around the sun).

■ Worum dreht es sich?
What is it?/What is the problem?

■ Ihr ganzes Gespräch drehte sich nur um Geld (/den Fußballspieler).
Their whole conversation revolved around nothing but money (/the soccer player).

■ Es dreht sich darum, ob.... (/daß....
The whole thing hinges on whether.... (/The point is that....

■ All ihre Gedanken drehen sich nur um ihn (/das Baby/ihre Arbeit).
All her thoughts revolve around him (/the baby/her work).

⟨**sich um sich (selbst) drehen**⟩   to rotate; to revolve on its axis; to turn
round

■ Der Planet dreht sich um sich selbst (/um die Sonne).
The planet rotates on its axis (/around the sun).

■ Das Auto hat sich auf der vereisten Straße (um sich selbst) gedreht.
The car turned (completely around) on the icy road.

■ Ich komme überhaupt nicht weiter. Ich habe das Gefühl, ich drehe
mich im Kreis. (*fig*)
I'm not making any progress. I feel like I'm going in circles.

dringen (+ prep)   to penetrate; to get through

■ Wasser ist in den Keller (/durch die Decke/durch meinen Mantel) gedrungen.
*Water has gotten into the basement (/has penetrated through the ceiling/has
drenched (or penetrated) my coat).*

■ Die Feuchtigkeit drang durch die Wand.
The dampness seeped through the wall.

■ Die Sonne dringt langsam durch den Nebel (/die Wolken).
The sun is slowly coming through the fog (/the clouds).

■ Das Gerücht drang bis zur höchsten Stelle.
The rumor rose to the highest place.

■ Die Kugel drang ihm in die Leber (/ins Herz).
The bullet penetrated (into) his liver (/heart).

■ Die Nachricht drang an (*or* in) die Öffentlichkeit.
The news leaked out and became public knowledge.

dringen auf + A ⟨auf etw d.⟩   to insist on (sth)

- Er drang darauf, in eine andere Abteilung versetzt zu werden.
  He insisted on being transferred to a different department.
- Die Bank dringt auf vollständige Zahlung (/auf eine Antwort).
  The bank is insisting on total payment (/on an answer).

drohen mit + D ⟨jdm/etw mit etw d.⟩   to threaten (sb/sth) with (sth)

- Libyen drohte den USA einst mit Krieg.
  Libya once threatened the USA with war.
- Der Chef drohte dem Angestellten mit Entlassung (/, ihn zu entlassen).
  The boss threatened the employee with dismissal (/to dismiss him).
- Die Arbeiter haben der Firma mit Streik gedroht.
  The workers threatened the company with a strike.
- Er drohte den Kindern mit der Faust (/einem Gewehr/einer Anzeige).
  He threatened the children with his fist (/a gun/going to court).

drücken (+ prep)   to push; to press; to squeeze

- Die Fahrerin drückte auf einen Knopf (/auf das Gaspedal).
  The driver pressed on a knob (/on the accelerator).
- Er drückte sie zur Seite (/nach hinten/in einen Sessel).
  He pushed her aside (/back/into an armchair).
- Er drückte einen Kuß auf ihre Lippen (/Stirn).
  He pressed a kiss on her lips (/forehead).
- Die Assistentin drückt das Siegel auf den Umschlag.
  The assistant is pressing the seal on the envelope.
- Christoph hat die Nase an die Scheibe des Spielwarenladens gedrückt.
  Christoph pressed his nose against the toy shop window.
- Die neuen Schuhe drücken sehr auf die Zehen.
  The new shoes are squeezing my toes.
- Er hat sie an sein Herz (/seine Brust) gedrückt.
  He gave her an affectionate hug. (idiom)

drücken auf/an + A/D ⟨auf/an etw d.⟩   to press (sth) on (sth); to dampen (sth); to depress (sth)

- Diese Musik von Dave Dudley drückt mir auf das Gemüt (/auf die Stimmung).
  This Dave Dudley music dampens (or depresses) my spirit (/mood).

■   Die Wurst drückt ihm auf den Magen.
The sausage lies (or sits) heavily on his stomach.

(s.) drücken um + A ⟨sich um etw d.⟩   to get out of (doing) (sth)

■   Immer wieder drückst du dich darum, den Abwasch zu machen.
You are always trying to get out of doing the dishes.

(s.) drücken vor + D ⟨sich vor etw d.⟩   to shirk *or* dodge (sth)

■   Er drückt sich gern vor der Arbeit (/seinen Verpflichtungen/offiziellen Einladungen).
He tends to dodge work (his obligations/official invitations).

■   Immer wenn es schwierig wurde, hat sie sich vor der Verantwortung gedrückt.
Whenever the going got tough, she dodged responsibility.

duften nach + D ⟨nach etw d.⟩   to smell *or* have a smell of (sth)

■   Unser Büro duftet immer nach Kaffee (/Parfüm).
There is always a smell of coffee (/perfume) in our office.

■   Er duftet nach Alkohol (/Whisky/Bier).
He smells of alcohol (/whisky/beer).

s. durchsetzen gegen + A ⟨sich gegen jdn/etw d.⟩   to assert o.s. against (sb/sth); to prevail against (sb/sth)

■   Obwohl er größer ist als sein Bruder, kann er sich nicht gegen ihn durchsetzen.
Although he is taller than his brother, he cannot best him.

■   Endlich setzte ich mich gegen meine Feinde durch.
I finally prevailed against my enemies.

s. durchsetzen mit + D ⟨sich mit etw d.⟩   to be successful with (sth).

■   Sie setzte sich in der Diskussion mit ihrer Meinung durch, weil sie die überzeugenderen Argumente hatte.
Her opinion prevailed in the discussion because she had the more convincing arguments.

■   Ich glaube, ich werde mich mit meinem Vorschlag durchsetzen können.
I think I have a chance to be successful with my proposal.

durchsuchen nach + D ⟨**jdn/etw nach jdm/etw d.**⟩   to search (sb/sth) for (sb/sth); to frisk (sb) for (sth)

■   Die Polizisten durchsuchten ihn (/das Haus) nach Waffen.
   The policemen searched him (/the house) for weapons.

■   Beim Zoll ist sein Koffer nach Heroin durchsucht worden.
   At customs his suitcase was searched for heroin.

■   Die Leute durchsuchten die ganze Stadt nach dem Verbrecher (/Kind).
   People searched the whole town for the criminal (/child).

(s.) duzen mit + D ⟨**sich mit jdm d.**⟩   to address sb with the "du"–form

■   Sie duzt sich mit ihr.
   She addresses her with (the informal form of "you") *"du."*

■   Ich habe mich mit deiner Freundin (/mit ihr/mit ihm) geduzt.
   I addressed your friend (/her/him) with (the) "du"(-form).

(s.) duzen (without prep)   to address with the familiar "du"–form

■   Er hat mich (/ihn) geduzt.
   He addressed me (/him) with (the) "du"(-form).

■   Ich duze Alex Schmidt.
   I address Alex Schmidt with (the) "du"(-form).

■   Die beiden duzen sich seit einiger Zeit.
   They have addressed each other with (the) "du"(-form) for a while.

E

s. eignen als/für/zu + N/A/D ⟨sich zu etw/als etw/für jdn/etw e.⟩ to be suitable *or* made for (sth), as (sth), for (sb/sth); to be appropriate for (sth)

- Der Mann eignet sich für diesen Job (/Beruf/diese Aufgabe).
  The man is suited for this job (/profession/task).

- Ich eigne mich fürs Kochen (/Nähen/Unterrichten).
  I'm made for cooking (/sewing/teaching).

- Der Schreiber, den du mir gegeben hast, eignet sich nicht für Folien (/die Tafel).
  The pen you have given me is not suitable for transparencies (/the blackboard).

- Diese Vase eignet sich fantastisch zum Verschenken (/als Geschenk).
  This book is suited splendidly for a gift (/as a gift).

- Dieser Film (/Dieses Buch) eignet sich nicht für Kinder.
  This film (/This book) is not suited for children.

eilen (+ prep) to hurry; to rush

- Er ist zur Arbeit (/nach Hause/zum Bus) geeilt.
  He rushed to work (/home/to the bus).

eilen mit + D ⟨es e. (mit etw)⟩ to be urgent *or* pressing

- Damit eilt es noch nicht.
  There's no great hurry (or rush) about it yet.

- Mit dieser Arbeit eilt es sehr (/nicht).
  This work is (/not) very urgent.

- Es eilt mir nicht mit dem Basteln der Geschenke. Weihnachten ist noch weit.
  Making the presents is not urgent. Christmas is still far away.

einbeziehen in + A ⟨jdn/etw in etw e.⟩ to include (sb/sth) in (sth)

- Wir bezogen ihn in die Diskussion ein.
  We included him in the discussion.

- Ich habe diese Beobachtungen in meine Forschung (/meinen Artikel) einbezogen.
  I have included these observations in my research (/article).

s. einbilden auf + A ⟨sich (D) etw auf etw e.⟩ to be conceited about *or* vain about (sth)

- Sie bildet sich viel darauf ein, daß sie all ihre Prüfungen mit der Note eins abgeschlossen hat.
  She is conceited about the fact that she finished all her examinations with the grade "one."
- Darauf kannst du dir etwas einbilden.
  You can be very proud of that.
- Er bildet sich nichts auf seinen Erfolg (/Reichtum) ein.
  He's not conceited about his success (/wealth).

einbrechen bei/in + D/A ⟨bei jdm/in etw e.⟩ to break into (sth) (*house, etc*)

- Sie haben bei unseren Nachbarn (/in unsere Wohnung) eingebrochen.
  They broke into our neighbors' home (/apartment).
- Gestern wurde in das Juweliergeschäft (/in den Tresorraum/bei ihm/eingebrochen).
  Yesterday the jeweler's shop (/the vault/his home) was broken into.

s. eindecken mit + D ⟨sich mit etw e.⟩ to stock up with (sth)

- Hast du dich für das Picknick mit Obst (/Getränken) eingedeckt?
  Did you stock up with fruit (/drinks) for the picnic?
- Haben Sie sich ausreichend mit Lebensmitteln für das Wochenende eingedeckt?
  Did you get enough groceries for the weekend?

> **⟨jdn/etw mit etw eindecken⟩** to be snowed under with (sth) *or* inundated with (sth)
>
> - Das Kind hat die Mutter mit so vielen Fragen eingedeckt.
>   *The child inundated her mother with so many questions.*
> - Mein Chef hat mich ganz schön mit Arbeit eingedeckt.
>   *My boss has really snowed me under with work.*

eindringen auf + A ⟨auf jdn e.⟩ to go for *or* attack (sb)

- Zwei Straßenräuber drangen (mit Messern und Knüppeln) auf sie ein.
  Two muggers attacked her (with knives and heavy sticks).

eindringen in + A ⟨in etw e.⟩   to force one's way into (sth); to force an entry into (sth); (*mil*) to penetrate (into) (sth); to study *or* examine (sth) thoroughly

- Der Dieb drang in das Geschäft ein und stahl die Juwelen.
  The thief forced his way into the store and stole the jewelry.
- Die Agenten drangen tief in die Regierung ein.
  The agents penetrated deeply into the government.
- Das Wasser drang schnell in die Erde (/den Keller/das Sofa) ein.
  The water penetrated quickly into the ground (/basement/sofa).
- Der Splitter (/Die Nadel) drang tief in meinen Finger ein.
  The splinter (/The needle) penetrated my finger deeply.
- Immer mehr amerikanische Wörter sind in die deutsche Sprache eingedrungen.
  More and more American words have found their way into the German language.

s. einfühlen in + A ⟨sich in jdn e.⟩   to empathize with (sb); to put oneself into (*the role of*) (sb)

- Der Pfarrer kann sich (/Ich kann mich) gut in andere Leute einfühlen.
  The minister is good (/I'm good) at putting himself (/myself) in other people's shoes (or at empathizing with other people.)
- Die Schauspielerin hat sich glänzend in die (Rolle der) Lady Macbeth eingefühlt.
  The actress put herself into the role of Lady Macbeth marvelously.

  ⟨sich in etw einfühlen⟩   to understand (sth)

  - Er hat sich sensibel in die Stimmung des Gedichtes eingefühlt.
    He really felt the mood of the poem.
  - Ich könnte mich in die Atmosphäre des 18. Jahrhunderts einfühlen.
    I could get (or project myself) into the atmosphere of the 18th century.

einführen bei + D ⟨jdn bei jdm e.⟩   to introduce (sb) to (sb)

- Ich habe meinen Freund bei ihnen (/dem Chef) eingeführt.
  I introduced my friend to them (/the boss).
- Sie wollen dieses dumme System bei uns einführen lassen.
  They want to have this dumb new system implemented here (at our place of work).

einführen in + A ⟨jdn in etw e.⟩   to introduce (sb) into (sth)

- Sie wird den neuen Angestellten in seine Arbeit (/seine Abteilung/ sein Amt) einführen.
  She will introduce the new employee to his job (/his department/his office).

- Sie hat ihn in die Familie (/in das gute Leben) eingeführt.
  She introduced him to her family (/to the good life).

- Er führte uns alle in den Umgang mit dem neuen Computer ein.
  He introduced us all to the workings of the new computer.

- Dostojewski führt immer sehr viele Personen in seinen Romanen ein.
  Dostoyevski always introduces numerous characters in his novels.

eingehen auf + A ⟨**auf etw e.**⟩   to go into (sth) (*a question, a point*); to respond to (sth)

- Darauf kann ich jetzt nicht eingehen. Später gehe ich darauf noch näher ein.
  I cannot go into that now. I'll go into that in more detail later.

- Sie konnten auf ihn (/seine Frage) nicht eingehen, weil die Zeit zu knapp war.
  They couldn't respond to him (/answer his question) because there was not enough time.

- Er ist auf die Frage eingegangen, weil ihn das Thema interessierte.
  He went (delved) into the question because it interested him.

  ⟨**auf jdn/etw eingehen**⟩   to give (one's) time and attention to (sb/sth)

  - Die Mutter geht intensiv auf die Bedürfnisse ihrer Kinder (/auf ihre Kinder) ein.
    The mother gives the needs of her children (/her children) all her time and attention.

  - Der Lehrer kann nicht nur auf schwierige Schüler (/die Probleme schwieriger Schüler) eingehen. Er muß allen eine Chance geben.
    The teacher cannot give his time and attention to only the (/problems of the) more difficult students. He must give all of them a chance.

  ⟨**auf etw (einen Vorschlag/Plan) eingehen**⟩   to agree to *or* to fall in with (sth) (*a suggestion/plan*)

  - Er geht auf das Problem (/den Vorschlag/die Wette) ein.
    He is addressing the problem (/accepts the suggestion/accepts the bet).

  - Er ist auf unseren Vorschlag, heute abend Schinken zu essen, eingegangen.
    He went along with our suggestion to have ham this evening.

  - Auf seine schmutzigen Gedanken ist sie nicht eingeganen.
    She ignored (or did not respond to) his dirty thoughts.

  - Er machte immer sexuelle Anspielungen, aber ich wollte nicht darauf eingehen.
    He kept making sexual innuendos, but I didn't care to respond to them.

eingehen in + A ⟨in etw e.⟩   to leave its mark on (sth) *or* to have some influence on (sth)

- Seine Tapferkeit (/Brutalität/Er) wird in die Geschichte eingehen.
  His courage (/brutality/He) will go down in (the annals of) history.
- Verschiedene musikalische Stilrichtungen sind in seine Musik eingegangen.
  Diverse musical styles have left some influence on his music.

s. eingewöhnen in + D ⟨sich in etw e.⟩   to settle down/in (sth); to get used to (sth)

- Ich habe mich in dieser Stadt eingewöhnt.
  I've gotten used to this city.
- Ich gewöhnte mich schnell in der neuen Schule ein.
  I quickly got used to the new school.

eingreifen in + A ⟨in etw e.⟩   to interfere or intrude in (sth); to encroach (up)on (sth)

- Er griff in das Gespräch (/den Wahlkampf/die Gesetzgebung) ein.
  He interfered in the conversation (/the election campaign/processes of the law).
- Er hat in meine Rechte eingegriffen.
  He encroached upon my rights.
- Er hat in meine Privatsphäre eingegriffen.
  He intruded into my privacy.
- Die Reise nach Bangladesh hat tief in mein Leben eingegriffen.
  The trip to Bangladesh left a deep impression on me.

eingreifen (without prep)   to make an intervention

- Der Schulleiter mußte bei der Schlägerei eingreifen.
  The principal had to intervene during the fight.
- Bei einer so schweren Krankheit muß ein Arzt eingreifen.
  In the case of such a serious illness a doctor must be consulted.

s. einigen (+ prep)   to agree

- Die Parteien einigten sich auf einen Kompromiß (/über die Steuerreform/auf eine gemeinsame Politik).
  The parties agreed on a compromise (/about the tax reform/on a common policy).
- Können wir uns auf ein Lustspiel (/ein chinesisches Restaurant/ein spätes Abendbrot) einigen?
  Can we agree on a comedy (/a Chinese restaurant/a late supper)?

s. einigen mit + D ⟨sich mit jdm e.⟩   to agree with (sb)

- Die Nachbarn haben sich gütlich miteinander geeinigt.
  The neighbors settled their disagreement amiably.

einladen (+ prep)   to invite (sb)

- Hans hat sie in seine Wohnung (/zum Picknick/zu einer Tasse Kaffee/zu einem Fußballspiel) eingeladen.
  Hans invited her to his apartment (/to a picnic/for a cup of coffee/to a soccer game).
- Er lädt uns für nächsten Samstag zum Essen (/zum Geburtstag seines Kindes/zu einem Besuch) ein.
  He is inviting us for dinner next Saturday (/to his child's birthday/for a visit).
- Hans lud mich ins Theater (/ins Kino/auf ein Bier/zu einem Spaziergang/zu einer Reise in die Schweiz) ein.
  Hans invited me to the theater (/to the movies/for a beer/for a walk/for a trip to Switzerland).
- Das offenstehende Garagentor lädt zum Stehlen (/Einbrechen) ein.
  The open garage door invites theft (/a break-in).

s. einlassen auf/in + A ⟨sich auf/in etw e.⟩   to get involved in (sth); to let oneself in for (sth)

- Ich will mich nicht auf diesen Streit (/auf ein Abenteuer) einlassen.
  I don't want to get involved in this dispute (/in an adventure).
- Er läßt sich nicht auf die Fragen ein.
  He doesn't let himself get involved with the questions. or *He doesn't respond to the questions.*
- Ich ließ mich nicht in ein Gespräch (/auf Verhandlungen) mit ihm ein.
  I didn't get involved in a conversation (/in negotiations) with him.
- Lasse dich nicht in diese hoffnungslose Affäre (/in keine Auseinandersetzung *or* keinen Konflikt) ein.
  Don't get mixed up in this hopeless affair (/a dispute or *any controversy).*
- Das Buch macht soviel Arbeit. Da habe ich mich aber auf etwas eingelassen!
  The book is so much work. I've really let myself in for something there!

s. einlassen mit + D ⟨sich mit jdm e.⟩   to get mixed up *or* involved with (sb)

- Sie will sich nicht mit ihm (/einem Spieler) einlassen.
  She doesn't want to get involved with him (/a gambler).
- Ich weiß nicht, warum du dich mit diesem fiesen Kerl einläßt.
  I don't know why you are carrying on with this bum.

- Ich habe gehört, daß sie sich mit jedem einläßt!
  I have heard that she'll go with anyone.
- Die CDU will sich nicht mit den Grünen einlassen.
  The CDU doesn't want to have dealings with the Greens.

s. einleben in/an + D ⟨sich in/an etw e.⟩   to settle down in (sth)

- Hast du dich hier in Hamburg (/an diesem Ort/in dieser Gemeinschaft) eingelebt?
  Have you gotten used to things here in Hamburg (/this place/this community)?
- Ich habe mich in Ihrer Stadt (/bei Ihnen/in Ihrer Familie) gut eingelebt.
  I feel at home in your city (/at your house/with your family).
- Ich fand es leicht, mich in dem modernen Wohnmobil einzuleben.
  I had no difficulty getting used to (living or *riding in) the modern motor home.*

s. einmischen in + A ⟨sich in etw e.⟩   to meddle in (sth); to interfere with (sth)

- Seine Frau mischt sich in alles ein.
  His wife sticks her nose into everything.
- Du sollst dich nicht in die Angelegenheiten anderer einmischen.
  You shouldn't meddle in the affairs of others.
- Das geht ihn nichts an, also soll er sich nicht darin einmischen.
  That's none of his business, so he shouldn't meddle.

einmünden in + A ⟨in etw e.⟩   to flow in (-to) (sth); to join in (sth)

- Die Mosel mündet bei Koblenz in den Rhein ein.
  The Mosel flows into the Rhine at Koblenz.
- Der Feldweg mündet in die Hauptstraße ein.
  The dirt road leads into the main road.

einnehmen für + A ⟨jdn für jdn/sich/etw e.⟩   to win (sb) over to oneself

- Mein Bruder nahm durch sein freundliches Wesen alle Leute für sich ein.
  Because of his friendly manners, my brother won everyone over.
- Ihre bescheidene Art nahm alle Kollegen für sie ein.
  Her modest manner won all of her colleagues over.
- Durch seine geschickte Argumentation hat er alle für seine Pläne eingenommen.
  He won everyone over to his plans with his clever arguments.
- Ihre Ehrlichkeit (/Hingabe) nimmt mich sehr für sie ein.
  Her honesty (/dedication) makes me think highly of her.

einpacken in + A ⟨etw in etw e.⟩   to pack (sth) in (sth); to wrap (up) (sth) in (sth)

- Andreas hat das Geschenk in buntes Papier eingepackt.
  Andreas packed the gift in colorful paper.
- Er packte die Badehose in den Koffer ein.
  He packed the swimsuit in the suitcase.
- Laß uns das Baby in eine Decke einpacken. Es wird kalt.
  Let's wrap the baby in a blanket; it's getting cold.

(s.) einschalten in + A ⟨sich in etw e.⟩   to include in (sth); to join in (sth); to intervene in (sth)

- Der Professor schaltete sich in die Unterredung (/das Verfahren) ein.
  The professor joined in the discussion (/proceedings).
- Der Verkehrsfunk schaltet sich oft in die Sendungen von Radio Hamburg ein.
  The broadcasts of Radio Hamburg are often interrupted by traffic news.

s. einschmeicheln bei + D ⟨sich bei jdm e.⟩   to ingratiate oneself with (sb); to chum up to (sb)

- Ich kann ihn nicht ausstehen. Er versucht immer wieder, sich bei seinen Vorgesetzten einzuschmeicheln.
  I can't stand him. He always tries to ingratiate himself with (or butter up to) his superiors.

s. einsetzen für + A ⟨(sich) für jdn/etw e.⟩   to fight for (sb); to support (sth)

- Ich habe mich sehr für sie (/ihre Beförderung) eingesetzt.
  I strongly supported her (/her promotion).
- Albert Schweitzer hat sich voll für die Kranken (/Bedürftigen) in Afrika eingesetzt.
  Albert Schweitzer lent his aid unreservedly to the sick (/needy) in Africa.
- Bitte setzen Sie sich dafür ein, daß....
  Please, see to it that....
- Ich setze mich für die 35-Stunden-Woche ein, weil....
  I support the 35-hour work-week because....
- Marion setzte sich für ihren schuldigen Jungen ein.
  Marion stood up for her guilty son.
- Er setzte seinen Einfluß (/seine Kraft/Energie) für diese (/für das Gelingen dieser) Aufgabe ein.
  He devoted all his influence (/power/energy) to the (/accomplishment of the) task.

einsetzen in + A ⟨jdn in etw e.⟩ to fit/set/place (sb) in (sth)

- Der Manager hat sie in der Damenabteilung eingesetzt.
  The manager put (or placed) her in the women's department.

- Die Studenten setzen die richtigen Wörter in die Lücken ein.
  The students are filling in the blanks with the right words.

- Nach dem Freispruch wurde er wieder in seine Rechte eingesetzt.
  After the acquittal his rights were restored.

einstehen für + A ⟨für jdn/etw e.⟩ to vouch for (sb/sth)

- Nicoles Eltern stehen dafür ein, daß sie die Arbeit heute abend zuende führt.
  Nicole's parents vouch (for the fact) that she will complete the work this evening.

- Ich stehe persönlich für meinen Sohn (/diesen Arbeiter) ein.
  I personally vouch for my son (/this worker).

- Ich habe immer behauptet, daß Brandt ein guter Kanzler war, und dafür stehe ich auch ein.
  I've always said that Brandt was a good chancellor, and I'll stand by it.

⟨**für etw einstehen**⟩ to make good on (sth); to answer for (sth); to take responsibility for (sth)

- Der Vater hat für den Schaden (/die Schulden) eingestanden.
  The father took responsibility for the damage (/the debts).

- Der Sohn hat kein eigenes Einkommen. Nun muß der Vater für seine unbezahlten Rechnungen einstehen.
  The son has no income of his own, so his father must assume responsiblity for his unpaid bills.

⟨**für jdn einstehen**⟩ to assume liability *or* responsibility for (sb)

- Die Eltern sind in einem Unfall gestorben. Der Onkel steht jetzt für die Kinder ein.
  The parents died in an accident. Their uncle now assumes responsibility for the children.

einsteigen in + A ⟨in etw e.⟩ to climb in(-to) (sth); to get in(-to) (sth); to get on(-to) (sth)

- Er ist in den Zug (/in das Auto) eingestiegen.
  He got onto the train (/into the car).

- Der Dieb stieg durch das Fenster (/über den Balkon) in die Wohnung (/ins Haus) ein.
  The thief climbed through the window (/over the balcony) into the apartment (/house).

- Die Bank (/Erbin) will durch den Kauf einer großen Menge von Aktien in die Computerfirma einsteigen.
  The bank (/heiress) wants to get into the (business of the) computer firm by buying a large number of shares.

einstellen auf + A ⟨etw auf etw e.⟩   to adjust (sth) to (sth); to aim (sth) at (sth); to focus (sth) on (sth); to tune (sth) to (sth)

- Die Artillerie hat die Kanonen auf den Feind eingestellt.
  The artillery aimed the cannons at the enemy.

- Die Fotografin stellt den Fotoapparat auf das Objekt in der Entfernung ein.
  The photographer is focusing the camera on the object in the distance.

- Ich muß den Wecker auf 8.00 Uhr einstellen.
  I must set the alarm for 8 o'clock.

- Du mußt das Radio (/die Stereoanlage) auf Zimmerlautstärke einstellen.
  You have to set the radio (/stereo) to normal listening volume.

- Er stellt das Radio auf einen anderen Sender ein.
  He's tuning the radio into another channel.

- Der Redner hat seinen Vortrag auf die jungen Universitätsstudenten eingestellt.
  The speaker tailored his lecture to the young university students.

s. einstellen auf + A ⟨sich auf jdn/etw e.⟩   to adapt oneself to (sb/sth); to prepare oneself for (sb/sth)

- Die Angestellten haben sich bereits auf die gleitende Arbeitszeit eingestellt.
  The office workers have already gotten used to the flexible working hours.

- Es fällt mir schwer, mich auf die neue Diät (/die schwierigen Schüler in meiner Klasse) einzustellen.
  I am having a hard time adjusting to the new diet (/the unruly students in my class).

- Man muß sich auf jeden neuen Lehrer einstellen.
  One has to adapt to each new teacher.

eingestellt sein auf + A ⟨auf etw e. sein⟩   to be prepared for *or* ready to do (sth)

- Sag mir, was ich tun soll. Ich bin auf viel Arbeit eingestellt.
  Tell me what I should do. I'm prepared for a lot of work.

- Nach zwei Stunden war das Bier alle. Wir waren nicht auf soviele Gäste eingestellt.
  After two hours the beer was gone. We weren't prepared for so many guests.

einstimmen auf + A ⟨**sich/jdn auf etw e.**⟩   to get *or* put (o.s./sb) in the (right) mood
for (sth)

- Durch eine witzige Rede stimmte der Chef seine Mitarbeiter auf einen
  vergnüglichen Abend ein.
  The boss put his employees in a jolly mood for the evening with a funny speech.
- Die Zuhörer waren auf das Konzert gut eingestimmt.
  The listeners were in the right mood for the concert.

eintauschen für/gegen + A ⟨**etw gegen/für etw e.**⟩   to exchange *or* swap (sth) for
(sth)

- Der Kunde tauschte den Rock für (*or* gegen) einen anderen ein.
  The customer exchanged the skirt for another one.
- Ich würde nie eine Dylan-Platte für (*or* gegen) eine von Johnny Cash eintauschen.
  I would never swap a Dylan record for one by Johnny Cash.

eintreten auf + A ⟨**auf jdn e.**⟩   to boot *or* kick (sb)

- Das böse Kind hat auf den Hund eingetreten.
  The mean kid kicked the dog (repeatedly).

eintreten für + A ⟨**für jdn/etw e.**⟩   to stand up for (sb/sth)

- Sting tritt für die Rechte der brasilianischen Indianer ein.
  Sting stands up for the rights of the Brazilian Indians.
- Viele Menschen sind für Nelson Mandela (/politische Reformen/diesen Plan)
  eingetreten.
  Lots of people stood up for Nelson Mandela (/political reforms/this plan).

eintreten in + A ⟨**in etw e.**⟩   to become a member of (sth); to join *or* go into (sth);
to enter (sth)

- Er ist in einen Verein (/in einen Orden/in eine Partei/in eine Sekte) eingetreten.
  He became a member of a club (/an order/a party/a sect).
- Er trat ins Haus (/in die Politik/in den diplomatischen Dienst) ein.
  He entered the house (/politics/joined the diplomatic service).

■   1941 traten die Vereinigten Staaten in den Krieg ein.
In 1941 the United States entered the war.

einverstanden sein mit + D ⟨mit jdm/etw e. sein⟩   to agree to *or* with (sb/sth)

■   Ich bin mit dir (/deiner Entscheidung/allem) einverstanden.
I agree with you (/your decision/everything).

■   Ich bin damit (/mit deinem Vorschlag) einverstanden, daß . . . .
I agree (/with your proposal) that. . . .

einwandern in/nach + A/D ⟨in ein Land; nach einem Land e.⟩   to immigrate to (*a country*)

■   Sie sind nach Amerika (/Kanada/Deutschland) eingewandert.
They immigrated to America (/Canada/Germany).

■   Sie wanderten in die Vereinigten Staaten (/in die Schweiz/in den Iran) ein.
They immigrated to the United States (/Switzerland/Iran).

einwechseln für + A ⟨jdn für jdn e.⟩   to substitute (sb) for (sb)

■   Ein neuer Spieler wurde für den verletzten Spieler eingewechselt.
A new player was substituted for the injured player.

einwechseln in (/gegen) + A ⟨etw für (*rarely* gegen) etw e.⟩   to change (sth) into (sth)

■   Der englische Tourist wechselte 200 Pfund in (*rarely*: gegen) Dollars ein.
The English tourist changed 200 pounds for dollars.

■   Könnten Sie diesen Tausendmarkschein in kleinere Banknoten einwechseln?
Could you break this 1000 Mark bill into smaller bills?

einwenden gegen + A ⟨gegen etw e.⟩   to object to (sth)

■   Willst du etwa gegen meinen Plan einwenden, daß er unrealistisch ist?
Are you really going to raise an objection to my plan by saying that it is unrealistic?

■   Er hat nichts degegen (/gegen meinen Vorschlag) einzuwenden.
He has no objection to it (/my proposal).

■   Dagegen ließe sich einwenden, daß . . . .
One objection to this could be that. . . .

■ Es ist nichts (/etwas) dagegen einzuwenden, daß wir unerfahrene Leute einstellen.
There is no (/some) objection to employing inexperienced people.

einwilligen in + A ⟨in etw e.⟩   to agree to (sth); to give consent to (sth)

■ Ich kann nicht darin einwilligen, daß in der Schule geraucht werden darf.
I cannot agree to the fact that smoking is permitted at school.

■ Sie willigte in die Scheidung ein.
She agreed to the divorce.

einwilligen (without prep)   to agree

■ Meinst du, wir dürfen per Anhalter fahren? Meine Eltern werden kaum einwilligen.
Do you think we will be allowed to hitchhike? My parents will hardly agree (or *give their consent*).

einwirken auf + A ⟨auf jdn/etw e.⟩   to have an effect on (sb/sth)

■ Diese Regierungsentscheidungen wirken günstig auf die Konjunktur ein.
These government decisions are having a favorable effect on the economic situation.

■ Die Kur (/Das Arzneimittel) wirkte günstig (/wohltuend/kräftigend) auf ihn ein.
The treatment (/medicine) had a favorable (/beneficial/strengthening) effect on him.

einziehen in + A ⟨in etw e.⟩   to move in (to) (sth); *(military, etc.)* march in (sth); to take office in (sth)

■ Die neuen Mieter sind letzte Woche in die neue Wohnung (/unser Haus) eingezogen.
Last week the new tenants moved into the new apartment (/our house).

■ Die Soldaten (/Truppen) zogen in die Stadt ein.
The soldiers (/troops) marched into the city.

■ Die Mannschaften der teilnehmenden Länder zogen in das Stadion ein.
The teams of the participating countries marched into the stadium.

■ Die Abgeordneten sind in das Parlament eingezogen.
The representatives took their seats in parliament.

einziehen in + A *or* **D** ⟨**in etw e.**⟩   *(fig)* to come in(-to) (sth)

■ Erst ein paar Wochen nach dem Umzug zog wieder Gemütlichkeit in unser (*or* in unserem) Haus ein.
A few weeks after we had moved, a feeling of comfort finally returned to our house.

(s.) ekeln vor + D ⟨**jdn e., jdn vor jdm/etw e.**⟩   to be disgusted *or* nauseated (at/by) (sb/sth)

■ Mir (*or* Mich) ekelt vor dieser Speise (/diesem Geschmack/seinem Verhalten).
This food (/taste/His behavior) is disgusting or revolting.

■ Ich ek(e)le mich vor diesem Film (/seiner Erscheinung/seinen unsensiblen Bemerkungen).
I am nauseated by this film (/his appearance/his insensitive remarks).

■ Ekelst du dich vor mir?
Do I disgust you?

enden auf/mit + A/D ⟨**auf/mit etw e.**⟩   to end with (sth)

■ Seine Rede (/Geschichte) endete mit Worten von Goethe.
His speech (/story) concluded with words from Goethe.

■ Im Deutschen enden viele Wörter auf (*or* mit) -heit.
In German many words end with (the suffix) -heit.

■ Die Demonstration (/Straße) endet auf dem Platz hinter dem Hauptbahnhof.
The demonstration (/street) ends in the square behind the main train station.

entgegnen auf + A ⟨**etw auf etw e.**⟩   to reply to (sth)

■ Auf ihre geistreiche Bemerkung konnte er nichts entgegnen.
He couldn't reply anything to her witty remark.

entgegnen (without prep) ⟨**jdm etw e.**⟩   to reply (sb/sth)

■ Als er sie danach fragte, hat sie ihm entgegnet, daß sie sich auf den Besuch freue.
When he asked her about it she replied that she was looking forward to the visit.

s. entrüsten über + A ⟨**sich über etw/jdn e.**⟩   to be indignant at (sth); to be(come) indignant with (sb); to fill (sb) with indignation, outrage, shock

■ Ich habe mich über die Zustände im Flüchtlingslager entrüstet.
I was indignant (or shocked) at the conditions in the refugee camp.

■ „Du solltest dich schämen," entrüstete sich der Pfarrer.
"You should be ashamed of yourself!" said the incensed preacher.

(s.) entrüsten (without prep) to incense; to anger

■ Warum entrüstet er sich so?
Why is he so enraged?

■ Wie diese Menschen behandelt werden, entrüstet mich sehr.
The way these people are treated really angers me.

entrüstet sein über + A ⟨über jdn/etw e. sein⟩ to be indignant about *or* with (s/sth)

■ Sie ist über seine Ernennung (/ihn/die erneute Verschmutzung des Rheins) entrüstet.
She is angry about his appointment (/with him/the renewed pollution of the Rhine).

(s.) entschädigen für + A ⟨sich/jdn für etw e.⟩ to compensate (sb) for (sth)

■ Wie wollen Sie uns für den Schaden (/Verlust) entschädigen?—Ich werde Sie dafür mit 2000 DM entschädigen.
How do you want to compensate us for the damage (/loss)?—I'll compensate you with 2000 marks.

■ Er brachte mich vor allen Leuten in Verlegenheit, aber ich habe mich reichlich dafür entschädigt.
He embarrassed me in front of all the people, but I got back at him with a vengeance.

■ Der Geschmack dieser Speise entschädigt uns für die Mühe des Kochens.
The taste of this food makes up for all the trouble of cooking it.

(s.) entscheiden für + A ⟨sich für etw/jdn e.⟩ to decide in favor of (sb/sth); to decide on (sth)

■ Der Direktor entschied sich für das neue kostensparende Verfahren.
The director decided in favor of the new cost-reducing procedure.

■ Ein großer Prozentsatz der Leute entschied sich für diese Partei.
A large percentage of people decided in favor of this party.

■ Ich habe mich für den anderen Bewerber entschieden.
I decided in favor of the other applicant.

■ Ich habe mich für das teurere Auto entschieden.
I settled for the more expensive car.

■ Hast du dich dafür entschieden, weiter in München zu studieren?
Have you decided to continue studying in Munich?

s. entscheiden gegen + A ⟨sich gegen jdn/etw e.⟩   to decide against (sb/sth)

- Er entschied sich gegen das Angebot.
  He decided against the offer.
- Wir haben uns dagegen entschieden, die Reise mit dem Auto zu machen.
  We have decided against making the trip by car.

entscheiden über + A ⟨über etw e.⟩   to decide (on) (sth); to rule (on) (sth)

- Der Präsident entschied über den Einsatz von Truppen in Kuwait.
  The President decided on the deployment of troops in Kuwait.
- Er soll selbst entscheiden, was er in der Zukunft machen will.
  He should decide for himself what he wants to do in the future.

s. entschließen zu + D ⟨sich zu etw e.⟩   to decide on (sth)

- Ich habe mich zu einer langen Reise (/zum Kauf dieses Kleides/zum Schreiben eines Briefes) entschlossen.
  I decided on a long trip (/to buy this dress/to write a letter).
- Die Partei hat sich zu einer alternativen Lösung entschlossen.
  The party decided on an alternative solution.
- Die Lehrer haben sich zur Durchführung einer Konferenz entschlossen.
  The teachers decided to hold a conference.

s. entschuldigen bei + D ⟨sich bei jdm wegen etw e.⟩   to apologize to (sb) for (sth)

- Ich entschuldigte mich bei seiner Frau (wegen meines Versehens/wegen meiner Störung).
  I apologized to his wife (for my oversight/for my interruption).
- Der Schüler hat sich bei der Lehrerin wegen seines Benehmens (/Herumblöd-elns/seiner fehlenden Hausaufgaben) entschuldigt.
  The student apologized to his teacher for his behavior (/his clowning around/his missing homework).

s. entschuldigen für + A ⟨sich für etw e.⟩   to excuse oneself for (sth); to apologize for (sth)

- Ich entschuldige mich für meine Verspätung (/Zerstreutheit/dafür).
  I apologize for my tardiness (/absent-mindedness/that).
- Du mußt dich nicht für die Fehler anderer entschuldigen.
  You needn't apologize for the mistakes of others.

s. entschuldigen wegen + G ⟨sich wegen etw e.⟩   to apologize for (sth)

■ Ich habe mich schon wegen meiner Verspätung (/deswegen) entschuldigt.
I have already apologized for my tardiness (/it).

■ Du solltest dich wegen deines schlimmen Verhaltens entschuldigen.
You ought to apologize for your bad behavior.

(s.) entschuldigen (without prep)   to excuse

■ Daß er Alkohol getrunken hat, entschuldigt sein Betragen (/seine Unhöflichkeit) nicht.
The fact that he drank alcohol doesn't excuse his behavior (/rudeness).

■ Entschuldigen Sie bitte den Lärm (/meine Fehler).
Please excuse the noise (/my mistakes).

■ Das entschuldigt nicht, daß du so lange nicht geschrieben hast.
That's no excuse for your not writing for so long.

entsetzt sein über/von + A/D ⟨über jdn/etw *or* von jdm/etw e. sein⟩   to be horrified *or* appalled at/with (sb/sth)

■ Die Mutter war über das Aussehen ihrer Tochter (/ihre Tochter) entsetzt.
The mother was appalled at her daughter's appearance (/with her daughter).

■ Ich bin von deinem (*or* über dein) Verhalten entsetzt.
I am horrified at your behavior.

enttäuscht sein von/über + D/A ⟨von jdm/etw *or* über jdn/etw e. sein⟩   to be disappointed in (sb/sth); to be let down by (sb/sth)

■ Jan ist sehr enttäuscht von seinem Verhalten (/ihm) (*or* über sein Verhalten/ihn).
Jan is disappointed in his behavior (/him).

■ Er ist vom (*or* über den) Klang seines neuen Recorders (/von seiner Note *or* über seine Note in Chemie) enttäuscht.
He is disappointed in the sound of his new (cassette) recorder (/his grade in chemistry).

(s.) entwickeln zu + D ⟨sich/jdn/etw zu etw e.⟩   to develop (sb/sth) into (sth)

■ Die Japaner haben Taschenrechner zu einem erschwinglichen Produkt entwickelt.
The Japanese have developed pocket calculators into an affordable product.

■ Der Trainer hat ihn zu einem der besten Fußballspieler der Welt entwickelt.
The coach made (or raised) him into one of the best soccer players in the world.

■ Er entwickelte seine spontanen Gedanken zu einer zusammenhängenden Theorie.
He developed his spontaneous thoughts into a coherent theory.

■ In den achtziger Jahren hat sich Korea zu einer Industriemacht entwickelt.
In the eighties Korea developed into an industrial power.

■ Julia entwickelt sich zu einer freundlichen, umgänglichen jungen Frau.
Julia is turning into a friendly, sociable young woman.

erachten für/als + A ⟨**jdn/etw für/als etw e.**⟩   to consider *or* deem (sb/sth) (to be) (sth).

■ Wir erachten sie dieser Ehrung für würdig.
We consider her to be worthy of this honor.

■ Er hat es als Zumutung (*or* für eine Zumutung) erachtet, daß er das Geschirr abwaschen mußte.
He considered washing the dishes to be an unreasonable demand.

■ Wir erachten es für (*or* als) nützlich (/schlecht/unsere Pflicht/wichtig), wiederverwendbare Verpackungen zu benutzen.
We consider it to be useful (/bad/our duty/important) to use recyclable packaging.

erfahren über + A ⟨**über etw e.**⟩   to learn about (sth)

■ Hast du Einzelheiten über das katastrophale Erdbeben erfahren?
Have you learned details of the catastrophic earthquake?

■ Ich habe eine ganze Menge über seine Krankheit erfahren.
I learned a lot about his illness.

erfahren über/von + A/D ⟨**über** *or* **von etw e.**⟩   to learn about (sth)

■ Ich habe nur Schlechtes von Karls neuem (*or* über Karls neuen) Job erfahren.
I learned or heard only bad things about Karl's new job.

erfahren von + D ⟨**von etw e.**⟩   to learn about (sth); to hear from *or* of (sth)

■ Leider erfuhr ich erst gestern von der Eröffnung des Hallenbades.
Unfortunately, I heard only yesterday about the opening of the indoor pool.

■ Ich habe von Kurts Krankheit (/vom Tod Kurts/von den Überschwemmungen/von den geplanten Reformen) erfahren.
I learned (or heard) about Kurt's illness (/death/the flood/the intended reforms).

s. erfreuen an + D ⟨sich an etw e.⟩   to enjoy (sth); to take pleasure in (sth)

■ Ich erfreute mich am Anblick der Kinder (/an der unberührten Natur/an den herr-lichen Nationalparks).
I took pleasure in the sight of the children (/untouched nature/the magnificent national parks).

erfreut sein über + A ⟨über jdn/etw e. sein⟩   to be pleased *or* delighted about *or* at (sb/sth)

■ Sie ist über das Geschenk (/die neue Babysitterin/seinen Besuch) erfreut.
She is delighted about the gift (/the new babysitter/his visit).

erfüllen mit + D ⟨jdn mit etw e.⟩   to fulfill (sb) with (sth)

■ Es erfüllt mich mit Freude (/Abscheu/Schrecken/Stolz), daß Kohl wieder Kanzler wurde.
The fact that Kohl became chancellor again fills me with joy (/disgust/horror /pride).

■ Ihre Kinder erfüllen sie (mit Befriedigung).
Her children give her fulfillment or satisfaction.

s. ergeben aus + D ⟨sich aus etw e.⟩   to result from (sth)

■ Die Notwendigkeit, umzuziehen, ergibt sich aus seinem Entschluß, für eine an-dere Firma zu arbeiten.
His decision to work for another company necessitates that he move.

■ Aus den politischen Veränderungen in Europa ergeben sich viele Möglichkeiten, den Frieden sicherer zu machen.
Many possibilities to make peace more secure result from the political changes in Europe.

■ Einige Vorteile (/Nachteile/unangenehme Folgen) können sich aus der Wahl dieses Mannes zum Präsidenten ergeben.
Some advantages (/disadvantages/unpleasant consequences) could result from the election of this man to the presidency.

s. ergeben in + A ⟨sich in etw e.⟩   to submit to (sth)

■ Ich ergebe mich in mein Schicksal (*or* Los).
I submit to my fate (or lot).

■ Er hat sich in Gottes Willen ergeben.
He submitted to the will of God.

(s.) ergehen (without prep)   to go for a walk *or* stroll; to fare (*well/badly*)

- Es wird den Armen schlecht (/gut) ergehen.
  The poor will suffer (/fare well).
- Wie ist es dir (/Herrn Schmidt/ihr bei der Fahrprüfung) ergangen?
  How did it go for you (/Mr. Schmidt/How did she fare in the driving test)?
- Ich erging mich in der Stadt (/am Strand/am Fluß entlang *(liter).*
  I went walking downtown (/at the beach/along the river).

ergehen an + A ⟨an jdn e.⟩   to go out to (sb); to be issued to (sb); to be sent to (sb)

- Befehle ergingen an alle Truppen.
  Orders were sent out to all troops.
- An welchen Professor ist ein Ruf an die Universität Hamburg ergangen?
  Which professor received a call to the University of Hamburg (or was offered a professorship at the University of Hamburg)?

s. ergehen in + D ⟨sich in etw e.⟩   to indulge in (sth)

- Bitte ergehen Sie sich nicht in Lobreden (/in Dankesworten). Wir haben nichts Besonderes für Sie getan.
  Please don't indulge in lavish praise (/in words of gratitude); we haven't done anything special for you.
- Er hat sich (/Du hast dich) in Beleidigungen gegen seinen (/deinen) Nachbarn ergangen.
  He (/You) poured forth insults against his (/your) neighbor.

⟨etw über sich ergehen lassen⟩   to let (sth) wash over (sb)

- Sie hat alles (/all seine kleinen Betrügereien) klaglos über sich ergehen lassen.
  She let everything (/all his little lies) simply wash over her without complaining.
- Trotz seiner Erkältung ließ sie seine Zärtlichkeit über sich ergehen.
  She suffered his affection in spite of his cold.

ergreifen bei + D ⟨jdn bei etw e.⟩   to grasp (sb) with (sth)

- Die Oma ergriff ihren Enkel bei der Hand.
  The grandmother took her grandson by the hand.
- Der Rettungsschwimmer ergriff den Ertrinkenden beim Arm.
  The lifeguard grasped the drowning person by the arm.
- Sie ergriff die Gelegenheit beim Schopf.
  She took advantage of the opportunity. (or She seized the opportunity with both hands.)

⟨**von etw ergriffen werden**⟩   to be seized with (sth)

■ Er wurde von einer Krankheit (/großer Angst vor der Prüfung/ unerklärlicher Unruhe) ergriffen.
He was seized or stricken by an illness (/fear of the test/an inexplicable restlessness).

■ Er wurde von Liebe zu ihr ergriffen.
He was overcome with love for her.

ergreifen (without prep)   to seize

■ Die Flammen ergriffen ein Zimmer nach dem anderen.
The flames engulfed one room after another.

■ Die Polizei hat den Dieb ergriffen.
The police seized the thief.

■ Angst (/Entsetzen/Freude/Schrecken/Unruhe/Begeisterung/Zorn) ergriff ihn, als er sah, was sein Sohn getan hatte.
He was overcome with fear (/rage/joy/fright/restlessness/enthusiasm/anger) when he saw what his son had done.

erheben (+ prep)   to lift; to raise

■ Es wird Zeit, daß du dich aus dem bequemen Sessel erhebst.
It's about time you got out of the comfortable armchair.

■ Ich möchte mein Glas erheben, um auf das Wohl von Jan zu trinken.
I'd like to raise my glass for a toast to Jan.

■ Du darfst deine Stimme nicht gegen deinen Vater erheben.
You must not raise your voice against your father.

s. erheben über + A ⟨**sich über jdn/etw e.**⟩   to elevate *or* place oneself above (sb/sth); to go beyond (sb/sth)

■ Ich verstehe nicht, wieso du dich immer wieder über andere erhebst.
I don't understand why you place yourself above others again and again.

■ Die Autorin erhob sich (/Ihre Bücher erhoben sich) nie über den Durchschnitt.
The author (/Her books) never went beyond the average.

erheben zu + D ⟨**sich/jdn/etw zu etw e.**⟩   to elevate (o.s./sb/sth) to (sth)

■ Nach dem Krieg wurde Bonn zur vorübergehenden deutschen Hauptstadt erhoben.
After the war Bonn was named the temporary capital of West Germany.

■ Sie haben ihre Ansicht zu einem Prinzip (/einer Regel) erhoben.
They made their view into a principle (/a rule).

s. erhitzen an/über + D/A ⟨sich an *or* über etw e.⟩   to become heated over (sth);
to get hot over (sth)

■ Das Gespräch erhitzte sich an dieser (*rarely* über diese) Streitfrage.
The conversation became heated over this controversial issue.

■ Die Gemüter erhitzen sich an der Frage, ob. . . .
Feelings run high concerning the question whether. . . .

erhitzen auf (Grad). . . ⟨auf (Grad) e.⟩   to heat (sth) to . . . degree

■ Wir erhitzen das Wasser auf 100 Grad.
We heat the water to 100 degrees.

erinnern an + A ⟨jdn an jdn/etw e.⟩   to remind (sb) of (sb/sth)

■ Dieser Junge erinnert mich an meinen alten Kumpel.
This boy reminds me of my old buddy.

■ Das erinnert mich an eine angenehme Begebenheit auf Föhr.
That reminds me of a beautiful incident on the island of Föhr.

■ Ich erinnerte ihn daran, daß er morgen einen Termin hat.
I reminded him that he has an appointment tomorrow.

s. erinnern an + A ⟨sich an jdn/etw e.⟩   to remember (sb/sth)

■ Ich erinnere mich nicht an meine Kindheit (/an meine Oma/daran, was du gesagt
hast).
I don't remember my childhood (/my grandma/what you said).

■ Sie wird sich wohl an dich (/diese Erfahrung) erinnern.
She'll probably remember you (/this experience).

■ An sein Gesicht kann ich mich beim besten Willen nicht mehr erinnern.
I can't remember his face for the life of me.

(s.) erinnern (without prep)   to remember; to remind

■ Wenn ich mich recht erinnere, hattest du ein blaues Kleid an.
If I remember correctly, you were wearing a blue dress.

■ Bitte erinnern Sie mich rechtzeitig.
Please remind me in time.

erkennen an + D ⟨jdn/etw an etw e.⟩   to know (sb/sth) by (sth)

■ Ich erkenne ihn an seinem Schritt (/Hut/an seiner Stimme).
I know him by his footstep (/hat/voice).

■ Der Detektiv hat ihn an seinem Fingerabdruck erkannt.
The detective knew him by his fingerprint.

■ Man erkennt diese Blume an ihrem Geruch.
One knows this flower by its smell.

erkennen auf + A ⟨auf etw e.⟩   to impose (sth); to grant (sth)

■ Der Richter hat auf zwei Monate Haft (/auf Freispruch/auf lebenslängliche Frei-
heitsstrafe) erkannt.
*The judge imposed a two-month sentence on him (/acquitted him/sentenced him
to life imprisonment).*

■ Der Schiedsrichter erkannte auf einen Schiedsrichterball (/einen Freistoß /zwei
Schüsse/abseits).
The referee called a jump ball (/a free kick/two shots/offside).

erklären für + A ⟨sich/jdn/etw für etw e.⟩   to declare (o.s./sb/sth) as (sth)

■ Die Polizei (/Armee) ließ den Vermißten für tot erklären.
The police (/army) had the missing person declared dead.

■ Er erklärte sie (/sich) für bankrott (/schuldig).
He declared her (/himself) bankrupt (/guilty).

s. erkundigen nach/über + D/A ⟨sich nach jdm/etw, über jdn/etw e.⟩   to ask *or*
inquire about (sb/sth)

■ Bevor du zu ihm gehst, solltest du dich über den neuen Chirurgen erkundigen.
Before you go to see him, you should inquire about the new surgeon.

■ Ich habe mich gerade nach dem Fahrplan (/ihrer Gesundheit/ihm/der Zeit)
erkundigt.
I have just inquired about the travel schedule (/her health/him/the time).

ermitteln gegen + A ⟨gegen jdn e.⟩   to investigate (sb)

■ Die Polizei ermittelt bereits seit einem Monat gegen ihn (/den Verdächtigen).
*The police have already been investigating (or making inquiries about) him for
a month.*

s. erschöpfen in + D ⟨sich in etw e.⟩   to amount to nothing more than (sth)

■ Seine Ausführungen vor Gericht erschöpften sich in der Behauptung, daß er unschuldig war.
His remarks in court amounted to nothing more than the contention that he was not guilty.

■ Mein Auftrag erschöpfte sich darin, dem Ausschuß einen Vorschlag zu unterbreiten.
My task was limited to (or amounted to nothing more than) submitting a proposal to the committee.

■ Seine Bildung erschöpft sich darin, die Namen der größten deutschen Dichter aufsagen zu können.
His education is limited to the ability to rattle off the names of the greatest German poets.

(s.) erschrecken bei + D ⟨(sich) bei etw e.⟩   to be alarmed *or* scared *or* shocked *or* startled at (sth)

■ Ich erschrak (mich) bei dem Gedanken, daß die Operation nicht erfolgreich sein könnte.
I was scared at the thought that the operation might not be successful.

■ Die Kinder haben sich bei der plötzlichen Explosion des Feuerwerkskörpers (/dem unerwarteten Eintreten des Mannes) erschrocken.
The sudden explosion of the firecracker (/unexpected entry of the man) made the children jump.

■ Wir erschraken uns bei der Nachricht, daß die Überschwemmung 20 Menschenleben kostete.
We were shocked at the news that the flood cost 20 people their lives.

erschrecken über + A ⟨(sich) über etw e.⟩   to be alarmed at (sth); to get scared at (sth)

■ Ich erschrak über seine Worte (/diese Entwicklung/die Nachricht).
I was alarmed at his words (/this development/the news).

ersetzen durch + A ⟨durch etw e.⟩   to replace (sth) with (sb) *or* (sth)

■ Ersetzen Sie die unterstrichenen Ausdrücke durch andere Wörter.
Replace the underlined expressions with other words.

■ Wir müssen dieses alte Sofa durch ein neues ersetzen.
We have to replace this old sofa with a new one.

■ Sie ist durch nichts (/niemanden) zu ersetzen.
She cannot be replaced by anything (/anyone).

s. erstrecken (+ prep)   to extend; to reach; to stretch

■ Chomskys Forschungsaktivitäten erstreckten sich (über einen Zeitraum von 40 Jahren) auch auf philosophische Fragen.
Chomsky's research activities also extended to philosophical questions (over a period of forty years).

■ Das Grundstück erstreckt sich bis zum Flußufer.
The lot extends to the bank of the river.

s. erstrecken auf + A ⟨sich auf jdn/etw e.⟩   to apply to (sb/sth)

■ Seine Kritik erstreckt sich nicht nur auf Details, sondern auf das ganze Werk.
His criticism does not merely apply to details, but to the work as a whole.

■ Ich weiß nicht ob, die Vorschriften sich auch auf Studenten erstrecken.
I don't know if the regulations apply to students, too.

ertappen bei + D ⟨jdn bei etw e.⟩   to catch (sb) *or* (o.s.) at *or* doing (sth)

■ Der Lehrer hat ihn bei einer Lüge (/beim Abschreiben/beim Kaugummi-kauen/beim Naschen/dabei/beim Schlafen) ertappt.
The teacher caught him in a lie (/cheating/chewing gum/snacking/at it/ sleeping).

■ Die Polizei ertappte den Verbrecher auf frischer Tat (/beim Stehlen).
The police caught the criminal red-handed (/while stealing).

■ Eben habe ich mich schon wieder beim Nasebohren ertappt!
I just caught myself picking my nose again.

(s.) erwarten von + D ⟨(sich) etw von jdm/etw e.⟩   to expect (sth) from (sb/sth)

■ Ich erwartete (mir) vielleicht zu viel von diesem Buch (/dieser Reise).
Perhaps I expected too much from this book (/this trip).

■ Ich glaube, wir können (uns) mehr von dieser Partei erwarten.
I believe we can expect more from this party.

■ Sie erwartet ein Kind von ihrem zweiten Mann.
She is expecting a child by her second husband.

■ Von diesem Jungen ist nicht viel Gutes zu erwarten.
No good can come of this boy.

erwidern auf + A ⟨auf etw e.⟩   to reply to (sth)

■ Was kann man auf ein solches Argument schon erwidern?
How can one respond to such an argument?

■ Auf seine unfreundliche Frage erwiderte sie, daß . . . .
In reply to his unfriendly question, she said that. . . .

erzählen über/von + A/D ⟨über jdn/etw, von jdm/etw e.⟩   to talk about (sb/sth)

■ Er erzählt immer über seine (*or* von seiner) Reise.
He always talks about his trip.

■ Ich habe meinem Vetter nie davon (*or* darüber) erzählt.
I never told my cousin about it.

■ Ich will nicht viel von ihm (*or* über ihn) erzählen.
I don't want to talk about him so much.

erziehen zu + D ⟨jdn zu etw e.⟩   to educate (sb) to (sth)

■ Eltern versuchen, ihre Kinder zu guten Menschen zu erziehen.
Parents try to bring up their children to be good people.

■ Er hat das Tier zur Sauberkeit (/zu gutem Benehmen) erzogen.
He trained (or taught) the animal to be clean (/to behave well).

■ Durch ihr gutes Vorbild erzogen sie das Kind zur Empfindsamkeit (/zur Sparsamkeit/zu einem guten Christen).
Through their good example they brought up their child to be sensitive (/economical/a good Christian).

F

fahren (+ prep) to travel; to go

- Er fuhr nach Hamburg (/nach Frankreich/in die Schweiz/in den Iran/ in die Berge/an die See/ins Grüne/ins Blaue/in *or* auf Urlaub/ in die Ferien/zu den Großeltern/zum Theater/ins Kino/an den Strand).
  He went or travelled to Hamburg (/to France/to Switzerland/to Iran/to the mountains/to the seaside/to the country/at random/on vacation/to his grandparents/to the theater/to the movies/to the beach).

fallen an + A ⟨**an jdn/etw f.**⟩ to go to (sb/sth); (become the property of)

- Die Insel (/Stadt) fiel an die Griechen (/Griechenland/die Türkei/ die Türken).
  The island (/city) fell to the Greeks (/Greece/Turkey/the Turks).

- Die Firma ist nach seinem Tod an seinen ältesten Sohn gefallen.
  After his death the firm went to his oldest son.

fallen auf + A ⟨**auf jdn/etw f.**⟩ to fall on (sb/sth)

- Er fiel von der Leiter auf die Erde (/den Boden).
  He fell from the ladder to the ground (/floor).

- Oft fällt die Schuld (/Entscheidung/Aufmerksamkeit/der Verdacht/ die Verantwortlichkeit) auf das älteste Kind.
  Often the fault (/decision/attention/responsibility/suspicion) falls on the oldest child.

- Das Kind fiel auf die Knie (/das Gesicht/den Rücken).
  The child fell on his knees (/face/back).

- Wieviel der Unkosten fällt auf mich?
  How much of the expenses falls on me?

- Es gab zwei Kandidatinnen für den Vorsitz im Elternrad; die Wahl fiel auf Frau Müller.
  There were two candidates for the presidency of the parental council; Frau Müller was elected.

- Sein Blick fiel auf ihr Gesicht (/ihre Halskette/ein Mädchen).
  His eyes fell on her face (/her necklace/a girl).

- Er hat den Gegenstand auf den Boden fallen lassen.
  He let the object fall to the floor.

fallen in + A ⟨**in etw f.**⟩   to get into a (certain) condition

■ Nach der Bombardierung fiel die Stadt in Trümmer.
After the bombing the city fell into ruins.

■ Gold (/Der Dollar/Die Mark) ist stark im Wert gefallen.
Gold (/The dollar/The mark) fell sharply in value.

fallen in/unter + A ⟨**in/unter etw f.**⟩   to come within (sth); to fall within *or* under (sth)

■ Dieses Verbrechen (/Die Entführung) fällt unter das Bundesgesetz.
This crime (/The kidnapping) falls under federal law.

■ Diese Kameras (/Parfüme) fallen nicht unter die Zollbestimmungen (/dieselbe Kategorie).
These cameras (/perfumes) don't fall under customs regulations (/under the same category).

■ Mein Geburtstag (/Der Vorfall) fällt in den Winter.
My birthday (/The event) falls in the winter.

■ Das fällt nicht in die Kompetenz der Vereinten Nationen.
That doesn't fall under the authority of the United Nations.

fehlen an + D ⟨**an jdm/etw f.**⟩   (sb) lacks (sb/sth)

■ Es fehlt mir an Geld (*or* Mir fehlt Geld). An Geld (/Daran) soll es nicht fehlen.
I'm short of money. Money (/That) should not be an object.

■ Es fehlt an Ärzten (/Spezialisten).
There is a shortage of doctors (/specialists).

■ Meine Mutter hat es mir (/meinem Vater) an nichts fehlen lassen.
My mother spared no pains for me (/my father).

■ Udo hat es an Sorgfalt (/am rechten Ernst/an Schamgefühl/an Humor) fehlen lassen.
Udo had a lack of concern (/seriousness/Udo had no shame/Udo had no sense of humor).

■ Den Menschen in Äthiopien fehlt es am Nötigsten (/an Nahrungsmitteln/Geld).
The people in Ethiopia suffer from a lack of the most basic things (/a lack of food/a lack of money).

■ Wie ist es möglich, daß es dir nie an einer Ausrede fehlt (/dir nie die Worte fehlen)!
How is it possible that you're never at a loss for an excuse (/for words)!

⟨**etw fehlt jdm/etw (without prep)**⟩   there is a lack of (sth); (sth) is missing

■ Mir fehlt ein Zehn-Dollarschein (/ein Zahn).
I am missing a ten-dollar bill (/a tooth).

■   Peter fehlt.
Peter is absent.

■   Du hast mir die ganze Woche gefehlt. Ich vermißte dich sehr.
I missed you the whole week. I missed you a lot.

■   Mein eigener Füller fehlt mir heute sehr. Ich habe ihn zu Hause gelassen.
I miss my pen today a lot; I left it at home.

festhalten an + D ⟨**an jdm/etw f.**⟩   to hold *or* stick to (sb/sth); to hold on to (sb/sth)

■   Sie hat eigensinnig an ihrer Ansicht (/ihrem religiösen Glauben/ihrem hohen Niveau) festgehalten.
She stood stubbornly by her view (/held on to her religious beliefs/stood by her high standards).

■   Engstirnige Leute halten oft am Rassismus fest.
Narrowminded people often hold on to racism.

■   Die Regierung hielt an dem umstrittenen Außenminister fest.
The government held on to (or stood by) the controversial foreign secretary.

(s.) festlegen auf + A ⟨**jdn/sich auf etw f.**⟩   to tie *or* commit (sb/o.s.) (down) to (sth)

■   Können Sie sich auf diese Aussage festlegen? —Nein, ich kann mich auch irren.
Can you swear to your testimony? —No, I might be wrong.

■   Du mußt dich darauf festlegen, den Artikel rechtzeitig fertigzustellen.
You must commit yourself to completing the article on time.

■   Eine Partei kann ihre Abgeordneten nicht auf eine Meinung festlegen. Sie sind nur ihrem Gewissen verpflichtet.
A party cannot commit its representatives to one opinion. They are responsible only to their conscience.

fischen auf + A ⟨**auf etw f.**⟩   to fish for (sth)

■   Die Fischer fischen auf Heringe.
The fishermen are fishing for herring.

■   In diesem See wird auf Forellen gefischt.
People fish for trout in this lake.

fischen aus + D ⟨**jdn/etw aus etw f.**⟩   to fish (sb/sth) out of (sth)

■   Der Rettungsschwimmer hat das Kind aus dem Becken gefischt.
The lifeguard got the child out of the pool.

■ Er fischt (sich) die Stücke Fleisch (/ein Haar) aus dem Eintopf.
He is fishing the pieces of meat (/a hair) out of the stew.

■ Ich habe (mir) ein Paar Socken aus dem Koffer gefischt.
I fished out a pair of socks from the suitcase.

flehen um + A ⟨um etw f.⟩   to plead for (sth)

■ Der Mörder flehte gegenüber dem Richter um sein Leben (/um Gnade).
The murderer pleaded to the judge for his life (/mercy).

flehen zu + D ⟨zu jdm/etw f.⟩   to plead with (sb)

■ Ich flehte eindringlich zu Gott, dem Herrn, um Hilfe (/baldige Genesung meines Sohnes).
I urgently beseeched the Lord God, for help (/for the speedy recovery of my son).

■ Die Gläubigen flehen zum Himmel um die Erlassung ihrer Sünden.
The faithful plead to heaven for the absolution of their sins.

fliegen (+ prep)   to fly

■ Er ist nach Chikago (/nach Hause/in die Vereinigten Staaten/zu einem fernen Ort/in den Urlaub) geflogen.
He flew to Chicago (/home/to the United States/to a distant place/on vacation).

■ Das Flugzeug ist über den Wolken (/die See) geflogen.
The plane flew over the clouds (/the ocean).

■ Der Pilot hat Medikamente (/das Flugzeug) nach Kurdistan geflogen.
The pilot flew medicine (/the plane) to Kurdistan.

■ Die Astronauten wollen mit dem Raumschiff zum Mond (/zu einem fernen Planeten) fliegen.
The astronauts want to fly to the moon (/to a far distant planet) in a spacecraft.

■ Im Sommer fliegen die meisten Vögel nach Norden (/nach Kanada).
In the summer most birds fly north(wards) (/to Canada).

fliegen auf + A ⟨auf jdn/etw f.⟩   to be mad *or* wild about (sb/sth)

■ Er fliegt auf Schokolade (/Michael Jordan/gute Fußballer).
He is mad about chocolate (/Michael Jordan/good soccer players).

■ Früher bin ich auch auf Krimis (/Comics) geflogen.
Once I, too, was wild about detective stories (/comics).

fliehen vor + D ⟨**vor jdm f.**⟩   to run away *or* escape from (sb)

- Er floh vor der Polizei (/der Gefahr/der Lawine).
  He escaped from the police (/danger/the avalanche).

- Der Teenager ist vor seinem bösen Stiefvater zu uns geflohen.
  The teenager ran away from his awful stepfather to us.

- Man kann vor seinem Schicksal (/seiner Zukunft) nicht fliehen.
  One cannot escape his fate (/future).

- Die Dissidenten flohen aus dem Lande (/nach Mexiko).
  The dissidents fled the country (/to Mexico).

- Ihre Kinder machten eine Party; sie floh vor dem Lärm aus der Wohnung.
  Her children were having a party; she fled the apartment to escape the noise.

fließen (+ prep)   to flow

- Der Mississippi (/Der Fluß) fließt in den Golf von Mexiko (/in die Ostsee /ins Meer).
  The Mississippi (/The river) flows to the Gulf of Mexico (/into the Baltic sea/into the ocean).

- Die Drogen fließen ins Ausland (/nach Deutschland).
  The drugs are flowing to foreign countries (/Germany).

- Der Schweiß floß ihm von den Achselhöhlen (/übers Gesicht/von der Stirn/vom Kopf/ins Hemd).
  The sweat ran from his armpits (/his face/his forehead/his head/into his shirt).

- Die Tränen flossen dem Kind über die Wangen.
  The tears flowed down the child's cheeks.

- Das Blut floß aus der Nase des Boxers (/dem Schnitt).
  The blood flowed from the boxer's nose (/cut).

- Das Wasser fließt mit Druck aus dem Wasserhahn (/der Leitung).
  The water is gushing from the faucet (/pipe).

fluchen auf/über + A ⟨**auf/über jdn/etw f.**⟩   to curse at (sb/sth)

- Sie hat auf (*or* über) ihren Manager geflucht.
  She cursed (or swore) at her manager.

- Die Putzfrau flucht über (*or* auf) die Unordnung im Kleiderschrank.
  The cleaning woman is swearing at the mess in the closet.

- Er fluchte über (*or* auf) den schlechten Kaffee des Restaurants.
  He cursed the restaurant's bad coffee.

flüchten (+ prep)   to run away, flee, escape

- Er ist aus den USA (/über die Grenze/ins Ausland/nach Kanada) geflüchtet.
  He escaped from the USA (/over the border/into a foreign country/to Canada).
- Die Katze konnte vor dem Hund auf einen Baum (/ein Dach) flüchten.
  The cat managed to escape from the dog up a tree (/onto a roof).

s. flüchten in + A ⟨sich in etw f.⟩   to resort to (sth); to take refuge in (sth)

- Wenn es schwierig wird, flüchtet er sich immer in Ausreden.
  Whenever it gets tough he resorts to excuses.
- Sie versucht ihren Problemen auszuweichen, indem sie sich in eine Traumwelt flüchtet.
  She tries to evade her problems by taking refuge in a dream world.

flüchten vor/aus + D ⟨vor jdm/etw f.⟩   to run away *or* flee *or* escape from (sb/sth)

- Er flüchtet vor der Presse (/seinen Problemen/der Wirklichkeit).
  He is running away from the press (/his problems/reality).
- Der Dissident flüchtete aus dem Land (/dem Gefängnis/Südafrika).
  The dissident fled the country (/escaped from the jail/escaped from South Africa).
- Sie sind vor der Mafia ins Ausland geflüchtet.
  They fled to a foreign country to escape the Mafia.

folgen auf + A ⟨auf jdn/etw f.⟩   to follow (sb/sth); to come *or* rank after (sb)

- Man sagt, daß auf einen (*or* einem) warmen Sommer ein kalter Winter folgt.
  People say that a cold winter will follow a warm summer.
- Ein toller Nachtisch (/Kuchen) folgte auf das Hauptgericht.
  A great dessert (/cake) followed the main course.

folgen aus + D ⟨aus etw f.⟩   (sth) follows *or* results from (sth)

- Aus seiner Aussage (/diesem Gesetzentwurf) folgt, daß. . . .
  From his statement (/this bill) it follows that. . . .
- Was folgt daraus für die Obdachlosen?
  What are the consequences of this for the homeless?

folgern aus + D ⟨aus etw f.⟩   to conclude from (sth)

- Aus seinen Darlegungen (/der Tatsache) folgerte ich, daß. . . .
  From his explanations (/the facts) I concluded that. . . .
- Daraus folgerte der Einbrecher, daß niemand zu Hause war.
  That led the burglar to conclude that no one was at home.

fordern von + D ⟨etw von jdm f.⟩   to demand *or* require (sth) from (sb)

- Der neue Schulleiter fordert viel von seinen Mitarbeitern.
  The new principal demands a lot from his staff.
- Die Entführer forderten Lösegeld von den Eltern des Kindes.
  The kidnappers demanded ransom from the child's parents.

forschen nach + D ⟨nach jdm/etw f.⟩   to search *or* seek after/for (sb/sth)

- Die Wissenschaftler forschen nach der Wahrheit (/nach dem Erreger der Krankheit).
  The scientists are searching for the truth (/the cause of the illness).
- Der Detektiv forschte nach dem Vermißten (/Verbleib der Pistole).
  The detective looked for the missing person (/whereabouts of the gun).
- Der Abenteurer hat nach dem Schatz geforscht.
  The adventurer searched for the treasure.

fragen nach + D ⟨(jdn) nach jdm/etw f.⟩   to ask *or* inquire about (sb/sth)

- Hat jemand nach mir (/nach den Büchern) gefragt?
  Did someone ask about me (/about the books)?
- Er fragte (sie) nach ihrem Namen (/ihrem Alter).
  He asked (her) about her name (/age).
- Sein Freund hat ihn nach seiner Mutter (/seinen Reiseplänen) gefragt.
  His friend asked him about his mother (/his travel plans).
- Ich fragte danach, ob der Opa schon zum Arzt gegangen sei.
  I asked if grandpa had seen the doctor yet.

s. freuen an + D ⟨sich an jdm/etw f.⟩   to get *or* derive a lot of pleasure from (sb/sth)

- Sie freute sich sehr an ihren Kindern (/Blumen/dem schönen Gesang).
  Her children (/Flowers/The beautiful singing) gave her a lot of pleasure.

■   Ich freue mich an deinem Glück (/an der Musik Beethovens).
I'm happy for you. (/Beethoven's music gives me pleasure.)

s. freuen auf + A ⟨**sich auf jdn/etw f.**⟩   to look forward to (sb/sth)

■   Die Kinder freuen sich auf die Ferien (/die Reise/dein Kommen).
The children are looking forward to the vacation (/the trip/your visit).

s. freuen für + A ⟨**sich für jdn f.**⟩   to be glad *or* pleased for (sb) *or* for (sb's sake)

■   Ich freue mich für euch, daß ihr dieses Haus kaufen konntet.
I am happy for you that you were able to buy this house.

■   Wir freuen uns für dich, daß du deinen Führerschein gekriegt hast.
We are happy for you that you got your driver's license.

s. freuen über + A ⟨**sich über jdn/etw f.**⟩   to be glad *or* pleased about (sb/sth)

■   Paul freut sich über seine erfolgreichen Kinder (/das Geschenk).
Paul is happy about his successful children (/the gift).

■   Ich freue mich über mein neues Auto (/ein Geschenk/meinen Erfolg).
I'm pleased about my new car (/a gift/my success).

■   Stefans Lehrerin freut sich darüber, daß er die 7. Klasse geschafft hat.
Stefan's teacher is happy that he passed the seventh grade.

s. fügen in + A ⟨**sich in etw f.**⟩   to be obedient to (sth); to obey (sth); to resign oneself to (sth)

■   Ich habe mich in mein Schicksal gefügt.
I have resigned myself to my fate.

■   Ich fügte mich—nach anfänglichem Widerstand—in das Unabänderliche.
After initial reluctance I bowed to the inevitable.

s. fügen (without prep)   to obey; to bow to

■   Du mußt dich deinem Vater (/Gott/meinen Anordnungen/mir) fügen.
You must obey your father (/God/my orders/me).

■   Es fügte sich, daß Nicole in jenem Augenblick ins Haus trat (*liter*).
It so happened that Nicole at that moment stepped into the house.

führen (+ prep)   to lead; to guide

- Er führte die Großmutter über den Hof.
  He helped the grandmother across the courtyard.

- Die Sekretärin führte ihn zum Direktor (/zur Chefin).
  The secretary led him to the director (/boss).

- Der Kellner (/Herr) wird die Dame zu ihrem Tisch führen.
  The waiter (/gentleman) will lead the lady to her table.

- Die alte Straße hat nach Kiel (/am Rhein entlang) geführt.
  The old highway went to Kiel (/ran along the Rhein).

- Eine neue Brücke führt über den Potomac (/den Fluß/die Straße).
  A new bridge crosses (or spans) the Potomac (/river/street).

- Sie haben uns mit Ihren widersprüchlichen Aussagen in die Irre geführt.
  You misled us with your contradictory statements.

- Die Frau führte ihr Kind (/einen Blinden/ihn) an der Hand.
  The woman led her child (/a blind man/him) by the hand.

- Der Urlaub führte sie in die Karibik (/nach China).
  The vacation took them to the Caribbean (/China).

- Deine Bemerkung führt uns auf die (*or* zu der) Frage. . . .
  Your remark brings (or leads) us to the question. . . .

- Unsere Mannschaft führt (mit) 4 : 2 (/führt mit zwei Punkten).
  Our team is leading 4 to 2 (/is leading by two points).

s. führen bei/mit + D ⟨etw bei/mit sich f.⟩   to carry (sth) with oneself

- Erich hat kein Geld (/kein Handwerkszeug) bei (*or* mit) sich geführt.
  Erich carried no money (/no tools) with him.

- Der Verbrecher führte einen geladenen Revolver mit (*or* bei) sich.
  The criminal carried a loaded gun with him.

führen durch + A ⟨jdn durch etw f.⟩   to show (sb) around; to give (sb) a (guided) tour of (sth)

- Der Mann führte die Gruppe durch das Museum (/die Stadt).
  The man showed the group around the museum (/city).

- Der Rektor hat den neuen Schüler durch die Schule geführt.
  The principal showed the new student around the school.

- Der Vorarbeiter selbst führte ihn durch die Fabrik.
  The foreman himself showed him around the factory.

führen in + A ⟨jdn/etw in etw f.⟩   to lead (sb/sth) to (sth)

- Gott, führe uns nicht in Versuchung!
  Lord, lead us not into temptation.
- Er hat das Land ins Elend (/in die Katastrophe/in den Ruin) geführt.
  He led (or reduced) the country to misery (/catastrophe/ruin).
- Der Politiker versprach, das Land in eine bessere Zukunft zu führen.
  The politician promised to lead the country to a better future.
- Der Alkohol führt ihn ins Verderben.
  Alcohol is leading him into ruin.

führen zu + D ⟨zu etw f.⟩   (sth) leads to (sth)

- Seine Faulheit führte zu dem Ergebnis, daß er die Versetzung nicht geschafft hat.
  His laziness resulted in his failing the class (i.e., he was held back).
- Das Vorgehen hat zu einer Katastrophe (/nichts Gutem/keinem Ergebnis) geführt.
  That action led to a catastrophe (/nothing good/didn't lead to any result).
- Diese Spur (/Dieser Fingerabdruck) hat zur Ergreifung des Schuldigen geführt.
  This clue (/fingerprint) led to the capture of the culprit.
- Ihre Beobachtung führte sie zu der Erkenntnis, daß. . . .
  Her observation made her realize that. . . .
- Das sehr heiße Wetter führte ihn dazu, die Klimaanlage einzuschalten.
  The very hot weather made him turn on the air conditioning.

  ⟨jdn/etw zu etw f.⟩   to lead (sb/sth) to (sth)

  - Der junge Trainer hat die Chicago Bulls zur Meisterschaft geführt.
    The young coach led the Chicago Bulls to the championship.
  - Der Lehrer führte all seine Schüler zum (*or* bis zum) Abitur.
    The teacher saw all of his students through the final graduating exams.

füllen in + A ⟨etw in etw f.⟩   to fill *or* stuff (sth) in (sth); to bottle (sth)

- Er füllt die Äpfel in Kästen.
  He is stuffing the apples into boxes.
- Der Bauer hat die Milch (/Sahne) in Flaschen gefüllt.
  The farmer put the milk (/cream) in bottles.

füllen mit + D ⟨sich/etw mit etw f.⟩   to fill with (sth)

- Bitte, füllen Sie die Vase (/das Glas) mit Wasser bis an den Rand!
  Please, fill the vase (/glass) with water all the way to the rim!

■ Sie füllte die Pute (/sich den Magen) mit Äpfeln.
  She filled the turkey (/her stomach) with apples.

■ Als sie ihren Sohn zum ersten Mal sah, füllten sich ihre Augen mit Tränen.
  When she saw her son for the first time, her eyes filled with tears.

fürchten um + A ⟨**um jdn/etw f.**⟩   to fear for (sb/sth)

■ Die Mutter fürchtet um die Gesundheit ihres Kindes.
  The mother fears for the health of her child.

■ Der Zeuge fürchtet um sein Leben.
  The witness fears for his life.

■ Mein Mann fürchtet um seine Arbeit (/seinen Job/seinen Posten).
  My husband fears for his job (/job/position).

s. fürchten vor + D ⟨**sich vor jdm/etw f.**⟩   to be afraid of (sb/sth)

■ Ich fürchte mich vor großen Hunden (/dem Tier da/niemandem).
  I am afraid of big dogs (/that animal/no one).

■ Hast du dich nicht vor ihm (/davor/vor deiner neuen Arbeit/vor einem Atomkrieg) gefürchtet?
  Were you not afraid of him (/it/your new job/an atomic war)?

■ Fürchtet ihr euch nicht vor der Dunkelheit (/dem Test/der Debatte/ der Arbeitslosigkeit)?
  Aren't you afraid of the dark (/test/debate/unemployment)?

G

geben (+ prep)   to give (sb/sth); to send (sb/sth)

- Sie gibt dem Kind jeden Samstag Geld für Bonbons (/eine Fahrkarte).
  She gives the child money for candy (/a ticket) every Saturday.

- Ich gab das Gepäck in die Gepäckaufbewahrung.
  I checked the luggage in the baggage room.

- Wilhelm hat das Auto zur Reparatur (/in die Werkstatt) gegeben.
  Wilhelm took the car in (/to the garage) to be repaired.

- Er gab den Brief (/das Päckchen) auf die Post.
  He mailed the letter (/package).

- Sie gaben das Kind in Pflege (/zur Adoption frei).
  They put (or placed) the child in foster care (/up for adoption).

- Ihr Mann gibt eine Decke auf den Tisch (/die Wäsche in die Waschmachine).
  Her husband is covering the table with a tablecloth (/putting the laundry in the washing machine).

- Ich gäbe viel darum, eine Karte für dieses Konzert zu bekommen.
  I'd give a lot to get a ticket for this concert.

geben auf + A ⟨etw auf etw g.⟩   to lay (value) upon (sth); give *or* think of (sth)

- Ich gebe nichts (/viel) auf seine Fußballkünste (/ihn/seinen Einfluß/lange Reisen /schnelle Autos).
  I think nothing (/highly) of his soccer skills (/him/his influence/long trips/fast cars).

- Wir gaben nicht viel auf seine Meinung (/seinen Rat/sein Urteil).
  We didn't think much of his opinion (/advice/judgment).

- Darauf ist nichts zu geben.
  That is of no importance whatsoever.

s. geben von + D ⟨etw von sich g.⟩   to utter (sth); to deliver (sth); to throw up, to vomit

- Mir war so schlecht. Ich habe das Essen (/alles) gleich wieder von mir gegeben.
  I felt so sick that I threw up the food (/everything) right away.

- Als sie gestern jene Bermerkung von sich gegeben hat, war sie total gestreßt.
  When she made that comment yesterday, she was totally stressed out.

gebrauchen zu/als + D/N ⟨jdn/etw zu/als etw g.⟩   to be useful for (sth)

■   Der Apparat ist völlig kaputt. Er ist zu nichts zu gebrauchen.
The apparatus is completely broken down. It is of no use to anybody.

■   Wir können das Altpapier gut als Rohstoff gebrauchen.
We can make good use of the waste paper as raw material.

■   Das Werkzeug läßt sich zu vielem gebrauchen.
That tool serves (or lends itself to) many purposes.

■   Das Buch ist sehr schwierig. Es läßt sich nicht als (*or* zur) Einführung in das Thema gebrauchen.
The book is very difficult. It is not suitable as an introduction to the subject.

geeignet sein für/zu/als + A/D/N ⟨jd/etw ist für/zu/als etw g.⟩   to be suited *or* right for (sth)

■   Sie ist zu diesem (*or* für diesen) Beruf nicht geeignet.
She's not suited to this profession.

■   Sie ist zum (*or* als) Vorschullehrerin gut (/schlecht) geeignet.
She makes (/doesn't make) a good kindergarten teacher.

■   Wozu (*or* Wofür) ist er geeignet? Wäre er für diesen Posten (zum *or* als Schauspieler) geeignet?
What is he suited for? Would he be suited for this position (/for becoming an actor)?

gehen (+ prep)   to go

■   Er geht in die Stadt (/auf den Berg/aufs Rathaus/aufs Standesamt/ins Büro/zur *or* in die Kirche/in die *or* zur Schule/in den Kindergarten/zur Arbeit/in die *or* zur Universität/zum Bahnhof/ins Ausland/nach Frankreich).
He goes downtown (/up or climbs the mountain/to the city hall/to the marriage office/to work in an office/to attend a church service/to school/to kindergarten/ to work/to the university/to the train station/to (work in) a foreign country/to France).

■   Er ging ins Kino (/ins Theater/an die Luft/nach Hause/zur Post/zum Fleischer/zum Bäcker/in Deckung/an den Strand/zu *or* ins Bett/zum Arzt).
He went to the movies (/to the theater/to take a walk in the fresh air/home/to the post office/to the butcher's/to the baker's/took cover/to the beach/to bed/to see the doctor).

■   Er ging in die Verwaltung (/in die Industrie/in die Politik/ins Kloster/in den Staatsdienst/zum Film/zum Theater/zum Militär/zur Polizei/zur See).
He went into administration (/into industry/into politics/joined a monastery (to become a monk)/into government service/to the movie to become an actor /to the theater/to the theater to become an actor /to join the military/to the police or to join the police force/to the sea or to join the navy).

■   Er ging über die Straße (/durch den Park/durch den Regen/nach Westen/in die falsche Richtung/die Treppe hinunter).

He went across the street (/through the park/through the rain/west/in the wrong direction/down the stairs).

- Felix ging mit 18 aus dem Haus.
  Felix left home at the age of 18.

- Das Schiff geht zweimal täglich nach Helgoland.
  The boat goes to Helgoland twice a day.

- Er ist unter die Sprachwissenschaftler (/Künstler/Säufer) gegangen.
  He joined the ranks of linguists (/artists/alcoholics).

- Er ging auf Zehenspitzen (/an *or* auf Krücken/an meinem Arm/im Zickzack).
  He went on his tip-toes (/on crutches/on my arm/in a zigzag).

- Unser Hotelzimmer ging auf den Wald (/auf eine verkehrsreiche Straße).
  Our hotel room faced the forest (/a busy street).

gehen an + A ⟨an etw g.⟩   to go to (sth)

- Die Passagiere gingen an Bord (/an Land).
  The passengers went on board (/ashore) (or (dis)embarked).

- Wir müssen sofort an die Arbeit gehen.
  We must get to work right away.

- Mein Sohn geht mir jetzt bis an das Kinn (/die Stirn).
  My son now reaches up to my chin (/forehead).

- Mit 15 ist sie ans Theater gegangen.
  She became an actress at the age of 15.

- Dieses Schreiben (/Angebot) geht an alle.
  This memo (/offer) goes to everybody.

- Bianka, geh nicht an das Geld (Du darfst nicht an das Geld gehen)!
  Bianka, keep your hands off the money!

gehen auf + A ⟨auf etw g.⟩   to approach (sth); to get on for (sth)

- Es ging auf 4 Uhr (/Mittag/Mitternacht).
  It approached 4 o'clock (/noon/midnight).

- Meine Tante geht auf (*or* gegen) 40.
  My aunt is almost 40.

gehen auf + A ⟨auf etw g.⟩   to go to (sth); to attend (sth)

- Wir gehen auf Urlaub (/Reisen/die Jagd).
  We are going on vacation (/a trip/hunting).

- Er geht auf die Universität Hamburg.
  He studies at the University of Hamburg.
- Der letzte Satz geht nicht mehr auf diese Seite.
  The last sentence does not fit on this page.

gehen auf/gegen + A ⟨**auf/gegen etw g.**⟩   to go for/against (sth)

- Das geht gegen meine Prinzipien (/Überzeugung/mein Gewissen).
  That goes against my principles (/convictions/conscience).
- Der Artikel ging gegen. . . .
  The article criticized. . . .
- Er ging auf einen Fenstertisch zu und setzte sich.
  He went to a table by a window and sat down.
- Es geht auf (*or* um) Leben und Tod!
  It's a matter of life and death.
- Das geht mir auf den Magen (/auf die Nerven).
  That upsets my stomach (/gets on my nerves).

gehen mit + D ⟨**mit jdm g.**⟩   (*inf*) to go steady with (sb); to date (sb)

- Sie geht mit meinem Bruder.
  She goes steady with my brother.
- Bevor sie heirateten, waren sie lange miteinander gegangen.
  Before they were married, they had dated each other a long time.

gehen nach + D ⟨**nach jdm g.**⟩   to go by (sth), to be up to (sb)

- Es kann nicht immer alles nach dir gehen.
  You can't expect to have your own way all the time.
- Wenn es nach mir ginge, ...
  If it was or *were up to me. . . .*

gehen über + A ⟨**über etw g.**⟩   to go beyond (sth)

- Das geht über meine Vollmacht (/Kräfte/seinen Horizont).
  That's beyond my authority (/power/his horizons).
- Seine Frau (/Sein Garten) geht ihm über alles.
  His wife (/garden) means more to him than anything else.

■ Nichts geht über frische Luft (/die Heimat).
Nothing beats (or There's nothing better than) fresh air. (/There is no place like home).

gehen um + A ⟨**um jdn/etw g.**⟩   to have concern for (sb/sth); to be about (sb/sth)

■ Es geht um seinen Antrag (/Entschluß).
It's about (or It concerns) his petition (/decision).

■ Worum geht es in diesem Film (/bei eurem Streit)?
What is this film (/your argument) about?

■ Es geht um meine Ehre (/Integrität).
My honor (/integrity) is at stake.

■ Es geht dem Mann nur um eins.
The man's only interested in one thing.

■ Es geht um 7 Millionen DM bei diesem Geschäft.
The deal involves DM 7 million (7 million is at stake in the deal).

■ Wenn es ums Lügen geht, ist er unübertrefflich.
When it comes to lying he is unbeatable.

gehen vor + D ⟨**vor sich g.**⟩   (sth) is going on

■ Was geht hier vor sich?
What's going on here?

■ Ich weiß nicht, wie das vor sich geht.
I don't know the procedure.

gehören (+ prep)   to belong

■ Die Flasche gehört in den Kühlschrank (/in die Schublade).
The bottle belongs (or goes) in the refrigerator (/drawer).

■ Ihre Bemerkung gehört nicht zu dieser Diskussion (/zur Sache).
Your comment is irrelevant to this discussion (/the matter).

■ Das Spielzeug gehört nicht in die Küche, Christoph!
The toy doesn't belong in the kitchen, Christoph!

gehören zu + D ⟨**zu jdm/etw g.**⟩   to be amongst (sb/sth); to be one of (sb/sth)

■ Der Austauschschüler gehört schon ganz zu unserer Familie.
The exchange student has already become one of our family.

■ Alle diese Menschen gehören zu seinen Anhängern.
All of these people are his followers.

■ Welche Pflichten gehören zu deiner Arbeit?
What duties are part of your work?

■ Zu diesem Rock gehören braune Strümpfe (/Teppich gehören helle Möbel).
Brown stockings go with this skirt (/Light-colored furniture goes with the rug).

■ Zum Hamburger gehört einfach Ketchup.
Ketchup is a must with hamburger.

■ Er hat zu den besten Psychologen seiner Zeit gehört.
He was among the best psychologists of his time.

gehören zu + D ⟨**zu etw g.**⟩   to be called for by (sth); (sth) takes (sth) (to be carried out/done)

■ Zu dieser Bastelarbeit hat viel Mühe (/Sorgfalt/Geduld) gehört.
Much effort (/care/patience) has gone into this handcraft.

■ Es gehört viel Mut dazu, diese Aufgabe zu übernehmen.
It takes a lot of courage to take on this task.

■ Es gehört große Dummheit dazu, über den Abgrund zu springen.
It takes a lot of stupidity to jump over the ravine.

■ Dazu gehört nicht viel (/einiges *or* etwas), von einem anderen Schüler abzuschreiben.
It doesn't take much (/It takes some doing) to cheat from another student.

gehören (without prep)   to belong

■ Das Auto gehörte meinem Bruder (/mir/der Bank).
My brother (/I/The bank) owned the car.

■ Ich wünschte, du gehörtest mir (/deine Liebe gehörte mir)!
I wish you belonged to me (/I had all your love)!

geizen mit + D ⟨**mit etw g.**⟩   to be stingy with (sth)

■ Er hat sehr mit dem Geld (/seinem Gehalt) gegeizt.
He was very stingy with the money (/his salary).

■ Ich geize mit jeder Minute (/der Zeit).
I am stingy with every minute (/with time).

■ Der Autor geizt nicht mit Worten (/mit der Beschreibung von Einzelheiten).
The author is not sparing with words (/the description of details).

- In ihrem letzten Film geizte sie nicht mit ihren Reizen.
  She didn't mind displaying her charms in her last film.

geizen nach + D ⟨nach etw g.⟩   to crave (for) (sth)

- Der Politiker geizt nach Ruhm (/Macht/Anerkennung) *(liter).*
  The politician craves fame (/power/recognition).

geizig sein mit + D ⟨mit etw g. sein⟩   to be stingy with (sth)

- Er ist mit dem Geld (/seinem Gehalt) geizig.
  He is stingy with the money (/his salary).

gelangen (+ prep)   to reach; to attain

- Wir sind ans Ziel gelangt.
  We have achieved our goal (or reached our destination).
- Mit diesem Bus gelangt man zum Flughafen.
  This bus takes you to the airport.
- Ist die Post in seine (/in die richtigen *or* falschen) Hände gelangt?
  Did the mail get into his (/fall into the right or wrong) hands?
- Das Gerücht (/Was die Leute über ihn redeten, /Die Nachricht) gelangte zu ihm (/an seine Ohren).
  The gossip (/What people said about him/The news) reached him (/his ears).
- Die Läufer gelangten an ihre Grenzen.
  The runners reached their limits.
- Durch die Diät bin ich an mein Idealgewicht gelangt.
  I attained my ideal weight on the diet.
- Er gelangte an die Macht.
  He came to power.

gelangen zu + D ⟨zu etw g.⟩   to reach *or* attain (sth)

- Er gelangte zur Macht (/zur Reife/zur Vernunft/zu Reichtum).
  He attained power (/maturity/came to his senses/acquired a fortune).
- Seine literarischen Werke (/Die Blumen) gelangten zur Blüte.
  His literary works (/The flowers) blossomed.

- Die Partei gelangte zu der Erkenntnis, daß. . . .
  The party came to the realization that. . . .

- Die Kommission gelangte zu folgender Beurteilung (/zum Abschluß ihrer Arbeit/zur Abstimmung/zu nichts).
  The commission arrived at the following assessment (/concluded its work/put to the vote/completed nothing).

- Die Geschworenen gelangten zu einem anderen Urteil als. . . .
  The jurors reached a different verdict than. . . .

- Der Vorschlag gelangte zur Abstimmung.
  The proposal was voted on.

- Das Stück wird am Broadway zur Aufführung gelangen.
  The play will be performed on Broadway.

- Die Lebensversicherung gelangt zur Auszahlung.
  The life insurance will be paid.

geraten (+ prep)   to get (into (sth) by chance, by accident or unwillingly)

- Unabsichtlich geriet ich in eine Gegend, die ich nicht kannte.
  Unintentionally, I got into an area that I wasn't familiar with.

- Er geriet in eine Falle (/ein Gewitter).
  He fell into a trap (/got caught in a storm).

- Die Katze geriet unter den Zug (/das Fahrzeug).
  The cat fell under (or was run over by) the train (/vehicle).

- Die Stadtregierung gerät unter den Einfluß der Mafia.
  The city government is coming under the influence of the Mafia.

- Der Junge gerät auf Abwege (*or* die schiefe Bahn).
  The boy is straying from the straight and narrow.

- Er geriet in Angst (/Begeisterung/Schwierigkeiten/Zorn/die Klemme/Wut/Not/Vergessenheit/Gefangenschaft).
  He got scared (/enthusiastic/into difficulties/mad/into a jam/fell into a rage/became needy/fell into oblivion/was taken prisoner).

- Ich bin heute in einen Stau geraten und mußte dreißig Minuten warten.
  I ran into a traffic jam today and had to wait thirty minutes.

- Der Kontrolleur war mit dem Fuß in ein Fließband geraten.
  The inspector had gotten his foot caught in a conveyor belt.

geraten nach + D ⟨nach jdm/etw g.⟩   to take after (sb)

- Die Tochter gerät ganz nach ihrer Mutter.
  The daughter really takes after her mother.

geraten (without prep)   to turn out

- Der Junge (/Das Rezept/Die Speise) ist gut geraten.
  The boy (/recipe/food) turned out well.

- Mein Aufsatz ist mir ausgezeichnet (/zu kurz) geraten.
  My essay turned out excellently (/too short).

- Mir gerät alles. Mir gerät alles, was ich tue.
  Everything I do turns out well. I succeed in everything I do.

- Sein neues Haus (/Die Speise) ist ihm nach Wunsch geraten.
  His new house (/The food) turned out exactly as he wished.

geschehen mit + D ⟨mit jdm/etw g.⟩   to be done with (sb/sth)

- Was ist mit dem Massenmörder (/damit) geschehen?
  What was done with the mass murderer (/it)?

- Ich verstehe nicht, warum du alles mit dir geschehen läßt.
  I don't understand why you let everything happen to you (you didn't object or defend youself).

- Was soll mit diesem unhöflichen Jungen (/diesem übriggebliebenen Essen) geschehen?
  What is to be done with this impolite boy (/this left-over food)?

geschehen um + A ⟨es ist um jdn/etw g.⟩   to be lost; to come to an end

- Als ich Sonia sah, war es um mich geschehen.
  I was lost the moment I set eyes on Sonia.

- Als Alexander die Beatles zum ersten Mal hörte, war es um ihn geschehen.
  When Alexander heard the Beatles for the first time, he went out of his mind.

gewinnen (+ prep)   to win; to gain; to obtain

- Sein Pferd hat gegen meines (/das andere) gewonnen.
  His horse won over mine (/the other one).

- Ich muß von diesem Fehlschlag Abstand gewinnen.
  I must get over this failure.

- Endlich hast du den Mut gewonnen zu tauchen!
  You finally gained enough courage to dive!

- Was ist damit gewonnen, wenn du so viel darüber weinst?
  What is the good of crying so much over it?

- Aus Öl kann man Benzin und Diesel gewinnen.
  One can obtain gasoline and diesel fuel from oil.

- Sie konnte viele Wähler für sich (/ihre Partei/ihr Programm) gewinnen.
  She could win a lot of voters for herself (/her party/her program).

gewinnen an (+ **noun without article**) ⟨**an etw g.**⟩   to gain (sth)

- Er gewann an Bedeutung (/Autorität/Ansehen/Gunst/Sicherheit).
  He gained importance (/authority/a reputation/favor/self-confidence).
- Der Vorschlag gewann an Popularität (/Wichtigkeit).
  The proposal gained popularity (/importance).
- Durch seine Reisen hat er viel Interesse an fremden Kulturen gewonnen.
  Through his travels he became very interested in foreign cultures.

gewöhnen an + **A** ⟨**jdn an jdn/etw g.**⟩   to accustom (sb) to (sth)

- Sie mußten ihr Kind an das frühe Aufstehen (/feste Nahrung/den neuen Babysitter) gewöhnen.
  They had to accustom their child to getting up early (/solid food/ the new babysitter).
- Der Lehrer gewöhnte die Schüler langsam an die neue Methode.
  The teacher slowly accustomed his students to the new method.
- Der Aufenthalt in Chile gewöhnte uns an heißes Klima.
  Our stay in Chile inured us to a hot climate.

s. gewöhnen an + **A** ⟨**sich an jdn/etw g.**⟩   to get used to (sb/sth); to adjust to (sb/sth)

- Ich kann mich nicht an diese Hitze (/dieses kalte Wetter) gewöhnen.
  I cannot get used to this heat (/cold weather).
- Meine Augen haben sich noch nicht an die Dunkelheit gewöhnt.
  My eyes haven't gotten used to (or adjusted to) the darkness yet.
- Wir haben uns an all den Komfort gewöhnt.
  We got used to all the comfort.
- Ich werde mich schnell an meinen neuen Lehrer (/dieses neue Haus/die Idee) gewöhnen.
  I'll quickly get used to my new teacher (/this new house/the idea).
- Das Haustier gewöhnt sich langsam an das Kind.
  The pet is slowly getting used to the child.
- Du mußt dich an Ordnung (/dieses Durcheinander/dieses Essen/dieses Wasser) gewöhnen.
  You must get used to being orderly (/to this mess/to this food/to this water).
- Ich habe mich daran gewöhnt, nur fünf Stunden zu schlafen.
  I got used to sleeping only five hours.

gewöhnt sein an + A ⟨an jdn/etw g. sein⟩   to be used to (sth)

- Ich bin jetzt an meine Arbeit (/an dieses Klima) gewöhnt.
  I am now used to this work (/this climate).

- An den neuen Lehrer (/diesen rauhen Ton) sind die Schüler noch nicht gewöhnt.
  The students are not yet used to the new teacher (/this rough tone).

glauben an + A ⟨an jdn/sich/etw g.⟩   to believe in (sb/o.s./sth); to swear to (sth)/sb

- Glauben Sie an Gott (/an Christus/an ihn/an die Bibel)?
  Do you believe in God (/Christ/him/the Bible)?

- Jeder glaubt an jemanden (/den Weihnachtsmann).
  Everyone believes in someone (/Santa Claus).

- Glaubst du an Wunder (/Gespenster)?
  Do you believe in miracles (/ghosts)?

- Wie kann ich an mich selbst glauben, wenn alle Leute mich kritisieren?
  How can I believe in myself if everybody keeps criticizing (or finding fault with) me?

- Sie glaubt an ihren Traum. An was glaubst du?
  She believes in her dream. What do you believe in?

glauben + D (jdm)/A (etw) (without prep)   to believe

- Ich habe davon kein Wort geglaubt.
  I didn't believe a word of it.

- Der Lehrer glaubte dem frechen Schüler nicht.
  The teacher didn't believe the smart-alecky student.

- Ich habe ihm jedes Wort geglaubt.
  I believed every word he said.

- Die skeptische Reporterin glaubte die Nachricht (/Geschichte) nicht.
  The skeptical reporter didn't believe the news (/story).

- Meine Mutter hat mich in Bremen (/im Kino/zu Hause) geglaubt.
  My mother thought I was in Bremen (/at the movies/at home).

graben in + A ⟨etw in etw g.⟩   to sink *or* bury (sth) into (sth)

- Sie graben wieder Löcher in die Straße.
  They are digging holes into the street again.

- Das Kind grub seine Zähne in den Apfel (/die Birne).
  The child sank her teeth into the apple (/pear).

s. graben in + A ⟨sich in etw g.⟩   to sink into (sth)

- Der Bohrer gräbt sich immer tiefer in die Erde. Da muß doch Öl sein.
  The drill is boring deeper and deeper into the ground; there must be oil there.
- Der Tod ihres Sohnes hat sich ihr tief ins Gedächtnis gegraben.
  The death of her son imprinted itself firmly in her memory.
- Die Krallen des Bären (/der Katze) gruben sich in seinen Rücken.
  The bear's (/cat's) claws sank into his back.

graben nach + D ⟨nach etw g.⟩   to dig for (sth)

- Sie graben nach Silber (/Uran/Gold/Wasser/Öl).
  They are digging for silver (/uranium/gold/water/oil).

gratulieren zu + D ⟨jdm zu etw g.⟩   to congratulate (sb) on (sth)

- Ich gratuliere dir zu deiner Zuverläßigkeit (/deinem Mut/deinem neuen Auto).
  I congratulate you on your reliability (/your courage/new car).
- Ich gratulierte ihm zum Geburtstag (/zur Heirat/zur bestandenen Abschluß-
  prüfung).
  I congratulated him on his birthday (/his marriage/passing the final exam).
- Wozu gratulierst du dem Mann?
  What are you congratulating the man on?

greifen (+ prep)   to take hold of, to grasp; to seize, to grab

- Ich griff in die Aktentasche und nahm ein Heft heraus.
  I reached into the briefcase and took out a notebook.
- Diese Schneeketten greifen gut in den Schnee. Sogar auf glatter Straße greift
  dieser Reifen gut.
  *These snow chains grasp well on the snow. This tire grips well even on a slippery
  road.*
- Die Musikerin hat in die Saiten (/Tasten) des Instruments gegriffen.
  The musician swept her hand over the strings (/keys) of the instrument.
- Als ich meinen Fehler bemerkte, griff ich mir an den Kopf (/an die Stirn).
  When I realized my mistake, I shook my head in disbelief.
- Er hat nach der Butter (/der Flasche/dem Buch/dem Hut) gegriffen.
  He reached for the butter (/bottle/book/his hat).
- Das Baby greift nach dem Schnuller (/dem Spielzeug/meinem Finger).
  The baby is reaching for the pacifier (/toy/my finger).
- Als das Licht ausging, griff sie suchend nach der Taschenlampe.
  When the light went out, she groped for the flashlight.

- Die Katze griff die Maus am Kopf (/am Schwanz).
  The cat grabbed the mouse by its head (/tail).
- Er griff die Sache (/das Messer/den Bleistift) mit der Hand.
  He grabbed the thing (/knife/pencil) with his hand.

greifen um + A ⟨**um sich g.**⟩   to expand; to spread

- Die Grippe (/Das Feuer) griff rasch um sich.
  The flu (/fire) spread quickly.
- Die Aids-Krankheit (/Der Geruch/Das Gerücht) greift schnell um sich.
  The AIDS virus (/The smell/The rumor) is spreading rapidly.

greifen zu + D ⟨**zu etw g.**⟩   to reach for (sth); to turn *or* resort to (sth)

- Der Gangster griff zu seiner Pistole.
  The gangster reached for his gun.
- Er griff zur Flasche (/zur Zigarette/zum Kokain).
  He took (or turned) to the bottle (/took up smoking or took a cigarette/to cocaine).
- Mein Vater mußte ein paar Mal zum Stock greifen, um mich zu disziplinieren.
  My father had to resort to the stick a few times to discipline me.
- Sie waren so hoch verschuldet, daß sie zur letzten Möglichkeit greifen mußten: dem Verkauf ihres Hauses.
  They were so far in debt that they had to consider the last resort of selling their house.

grinsen (+ prep)   to grin; to smirk

- Die Schüler haben heimlich über den Lehrer gegrinst.
  The students smirked secretly at the teacher.
- Ich wußte, daß das Kind schuldig war, weil es übers ganze Gesicht grinste.
  I knew the child was guilty because he had a smirk on his face.
- Worüber grinsten die Jungen? —Sie haben über ihn (/über seinen komischen Hut) gegrinst.
  What were the students grinning about? —They were grinning at him (/about his funny hat).

grenzen an + A ⟨**an etw. g.**⟩   to border on (sth), to verge on (sth)

- Das Land grenzt im Norden an Frankreich (/die Schweiz/den Irak).
  In the north the country borders on France (/Switzerland/Iraq).

- Sein Haus hat an unser Grundstück gegrenzt.
  His house bordered on our land.
- Seine Tat grenzte an Unverschämtheit (/Geistesgestörheit/Dummheit).
  His deed bordered on impudence (/suggested mental illness/stupidity).

s. grüßen mit + D ⟨**sich mit jdm g.**⟩   to say hello to (sb); to greet (sb)

- Ich grüße mich nicht mehr mit ihm. Wir grüßen einander nicht mehr.
  I don't say hello to him any more. We don't greet each other anymore.

grüßen (without prep)   to greet

- Warum grüßt er dich nicht?
  Why doesn't he say hello to you?
- Grüßen Sie Ihre Familie von mir! (*or* Grüßen Sie mir Ihre Familie!)
  Give my regards to your family.

gucken (+ prep)   to look; to peep

- Guck doch mal auf den Stadtplan (/durch das Fernglas)!
  Why don't you have a look at the (street) map of the town (/through the binoculars).
- Der Spieler hat ihm in die Karten geguckt.
  The gambler sneaked a look at his cards.
- Er guckte vom Balkon (/aus dem Zimmer/aus dem Turm).
  He took a peek from the balcony (/room/tower).

H

haften (+ prep)   to stick; to cling

- Dieses Lied (/Ihr schönes Gesicht) haftet in meinem Gedächtnis.
  This song (/Her beautiful face) sticks in my memory.
- Die Lehrerin klagte, daß bei ihren Schülern nichts haftet.
  The teacher complained that nothing sinks in with her students.

haften an + D ⟨an etw h.⟩   to stick to; to cling to (sth)

- Das Papier haftet an dem Brett mit einer Reißzwecke.
  The paper is sticking to the board with a thumbtack.
- Der Klebstoff haftete an der Hand des Kindes.
  The glue stuck to the child's hand.
- Dem Wanderer haftet nasse Erde an den Stiefeln.
  The damp earth stuck to the hiker's boots.
- Der Zigarettengeruch hat an allen seinen Sachen gehaftet.
  The smell of cigarettes clung to all of his things.
- Er war ein vortrefflicher Redner. Alle hafteten an seinen Lippen.
  He was an excellent orator. Everyone's attention was fixed on him.

haften für + A ⟨für jdn/etw h.⟩   to be (legally) responsible for (sb); to be (legally) liable for (sth); to be responsible to (sb) for (sb/sth)

- Er haftet für ihre Schulden (/sein Kind).
  He's responsible for her debt (/his child).
- Ich hafte persönlich dem Nachbarn für den Schaden.
  I am personally responsible (or *I personally accept liability) to my neighbor for the damages.*
- Der Hausmeister haftet dafür, daß um 10.00 Uhr die Türen der Schule zugeschlossen werden.
  The janitor is responsible for locking the doors of the school at 10 o'clock.
- Auf dem Schild steht: „Eltern haften für ihre Kinder."
  The sign says (or indicates): "Parents are responsible for their children."

halten (+ prep)   to hold

- Er hält den Gegenstand in der Hand (/unterm Arm).
  He is holding the object in his hand (/under his arm).

■ Sie hat das Kind im Arm (*or* auf dem Arm/ins Wasser/bei *or* an der Hand) gehalten.
She held the child in her arms (or put the child in the water/by the hand).

■ Mein Bruder hält immer die Zeitung vor das Gesicht.
My brother always holds the newspaper in front of his face.

■ Halt doch nicht immer deinen Kopf vor den Fernseher.
Don't always stick your head in front of the TV.

■ Halt das Dia gegen das Licht, so daß....
Hold the slide up to the light, so that....

■ Connie hielt den Arm (/die Sache/das Baby) in die Höhe.
Connie held her arm (/the thing/the baby) up.

halten (+ prep)   to stop

■ Dieser Zug hält auf dem nächsten Bahnhof.
This train stops at the next station.

■ Ich hielt vor dem Haus (/Bahnhof).
I stopped in front of the house (/train station).

s. halten an + A ⟨sich an jdn h.⟩   to ask (sb); to turn to (sb)

■ Mit dieser Frage mußt du dich an den Lehrer halten.
For this question you ought to ask the teacher.

■ Er hielt sich an den Pressesprecher, um die Informationen zu bekommen.
He turned to the spokesperson to get the information.

s. halten an + A ⟨sich an etw h.⟩   to stay with *or* stick to (sth)

■ Alkohol schmeckt mir nicht. Ich halte mich lieber an Cola.
I don't particularly like alcoholic beverages. I'd rather stick to Coke.

■ Ich habe mich immer an bewährte Verfahren (/die alte Methode/meinen alten Mechaniker) gehalten.
I have always stuck to (or stayed with) established procedures (/the traditional method/my old mechanic).

■ Du mußt dich an die Vorschriften (/den Vertrag/die Regeln/dein Versprechen) halten.
You must stick to the regulations (/the contract/rules/keep your promise).

■ Halten Sie sich bitte an die Tatsachen (/die Verfahren/die Redezeitbegrenzung/ans Thema).
Keep (or stick to) the facts (/procedures/time limit/subject), please.

halten auf + A ⟨auf sich/jdn/etw (etw) h.⟩   to attach (a lot of importance) to (sb/sth); to take pride in (sb/sth)

- Volker hält auf frische Luft.
  Fresh air is important to Volker.
- Sie hält gar nicht viel (/einiges) auf sich.
  She doesn't take much (/She takes some) pride in herself.
- Er hält sehr auf sein Aussehen (/seine Mitarbeiter/seine Arbeit/seine Familie/seine Kleidung).
  He attaches a lot of importance to his appearance (/employees/work/family/ clothes).
- Diese Leute hielten viel auf ihre Religion (/Traditionen/alte Menschen/Vorfahren/ Rasse).
  These people attached a lot of importance to their religion (/traditions/old people/their ancestors/their race).
- Wenn man etwas auf sich hält, wird man Mitglied in einem „country club."
  If you think you're somebody, you become a member of a country club.

halten auf/nach + A/D ⟨auf/nach etw h.⟩   to aim at (sth); to head for (sth)

- Die Segler halten auf New York.
  The sailors are heading for New York.
- Das Schiff hielt nach Norden (/or nordwärts).
  The ship headed north.
- Halt das Auto nach links!
  Keep the car to the left.

halten für + A ⟨jdn/sich/etw für etw h.⟩   to take (sb/sth) for (sth), to consider (sb) to be (sth)

- Die meisten Leute halten es für unverantwortlich (/angebracht/ratsam/falsch).
  Most people consider it irresponsible (/appropriate/advisable/false).
- Ich halte ihn für einen Dummkopf (/meinen Feind/klug).
  I consider him to be stupid (/my enemy/smart).
- Sie hat mich (irrtümlich) für ihren alten Lehrer gehalten.
  She (mis)took me for her old teacher.
- Für wen (/Wofür) hältst du mich? Hältst du mich nicht für deinen Freund (/ehrlich)?
  Who (/What) do you take me for? Don't you consider me to be your friend (/honest)?
- Ich möchte nicht für rücksichtslos (/wahnsinnig/einen Feigling) gehalten werden.
  I wouldn't like to be considered inconsiderate (/crazy/ridiculous/a coward).

halten mit + D ⟨es mit jdm/etw h.⟩   to prefer (sb/sth); to agree with (sb/sth)

- Meine Töchter halten es mit der Bequemlichkeit (/Sauberkeit).
  My daughters like things to be comfortable (/clean).

- Dieser Anwalt hält es immer mit den Armen (/Obdachlosen).
  This lawyer always sides with the poor (/homeless).

halten von + D ⟨etw von jdm/sich/etw h.⟩   to have an opinion of (sb/sth)

- Was hältst du von seiner Frau (/dem Programm/vom Beten/vom Sparen)?
  What do you think of his wife (/the program/praying/saving)?

- Ich halte nichts davon, mit Peter zu sprechen.
  I don't think much of talking to Peter.

- Ich hielt nichts von seinen tollen Plänen (/jenem Lehrer).
  I didn't think much of his grandiose plans (/that teacher).

halten zu + D ⟨zu jdm h.⟩   to stand *or* stick by (sb); to support (sb)

- Die Arbeiter hielten zu ihren Führern (/dem Vorsitzenden).
  The workers supported their leaders (/the chairman).

- Obwohl der Torhüter mehrere mittelmäßige Spiele geliefert hatte, hielt der Trainer zu ihm.
  In spite of several mediocre games, the coach stuck by his goalie.

handeln gegen + A ⟨gegen etw h.⟩   to act against (sth); to act not in accordance with

- Er handelte gegen das Gesetz (/die Vorschriften/seine Überzeugungen /jede Vernunft).
  He acted against the law (/the regulations/his convictions/all reason).

handeln mit + D ⟨mit jdm/etw h.⟩   to trade in (sth); to trade with (sb)

- Er handelt mit Antiquitäten (/Lebensmitteln/Computern).
  He trades in antiques (/groceries/computers).

- Die Polizei weiß, daß er mit Drogen handelt.
  The police know that he is a drug dealer.

- Die USA handeln viel mit Übersee (/Deutschland).
  The USA trades a lot with countries overseas (/Germany).

- Sie haben mit den Franzosen (/Waffenhändlern) gehandelt.
  They traded with the French (/arms dealers).

handeln über/um + A ⟨über *or* um etw h.⟩   to negotiate *or* bargain *or* haggle over (sth)

■ In Mexiko soll man über (*or* um) den Preis (/die Waren) handeln.
In Mexico one has to negotiate (or haggle) over the price (/goods).

■ Ich lasse schon mit mir handeln.
(In reference to price) I'm open to persuasion/I'm open to offers.

s. handeln um + A ⟨es handelt sich um jdn/etw⟩   to be about (sb/sth); to be a question *or* matter of (sth); to deal with (sth)

■ Es handelte sich bei der Konferenz um eine wichtige Angelegenheit.
The conference was an important event.

■ Darum handelt es sich ja! Darum handelt es sich nicht.
That's just the point! That's not the point.

■ Worum (/Um wen) handelt es sich?
What is it (all) about (/About whom is it)?

■ Es handelt sich darum, daß ich mehr Geld haben möchte.
It is about (or concerns) the fact that I would like to have more money.

■ Das Geschäft, um das es sich handelt, liegt in einem Vorort.
The store in question is located in a suburb.

■ Wo es sich um sein Geld handelt, ist er sehr empfindlich.
Where his money is concerned, he is very sensitive.

handeln von/über + D/A ⟨von *or* über etw h.⟩   to deal with (sth), to be about (sth)

■ Der Film handelt vom (*or* über den) Untergang der Titanik.
The film is about the sinking of the Titanic.

■ Sein Vortrag heute handelte von sozialen Problemen (*or* über soziale Probleme).
His lecture today dealt with social problems.

■ Wovon (/*or* Worüber) handelt dieses Buch? Handelt es von Politikern (*or* über Politiker) (/Liebe/George Bush)?
What is this book about? Is it about politicians (/love/George Bush)?

(1) hängen (+ prep)   to hang, to be hanging (intransitive verb: *pret* **hing,** *ptp* **gehangen**)

■ Das Poster hängt an der Wand (/am Nagel/über dem Sofa/an einem Haken).
The poster is hanging on the wall (/on the nail/above the sofa/on a hook).

■ Die Kleider hingen auf der Wäscheleine zum Trocknen (/im Schrank).
The clothes were hanging on the clothesline to dry (/in the closet).

- Die Nachbarn (/Fahnen) haben aus den Fenstern gehangen.
  The neighbors (/flags) were hanging out of the windows.

- Das Kind hängt ihr am Hemd (/am Hals/an der Schürze).
  The child is hanging onto her shirt (/around her neck/her apron).

- Der Blumentopf hängt an der Decke.
  The flower pot is suspended from the ceiling.

- In der Klasse hing der Junge lustlos auf seinem Stuhl.
  The boy slouched listlessly in his chair in the class.

- Sie hat dauernd vorm Fernseher (/am Telefon/am Radio) gehangen.
  She spent hours in front of the television (/on the telephone/listening to the radio).

- Die Kleider hingen mir nur so am Leibe, nachdem ich 20 Pfund abgenommen hatte.
  My clothes hung on me after I had lost 20 pounds.

- Jens, häng nicht wie eine Klette an mich!
  Jens, don't hang on me like a nuisance!

- Seine Blicke (/Augen) hingen an dem Essen.
  His gaze was (/eyes were) fixed on the food.

- Der Smog hing in (/über) der Stadt.
  The smog hung over the city.

- Der Rauch des Bratens hing noch in der Luft (/meinem Kleid).
  The smell of the roast still hung in the air (/clung to my clothes).

- Die Leiter hing nach einer Seite.
  The ladder was leaning to one side.

hängen an + D ⟨**an jdm/etw h.**⟩   to depend on (sb/sth); to be connected (up) to (sth)

- Die ganze Planung hängt an ihm.
  He's responsible for all the planning.

- Ihr Mann hängt an der künstlichen Niere (/am Tropf).
  Her husband is dependent on the kidney machine (/connected (up) to the I.V.).

- Woran hängt es denn? —Alles hängt daran, ob wir das Auto kriegen.
  What's the matter (or problem)? —Everything depends on whether we can get the car.

- An dem Projekt hängt viel Arbeit.
  There's a lot of work involved in that project.

hängen an + D ⟨**an jdm/etw h.**⟩   to be fond of (sb/sth); to cling on (to)

- Sie hängt am Geld (/an den Antiquitäten/sehr an ihrem Auto).
  She loves money or *She doesn't like parting with her money (/She collects antiques/She is very fond of her car).*

■ Sie hängt sehr an ihren Kindern (/am Leben).
She dotes on (or is fond of) her children (/loves life).

■ Nach so vielen Jahren hängt er noch an seiner Heimatstadt (/seinem alten Sessel).
After so many years he still is fond of (or tied emotionally to) his hometown (/his old chair).

(2) hängen (+ prep)   to hang (transitive verb: *pret* **hängte,** *ptp* **gehängt**)

■ Er hängt das Poster an die Wand (/an den Nagel/über das Sofa).
He's hanging the poster on the wall (/on the nail/above the sofa).

■ Die Mutter hängte die Kleider auf die Wäscheleine (zum Trocknen).
The mother hung the clothes on the clothesline (to dry).

sich hängen (+ prep)   to hang

■ Häng dich nicht so über das Gitter (/aus dem Fenster).
Don't hang over the railing (/out of the window) like that.

■ Ich hängte mich sofort ans Telefon (*or* an die Strippe), um den Arzt anzurufen.
I got right on the phone to call the doctor.

sich hängen an + A ⟨sich an jdn/etw h.⟩   to cling *or* stick to (sb/sth); to set off in pursuit of (sb) *or* a vehicle

■ Das Kind hängte sich dem Vater an den Hals (/Arm/Gürtel).
The child hung on to (or clung to) his father's neck (/arm/belt).

■ Der Polizist hat sich an den Gauner (/das Auto) gehängt. (*inf*)
The policeman pursued the crook (/the car).

hapern an + D ⟨es hapert an etw⟩   there is a shortage *or* lack of (sth)

■ Es hapert am Geld (/guten Willen/Einsatz).
There is a shortage of money (/good will/lack of commitment).

hapern mit/in + D ⟨es hapert mit etw/jdm/in etw⟩   to be short of (sth); to be badly off for/with (sth)

■ Mit (*or* An) Vokabeln hapert es bei ihr (*or* Bei ihr hapert es mit *or* an Vokabeln).
She's weak in (or poor at) vocabulary.

■ Es hapert (in Tansania) mit den Vorräten (/Spezialisten/Ärzten).
There is a shortage of supplies (/specialists/doctors) (in Tanzania).

- Im Rechnen (/Spanischen) haperte es bei him.
  He was weak in arithmetic (/Spanish).

harmonieren mit + D ⟨mit jdm/etw h.⟩   to harmonize; to go together; to match

- Das Hemd harmoniert (gut/schlecht) mit der Hose.
  The shirt matches the pants (well/badly).
- Die Klänge (/Instrumente/Farben) harmonieren gut miteinader.
  The sounds (/instruments/colors) go well together.
- Die Geschwister (/Freunde/Kinder) harmonieren gut miteinander.
  The siblings (/friends/children) get along well with one another.

haushalten mit + D ⟨mit etw h.⟩   to be economical with (sth); to use (sth) economically; to conserve (sth)

- Du mußt mit deinem Geld (/deiner Zeit/den Lebensmitteln/der Elektrizität) besser haushalten.
  You have to utilize your money (/time/groceries/electricity) more economically.
- Ich halte mit meiner Energie jetzt besser haus.
  I am conserving (or sparing) my energies better now.

heften an + A ⟨etw an etw h.⟩   to fasten (sth) onto (sth); to staple (sth) to (sth); to tack (sth) to (sth) (with clip); to pin (sth) to (sth)

- Er hat das Blatt mit Klebstoff (/Stecknadeln/Reißzwecken) ans Schwarze Brett geheftet.
  He fastened the sheet to the bulletin board with glue (/pins/thumb tacks).
- Ich heftete einen Kalender mit Reißzwecken an die Tür.
  I tacked a calendar on the door.
- Sie haben ihm ein Abzeichen an die Brust (/den Mantel) geheftet.
  They pinned a badge to his chest (/coat).

s. heften an + A ⟨sich an jdm/etw h.⟩   to latch onto (sb); to follow (sth) (sb's trail, etc.)

- Der Detektiv heftete sich an die Spur des Verbrechers.
  The detective followed the criminal's trail.

heften auf + A ⟨etw auf jdn/etw h.⟩   to fix onto (sb/sth)

- Das Baby heftete seine Augen auf das Mobile.
  The baby fixed its eyes on the mobile.

heiraten (+ prep)   to marry (sb); to get married

- Arnold Schwarzenegger heiratete in eine reiche (/alte) Familie.
  Arnold Schwarzenegger married into a rich (/old) family.
- Ich habe nach London (/nach Kanada/aufs Land/in die Stadt) geheiratet.
  I got married and settled in London (/in Canada/in the country/in the city).
- Sie hat in London (/in Amerika/auf dem Land/in der Stadt/in einer Kirche) geheiratet.
  She got married in London (/America/in the country/in the city/in a church).
- Sie hat ihn aus Vernunft (/aus Liebe/wegen des Geldes) geheiratet.
  She married him because it seemed the reasonable thing to do (/for love/for money).

helfen (+ prep)   to help

- Er half mir in den Mantel (/aus dem Mantel/in den Wagen/aufs Pferd).
  He helped me into my coat (/out of my coat/to get into the car/to get on the horse).
- Die Tabletten helfen gegen (*or* bei) Kopfschmerzen (/Beschwerden).
  The tablets are good for (or help to relieve) headaches (/pains).
- Seine Frau hilft ihm mit Rat (/im Haushalt/auf dem Feld/in der Not).
  His wife helps him with advice (/in the house/in the field/in emergencies).

helfen bei + D ⟨jdm bei etw h.⟩   to help (sb) with (sth)

- Sie hat ihm bei den Schulaufgaben (/bei der Arbeit/beim Tragen der Koffer/beim Aussteigen) geholfen.
  She helped him with his school work (/the work/to carry the suitcases/to get out).

herabblicken auf + A ⟨auf jdn/etw h.⟩   to look down on (sb/sth) (from a higher position)

- Er blickte von dem Berg auf die Stadt herab.
  He looked down from the mountain on the city.
- Der Eingebildete blickte auf alle seine Kollegen herab.
  The conceited man looked down on all his co-workers.
- Sie hat auf ihn herabgeblickt, weil er nicht gebildet war.
  She looked down on him because he wasn't well-educated.

s. herablassen zu + D ⟨sich zu etw h.⟩   to deign *or* condescend to do (sth)

- Wirst du dich endlich zur Beantwortung meiner Frage (/zum Geschirrspülen) herablassen? *(ironisch)*
  Will you condescend (or deign) to answer my question (/to do the dishes)? (ironic)

- Sie ließ sich nur selten zum Umgang mit sogenannten einfachen Menschen (/zu Interviews) herab.
  Only rarely did she condescend to associate with so-called simple people (/inter-views).

herabsetzen (+ prep)   to reduce; to lower; to disparage

- Der Laden hat Schuhe im Preis herabgesetzt.
  The shop marked down the the price of shoes.
- Der Politiker setzte die Leistungen seines Gegners bei den Wählern (/in den Augen der Wähler) herab.
  The politician belittled the achievements of his opponent in the voters' view (/in the eyes of the voters).
- Immer wieder setzen Menschen die Mitglieder von Minderheiten herab.
  Again and again people disparage members of minorities.

herankommen an + A ⟨an jdn/etw h.⟩   to come *or* draw near to; to approach (sth)

- Es ist schwer, an Drogen (/an diesen Motor/an den Kram auf dem Boden/ans Spielzeug in der Kiste) heranzukommen.
  It is difficult to get hold of drugs (/to get to the engine/to get to the junk in the attic/to get to the toys in the box).
- Das Feld kam dicht an den führenden Läufer (/ihn) heran.
  The pack was close to catching up to the leader (/him).
- Laß die Sache (/das Problem) erst einmal an dich herankommen.
  Cross that bridge when you get to it.
- Es ist nicht leicht, an die Schuldigen heranzukommen.
  It's not easy to get to (or get) those who are guilty.
- An sie (/den Direktor) ist nicht heranzukommen.
  It is impossible to get through to her (/the director) or It is impossible to measure up to her (/the boss).

s. heranmachen an + A ⟨sich an etw h.⟩   to get down to (sth); to get going on (sth)

- Ich habe mich endlich ans Schreiben des Briefes (/an meine Hausaufgabe) herangemacht.
  I finally got down to writing the letter (/doing my homework).

s. heranmachen an + A ⟨sich an jdn h.⟩   to approach (sb); to have a go at (sb)

- Hast du dich endlich an das Mädchen herangemacht?
  Did you finally approach (i.e., make a pass at) the girl?

■ Der Spion machte sich an den Minister heran, um geheime Informationen zu bekommen.
The spy made up to the governmental minister in order to obtain secret information.

heranziehen zu + D ⟨etw zu etw h.⟩   to draw *or* pull nearer to (sth); to consult (sth); to use (sth)

■ Sie zogen das Boot näher zum Ufer heran.
They pulled the boat closer to the shore.

■ Zur Lektüre dieses Buches solltest du ein Wörterbuch heranziehen.
When reading this book you should consult a dictionary.

■ Man kann die Arbeitslosenrate in England zum Vergleich heranziehen.
You can use the unemployment rate in Great Britain as a comparison.

⟨**jdn zu etw heranziehen**⟩   to call upon (sb) to do (sth); to enlist (sb's) services

■ Sie zogen Fachleute zur Beratung heran.
They called upon experts for advice.

■ Während der Flutkatastrophe zog die Regierung Soldaten zur Unterstützung heran.
During the flood the government called in soldiers for support.

herauskommen aus + D ⟨aus etw h.⟩   to come out of (sth)

■ Die Pflanzen (/Blumen) kommen dieses Jahr früh (aus der Erde) heraus.
The plants (/flowers) are coming out (of the ground) early this year.

■ Er ist drei Tage aus den Kleidern (/der Wohnung) nicht herausgekommen.
He hasn't taken his clothes off (/been out of the apartment) for three days.

■ Der Autor kam nie aus seiner Stadt (/seinem Heimatland) heraus.
The author never came out of (or left) his city (/homeland).

■ Er kam aus dem Weinen (/Staunen/den Sorgen) nicht heraus.
He couldn't stop crying (/from being surprised/worrying).

■ Er konnte nicht aus seinen Schwierigkeiten (/Problemen/Schulden) herauskommen.
He couldn't get out of his difficulties (/away from his problems/debt).

⟨**aus sich herauskommen**⟩   to come out of one's shell

■ Das Mädchen kam endlich aus sich heraus.
The girl finally came out of her shell.

herauskommen bei + D ⟨**bei etw h.**⟩ to come of (sth); to emerge from (sth)

- Was kam bei dieser Rechenaufgabe (/Addition) heraus? Kam dabei 60 heraus?
  What was the answer to this (math) problem (/addition)? Was it 60?
- Was ist schließlich bei dieser Angelegenheit (/dummen Sache) herausgekommen? Kam etwas Gutes heraus?
  What finally came of this matter (/dumb thing)? Did anything good come of it?
- Es kommt nichts dabei heraus (*or* Dabei kommt nichts heraus).
  It doesn't lead anywhere (or get us anywhere).

herauskommen mit + D ⟨**mit etw h.**⟩ to come out with (sth); to bring (sth) out

- Dieses Jahr kam Volkswagen mit einem neuen Modell heraus.
  This year Volkswagen brought out a new model.
- Wo warst du gestern abend? Komm mit der Sprache heraus!
  Where were you last night? Come out with it!
- Der kleine Junge kam mit dem Geständnis heraus, daß er die Vase kaputt gemacht hatte.
  The little boy (finally) admitted that he had broken the vase.

hereinfallen auf + A ⟨**auf jdn/etw h.**⟩ to be taken in by (sb/sth); to be taken for a ride (by sb); to fall for (sth)

- Er ist auf den Scherz (/ihre Schmeichelei/jede Lüge) hereingefallen.
  He fell for the joke (/her flattery/every lie).
- Das alte Ehepaar fiel auf einen Betrüger (/ein irreführendes Angebot) herein.
  The old couple was taken for a ride by a con man (/a deceptive offer).
- Darauf (/Auf sie) falle ich nicht herein.
  I am not falling for that (/for her).

hereinfallen mit + D ⟨**mit jdm/etw h.**⟩ to have a bad deal with (sb/sth)

- Mit unserer neuen Waschmaschine (/unserem neuen Auto) sind wir hereingefallen.
  We got a bad deal with our new washing machine (/new car).
- Alles war schön im Urlaub. Nur mit dem Wetter sind wir hereingefallen.
  Everything was fine during our vacation. We only had bad luck with the weather.
- Mit der neuen Sekretärin ist die Firma (/der Boß) hereingefallen.
  The new secretary was a disappointment to the firm (/boss).

s. herleiten von + D ⟨**sich von etw h.**⟩ to come from (sth); to be derived from (sth)

- Das Wort „Sklave" leitet sich vom griechischen „Sklabos" her.
  The word "Sklave" (slave) is derived from the Greek "Sklabos."

- Viele Worte im heutigen Deutsch leiten sich von amerikanischen Einflüssen her.
  Many words in contemporary German are derived from American influences.
- Das Wort leitet sich vom Griechischen her.
  The word comes from Greek.

s. hermachen über + A ⟨sich über jdn/etw h.⟩   to attack *or* lay into (sb/sth)

- Die Gäste machten sich über die Geburtstagstorte her. *(inf)*
  The guests attacked the birthday cake. (inf)
- Die Eindringlinge haben sich über die Einwohner des besetzten Landes hergemacht.
  The invaders attacked (or fell upon) the inhabitants of the occupied country.
- Warum hast du dich über ihn hergemacht? *(inf)*
  Why did you lay into him? (inf)

herrschen über + A ⟨über jdn/etw h.⟩   to rule (over) (sb/sth); to govern (a country)

- Er (/Die Königin) herrscht nur noch nominell über dieses Land (/50 Millionen Menschen).
  He (/The queen) governs this country (/rules over 50 million people) in name only.
- Der Diktator herrschte grausam über seine Untertanen.
  The dictator ruled cruelly over his subjects.

herumdrücken an + D ⟨an etw h.⟩   to squeeze (sth)

- Warum drückst du immer noch an der Plastikflasche herum?
  Why do you keep squeezing the plastic bottle?

s. herumdrücken um + A ⟨sich um etw h.⟩   to dodge (sth)

- Der Teenager hat sich um seine Arbeit (/die schwierige Aufgabe/das Aufräumen seines Zimmers/die Prüfung/den Militärdienst) herumgedrückt.
  The teenager dodged his work (/the difficult task/cleaning his room/the examination/military service).

s. herumdrücken (without prep)   to hang out, idle

- Wo hast du dich gestern abend herumgedrückt? Warst du wieder in der Kneipe?
  Where did you hang out yesterday? Were you in the bar again?

herumkommen um + A ⟨um etw h.⟩   to come around (sth); to get around (sth)

- Er ist um die Ecke (/Kurve/das Stadion) herumgekommen.
  He came around the corner (/curve/stadium).

herumkommen um + A ⟨um etw h.⟩   to get out of *or* avoid (sth)

- Man kommt nicht darum herum (*or* Du kannst nicht darum herumkommen).
  You can't get around that (or *overlook that*).
- Um diese Unkosten (/die Arbeit) können wir nicht herumkommen.
  We can't avoid these expenses (/this work).
- Wir kommen nicht darum herum, seine Schwiegermutter einzuladen.
  We cannot avoid inviting his mother-in-law.
- Hoffentlich werde ich um die Prüfung (/Operation) herumkommen.
  Hopefully, I will get out of taking the test (/having the operation).

herumnörgeln an + D ⟨an jdm/etw h.⟩   to find fault with (sb/sth); to crab about (sb/sth)

- An allem mußt du herumnörgeln!
  You have to find fault with everything!
- Es hat keinen Zweck, am Wetter (/an deinen Lehrern) herumzunörgeln.
  There is no point in crabbing about the weather (/your teachers).

herumreiten auf + D ⟨auf jdm/etw h.⟩   to keep on at (sb/sth); to keep bringing (sth) up

- Der dumme Mann ist immer wieder auf der gleichen Frage (/dem gleichem Thema) herumgeritten.
  The stupid man brought up the same question again and again (/kept bringing up the same topic).
- Ihr müßt nicht immer darauf herumreiten, daß er nicht schwimmen kann.
  You don't have to keep bringing up the fact (or *rub it in) that he can't swim.*

s. herumschlagen mit + D ⟨sich mit jdm/etw h.⟩   *(mainly fig)* to fight *or* scuffle with (sb); to struggle with (sb/sth)

- Die Polizei schlägt sich mit der Drogenkriminalität in Berlin herum.
  The police are struggling with drug-related crimes in Berlin.
- Jeden Tag muß ich mich mit meinen faulen Schülern herumschlagen.
  Every day I have to struggle with my lazy students.

herumspielen an/mit + D ⟨an/mit etw h.⟩   to fiddle around with (sth)

- Peter spielt gerne an der Fernbedienung herum.
  Peter likes fiddling around with the remote control.

- Hör auf, mit dem Fußball in der Wohnung herumzuspielen! Es macht mich ganz verrückt.
  Stop playing around with the soccer ball in the apartment. It's driving me nuts.

herumspielen auf + D ⟨auf etw h.⟩   to play around on (sth)

- Es entspannt ihn, auf dem Klavier (/der Gitarre) herumzuspielen.
  He finds it relaxing to play around on the piano (/guitar).

s. herumtreiben (+ prep)   to hang around *or* about in (bad places/company)

- Hast du dich wieder in Lokalen (/Kneipen) herumgetrieben?
  Did you hang around again in cafes (/bars)?

- Ihr Mann treibt sich den ganzen Tag auf der Straße mit anderen Männern herum.
  Her husband hangs around all day on the streets with other men.

- Er treibt sich immer bei anderen Leuten herum.
  He always hangs around with other people.

- Er treibt sich mal wieder irgendwo in der Welt (/mit seinen Freunden) herum.
  He's off traipsing around again somewhere in the world (/with his friends).

herunterkommen (+ prep)   to come *or* get down

- Komm sofort vom Tisch (/Baum) herunter!
  Get down from the table (/Come down from the tree) immediately!

- Die Gesellschaft wird unter seinem Vorsitz völlig herunterkommen.
  The company will be ruined completely under his chairmanship.

- Die Dame kam die Treppe herunter (und auf mich zu).
  The lady came down the steps (and toward me).

- Nach seinem (/Durch seinen) Herzanfall ist er sehr heruntergekommen.
  He has really become run-down after (/from) his heart attack.

- Die Bank ist durch schlechtes Management (/falsche Entscheidungen) völlig heruntergekommen.
  Through bad management (/wrong decisions), the bank has really gone downhill.

herunterkommen von + D ⟨von etw h.⟩   *(fig)* to get over something; to kick a habit.

- Hoffentlich wirst du von deinen schlechten Noten herunterkommen.
  Hopefully you'll be able to get over your bad grades.

■ Der Schüler muß versuchen, von seiner 5 in Mathe herunterzukommen, wenn er die Versetzung schaffen will.
The boy must try to improve his (poor grade) 5 in math in order not to fail the class.

■ Er ist vom Heroin (/Alkohol) heruntergekommen. *(fig)*
He has kicked (the habit of) (or gotten off) heroin (/alcohol).

heruntersein (+ prep)   to be (run) down *(inf)*

■ Er ist durch seine viele Arbeit (/durch Mangel an Schlaf/wegen seines Studiums/wegen des Abiturs) sehr herunter.
He is very weak (or run-down) due to so much work (/lack of sleep/because of his studies/because of the "Abitur").

■ Ich war völlig mit den Nerven (/mit der Gesundheit) herunter.
I was a nervous wreck (/physically run-down).

■ Sie war nach dem Tod ihres Sohnes psychologisch sehr herunter.
She was psychologically run-down after the death of her son.

hervorgehen aus + D ⟨aus etw h.⟩   to result from (sth); to come out of (sth); to follow from (sth)

■ Aus diesem Brief (/Daraus) geht hervor, daß sie nicht zu uns zu Besuch kommen können.
From this letter (/this) it follows that they cannot come to visit us.

■ Wieviele Kinder gingen aus dieser Ehe hervor?
How many children resulted from this marriage?

■ Ali ist als Sieger (/Verlierer) aus dem Wahlkampf hervorgegangen.
Ali came out of the election campaign as the winner (/loser).

■ Er ist aus sehr streng religiösen Verhältnissen hervorgeganen.
He comes from a very religious background.

herziehen hinter + D ⟨jdn/etw hinter sich h.⟩   to pull *or* drag (sb/sth) (along) behind one

■ Ich habe den Karren hinter mir hergezogen.
I pulled the cart behind me.

■ Der Abschleppwagen zog das Auto (/den Anhänger) hinter sich her.
The tow car pulled the car (/trailer) behind itself.

■ Die Mutter zog das müde Kind (/das schwere Gepäck) hinter sich her.
The mother dragged the tired child (/heavy luggage) along with her.

herziehen über + A ⟨über jdn/etw h.⟩   to put (sb/sth) down; to denigrate (sb/sth)

- Sie war nur neidisch auf deinen Erfolg, deshalb ist sie über dich hergezogen.
  She was only jealous of your success. That's why she denigrated you.

- Alle ziehen über mich her!
  Everybody puts me down!

hetzen auf + A ⟨ein Tier auf jdn/etw h.⟩   to hound; to set an animal on(to) (sb/sth)

- Die Gefängniswärter haben ihre Hunde auf den entwichenen Häftling gehetzt.
  The prison guards set their dogs on(to) the escapee.

hetzen gegen + A ⟨gegen jdn/etw h.⟩   to agitate against *or* stir up hatred against (sb/sth)

- Ich weiß nicht, warum er immer gegen mich (/seine Schwiegermutter) hetzt.
  I don't know why he's always running me (/his mother-in-law) down.

- Der Politiker hetzt (bei den Leuten) gegen Minderheiten (/Ausländer).
  The politician agitates (or stirs up hatred) (among people) against minorities (/foreigners).

hetzen (without prep)   to hurry; to race; to dash

- Ich bin ganz schön gehetzt, um den Bus nicht zu verpassen.
  I rushed like mad not to miss the bus.

- Warum mußt du hetzen? Du hast noch Zeit.
  Why do you have to hurry? You still have time.

- Eleanor ist von der Schule (/vom Arzt) zur Haltestelle gehetzt.
  Eleanor raced from the school (/doctor) to the bus stop.

hinausfliegen aus + D ⟨aus etw h.⟩   to get kicked out; to get the sack

- Nach der dritten Verwarnung flog er aus der Schule hinaus.
  After the third warning he was kicked out of the school.

- Es sind nicht viele Aufträge da. Viele Arbeiter werden wohl hinausfliegen.
  There aren't many orders there. A lot of workers will probably get the sack.

hinauslaufen auf + A ⟨auf etw h.⟩   to amount to (sth)

- Alles läuft auf dasselbe (*or* auf eins *or* aufs gleiche/auf seine Nominierung) hinaus.
  It all comes down to the same thing (/his nomination).

■ Das Ganze wird darauf hinauslaufen, daß wir die Hotelreservierung abbestellen müssen.
The whole thing comes down to the fact that we will have to cancel our hotel reservation.

■ Der Vorschlag läuft darauf hinaus, ein Steuerparadies für die Reichen zu haben.
The proposal amounts to providing a tax haven for the rich.

■ Ich kann nicht vorhersagen, worauf dieser Plan hinauslaufen wird.
I can't predict what this plan will amount to.

hinauswerfen (+ prep)   to throw *or* cast out

■ Der Gastwirt hat ihn (aus der Kneipe) hinausgeworfen.
The innkeeper threw him out (of the bar).

■ Der Schmutzfink warf den Abfall und das Papier (aus dem Wagen) hinaus.
The dirty slob threw the garbage and the paper out (of the car).

■ Der Lehrer hat den frechen Jungen (aus der Klasse) hinausgeworfen.
The teacher kicked the rude boy out (of the classroom).

■ Nach zehn Jahren haben sie ihn ohne Grund aus der Firma (/den Mieter aus der Wohnung) hinausgeworfen.
After ten years they sacked him without (giving) any reason (/threw the tenant out of the apartment).

hindern an + D ⟨jdn an etw h.⟩   to prevent (sb) from (sth)

■ Eva hindert mich am Schreiben (/am Trinken/am Verlassen des Hauses/daran/an meinem Vorhaben).
Eva prevents me from writing (/drinking/leaving the house/it/my plan).

■ Der Bahnstreik hat ihn an seiner Urlaubsreise gehindert.
The railroad strike prevented him from taking his vacation.

■ Eine Krankheit hinderte sie am Einschlafen (/Kommen).
An illness made it impossibe for her to sleep (/come).

hindeuten auf + A ⟨auf jdn/etw h.⟩   to point at *or* to (sb/sth); to suggest *or* indicate to (sb/sth)

■ Es deutet alles darauf hin, daß er an Krebs leidet.
Everything points to the fact that he's suffering from cancer.

■ Der Zeuge deutete auf den Angeklagten (/die Waffe) hin.
The witness pointed to the accused (/the weapon).

■ Die Symptome haben auf ein Herzversagen hingedeutet.
The symptoms pointed to a coronary failure.

s. hineinsteigern in + A ⟨**sich in etw h.**⟩   to work o.s. up into a state

■   Er steigerte sich immer mehr in seine Wut (/seinen Ärger/seine Hysterie) hinein.
   He worked himself up into a rage (/a temper/hysterics).

s. hineinversetzen in + A ⟨**sich in jdn/etw h.**⟩   to put oneself in (sb's) position; to empathize with (sth)

■   Es ist schwer, sich in seine Lage hineinzuversetzen.
   It is difficult to put oneself in his position.

■   Ich kann mich in ihn (/die Hauptperson des Romans) nicht hineinversetzen.
   I can't empathize with him (/the protagonist of the novel).

hinwegkommen über + A ⟨**über etw h.**⟩   to get over (sth)

■   Sie kam nicht darüber hinweg, daß ihr Sohn nach Amerika zog.
   She couldn't get over the fact that her son moved to America.

■   Er ist über den Tod seiner Mutter (/diese Enttäuschung) nicht hinweggekommen.
   He didn't get over the death of his mother (/this disappointment).

hinwegsetzen über + A ⟨**über etw h.**⟩   to jump *or* leap over (sth)

■   Er setzte über den Bach (/den Zaun/das Hindernis) hinweg.
   He jumped over the brook (/fence/obstacle).

s. hinwegsetzen über + A ⟨**sich über etw h.**⟩   to disregard, to dismiss *or* ignore (sth)

■   Ich habe mich über alle Warnungen (/Tatsachen/Auskünfte) hinweggesetzt.
   I disregarded all the warnings (/facts/information).

■   Warum mußt du dich immer über meine Bitten (/diese Anordnungen/meine Vorschläge/die Vorschriften) hinwegsetzen?
   Why do you always have to disregard (or ignore) my requests (/these orders/my suggestions/the regulations)?

hinweisen auf + A ⟨**jdn auf jdn/etw h.**⟩   to point (sth) out to (sb)

■   Ich will Sie darauf hinweisen, daß. . . .
   I want to draw your attention to the fact that. . . .

■   Der Experte wies die Senatoren auf die Gefahren des Ozonloches hin.
   The expert drew the attention of the senators to the dangers of the hole in the ozone layer.

⟨auf jdn/etw hinweisen⟩   to point to (sb/sth)

■   Ich möchte auf die Tatsache (/Gefahr) hinweisen, daß. . . .
I would like to draw your attention to the fact (/danger) that. . . .

■   Er wies mit dem Finger auf den Laden (/die elegant gekleidete Dame)
hin.
He pointed to the store (/the elegantly-dressed lady).

(s.) hocken (+ prep)   to squat; to crouch

■   Warum hockst du dich auf die Treppe (/auf den gleichen Platz)?
Why are you squatting on the steps (/in the same place)?

■   Ich habe mich auf den Boden (/ins Gras/auf den Bürgersteig) gehockt.
I squatted on the floor (/in the grass/on the sidewalk).

■   Er hockt über seinen Büchern.
He is poring over his books.

■   Er hockt immer nur bei anderen Leuten (/in seinem Zimmer/immer zu Hause).
He spends all his time with other people (/in his room/at home).

hoffen auf + A ⟨auf jdn/etw h.⟩   to set one's hopes on (sb); to hope for (sth)

■   Ich hoffte auf ein glückliches Ereignis (/Ende/eine baldige Genesung).
I was hoping for a happy event (/an end/a speedy recovery).

■   Wir hoffen auf den Sieg unserer Mannschaft (/Regen/gutes Wetter).
We are hoping for the victory of our team (/rain/good weather).

■   Sie hoffen auf ihre Kinder (/auf Gott).
They set their hope on their children (/God).

■   Die Bevölkerung hat auf die Besatzungstruppen gehofft.
The population set its hopes on the occupying troops.

■   Er hofft (darauf), daß er gewählt wird.
He hopes that he will be elected.

(s.) holen (+ prep)   to fetch; to get

■   Hol doch die Stühle aus dem Keller!
Fetch the chairs from the basement.

■   Er holt seinen Anzug vom Schneider (/aus seinem Schrank/von der Reinigung).
He will fetch his suit from the tailor (/out of his closet/from the dry cleaner).

■   Die Mutter hat ihn aus dem Bett geholt.
The mother got (or dragged) him out of bed.

■ Könnten Sie bitte Herrn Müller ans Telefon holen?
Could you call Mr. Muller to the phone, please?

■ Ich habe mir (/Meine Mannschaft hat sich) die Meisterschaft im Schwimmen geholt.
I (/My team) won the swimming championship.

hören (+ prep)   to hear

■ Sie hat an der Tür (/am Eingang) gehört *(more common: gehorcht).*
She was listening at the door (/entrance).

■ Man kann dich (/deine Aussage/sein eigenes Wort) vor lauter Lärm nicht hören.
One cannot hear you (/your statement/one's own voice) because of all that noise.

■ Mit diesem Radio höre ich ganz Nordamerika.
I can get all the North American stations with this radio.

■ Ich habe diese Werbung (/diesen Mann/das Hörspiel) schon mal im Radio gehört.
I've heard this advertisement (/man/the play) on the radio before.

■ Auf dem Ohr hört mein Opa nicht (gut).
My grandpa cannot hear (well) with that ear.

hören an + D ⟨etw an etw h.⟩   to hear; to tell

■ Wir konnten am Schritt hören, daß es unser Lehrer war.
We could hear that it was our teacher by his step.

■ An ihrer Stimme konnte man hören, daß sie log (/traurig war).
You could tell from her voice that she was lying (/was sad).

hören auf + A ⟨auf jdn/etw h.⟩   to listen to *or* heed (sb/sth)

■ Das Mädchen hört einfach nicht auf seine Eltern (/meine Bitten).
The girl simply won't listen to her parents (/my entreaties).

■ Ich höre auf Rolfs Rat, aber warum soll ich auf dich hören!
I'll listen to Rolf's advice, but why should I listen to you?

■ Meine Katze hört auf den Namen Kelly.
My cat answers to the name of Kelly.

■ Ich habe ihn zweimal gewarnt, aber trotzdem hörte er nicht auf mich.
I warned him twice, but he still didn't listen to me.

hören von + D ⟨von jdm h.⟩   to hear of/from (sb)

■ Wir haben von ihm (*or* über ihn) viel (/nichts) Gutes gehört.
We have heard a lot of good things (/nothing good) about him.

- Ich habe lange nicht (nichts mehr) von ihm gehört.
  I haven't heard (anything) from him in/for a long time.

- Laß bald von dir hören.—Ich lasse von mir hören.
  Keep in touch.—I'll be in touch.

- Mein alter Mitschüler hat nichts von sich hören lassen.
  I haven't heard from my old schoolmate/No one has heard anything from my old schoolmate.

hören von + D ⟨von etw h.⟩   to hear about *or* of (sth)

- Ich will davon (/von deinem Plan/diesem Angeber) nichts hören.
  I don't want to hear anything about it (/your plan/this braggart).

- Hast du von dem Unfall (/diesem Ereignis/seiner Beförderung) gehört?
  Did you hear about the accident (/this event/his promotion)?

hören (without prep)   to hear

- Sie hören dich nicht. Bitte sprich lauter (/am Mikrophon *or* am Telefon)!
  They can't hear you. Please speak louder (/into the microphone or *on the phone).*

- Sei mal still! Ich will das (/den Sänger/seine Stimme/die Musik) hören.
  Be quiet. I want to hear this or *listen to this (/the singer/his voice/the music).*

- Ich hörte sie gehen (/sprechen/lachen).
  I heard her leave (/speaking/laughing).

(s.) hüllen in + A ⟨sich/jdn/etw in etw h.⟩   to wrap (sb/sth) (up) in (sth)

- Würden Sie bitte den Blumenstrauß (/das Päckchen) in Papier hüllen?
  Would you please wrap the bouquet of flowers (/package) in paper?

- Hüll dich fest in deinen Mantel, dann wird dir wärmer!
  Wrap yourself up tight in your coat; then you'll get warmer!

- Ich hüllte mich fester in meinen Mantel.
  I wrapped my coat more tightly around me.

- Hätte sie nicht das Kind in eine Decke gehüllt, hätte es sich erkältet.
  If she hadn't wrapped the child in a blanket, he would have caught cold.

- Die Leute hüllten sich in Schweigen (über das Verbrechen der Mafia).
  The people remained silent (about the Mafia's crime).

s. hüten vor + D ⟨sich vor jdm/etw h.⟩   to watch out for, guard against (sb/sth)

- Hüte dich vor dem Hund! Er ist sehr böse.
  Beware of the dog. He is very mean.

■ Du sollst dich vor Erkältungen (/ihm/bösen Einflüssen/davor) hüten.
You should guard against catching cold (/beware of him/evil influences/that).

■ Die kleinen Ziegen hüteten sich nicht vor dem Wolf.
The little goats weren't on guard against the wolf.

■ Diese Länder (/Diese Leute) müssen sich vor Ausbeutung hüten.
These countries (/people) must protect themselves against exploitation.

I

identifizieren als + A ⟨jdn/etw als etw i.⟩   to identify (sb/sth) as (sth)

- Der Zeuge konnte den Mann als Täter identifizieren.
  The witness was able to identify the man as the perpetrator.
- Ich kann den Koffer leicht (als meinen) identifizieren.
  I can easily identify the suitcase (as mine).

s. identifizieren mit + D ⟨sich mit jdm/etw i.⟩   to identify o.s. with (sb/sth)

- Ich habe mich nie mit Hamlet identifiziert. Er ist mir zu unentschlossen.
  I have never identified myself with Hamlet. He is too indecisive for my taste.
- Nur wenige Menschen identifizierten sich wirklich mit der Philosophie (/der Meinung/den Gedanken/den Ansichten) Maos.
  Only a few people really identified themselves with Mao's philosophy (/opinion/thoughts/views).
- An der Grenze mußte ich mich mit meinem Paß identifizieren.
  At the border I had to prove my identity with my passport.

imponieren (+ prep)   to make an impression; to impress

- Sie hat mir durch ihr Wissen (/ihre Leistungen) imponiert.
  She impressed me by her knowledge (/achievements).
- Vor allem imponierte den Leuten an ihm seine Tapferkeit (/sein Humor/seine Energie/sein Vermögen).
  His bravery (/sense of humor/energy/wealth) most impressed people.

imponieren (without prep)   to impress

- Seine Haltung imponiert mir nicht im geringsten.
  His attitude doesn't impress me in the least.

s. infizieren bei/mit + D ⟨sich bei jdm/etw, mit etw i.⟩   to be *or* get infected by (sb/sth)

- Sie hat sich bei einer flüchtigen Bekanntschaft mit Windpocken infiziert.
  She was infected with chicken pox by a casual acquaintance.
- Ich infizierte mich bei dem schlechten Wetter mit einer Lungenentzündung.
  I caught pneumonia during the bad weather.

(s). informieren über + A ⟨sich/jdn über jdn/etw i.⟩   to inform (o.s./sb) about (sb/sth)

■ Er hat mich (/den Mann) darüber nur unvollständig informiert.
He only gave me (/the man) incomplete information about that.

■ Ich möchte mich über die neuen Entwicklungen (/alles) informieren.
I would like to become informed (or *acquire knowledge) about the new developments (/everything).*

■ Der Außenminister informierte den Präsidenten über die Verhandlungen mit der Sowjetunion.
The Secretary of State informed the President about his negotiations with the Soviet Union.

inspirieren zu + D ⟨jdn zu etw i.⟩   to inspire (sb) to (sth)

■ Das Ereignis inspirierte mich zu einem Roman (/zu täglichen Leibesübungen).
That incident inspired me to write a novel (/to exercise daily).

■ Eine Reise mit dem Zug inspirierte Einstein zu seiner Relativitätstheorie.
A train trip inspired Einstein to develop his theory of relativity.

s. inspirieren lassen von + D ⟨sich von jdm/etw i. lassen⟩   to get one's inspiration from (sb/sth)

■ Der Maler hat sich von der wunderschönen Umgebung seines Hauses (/seiner Frau) inspirieren lassen.
The painter got his inspiration from the beautiful surroundings of his house (/his wife).

s. interessieren für + A ⟨sich für jdn/etw i.⟩   to be interested in (sb/sth)

■ Ich interessiere mich für klassische Musik (/Basketball/sie).
I'm interested in classical music (/basketball/her).

■ Er hat sich für den Dichter (/den Komponisten) interessiert.
He was interested in the writer (/the composer).

■ Interessierst du dich für Briefmarken (/dieses Buch/das Theaterstück)?
Are you interested in stamps (/this book/the play)?

■ Ich interessiere mich für ein neues Auto (/eine neue Küchenmaschine).
I am in the market for a new car (/for a new kitchen appliance).

interessieren für/an + A/D ⟨jdn für/an etw i.⟩   to interest (sb) in (sth)

■ Er hat mich für diesen Roman (/an diesem Geschäft) interessiert.
He made me interested in this book (/in a business proposition).

■ Ich interessierte ihn für das (*or* an dem) Projekt (/Auto).
I interested him in the project (/car).

interessiert sein an + D ⟨an jdm/etw i. sein⟩   to be interested in (sb/sth)

■ Der Junge ist an dem Mädchen (/dem Buch) interessiert.
The boy is interested in the girl (/book).

■ Daran bin ich nicht interessiert. Interessiert es dich überhaupt?
I'm not interested in that. Does that interest you at all?

interviewen zu + D ⟨jdn zu etw i.⟩   to interview (sb) on *or* about (sth)

■ Der Finanzminister wurde zu der Frage (/dem Problem) höherer Steuern interviewt.
The Secretary of the Treasury was interviewed about the question (/the problem) of higher taxes.

■ Der Reporter interviewte den Popstar zu seiner letzten Langspielplatte.
The reporter interviewed the pop star about his latest album.

investieren in + A ⟨in jdn/etw i.⟩   to invest in (sb/sth)

■ Ich habe so viel Kraft (/Zeit) in meine Forschung investiert.
I invested so much energy (/time) in my research.

■ Die Spekulantin investierte etwas Geld an der Börse.
The speculator invested some money in the stock market.

■ Ich habe meine Gefühle in sie investiert.
I became (emotionally) involved with her.

■ Die osteuropäischen Länder investierten viel Geld in ihre Sportler.
The eastern European countries invested a lot of money in their athletes.

irreführen (without prep)   to mislead; to lead astray

■ Er hat mich durch falsche Angaben (/ungenaue Auskünfte/sein Verhalten) irregeführt.
He misled me by giving me wrong information (/imprecise information/by his action).

■ Deine Beschreibung des Weges hat uns total irregeführt.
Your directions completely misled us.

irregehen (+ prep)   to go astray; to lose one's way; to be wrong

■ Du gehst irre in der Annahme, daß. . . . (*fig*)
You're wrong in your assumption that. . . .

irren (+ prep)   to wander; to stray; to roam

■ Ich irrte durch den Wald (/die Straßen).
I wandered through the forest (/streets).

■ Sie sind von einem Ort zum andern geirrt.
They wandered from one place to another.

s. irren in + D ⟨**sich in jdm/etw i.**⟩   to be mistaken in *or* about (sb/sth); to be wrong about (sb/sth)

■ In dieser Hinsicht (/In dieser Sache) irrte ich mich.
I was mistaken in this respect (/matter).

■ Ich habe mich in der Telefonnummer (/in der Zeit/im Datum/im Termin) geirrt.
I was wrong about the phone number (/time/date/appointment).

■ Sie hatte sich gründlich in ihrem ersten Mann geirrt.
She had really been wrong about her first husband.

s. irren um + A ⟨**sich um etw i.**⟩   to be mistaken about (sth)

■ Ich glaube, daß die Kellnerin sich um fünf Mark geirrt hat.
I think the waitress made a mistake of five marks.

■ Entschuldigung! Ich habe mich um eine Stunde geirrt.
Sorry! I'm an hour late (or early).

J

jagen (+ prep)   to hunt; to chase; to drive (wildly); to hound

- Sie wollen Tiger in Afrika jagen.
  They want to hunt tigers in Africa.
- Die Aufseher haben die Entflohenen mit Hunden durch den Wald gejagt.
  The guards chased the escapees through the forest with dogs.
- Sein Freund hat ihn aus dem Bett gejagt. *(inf)*
  His friend rousted (or roused) him out of his bed. (inf)
- Sie jagte ihn aus dem Haus (/dem Dienst). *(inf)*
  She kicked (or drove) him out of the house (/fired him). (inf)
- Er hat das Volk in einen Krieg gejagt.
  He drove the people into a war.
- Sie hat die Kinder ins Bett gejagt.
  She hustled the children off to bed.
- Der Wind jagte den Regen über die Autobahn.
  The wind drove the rain across the expressway.
- Die Anstrengung jagte mir das Blut in den Kopf.
  The exertion made the blood rush to my head.
- Das Auto jagte über die Brücke (/durch die Nebenstraße) und gegen eine Mauer.
  The car darted across the bridge (/through the side-street) and smashed into a brick wall.

jagen auf (+ singular)/nach (+ plural) + A/D ⟨auf ein Tier/nach Tieren j.⟩   to hunt (animal)

- Sie haben auf Fuchs (/Fasan) (*or* nach Füchsen/Fasanen) gejagt.
  They hunted fox (/pheasant) (or foxes/pheasants).

jagen nach + D ⟨nach etw j.⟩   *(fig)* to chase after (sth); to chase for (sth)

- Wie immer jagt er nach dem Geld (/dem Glück).
  As always, he is chasing after money (/happiness).
- Er jagt nach dem Ruhm (/Genuß/wahrer Liebe).
  He's chasing after fame (/pleasure/true love).

(s.) jagen in/durch + A ⟨sich/jdm/etw in/durch etw j.⟩   to stab (o.s./sb/sth) in/through (sth); to stick (o.s./sb/sth) with (sth)

- Er jagte sich zufällig ein Messer in (/durch) die Hand (/den Magen).
  He accidentally stabbed himself in the hand (/stomach).

■ Die Krankenschwester hat mir eine Spritze in die Hüfte gejagt. *(inf)*
The nurse stuck a needle in my hip. (inf)

■ Ich habe mir beim Reparieren des Autos einen Schraubenzieher durch die Hand gejagt.
While repairing the car, I ran a screwdriver through my hand.

jammern nach + D ⟨**nach jdm/etw j.**⟩   to whine *or* yammer for (sb/sth)

■ Das Kind hat den ganzen Tag nach Eis gejammert.
The child whined for ice cream all day.

■ Der Gefangene jammerte nach Wasser.
The prisoner begged pitifully for water.

jammern über + A ⟨**über jdn/etw j.**⟩   to moan *or* lament *or* wail over/about (sb/sth)

■ Mein Bruder ist nie zufrieden und jammert immer (über irgendetwas).
My brother is never happy and is always moaning (about something).

■ Die Frau jammerte bitterlich über den Tod ihres Sohnes.
The woman wailed bitterly over the death of her son.

jammern um + A ⟨**um Gnade/Vergebung j.**⟩   to beg for mercy/a remission of sins

■ Der sterbende Mann jammerte um Gnade (/Vergebung/Verzeihung/Hilfe).
The dying man begged for mercy (/remission of his sins/forgiveness/help).

jonglieren mit + D ⟨**mit etw j.**⟩   to juggle (sth)

■ Der Clown kann hervorragend mit Bällen jonglieren.
The clown can juggle balls excellently.

■ Als Buchhalter mußt du gut mit Zahlen jonglieren können. *(fig)*
As an accountant you must be able to juggle figures. (fig)

jubeln über + A ⟨**über etw j.**⟩   to cheer *or* rejoice about (sth)

■ Seine Mutter jubelte vor Freude (über seine Ankunft).
His mother rejoiced with pleasure (over his arrival).

■ Du hast zu früh über deinen Gewinn (/darüber) gejubelt.
You rejoiced too soon about your prize (/about it).

K

s. kämpfen durch + A ⟨sich durch etw k.⟩   to fight one's way through (sth)

- Der Anwalt kämpfte sich durch einen Berg von Akten.
  The lawyer fought his way through a mountain of files.
- Ich habe mich durch die Bürokratie gekämpft.
  I fought my way through the bureaucracy.

kämpfen für + A ⟨für etw k.⟩   to campaign *or* fight for/against (sth)

- Sie kämpfen für Frieden (/ihren Glauben/den Erhalt eines Naturschutzgebietes).
  They are fighting for peace (/their beliefs/to keep a wildlife preserve).
- Er kämpft dafür, daß alle Frauen die Gleichberechtigung mit den Männern erhalten.
  He's fighting so that all women have equal rights with men.
- Die Kongreßabgeordnete kämpfte für ihre Wähler (/den Gesetzentwurf).
  The Congresswoman fought for her constituents (/the bill).

kämpfen gegen + A ⟨gegen jdn/etw k.⟩   to fight against (sb/sth)

- Wir kämpfen heute abend gegen eine starke Mannschaft.
  We are playing against a strong team this evening.
- Er kämpte gegen Apartheid (/seine Feinde/für die Freiheit).
  He fought against apartheid (/his enemy/for freedom).
- Viele Frauen kämpfen dagegen, diskriminiert zu werden.
  Many women are fighting discrimination against them.
- Die Linken kämpfen gegen die Ausbeutung des Menschen durch die Menschen.
  The leftists are fighting against the exploitation of men by men.
- Sie kämpfen gegen Korruption und Ämtermißbrauch.
  They're fighting against corruption and misuse of office.

kämpfen mit + D ⟨mit sich/jdm/etw k.⟩   to fight with (o.s./sb/sth)

- Sie kämpften mit Kanonen.
  They fought with cannons.
- Tennis: Er kämpfte mit seinem Partner gegen das amerikanische Doppel.
  Tennis: He and his partner battled the American pair.

■ Sie hat mit dem Tod (/den Tränen/ihren Gefühlen) gekämpft.
She fought for her life (/back her tears/back her emotions).

■ Ich kämpfte mit mir, ob ich die Konferenz besuchen sollte.
I struggled to decide whether I should attend the conference.

■ Ich versuchte, mit dem (*or* gegen den) Schlaf zu kämpfen. (*fig*)
I tried hard to keep awake.

kämpfen um + A ⟨um jdn/etw k.⟩   to fight for (sb/sth)

■ Das kleine Land kämpfte lange um seine Unabhängigkeit (/Freiheit).
The small country fought a long time for its independence (/freedom).

■ Die beiden Männer kämpfen um dieselbe Frau.
Both men are fighting for the same lady.

■ Die Arbeiter kämpfen um höhere Löhne (/mehr Geld/kürzere Arbeitszeit).
The workers are fighting for higher wages (/more money/a shorter work week).

■ Der Sportler kämpfte um den Davis-Cup.
The athlete fought for the Davis Cup.

■ Die Truppen kämpften um jeden Ort (/jede Straße der Stadt/jeden Meter Boden).
The troops fought for every town (/every street of the city/for every inch of ground).

kandidieren für + A ⟨für etw k.⟩   to run for (office), to be a candidate for

■ Er kandidierte für das Amt des Präsidenten (/für den Senat).
He ran for president (/the Senate).

■ Sie wird für die Konservativen kandidieren.
She will run for the Conservatives.

kandidieren gegen + A ⟨gegen jdn k.⟩   to run against (sb)

■ Sie hat gegen einen anderen Bewerber kandidiert.
She competed with another applicant.

kapitulieren vor + D ⟨vor etw k.⟩   to give up (sth); to capitulate in the face of (sth); to yield to (sth)

■ Er kapituliert vor den Schwierigkeiten.
He is giving up in the face of (implied: *insurmountable) difficulties.*

■ Sie kapitulierten vor der Übermacht ihrer Gegner.
They yielded to the superiority of their opponents.

kauen an/auf + D ⟨**an** *or* **auf etw k.**⟩   to chew (on) (sth)

- Sie kaut an (*or* auf) den Lippen.
  She's chewing her lips.

- Anne kaute vor Langeweile an (*or* auf) den Nägeln.
  Anne was chewing on her fingernails because of boredom.

- Der Hund kaute an (*or* auf) dem Knochen (/an *or* auf dem Schuh).
  The dog chewed on the bone (/shoe).

- An deiner Entscheidung werde ich länger zu kauen haben. (*fig*)
  Your decision will really give me food for thought (or something to think about).

kaufen (+ prep)   to buy

- Ich kaufte ihr (*or* für sie) ein Hemd.
  I bought her a shirt (or I bought a shirt for her).

- Ich habe den Mantel für 300 Mark bei Karstadt (/auf Raten) gekauft.
  I bought the coat at Karstadt (/in installments) for 300 marks.

- Kannst du den Fernseher auf Kredit kaufen?
  Can you buy the television on credit?

- Ich kaufe meine Anzüge (/den Wein) immer bei ihm (/in diesem Laden).
  I always buy my suits (/the wine) at his place (/in this store).

ketten an + A ⟨**jdn/etw an sich/jdn/etw k.**⟩   to chain *or* bind (sb/sth) to (sb/sth/o.s.)

- Sie ketteten den Hund an seine Hundehütte.
  They chained the dog to his kennel.

- Es gelang ihr, ihn völlig an sich zu ketten. (*fig*)
  She succeeded in making him completely dependent on her.

- Die Sklaven wurden aneinander gekettet, so daß sie nicht fliehen konnten.
  The slaves were chained to each other so that they were unable to escape.

s. ketten an + A ⟨**sich an jdn/etw k.**⟩   to tie *or* bind oneself to (sb/sth)

- Die Demonstranten haben sich an das Tor der Botschaft (/aneinader) gekettet.
  The demonstrators chained themselves to the gate of the embassy (/to each other).

klagen gegen + A ⟨**gegen jdn/etw k.**⟩   to sue *or* file a suit against (sb/sth)

- Er will gegen die Firma klagen, wenn der Vertrag nicht erfüllt wird.
  He wants to file a suit against the firm if the contract is not fulfilled.

■ Sie klagte gegen ihren Chef, weil er sie sexuell belästigt hatte.
She filed a suit against her boss because he had sexually harrassed her.

klagen über + A ⟨über jdn/etw k.⟩   to complain about

■ Er klagt über die laute Musik (/den Lärm/den neuen Boß).
He's complaining about the loud music (/noise/new boss).

■ Er hat nie darüber geklagt, daß sie abends oft ausging.
He has never complained about the fact that she often went out in the evenings.

■ Sie klagt über Kopfschmerzen (/Halsweh).
She is complaining of a headache (/sore throat).

klagen um + A ⟨um jdn/etw k.⟩   to complain *or* moan *or* lament over/about (sb/sth)

■ Erika klagt um ihr verlorenes Glück (/ihr Unglück/ihren ersten Ehemann).
Erica is lamenting over her loss of luck (/accident/first husband).

■ Über Hitler haben sicher viele geklagt, aber wenige um ihn.
Many people surely complained about Hitler, but only a few people were sorry when he died.

■ Die Mutter konnte nicht aufhören, um ihr totes Kind zu klagen.
The mother could not stop lamenting her dead child.

s. klammern an + A ⟨sich an jdn/etw k.⟩   to cling to (sb/sth)

■ Der Schüler klammerte sich an die Formulierungen des Textes, anstatt etwas freier zu schreiben.
The student clung to the wording of the text instead of writing more freely (by using his own words).

■ Der Totkranke klammerte sich an das Leben (/eine Hoffnung/die Illusion, noch geheilt werden zu können).
The very sick man clung to life (/hope/the illusion that he could still be cured).

■ Er hat sich an seine Freundin geklammert.
He clung to his girlfriend (i.e., she didn't want him any more, but he wanted her).

klappen (+ prep)   to turn *or* move (sth) (in a certain direction)

■ Das Fenster klappt nach außen (/innen).
The window opens to the outside (/inside).

■ Er hat seinen Sitz nach vorn (/hinten) geklappt.
He tipped his seat forward (/back).

- Er klappte den Deckel in die Höhe (, um in den Kasten hineinsehen zu können).
  He lifted the lid (in order to be able to look into the box).

klappen (+ prep)   to make a banging sound

- Der Junge klappte wieder mit der Tür.
  The boy banged the door again.

- Die ganze Nacht über klappten die Fensterläden an (*or* gegen) die Hauswand.
  The shutters banged against the wall of the house all night.

klappen (+ prep)   to work; to work out (*inf*)

- Mit dem Flug hat alles geklappt.
  The flight went all right/There was no problem with the flight.

- Hat es mit der Reservierung (/Arbeit/Bestätigung/Rechnung) geklappt?
  Did you get the reservation (/job/confirmation/bill)?

(s.) klatschen (+ prep)   to smack; to go smack; to slap; to throw; to clap

- Sie klatschte in die Hände.
  She applauded.

- Ich habe mir vor Überraschung auf die Schenkel (/auf die Wange/gegen die Stirn) geklatscht.
  I slapped my thighs (/cheek/forehead) with surprise.

- Er hat ihm (mit der rechten Hand) eine Ohrfeige geklatscht. *(inf)*
  He slapped (or smacked) him in the ear (/with his right hand).

- Sie klatschte auf den Tisch (vor Wut).
  She smacked the table (in rage).

- Der Hagel (/Regen) klatscht gegen die Fensterscheibe.
  The hail (/rain) is beating against the window pane.

- Das Ei (/Glas/Die Torte) ist zu Boden geklatscht.
  The egg (/glass/cake) went smack on(to) the floor.

klatschen über + A ⟨über jdn k.⟩   to gossip, *or* spread gossip about (sb) *(inf)*

- Er klatscht immer über andere Leute.
  He always gossips (or spreads gossip) about other people.

kleben (+ prep)   to stick; to glue

- Kleb die Marke auf den Briefumschlag!
  Stick the stamp on the envelope!

■ Sie hat die Photos in das Album (/auf die Pappe/über ihr Bett an die Wand) geklebt.
She stuck the photos in the album (/on the posterboard/on the wall above her bed).

kleben an + D ⟨an jdm/etw k.⟩   to stick to (sb/sth); to cling to (sth)

■ Er klebte das Plakat (/den Zettel) an die Mauer.
He stuck (or glued) the poster (/slip of paper) to the wall.

■ Sie kleben an den Traditionen (/ihren Ideen/am Text).
They cling to traditions (/their ideas/stick to the text).

■ Dieses Material klebt fest an (or auf) der Haut (/dem Holz).
This material sticks fast to your skin (/wood).

■ Er klebt an seiner Arbeit (/an seiner Mutter).
He's glued to his work (/his mother).

klettern (+ prep)   to climb

■ Er ist auf die Leiter (/den Baum/vom Baum/auf das Dach/auf den Berg/über den Zaun/in den Ring/aus dem brennenden Flugzeug) geklettert.
He climbed the ladder (/the tree/down from the tree/onto the roof/the mountain/over the fence/into the ring/out of the burning plane).

klopfen an/auf + A ⟨an/auf etw k.⟩   to knock at/on (sth); *(quietly)* to tap at/on (sth); to rap at/on (sth); to slap (sb) on *(the shoulder, back, etc.)*

■ Er klopfte an die Tür (/an das Fenster).
He knocked (or tapped) at the door (/window).

■ Er klopfte an das Barometer (/auf das Heft/an die Tafel/an die Wand).
He tapped at the barometer (/on the notebook/at the blackboard/at the wall).

■ Er klopfte auf den Tisch (/mit dem Messer ans Glas) (, um eine Rede zu halten).
He rapped (on) the table (/(on) his glass with a knife) (in order to give a speech).

■ Meine Freundin klopfte mir auf die Schulter (/auf den Rücken).
My friend slapped (or tapped or patted) me on the shoulder (/on the back).

■ Der Specht klopft (mit dem Schnabel an den Baum).
The woodpecker is tapping ((on) the tree with its beak).

klopfen durch/in + A ⟨etw durch/in etw k.⟩   to knock *or* drive (sth) into (sth)

■ Er klopft einen Nagel in das Holz (/durch das Brett).
He's driving a nail into the wood (/through the board).

klopfen von + D ⟨etw von/aus etw k.⟩   to beat *or* knock (sth) out of (sth)

- Sie klopfte den Staub aus dem Teppich (/aus *or* von dem Mantel).
  She beat the dust out of the rug (/out of or *from the coat).*

- Der Pfeifenraucher hat die Asche aus seiner Pfeife geklopft.
  The pipe smoker knocked the ashes out of his pipe.

knabbern an + D ⟨an etw k.⟩   to nibble on (sth)

- Das Kaninchen knabbert an Karroten.
  The rabbit is nibbling on carrots.

- Vor dem Essen solltest du nicht an Keksen (/Nüssen) knabbern.
  You shouldn't nibble on cookies (/nuts) before the meal.

knallen (+ prep)   to bang; to crack; to ring out

- Er knallte mit der Tür (/der Peitsche/den Absätzen).
  He banged (or slammed) the door (/cracked the whip/clicked his heels).

- Der Fahrer (/Wagen) ist gegen die Mauer geknallt.
  The driver (/car) hit the wall.

- Peter, knall nicht den Ball (/das Spielzeug) gegen die Wand!
  Peter, don't bang (or bounce) the ball (/toy) against the wall!

- Aus Zorn hat er das Buch (/Geld) auf den Tisch geknallt.
  He banged (or slammed) the book (/money) on the table out of anger.

- Sie knallte den Hörer auf die Gabel. *(inf)*
  She slammed (or banged) down the receiver.

kneifen in + A ⟨jdn *or* jdm in den Arm, usw k.⟩   to pinch (sb/sb's) arm, etc.

- Sie kniff ihm (*or* ihn) in den Arm (/die Schulter/den Hintern).
  She pinched his arm (/shoulder/buttocks).

- Er hat ihr (*or* sie) (/in die Wange/in den Schenkel) gekniffen.
  He pinched her (/her cheek/her thigh).

- Der Entschluß, dieses teuere Kleid zu kaufen, kneift mich im Magen. *(fig)*
  The decision to buy this expensive dress makes my stomach turn.

kneifen vor + D ⟨vor jdm/etw k.⟩   to get *or* back out of (sth); to duck out of (sth); to dodge (sth)

- Sie kniff vor jeder Entscheidung (/ihrem Chef).
  She avoided making any decisions (/her boss).

knüpfen an + A ⟨etw an etw k.⟩ to tie *or* knot (sth) to (sth)

- Die Liebe zur bayerischen Landschaft knüpft ihn an seine Heimat.
  His love of the Bavarian countryside ties him (or links him) to his homeland.
- Viele Menschen knüpfen an seine Kandidatur große Hoffnungen (/Erwartungen).
  A lot of people attach great hopes (/expectations) to his candidacy.
- Ich knüpfe daran die Bedingung, daß du rechtzeitig nach Hause kommst.
  I am adding the condition that you get home on time.
- Ich knüpfe keine Bedingung an diesen Vorschlag.
  I attach no condition to this proposal.

s. knüpfen an + A ⟨sich an etw k.⟩ to be linked or connected with (sth)

- An die alte Stadt knüpfen sich für mich viele Erinnerungen.
  Lots of memories bind (or connect) me to this old city.
- An diesen Vorgang (/diese Entscheidung) haben sich viele Gerüchte geknüpft.
  This event (/decision) has raised many rumors.

kokettieren mit + D ⟨mit etw k.⟩ to flirt with (sth)

- Sie kokettierte mit ihren hübschen Augen (/einem Lächeln).
  She flirted with her lovely eyes (/a smile).
- Deine Freundin kokettiert mit einem anderen.
  Your girlfriend is flirting with another guy.
- In letzter Zeit kokettiert er mit dem Gedanken, nach Amerika auszuwandern. *(fig)*
  Lately he's been toying with the idea of emigrating to America.
- Er kokettiert gern mit seinem Alter.
  He likes to play up his age.

kommen (+ prep) to come to, to get to, to reach *(one's destination)*

- Er kam nach Hause (/ins Kino/zum Theater/in *or* auf die Toilette/aufs Klo/in die Stadt/nach Hamburg/in die Türkei/nach Deutschland/in den Iran/zur Haltestelle/zur Arbeit/zur Schule/regelmäßig zum Training/zu meinem Geburtstag/in die Kirche/zum Frühstück/ins Zimmer/in das Alter).
  He came home (/to the cinema/to the theater/to the toilet/to the john/to the city center/to Hamburg/to Turkey/to Germany/to Iran/to the bus stop/to work/to school/to practice regularly/to my birthday party/to church/for breakfast/He entered the room/He reached the age).
- Dann kommen Sie an eine Kreuzung (/zu einem Kaufhaus/in eine Fußgängerzone).
  Then you will get to an intersection (/a department store/a pedestrian area).

- Sie kam neben mich zu sitzen.
  She happened to sit beside me.

- Ich bin an einen Punkt gekommen, an dem ich nicht mehr weiter weiß.
  I have gotten to a point where I don't know how to go on.

- Das Kind kommt mit seiner Hand bis an die Deckenlampe.
  The child can reach the ceiling light with his hand.

- Wie kommen wir (von hier) nach Hamburg (/ans Ziel/ans Ufer/zum Bahnhof/ins Theater/an den See)?
  How do we get (from here) to Hamburg (/the destination/the shore/the train station /the theater/the lake)?

- Diesen Monat kommen keine guten Filme ins Kino.
  No good films are coming to the cinema this month.

kommen (+ prep)   to come (into), to enter

- Er kam in Gefahr (/Wut/Verlegenheit/eine schwierige Lage /Fahrt/Schwung).
  He got into danger (/a rage/an embarrassing situation/a difficult situation/going /hit his stride).

- Er kam ins Krankenhaus (/in ein Heim/ins Gefängnis).
  He was hospitalized (/sent to a home/imprisoned).

- Der Teppich kommt in die Mitte (/unter die Lampe).
  The rug belongs (goes) in the middle (/under the light).

kommen (+ prep)   to come

- Er kam von der Arbeit (/aus England/mit dem Wagen/aus dem Kino/vom Arzt/vom Spaziergang/durch die Stadt/durch München/um die Ecke/vor mir/nach mir/an die frische Luft/bis vor die Tür/aus dem Knast *or* aus dem Gefängnis).
  He came from work (/from England/by car/from the cinema/from the doctor/from a walk/through the city/through Munich/around the corner/before me/after me/to get fresh air/up to the front of the door/was released from the clink or *jail).*

- Das Geschenk ist von meinem Freund gekommen.
  The present was from my friend.

- Das kommt davon (*or* daher), daß du nicht gut aufpaßt.
  That's because (or That's what happens when) you don't pay attention.

kommen auf + A ⟨auf etw k.⟩   to come on(to)/upon (sth), to get on(to) (sth); *(school)* to go to; *(memory)* to think of (sth)

- Viele neue Produkte sind auf den Markt gekommen.
  Lots of new products came out on (or into) the market.

- Er kam plötzlich auf die Idee, das alte Auto zu verkaufen.
  He suddenly got (or thought of) the idea of selling the old car.

■ Die Diskussion kam zufällig auf dieses Thema (/diesen Punkt).
The discussion accidentally turned to this subject (/point).

■ Ich wäre nie auf so etwas gekommen.
I would never have thought of such a thing.

■ Wie bist du darauf gekommen? Weißt du, wie du auf diese Idee (/Erkenntnis) gekommen bist?
How did you get (to) that? (or How did you come to (or reach) that conclusion?) Do you know how you arrived at this idea (/insight)?

■ Wie kommen Sie darauf? —Ich kam auf die Idee, als. . . .
What makes you think that? —I came upon the idea when. . . .

■ Konntest du schließlich auf die richtige Landstraße kommen?
Were you finally able to get on the right highway?

■ Er kommt aufs Gymnasium (/auf die Schule/auf die Univerität).
He will go to (attend) the "Gymnasium"(/to school/to the university).

■ Die Blumen kommen auf den Tisch.
The flowers go on the table.

kommen auf + A ⟨auf etw k.⟩   to come to *or* add up to *or* amount to

■ Wie hoch kommt das? —Das Renovieren kommt auf etwa 10.000 Mark.
What does that come to? —The renovation comes to about 10,000 marks.

■ Ich habe zweimal gerechnet. Ich komme nur auf 19.
I have calculated twice. I only get 19 (or come to 19).

■ Worauf kommst du im Monat? —Ich komme auf 3.000 Mark im Monat.
How much do you make a month? —I get (make) 3,000 marks a month.

■ Die Unkosten kommen auf die Rechnung (/dein Konto).
The expenses go onto the bill (/into your account).

kommen auf + A ⟨auf jdn/etw k⟩   there is *or* there are (sth) for (sb)

■ Auf jeden Gewinner beim Spielen kommen zwei Verlierer.
In gambling there is one winner for every two losers.

■ In Kuba kommt auf jeden vierten Einwohner ein Kühlschrank.
In Cuba there is one refrigerator for every fourth person.

■ Auf jeden Haushalt kam nur ein Kilo Zucker pro Monat.
Each household could consume only one kilogram of sugar per month.

kommen aus + D ⟨aus etw k.⟩   to come from (sth); to originate from (sth)

■ Woher kommt er? —Er kommt aus Deutschland (/aus Chikago/aus der Tschechoslowakei/aus dem Irak).
Where is he from? —He is from Germany (/Chicago/Czechoslovakia/Iraq).

- Das Wort kommt aus dem Sanskrit.
  The word comes from Sanskrit.

- Die Information kam aus seinem Buch (/einer verläßlichen Quelle).
  The information came from his book (/a reliable source).

kommen mit + D ⟨jdm mit etw k.⟩   to come to (sb) with *or* for (sth)

- Ich komme (Ihnen) mit einer Bitte (/einer Frage/einem Rätsel/einem Problem).
  I have a request (/question/riddle/problem) for you.

- Wenn du (mir) noch einmal mit derselben Entschuldigung kommen würdest, würde ich dich schlagen.
  If you were to try the same excuse on me again, I would smack you.

- Komm mir nicht mit deinen sarkastischen Bemerkungen (/Komm mir nicht wieder damit)!
  Spare me your sarcastic remarks (/Don't start that all over again)!

kommen über + A ⟨über jdn k.⟩   to befall (sb); to come over (sb)

- Ein schweres Unglück ist über sie gekommen.
  She had awfully bad luck.

- Zorn (/Wut/Ekel) kam über sie.
  Anger (/rage/disgust) came over her.

- Was ist denn über dich gekommen?
  What has come over (or gotten into) you?

kommen um + A ⟨um etw k.⟩   to lose (sth); to be deprived of (sth)

- Durch euren Lärm bin ich um meinen Schlaf (/um meine wohlverdiente Ruhe) gekommen.
  Due to the noise you made, I couldn't sleep (/get my well-deserved rest).

- Er kam ums Leben (/um sein Vermögen/um sein ganzes Geld).
  He lost his life (/fortune/all his money).

- Durch seine Alkoholabhängigkeit kam er um seinen Führerschein.
  He lost his driver's license because of his alcoholism.

- Durch ihre Krankheit kommen wir um das Vergnügen, sie kennenzulernen.
  Due to her illness, we're deprived of the pleasure of getting to know her.

- Durch häufiges Zuspätkommen kam das Mädchen um das Privileg, allein ins Kino gehen zu dürfen.
  Because of her frequent tardiness, the girl lost the privilege of being allowed to go to the movies alone.

kommen unter + A ⟨**unter etw k.**⟩   to get under (sth); to be run over (by) (sth); to mix with (sth)

- In Paris ist er unter die Räder gekommen. *(idiom)*
  In Paris he went to the dogs.
- Du mußt mal wieder unter Leute kommen.
  You must mix with people again.

kommen zu + D ⟨**zu etw k.**⟩   to attain *or* gain *or* reach (sth); to come to (sth)

- Sie kamen zu einem Entschluß (/einer Entscheidung/einer Einigung).
  They came to (or reached) a conclusion (/a decision/an agreement).
- Er kam plötzlich zu Kräften (/einem großen Vermögen/Geld).
  He suddenly recovered (/came into a large fortune/money).
- Ich habe mich ausgeruht, und nachdem ich zu Atem gekommen war, setzte ich meinen Lauf fort.
  I rested and after I had gotten my breath, I continued my run.
- Der Teenager kam endlich zur Besinnung.
  The teenager finally came to his senses.
- Der Junge kam zu sich. Ich muß zu mir kommen.
  The boy came around. I must come to my senses.
- Die Pflanzen kommen schnell zum Blühen (/zum Wachsen).
  The plants are blossoming (/growing) quickly.
- Das Auto ist zum Stehen (/Stillstand) gekommen.
  The car came to a halt (/to a stop).

kommen zu + D ⟨**zu jdm k.**⟩   to visit (sb)

- Ich will morgen zu euch kommen. Soll ich (zum Essen) zu euch kommen?
  I want to visit you tomorrow. Should I come to visit (to eat with) you?
- Hoffentlich kommt er nicht betrunken zu euch (/eurer Party).
  Hopefully, he won't get to your home (/party) drunk.

kommen zu + D ⟨**zu etw k.**⟩   to occur *or* to happen, to result in (sth)

- Niemand weiß, ob es zum Streit (/Krieg) kommen wird.
  No one knows if it will come to a fight (/war).
- Daß es zu einem Prozeß (/zu ihrer Entlassung/dazu) kommen mußte, machte uns alle traurig.
  That it had to come to a trial (/end in her dismissal/that) made all of us sad.

■ Es kam eins zum anderen.
One thing led to another.

■ Es wird hoffentlich noch dazu kommen, daß niemand auf der Welt mehr mit Hunger ins Bett gehen muß.
Hopefully, the day will come when no one in the world will have to go to bed hungry.

konkurrieren mit + D ⟨mit jdm/etw k.⟩   to compete with (sb/sth); to be in/go into competition with (sb/sth)

■ Mit diesen Preisen (/Marken/Damit) können sie nicht konkurrieren.
They cannot compete with these prices (/brands/that).

■ Uwe konkurriert immer (/in allem/in der Schule/im Sport) mit seinem Bruder.
Uwe is always in competition with his brother (/is competitive in everything/in school/in sports).

■ Es ist schwer, mit den Produkten aus Japan zu konkurrieren.
It is difficult to compete with the products from Japan.

konkurrieren um + A ⟨um etw k.⟩   to compete for (sth)

■ Er konkurrierte mit ihm um den ersten Preis (/die Anerkennung/die Ehre/die Tennismeisterschaft).
He competed with him for first prize (/the recognition/the honor/the tennis championship).

■ Sie konkurrierten miteinander um die übrigen Stellen.
They competed with each other for the remaining jobs.

(s.) kontrollieren (+ prep)   to control; to check

■ Sie ließ sich von ihrem Mann kontrollieren.
She let herself be controlled by her husband.

■ Dieser Lehrer kann die Schüler in seiner Klasse einfach nicht kontrollieren.
This teacher simply cannot control the students in his class.

■ Du sollst mich nicht (bei allem) immer kontrollieren!
Stop trying to control me (in everything).

■ Ich muß alles unter der Haube kontrollieren, bevor ich abfahre.
I have to check everything under the hood before I leave.

kontrollieren nach/auf + D/A ⟨jdn/etw nach etw *or* auf etw k.⟩   to check (sb/sth) for (sth)

■ Sie haben die Ausweise (/die Pässe) auf Gültigkeit kontrolliert.
They checked the identifications (/passports) for (their) validity.

- Die Polizei hat den Verdächtigen nach (*or* auf) Waffen (/Drogen) kontrolliert.
  The police checked the suspect for weapons (/drugs).
- Der Lehrer kontrollierte die Hausaufgaben der Schüler auf Richtigkeit.
  The teacher checked the students' homework for accuracy.

konzentrieren auf + A ⟨etw auf jdn/etw k.⟩   to concentrate on (sth)

- Sie konzentriert ihre ganze Kraft und Zeit auf ihren ungebärdigen Sohn.
  She concentrates all her strength and time on her unruly son.
- Ich muß alle Gedanken (/meine ganze Energie) auf dieses Problem (/ihn/die Fertigstellung dieses Aufsatzes) konzentrieren.
  I have to concentrate all my thoughts (/energy) on this problem (/him/the completion of this essay).

s. konzentrieren auf + A ⟨sich auf jdn/etw k.⟩   to concentrate on (sb/sth)

- Er konzentriert sich auf die Arbeit (/Aufgaben/Untersuchung).
  He's concentrating on the work (/tasks/investigation).
- Ich konzentrierte mich ganz auf die Prüfung (/mein Studium/die Frage).
  I concentrated completely on the exam (/my studies/the question).
- Seit seinem Herzinfarkt konzentriert er sich mehr auf seine Kinder (/seine Frau/seine Familie).
  Since his heart attack he has concentrated more on his children (/his wife/his family).

kranken an + D ⟨an etw k.⟩   to suffer from (sth)

- Sie krankt an einem schlechten Erinnerungsvermögen.
  She suffers from a bad memory.
- Der Plan (/Es) krankt daran, daß niemand mitmachen will.
  The plan (/It) suffers from the fact that no one wants to participate.

s. kümmern um + A ⟨sich um jdn/etw k.⟩   to look after (sb/sth); to take care of (*sick person/sb's children*); to care *or* be worried about (sb/sth)

- Ich habe mich um meinen Großvater gekümmert, als die Oma starb.
  I looked after my grandfather when my grandma died.
- Die Krankenschwester kümmert sich um die Kranken (/das Essen).
  The nurse is looking after the sick people (/the food).
- Wer kümmert sich um ein Geschenk für unsere Sekretärin?
  Who's going to see about (getting) a present for our secretary?

- Ich kümmere mich nicht um Politik (/Philosophie/Geld/mein Ansehen).
  I don't care about politics (/philosophy/money/my reputation).
- Kümmere dich um deine eigenen Angelegenheiten!
  Mind your own business!
- Ich kümmere mich nicht darum, was die anderen tun.
  I don't mind (or don't care) what other people do.
- Kümmern Sie sich nicht um die Kinder (/mich)!
  Don't worry about the children (/me).
- Der Chef wird sich selber um die ordnungsgemäße Bearbeitung der Bestellung kümmern.
  The boss will see to it himself that the order is properly processed.

küssen (+ prep)   to kiss

- Er küßte sie (zärtlich) auf den Mund (/die Wange/die Stirn/den Hals).
  He kissed her (tenderly) on the lips (/cheek/forehead/neck).

L

lachen (+ prep) to laugh

- Er lachte in sich (/Ich lachte in mich) hinein.
  He laughed to himself. (/I laughed to myself.)
- Er lachte ihm (/ihnen) ins Gesicht.
  He laughed in his (/their) face(s).
- Es ist zum Lachen. Mir ist heute nicht zum Lachen zumute.
  That is ridiculous! I'm not in a mood for laughing today.
- Er lachte leise vor sich hin (/Ich lachte vor mich hin).
  He chuckled (to himself). (/I chuckled to myself.)
- Das Publikum lachte aus vollem Halse.
  The audience roared with laughter.
- Das Kind lachte über das ganze Gesicht.
  The child smiled from ear to ear.
- Sie (/Ihre Witze) bringen mich (/uns/sie) immer zum Lachen.
  They (/Her jokes) always make me (/us/her) laugh.

lachen über + A ⟨über jdn/etw l.⟩ to laugh at (sb/sth)

- Er lachte über diese Anekdote (/jeden blöden Witz).
  He laughed at this anecdote (/every silly joke).
- Er lacht über seine Schwester, weil sie immer merkwürdige Kleidungsstücke trägt.
  He laughs at his sister because she always wears odd clothes.
- Die Schüler lachten über den eigenartigen neuen Lehrer.
  The students laughed at the peculiar new teacher.
- Ich lache immer darüber, daß die Leute dieses Thema so ernst nehmen.
  I always laugh about people taking this issue so seriously.

landen (+ prep) to land

- Sie sind sicher auf dem Mond (/der Erde/der Landebahn) gelandet.
  They landed safely on the moon (/earth/runway).
- Er hat eine kräftige Linke am Kinn (/im Gesicht) des Gegners gelandet.
  He landed a powerful left on his opponent's chin (/face).
- Nach einem einzigen Schlag landete der Boxer auf dem Boden (/auf seinem Hintern).
  After one blow the boxer landed on the floor (/on his behind).

- Unsere Mannschaft (/Er) ist auf dem zweiten Platz gelandet.
  Our team (/He) placed (or came in) second.

- Seine schriftliche Bitte landete im Papierkorb.
  His written request ended up in (or landed in) the wastepaper basket.

- Mit seinen Versprechen und Schmeicheleien konnte er bei ihr nicht landen.
  His promises and flattery didn't get him anywhere with her.

- Bei ihr kannst du nicht landen.
  You haven't got a chance with her.

- Schließlich landete er bei Freunden (/im Kino/im Gefängnis).
  He finally ended up at the home of friends (/at the movies/in jail).

- Das Auto landete an einem Baum (/an einer Mauer/im Graben/auf einem Schrottplatz).
  The car crashed into a tree (/wall/landed in a ditch/ended up in a junkyard).

lassen (+ prep)   to let; to leave

- Der Hund läßt niemanden in die Wohnung (kommen).
  The dog doesn't let anyone into the apartment.

- Ich lasse meine Kinder nicht allein zu Hause (/bei den Großeltern/auf die Straße/auf das neue Sofa).
  I don't let my children (stay) alone at home (/with their grandparents/walk on the street/get onto the new sofa).

- Sie ließ Wasser in die (/aus der) Badewanne (laufen).
  She ran water into the bathtub (/let the water out of the bath).

- Er ließ den Verdächtigen (/das Kleinkind) nicht aus den Augen.
  He didn't let the the suspect (/toddler) out of his sight.

- Laß den Opa in Ruhe, Nils!
  Leave Grandpa alone, Nils!

- Der Kranke will niemanden (/nur seine Ehefrau) zu sich lassen.
  The sick man doesn't want to see anyone (/but his wife).

- Ich werde es dabei lassen.
  I'll leave it at that.

- Ich verstehe nicht, warum sie alles mit sich (/du alles mit dir) machen läßt.
  I don't understand why she puts (/you put) up with everything.

lassen von + D ⟨von jdm/etw l.⟩   to give (sb/sth) up

- Laß von den widerlichen Angewohnheiten!
  Give up your disgusting habits!

- Er kann von seiner Spielleidenschaft nicht lassen.
  He can't give up his passion for gambling.

■   Am Anfang konnte er von dem Mädchen nicht lassen. Aber nach einigen Enttäuschungen ließ er schließlich doch von ihr.
At first he couldn't give the girl up. But after a number of disappointments, he did, indeed, give her up.

lasten auf + D ⟨auf jdm/etw l.⟩   to weigh heavily on (sb/sth)

■   Der Entschluß, in den Krieg einzutreten, lastet schwer auf dem Prädidenten (/seinem Gewissen).
The decision to enter the war weighs (or lies) heavily on the President (/his conscience).

■   Diese Arbeit (/Verantwortung) lastet schwer auf mir (/meinen Schultern).
This work (/responsibility) weighs heavily on me (/my shoulders)

■   Auf dem Grundstück lastet eine hohe Schuld (/Hypothek).
There is a large debt (/mortgage) on the property.

■   Auf wem lastet die Verantwortung für diese Aufgabe?
Whose responsibility is it to do this task?

lästern über + A ⟨über jdn/etw l.⟩   to make nasty remarks about (sb/sth)

■   Seine Mitarbeiter lästerten über ihn (/seine Heirat/seine Frau/seine lockere Moral).
His co-workers made nasty remarks about him (/his marriage/his wife/his loose morals).

laufen (+ prep)   to run

■   Er läuft dauernd ins Kino (/ins Restaurant/zur Polizei).
He's always off to the movies (/to a restaurant/running to the police).

■   Er lief nach Hause (/zum Fleischer/zur Post/an den Strand/am Strand entlang/auf die Straße/auf den Rasen/zum Bahnhof/die Straße entlang/ durch den Park/in den Park/auf den Teppich).
He ran home (/to the butcher/to the post office/to the beach/along the beach/ into the street/onto the lawn/to the train station/along the road/ through the park/into the park/onto the rug).

■   Das Wasser ist durch die Decke (/über das Dach in den Gully/in die Rinnen) gelaufen.
The water ran through the ceiling (/over the roof into the drain/into the gutter).

■   Das Haus (/Auto/Konto) läuft auf den Namen meines Sohnes.
The house (/car/bank account) is in my son's name.

■   Mir lief der Schweiß über das Gesicht (/den Rücken).
Sweat ran down my face (/back).

■   Wann läuft der Film in diesem Kino (/im siebten Programm)?
When does the film run in this theater (/on Channel Seven)?

lauschen (+ prep)   to listen (for); to eavesdrop

- Er lauschte an der Tür, um das Gespräch seiner Eltern zu hören.
  He eavesdropped at the door in order to hear his parents' conversation.
- Sie hat am Fenster auf verdächtige Geräusche gelauscht.
  She listened at the window for suspicious sounds.

lauten auf + A ⟨auf etw l.⟩   to be (made out) for (sth); to be charged with (sth); to go for (sth)

- Der Scheck (/Paß/Ausweis) lautet auf den Namen Röhrs.
  The check (/passport/I.D. card) is made out in the name of Röhrs.
- Dieser Scheck lautet auf den Betrag von $100.
  This check is made out for (the amount of) $100.

leben (+ prep)   to live

- Er lebt bei seinen Eltern (/uns).
  He lives with his parents (/at our house).
- Er lebt nur für andere (/seine Frau/die Kunst/sich).
  He lives only for (or devotes his life to) others (/his wife/art/himself).
- Er lebte in Berlin (/in Amerika/in der Stadt/auf dem Lande/an der Küste/in der Vergangenheit/in einer Traumwelt).
  He lived in Berlin (/in America/in the city/in the country/at the coast/in the past/in a dream world).
- Er lebt über seine Verhältnisse.
  He lives beyond his means.
- Er lebt nach dem Grundsatz: „Jedem das Seine."
  He lives according to the principle, "To each his own."

leben von + D ⟨von etw l.⟩   to live *or* subsist (up)on (sth)

- Er lebt von seiner Arbeit (/seiner Rente/den Zinsen/seinem Sohn).
  He lives by (or subsists (on)) his work (/lives on his pension/lives on the income from the interest/subsists on his son's income).
- Man lebt nicht (nur) vom Brot allein. *(idiom)*
  One doesn't live on bread alone.
- Er hat einmal vom Malen (/Fußballspielen/Musizieren) gelebt.
  He once made a living by painting (/playing soccer/making music).

(s.) legen (+ prep)   to lay down; to lay; to put; to lie down

■   Ich muß das Tuch auf den Tisch (/über die Kommode) legen.
I have to lay the cloth on the table (/over the chest of drawers).

■   Sie hat die Wäsche in den Schrank gelegt.
She put the laundry in the closet.

■   Leg das in den Kühlschrank (/in das Wasser/über die Wunde/um deine Schultern/um den Hals)!
Put that in the refrigerator (/in the water/over the wound/around your shoulders/around your neck)!

■   Ich legte mich an den Strand (/in den Sand/auf den Sand/auf das Sofa/auf die Terrasse/in die Sonne/unter die Decke/auf den Bauch/auf den Rücken/auf die Seite/ins Bett/zu Bett).
I lay down at the beach (/in the sand/on the sand/on the sofa/on the terrace/in the sun/under the blanket/on my stomach/on my back/on my side/in the bed/went to bed, retired to bed).

(s.) lehnen an/gegen + A ⟨(sich) an/gegen jdn/etw l.⟩   to lean against/on (sth)

■   Ich lehnte mich an (*or* gegen) die Mauer (/den Baum).
I leaned against the wall (/tree).

■   Sie lehnte sich (/den Kopf) an die Schulter ihres Mannes.
She leaned (/her head) on her husband's shoulder.

■   Sie lehnte ihr Fahrrad an den Zaun (/an die Wand).
She leaned her bike against the fence (/wall).

s. lehnen über/aus + A/D ⟨sich über/aus etw l.⟩   to lean over/out of (sth)

■   Er lehnt sich über das Geländer (/ihn).
He's leaning over the railings (/him).

■   Sie hat sich aus dem Fenster gelehnt. Nicht aus dem Fenster lehnen!
She leaned out of the window. Do not lean out of the window!

leiden an + D ⟨an etw (Krankheit etc.) l.⟩   to suffer from (sth) (an illness)

■   Sie leidet an einer unbekannten Krankheit (/an Krebs/an Kopfschmerzen/an Heimweh).
She suffers from an unknown illness (/cancer/headaches/homesickness).

■   Leiden Sie an ansteckenden Krankheiten (/an Lungenentzündung)?
Do you suffer from any infectious diseases (/pneumonia)?

■   Er litt an Tuberkulose (/Altersbeschwerden).
He suffered from tuberculosis (/complaints of old age).

leiden unter + D ⟨unter jdm/etw l.⟩　to be suffering from (sb/sth)

- Sie leidet sehr unter ihren Kopfschmerzen (/ihrer Migräne).
  She is suffering a lot from her headaches (/migraine headaches).

- Sabine leidet unter der Hitze (/einem Minderwertigkeitskomplex/ihrem strengen Vater).
  Sabine is suffering from (or because of) the heat (/an inferiority complex/her strict father).

- Die Leute litten sehr unter den Auswirkungen des Erdbebens (/Tornados).
  The people suffered a lot from the effects of the earthquake (/tornado).

- Unsere Bilder (/Dias) haben unter der Feuchtigkeit im Keller gelitten.
  Our pictures (/slides) deteriorated because of the dampness in the basement.

leiten (+ prep)　to lead; to conduct

- Der Hinweis eines Zeugen leitete die Polizei an die richtige Stelle.
  A witness's tip led the police to the right place.

- Der Beamte hat den Antrag an die richtige Stelle weitergeleitet.
  The civil servant passed the application on to the proper authority.

- Mein Instinkt (/Weitblick) leitete mich zum Kauf des Hauses (/zu diesem Entschluß).
  My instinct (/insight) brought (or led) me to purchase this house (/make this decision).

- Das Öl (/Gas/Der Dampf) wird (durch Rohre) zum Hafen geleitet.
  The oil (/gas/steam) flows to the port (by pipeline).

s. leiten von + D ⟨sich von jdm/etw l. lassen⟩　to let oneself be guided by (sb/sth)

- Ich habe mich dabei von folgenden Erwägungen leiten lassen.
  I let myself be guided by the following considerations.

- Sie läßt sich von ihren Gefühlen (/Emotionen/ihrer Intuition) leiten.
  She is guided (or governed) by her feelings (/emotions/intuition).

lenken (+ prep)　to direct; to guide; to turn; to steer

- Ich mußte den Wagen nach links (/rechts) lenken.
  I had to steer the car to the left (/right).

- Der Verkäufer lenkte die Aufmerksamkeit des Kunden auf die neuen Computer (/Spielzeuge).
  The salesperson directed the customer's attention to the new computers (/toys).

- Sehr geschickt hat er die Unterhaltung auf sein Lieblingsthema gelenkt.
  He cleverly steered the conversation to his favorite topic.

- Sie versuchte, seine Aufmerksamkeit auf sich zu lenken.
  She tried to attract (or catch) his attention.
- Susannes Kind war schwer zu lenken.
  Suzanne's child was difficult to control.

lernen (+ prep)   to learn

- Er lernte aus dieser Erfahrung.
  He learned from this experience.
- Sein Bruder lernt jeden Tag mit ihm.
  His brother studies with him every day.
- Sie lernt bei der Firma Schmidt (/einem Schneider/einem Tischler).
  She's being trained (or doing an apprenticeship) at Schmidt's (/at a tailor's/at a carpenter's).
- In der Schule habe ich nichts über Verhütungsmittel (/das Mittelalter) gelernt.
  I learned nothing about contraceptives (/the Middle Ages) in school.

lernen von/bei + D ⟨etw von/bei jdm l.⟩   to learn (sth) from (sb)

- Bei (*or* von) wem lernst du Englisch? Bei (*or* Von) deinem Freund?
  Who teaches you English? Your friend?
- Er hat es von (*or* bei) seinem Vater gelernt. Von (*or* Bei) ihm lernte er viel.
  He learned it from his father. He learned a lot from him.

lesen (+ prep)   to read

- Mark liest gern Bücher (/Artikel) über deutsche Literatur.
  Mark likes to read books (/articles) about German literature.
- Ich habe den Bericht in der Zeitung (/im Buch) gelesen.
  I read the report in the newspaper (/book).
- Ich las in seinen Augen (/seinem Gesicht) pure Wut.
  I saw pure rage in his eyes (/face).
- Ich möchte jetzt das Gedicht aus dem Buch lesen.
  Now I would like to read the poem from the book.
- Aus (/In) seinen Zeilen (/diesem Brief) lese ich ein bißchen Sarkasmus (/eine Menge Neid).
  I detect a bit of sarcasm (/a lot of envy) from (/in) his lines (/this letter).
- Er liest mit Mühe.
  He has difficulty reading.
- Dieser Brief (/Rolfs Handschrift) ist schwer zu lesen.
  This letter (/Rolf's handwriting) is difficult to read.

liefern (+ prep)   to supply; to deliver

- Liefern Sie Ihre Güter ins Haus (/ins Ausland/nach Schweden)?
  Do you make home deliveries?(/Do you deliver your goods to the foreign market /Sweden)?

- Die Amerikaner haben den Flüchtlingen Vorräte mit dem Flugzeug geliefert.
  The Americans delivered supplies by plane to the refugees.

liegen (+ prep)   to lie; to be (in a certain place, position, *or* condition)

- Die Sache (/Katze) liegt unter (/vor/auf/in) dem Koffer.
  The thing (/cat) is under (/in front of/on/in) the suitcase.

- In der Stadt (/Auf dem Dach) lag viel Schnee.
  There was a lot of snow in the city (/on the roof).

- Meine Allergien (/Probleme) liegen hinter mir.
  My allergies (/problems) are behind me.

- Ich lag ganz nahe vor (/hinter) dem vierten Läufer. Später lag ich auf dem 5. Platz (/an der Spitze).
  I was not far in front of (/behind) the fourth runner. Later I was in fifth place (/in first place).

liegen an + D ⟨an jdm/etw l.⟩   to lie on (sb/sth); to depend on (sb/sth); to be up to (sb/sth)

- Er lag am Strand.
  He was lying at the beach.

- Diese Woche liegt die Platte an zweiter Stelle (der Hitparade).
  The record is number two this week (in the charts or hit parade).

- Der Hund hat an der Kette gelegen, als der Postbote kam.
  The dog was chained (up) when the postman arrived.

- Es liegt (ganz) an ihr (/meiner Arbeit/meiner Frau). Es lag an ihm (/meiner Arbeit/meiner Frau), daß. . . .
  It depends (totally) on (or is up to) her (/my work/my wife). It was because of him (/my work/my wife) that. . . .

- Soweit es an mir liegt, können wir jetzt gehen.
  As far as I'm concerned we can leave now.

- Woran liegt es? —Es liegt daran, daß. . . . —Daran liegt es. —An seiner Frechheit liegt es.
  What is the reason for that? —The reason is that. . . . — That's (the reason) why. —It's (because of) his impudence.

⟨jdm liegt an etw⟩   to be interested in (sth)

- Mir liegt nichts daran. Mir liegt an der schnellen Durchführung dieser Maßnahme.
  It's of no interest to me. or *I don't care about it. I'm concerned about the rapid execution of this measure.*

- Wem (/Was) liegt schon daran?
  Who cares (about it)? (/What does it matter?)

- Es liegt mir daran, zu. . . . *or* Mir ist daran gelegen, ...
  I'm anxious to. . . . or *I'm concerned about. . . .*

- Mir liegt viel (/wenig/nichts) an ihm.
  He means a lot (/little/nothing) to me.

liegen auf + D ⟨auf etw l.⟩   to lie *or* rest on (sth)

- Er liegt auf dem Sofa (/Sand/Bett/Boden).
  He is lying on the sofa (/sand/bed/floor).

- Ich lag auf dem Boden (/dem Bett/der Couch), um ein kleines Schläfchen zu machen.
  I was lying on the floor (the bed/the couch) to take a little nap.

- Sein Haus (/Der Laden) liegt nicht auf meinem Weg zur Schule.
  His house (/The store) is not on my way to school.

- Mein Geld liegt auf der Bank (/auf dem Sparkonto).
  My money is (deposited) in (or at) the bank (/in the savings account).

- Warum lag ein Lächeln auf seinem Gesicht?
  Why did he have a smile on his face?

- Wieviel Steuer liegt auf Alkohol (/ausländischen Produkten)?
  How much tax is there on alcohol (/foreign products)?

liegen bei + D ⟨bei jdm/etw l.⟩   to be up to (sb/sth); to lie with (sb/sth)

- Es liegt bei meinem Vater zu entscheiden, ob wir einen neuen Computer kaufen können.
  It is up to my father to decide if we can buy a new computer.

- Niemand weiß, bei wem die Verantwortung (/Schuld) liegt.
  No one knows with whom the responsibility (/fault) lies.

- Der Gewinn lag bei 2.000 Mark.
  The prize amounted to about 2,000 marks.

- Der amerikanische Soldat lag bei Berlin (/Honolulu).
  The American soldier was stationed near Berlin (/Honolulu).

liegen in + D ⟨in etw l.⟩   to lie in (sth)

- Wo liegt dein Hut? Im Schrank?
  Where is your hat? In the closet?

- Sie liegt im Krankenhaus (/in Zimmer 10/in der Sonne/im Schatten).
  She is in the hospital (/in room 10/lying in the sun/lying in the shade).

- Das Schiff lag im Hafen (/in der Nähe).
  The ship lay in the harbor (/nearby).

- Der Unterschied liegt in der Tatsache, daß. . . .
  The difference lies in the fact that. . . .

- In seiner Stimme lag Angst (/Wut/Freude).
  There was fear (/rage/joy) in his voice.

- Die Entscheidung hat in ihrer Kompetenz (/Hand) gelegen.
  The decision was (or lay) within her authority (/in her hands).

liegen nach + D ⟨nach etw l.⟩   to face (on) (sth)

- Der Balkon liegt nach der Straße (/den Bergen/Norden/hinten).
  The room faces (or looks) onto the street (/mountains/north/back).

locken (+ prep)   to lure

- Sie locken Kunden mit Sonderangeboten.
  They lure customers with special sales.

- Es (/Der Geruch/Das wunderbare Wetter) hat uns ins Freie (/zum See) gelockt.
  It (/The smell/The wonderful weather) lured us outside (/to the lake).

- Ich habe das Tier (mit Futter) ins Haus (/zu mir/in den Käfig/in einen Hinter-
  halt/aus dem Bau) gelockt.
  *I lured the animal (with food) into my house (/to me/into the cage/into a trap/out
  of the foxhole).*

- Sie lockten den Experten mit einem hohen Gehaltsangebot zu ihrer Firma.
  They lured the expert to their company with the offer of a high salary.

(s.) lösen aus + D ⟨sich/jdn/etw aus etw l.⟩   to extract (o.s./sb/sth) from (sth); to
free

- Er löste ein Blatt aus dem Heft.
  He tore out a page from the notebook.

- Hast du dich aus der Gruppe (/Menge/Verlobung/dem Vertrag) gelöst?
  Did you break away from the group (/crowd/your engagement/contract)?

■ Sie löste sich aus der Bevormundung durch ihre Mutter.
She freed herself from her mother's decision making.

(s.) lösen in + D ⟨**sich/etw in etw l.**⟩   to dissolve (sth) in (sth)

■ Zucker (/Dieses Medikament) löst sich leicht in Wasser (/in Milch). Du kannst Zucker leicht in Wasser lösen.
Sugar (/This medicine) dissolves easily in water (/milk). You can easily dissolve sugar in water.

■ Meine Angst löste sich in einem Seufzer (/in Lachen).
My fear found relief in a sigh (/laughter).

(s.) lösen von + D ⟨**(sich) von jdm/etw l.**⟩   to free oneself from (sb/sth); to break away from (sb/sth)

■ Sie hat sich von ihm (/ihren Verpflichtungen/Vorurteilen) gelöst.
She freed herself (or broke away) from him (/her obligations/prejudices).

■ Ich kann mich nur schwer von liebgewordenen Traditionen (/meiner Partei/alten Bindungen/meiner Heimat) lösen.
I have a hard time breaking away from cherished traditions (/my party/old ties/my home country).

■ Der Fleischer löste das Fleisch vom Knochen.
The butcher separated the meat from the bone.

■ Das Problem (/Die Schwierigkeit) wird sich von selbst lösen.
The problem (/difficulty) will resolve itself.

s. lustig machen über + A ⟨**sich über jdn/etw l. machen**⟩   to laugh at *or* make fun of (sb/sth)

■ Er machte sich über seine Schwester lustig, weil. . . .
He made fun of his sister because. . . .

■ Du sollst dich über ihren Haarschnitt nicht lustig machen.
You shouldn't make fun of her haircut.

M

s. machen (+ prep) ⟨sich auf den Weg/die Reise m.⟩   to set off for

- Du mußt dich bald auf den Weg (zur Schule) machen. Sonst kommst du zu spät.
  You will have to leave (for school) pretty soon. Otherwise, you'll be late.
- Im Juli machten sie sich auf die Reise nach Frankreich.
  In July they set off for France.

s. machen an + A ⟨sich an etw m.⟩   to get down to doing (sth); to tackle (sth)

- Ich muß mich jetzt an die Arbeit (/ans Kochen/ans Putzen) machen.
  I must set (or get down) to work (/cooking/cleaning).
- Wann wirst du dich endlich ans Mittagessen machen?
  When will you finally get down to making lunch?

machen auf + A ⟨auf etw m.⟩   to play (sth) *or* pretend (*inf*)

- Jetzt macht sie auf großen Star (/elegant/pazifistisch).
  She's pretending to be the star now (/elegant lady/pacifist).
- Nie kann er mal er selbst sein. Er macht immer auf Schau.
  He just cannot be himself. He's always out for effect.

machen aus + D ⟨etw aus sich/jdm/etw m.⟩   to make (sth) of (o.s./sb/sth); to make (sth) (out) of (o.s./sb/sth); to turn *or* make (o.s./sb/sth) into (sth)

- Was kann man aus diesem Material machen?—Daraus kannst du ein Puppenhaus (/einen Rock) machen.
  What can one make out of this material?—You can make a doll house (/skirt).
- Er macht eine große Sache aus seinen Platten (/seiner Fähigkeit, Schach zu spielen).
  He makes a big thing of his albums (/his ability to play chess).
- Der Lehrer hat aus ihm schließlich einen sehr fleißigen (/toleranten) Jungen gemacht.
  The teacher finally made a very industrious (/tolerant) boy out of him.
- Er ist eigentlich nicht sehr begabt. Aber er macht viel aus seinen geringen Anlagen.
  Actually, he is not very gifted. But he makes a lot of the little talent he has.

- Der Tisch ist aus Aluminium (/Holz) gemacht.
  The table is made from aluminum (/wood).

- Er ist nicht das, was die Leute aus ihm machen.
  He isn't what people try to make him out to be.

- Man macht Brot aus Mehl. Der Tisch ist aus Eiche gemacht.
  One makes bread from flour. The table is made of oak.

s. machen aus + D ⟨**sich etw aus jdm/etw m.**⟩   to care *or* worry about (sb/sth)

- Ich mache mir nicht viel aus Bohnen (/Schinken).
  I don't care much for beans (/ham).

- Mach dir nichts aus dem Gerede (/Quatsch)!
  Don't let the gossip (/nonsense) worry you!

- Mach dir nichts daraus!
  Don't worry! Don't let it bother you!

- Sie macht sich nichts aus ihm.
  She doesn't like him.

- Ich mache mir ein Vergnügen aus diesem Treffen (/dieser Arbeit/dieser Wanderung).
  [I've made up my mind that] this meeting (/work/hiking) is going to be enjoyable.

machen mit + D ⟨**etw mit jdm m.**⟩   to make *or* do (sth) with (sb)

- Du kannst mit ihm (/der übriggebliebenen Speise) machen, was du willst.
  You can do what you like with him (/the left-over food).

- Immer kriege ich die meiste Arbeit. Mit mir kann man's ja machen.
  I always get the biggest workload. I just get pushed around.

- Warum läßt du alles mit dir machen?
  Why do you submit to (or put up with) everything?

- Er machte mit ihm einen Vertrag (/ein Geschäft/eine Abmachung).
  He made a contract (/deal/an arrangement) with him.

- Was kann man mit diesem Werkzeug machen?
  What can one do (accomplish) with this tool?

machen zu + D ⟨**jdn/etw zu jdm/etw m.**⟩   to make (sb/sth) (sb/sth); to turn (sb/sth) into (sb/sth)

- Er machte sie zu seiner Frau (/zur Sprecherin/zur Sekretärin/zur Geliebten/zur Partnerin/sich zum Feind/zur Sklavin/zur Gefangenen).
  He made her his wife (/spokeswoman/secretary/mistress/partner/enemy/slave/ prisoner).

■ Sie machen den schönen Wald zur Wüste.
They're turning the beautiful forest into a desert.

mahnen wegen + G ⟨**jdn wegen etw m.**⟩ to warn (sb) on account of (sth)

■ Die Firma hat ihn wegen eines Zahlungsversäumnisses gemahnt.
The company warned him about a missing payment.

mahnen zu + D ⟨**jdn zu etw m.**⟩ to admonish *or* warn (sb) (for sth)

■ Die Zeit (/Uhr) mahnt uns zum Aufbruch (/zur Eile).
The time (/clock) reminds (or warns) us that we must leave (/hurry).

■ Ich habe ihn zur Geduld (/Eile/Ruhe) gemahnt.
I warned (or urged) him to be patient (/to hurry/to be quiet).

mangeln an + D ⟨**an jdm/etw m.**⟩ to be lacking in (sb/sth)

■ Es mangelte an nichts.
Nothing was wanting. There was plenty of everything.

■ Es mangelte an Medikamenten (/Wasser/Geld/Arbeitskräften/Vorräten).
There was a shortage of medicine (/water/money/a work force/supplies).

⟨**es mangelt jdm an jdm/etw**⟩ to be lacking (in) (sb/sth)

■ Es mangelt ihm an Vernunft (/Verständnis/Einsicht).
He is lacking in (or he lacks) reason (/understanding/insight).

■ Es mangelt Ihnen an guten Vorschlägen (/Einfällen/nichts).
You are lacking in good suggestions (/ideas/You lack nothing).

■ Es mangelt ihm an Selbstvertrauen.
He lacks self-confidence.

meinen mit + D ⟨**etw mit etw/es mit jdm m.**⟩ to mean by (sth); to mean well by (sb)

■ Was meinst du damit (/mit dieser Bemerkung)?
What do you mean by that (/this remark)?

■ Was meint er mit diesem teuren Geschenk?
What does he intend (or is he up to) with this expensive gift?

■ Was meint der Autor mit diesem Wort?
What does the author intend to say with this word?

■ Der Junge hat es nicht ehrlich mit dem Mädchen (/ihr) gemeint.
The boy's intentions towards the girl (/her) were not honorable.

■ Sie meint es gut mit dir.
She means well by you.

(s.) melden (+ prep)   to report; to answer; to sign up for

■ Er will sich zum Dienst (/zum Wehrdienst/zur Prüfung/zu einer Aufgabe/zu Wort) melden.
He wants to report for duty (/military service/the examination/a task/to speak or ask for the floor).

■ Ich möchte mich für diesen Lehrgang (/den Psychologiekurs) melden.
I would like to sign up for this course (/the psychology workshop).

■ Wie diese Zeitung aus Frankfurt meldet,. . . .
As this newspaper from Frankfurt reports, . . .

■ Ich werde mich auf diese Anzeige melden.
I will answer this advertisement.

■ Der Nachbar hat ihn wegen eines Vergehens (/einer ansteckenden Krankheit) gemeldet.
The neighbor reported him because of an offense (/a contagious disease).

■ Ich habe mich sofort am Telephon gemeldet.
I answered the telephone right away.

■ Für das Wochenende ist Schnee gemeldet.
Snow is forecast for the weekend.

(s.) melden bei + D ⟨(sich) bei jdm m.⟩   to report to (sb); to register by (sb)

■ Wir müssen den Vorfall (/Verlust) bei der Behörde melden.
We must report the incident (/loss) to the authorities.

■ Wir müssen uns bei der Polizei melden.
We must register with the police.

■ Er hat ihn (/den Unfall) bei der Polizei gemeldet.
He reported him (/the accident) to the police.

■ Ich werde Sie beim Direktor (/Chef) melden.
I will tell the director (/boss) that you are here.

(s.) messen an + D ⟨jdn/etw an jdm/etw m.⟩   to compare (sb/sth) with (sb/sth)

■ Du kannst dich mit ihm an Wissen (/Körperkraft) sicherlich messen.
You can certainly compare with (or match) him in knowledge (/physical power).

■ Gemessen an ihren Bodenschätzen hat die Sowjetunion eine geringe Wirtschaftskraft.
Considering its natural resources, the Soviet Union's economic power is minimal.

■ An dir gemessen, ißt er wenig.
Compared to you, he eats little.

■ Es wäre nicht richtig, ihn an seinem älteren Bruder zu messen.
It wouldn't be appropriate to compare him with his older brother.

messen mit + D ⟨jdn/etw mit etw m.⟩   to measure (sb/sth) with/against (sth)

■ Er mißt die Größe (/Länge/Breite) des Fensters (mit einem Maßband).
He's measuring the height (/length/width) of the window (with a tape measure).

■ Ich habe mich (/meine Tochter) mit dem Zollstock gemessen.
I measured myself (/my daughter) with the yardstick.

■ Der Arzt maß die Temperatur des Jungen mit einem Thermometer.
The doctor took the boy's temperature with a thermometer.

■ Ihr dürft nicht mit zweierlei Maß messen.
You mustn't judge by (two) different standards.

(s.) messen mit + D ⟨sich/etw mit jdm/etw m.⟩   to be a match for (sb/sth); to compare one's power *or* ability with (sb/sth)

■ Er mißt sich (/seine Kraft) mit seinem älteren Bruder (/mit der seines älteren Bruders).
He measures himself (/his power) against his older brother (/with that of his older brother).

■ Sie maß sich mit ihm (/dem Herausforderer) im Laufen.
She ran (or raced) against him (/the challenger).

■ In Mathematik kann ich mich mit jedem messen.
I can hold my own with anyone in math.

■ Ich kann mich nicht mit ihm messen. Er ist viel klüger (/kräftiger).
I am no match for him. He is much smarter (/stronger).

messen nach + D ⟨etw nach etw m.⟩   to measure (sth) in (sth)

■ In diesem Land mißt man Flüßigkeiten nach Gallonen (/Litern).
In this country people measure liquids in gallons (/liters).

■ Ich maß den Stoff einmal nach Zentimetern und einmal nach Zoll.
I measured the material once in centimeters and once in inches.

mitmachen bei + D ⟨bei etw m.⟩   to join in (sth); to participate in (sth)

- Der gute Schüler macht beim Unterricht (/Rechnen/Lesen/Schreiben) immer mit.
  The good student always takes an active part (or participates) in class (/math/ reading/writing).
- Sie hat bei allen Spielen (/bei dem Ausflug) mitgemacht.
  She took part in all games (/joined in the excursion).
- Bei der Mode machen einige Leute immer mit.
  Some people always follow the fashion.
- Willst du dabei (/beim Spielen) mitmachen?
  Do you want to join in (/join in the play)?

mitmachen (without prep)   to join in; to participate

- Machst du mit?—Ja, ich mache alles mit.
  Are you going to join in?—Yes, I'm game for anything.
- Ich habe den Ausflug mitgemacht.
  I joined the excursion.

mitwirken an/bei + D ⟨an/bei etw m.⟩   to play a part in (sth); to contribute to (sth); to be involved in (sth); to collaborate on (sth)

- Diese Autoren wirken an (*or* bei) dem Buch auch mit.
  These authors are also contributing to the book.
- Er wollte bei der Organisation der Festlichkeiten mitwirken.
  He wanted to be involved in the organization of the festivities.
- Sie wirkten an der Gründung der Jugendbewegung mit.
  They played a part in the founding of the youth movement.
- Der Zeuge hat an (*or* bei) der Auklärung des Diebstahls mitgewirkt.
  The witness played a part in solving the theft.
- Hast du daran (*or* dabei) auch mitgewirkt?
  Were you also involved in that?

N

nachdenken über + A ⟨**über jdn/etw n.**⟩ to reflect on (sth); to ponder on/over (sth)

- Ich dachte gründlich über meine Antwort (/die Frage) nach.
  I thought over my answer (/the question) carefully.

- Bevor ich etwas zu diesem Problem sage, möchte ich erst einmal darüber nachdenken.
  Before I say anything about this problem, I would like to think about it first.

- Ich dachte lange darüber nach, wie ich den Essay schreiben (/den Brief beginnen) sollte.
  I pondered a long time over how I should write the essay (/how I should begin the letter).

- Ich habe intensiv über den Tod meines Freundes (/das Erlebnis) nachgedacht.
  I spent a lot of time thinking about the death of my friend (/experience).

- Denk doch mal nach! Darüber darf man gar nicht nachdenken.
  Think about it! It doesn't bear thinking about.

- Er dachte lange über das Mädchen nach, dem er gerade begegnet war.
  He thought a long time about the girl he had just met.

nachkommen mit + D ⟨**mit etw n.**⟩ to keep up with (sth)

- Die Firma kam mit den Lieferungen (/der Herstellung) nicht nach.
  The company didn't keep up with deliveries (/the production).

- Das Kind konnte mit seinen kurzen Beinen nicht nachkommen.
  The child wasn't able to keep up because of his short legs.

- Die Schüler sind mit dem Diktat nicht nachgekommen.
  The students didn't keep up with the dictation.

- Karl fährt zu schnell. Wir können mit unserem Auto nicht nachkommen.
  Karl is driving too fast. We can't keep up with our car.

nähen (+ prep) to sew

- Sie nähte das Kleid mit der Maschine (/mit der Hand).
  She sewed the dress by machine (/hand).

- Der Arzt hat die Wunde (mit einem Faden) genäht.
  The doctor stitched the wound.

nähen an/auf + A ⟨etw an/auf etw n.⟩   to sew (sth) (on)to (sth)

- Er nähte den Knopf (/den Ärmel/den Reißverschluß) an die Jacke.
  He sewed the button (/sleeve/zipper into) on(to) the jacket.
- Die Mutter hat eine Blume auf die Bluse genäht.
  The mother sewed a flower on the blouse.

naschen an/von + D ⟨an/von etw n.⟩   to eat sweet things; (*secretly*) to pinch a bit of (sth); to nibble at (sth)

- Ich naschte Schokolade (*or an or* von der Schokolade).
  I nibbled on chocolate.
- Wer hat von (*or* an) den Süßigkeiten genascht?
  Who's been at the sweets?

necken mit + D ⟨jdn mit jdm/etw n.⟩   to tease (sb) about (sb/sth)

- Nun necke ihn doch nicht immer mit seiner jüngeren Schwester (/seiner Glatze)!
  Stop teasing him about his younger sister (/bald head)!
- Sein Freund neckt ihn mit seiner Schwäche für gute Weine.
  His friend teases him about his weakness for good wines.

s. necken mit + D ⟨sich mit jdm n.⟩   to tease each other

- Du solltest dich nicht so viel mit ihm necken.
  You and he shouldn't tease each other so much.

nehmen (+ prep)   to take

- Ich habe die Kiste an Bord (/unter den Arm/ins Auto) genommen.
  I took the box on board (/under my arm/into the car).
- Wieviel hat er für den Hut genommen?—Er nahm acht Mark dafür.
  How much did he take (or charge you) for the hat?—He charged eight marks for it.
- Er nimmt Nachhilfe in Englisch und Mathe.
  He's getting help in English and math.
- Sie haben ihn in die Mitte (*or* zwischen sich) genommen.
  They put him between them.

nehmen an + A ⟨etw an sich n.⟩   to take (sth); to (mis)appropriate (sth)

- Ich werde das Paket (/den Brief) vorläufig an mich nehmen.
  I'll take (or accept) the package (/letter) temporarily.
- Er hat das Geld an sich genommen. (Ich habe keine Ahnung, wo es ist.)
  He took the money. (I have no idea where it is.)

nehmen auf + A ⟨etw auf sich n.⟩   to take (sth) upon oneself; to undertake (to do) (sth)

- Ich habe es auf mich genommen, den Arbeiter zu entlassen.
  I took it upon myself to fire the worker.
- Der Polizist nahm es auf sich, die Ehefrau über den Unfall ihres Mannes zu unterrichten.
  The policeman took it upon himself to notify the wife of her husband's accident.
- Ich nahm die Folgen (/Bürde/Last) auf mich.
  I took the consequences (/burden/weight) upon myself.
- Du mußt selbst die Verantwortung dafür auf dich nehmen.
  You have to take the responsibility for that yourself.

nehmen auf + A ⟨jdn/etw auf etw n.⟩   to take (sb/sth) on/upon (sth)

- Sie hat das Kind auf den Arm (/auf den Schoß/auf die Schulter) genommen.
  She took the child in her arms (/on her lap/on her shoulder).
- Er nahm den Sack auf den Rücken.
  He put the sack on his back.

nehmen aus/von + D ⟨jdn/etw aus/von etw n.⟩   to take (sth) out of/from (sth)

- Er nahm ein Buch aus (*or* von) dem Regal.
  He took a book from the shelf.
- Sie nahm das Portemonnaie aus der Tasche.
  She took the purse out of the bag.
- Sie mußten ihr Kind aus der Schule nehmen, weil es nur Ärger machte.
  They had to take their child out of the school because he only caused trouble.
- Er nimmt die Vase vom (/aus dem) Schrank.
  He's taking the vase from (/out of) the closet.

nehmen für + A ⟨etw für etw n.⟩   to take (sth) for (sth)

- Er hat seine Ankunft für (*or* als) ein günstiges Omen (/Zeichen) genommen.
  He took his arrival for (or as) a good omen (/sign).

- Er hat mein Gerede (/meine Aussagen) für bare Münze (/als Scherz) genommen.
  He took my gibberish (/statements) for the truth (/as a joke).

nehmen zu + D ⟨etw zu sich n.⟩   to eat (sth)

- Der Patient nahm nichts (/zwei Tabletten/ein Glas Wasser) zu sich.
  The patient didn't eat anything (/took two pills/had a glass of water).
- Ich nahm eine Kleinigkeit (/eine Gewürzgurke) zu mir.
  I had (or helped myself to) a little snack (/a pickle).

nehmen zu + D ⟨jdn zu sich n.⟩   to adopt (sb); to take a spouse

- Ich habe ein Waisenkind (/meinen alten Opa) zu mir genommen.
  I adopted an orphan child (/had my old grandpa living with me).
- Er nahm sie zur Frau. Sie nahm ihn zum Mann.
  He married her. (or He took her as his wife.) She married him. (or She took him as her husband.)
- Gott hat sie zu sich genommen.
  God took her away.

(s.) neigen (+ prep)   to bend

- Ich neigte mich nach vorne (/hinten).
  I leaned (or bent) forward (/backwards).
- Die Leiter neigt sich leicht zur Seite.
  The ladder is leaning (or tilting) over slightly.
- Er neigte das Haupt (*or* den Kopf) als Zeichen der Demut.
  He bowed his head as a sign of humility.
- Ich habe mich über mein Kind (/die Wiege des Babys) geneigt.
  I leaned over my child (/the baby's cradle).

neigen zu + D ⟨zu etw n.⟩   to tend to (sth); to be prone *or* susceptible to (sth)

- Der Autor neigte zu kommunistischen Anschauungen (/zur sozialistischen Partei).
  The author leaned towards communist ideas (/the socialist party).
- Ich neige dazu, das Angebot abzulehnen.
  I tend to think I'll refuse the offer.
- Ich neige zu der Annahme, daß die Bears Meister werden.
  I tend to think that the Bears will be champs again.

- Sie neigt zur Rockmusik (/zu sportlichen Autos).
  She rather leans towards rock music (/sport cars).

- Ich neige im Winter zu verschiedenen Krankheiten (/zur Grippe).
  I'm susceptible to different illnesses (/getting the flu) in winter.

- Sein Freund neigt zum Ausgleich (/zur Verschwendung/zum Alkohol/zur Lüge).
  His friend is prone to finding compromises (/wasting money/is prone to drink/tends to lie).

s. niederlassen (+ prep)   to sit down; to settle; to set up (sth)

- Das Unternehmen hat sich in Chikago niedergelassen.
  The firm set up (a business) in Chicago.

- Die Taube ließ sich auf dem (*or* auf den) Zweig nieder.
  The pigeon was sitting (or alighted) on the branch.

- Ich ließ mich in dem Sessel (/am Tisch) nieder.
  I sat down in the armchair (/at the table).

s. niederlassen als + N ⟨**sich als etw (Arzt, Rechtsanwalt, usw) n.**⟩   to set up as

- 1989 habe ich mich als Arzt (/Rechtsanwalt/Geschäftsmann) in dieser Stadt niedergelassen.
  In 1989 I set up (a practice) as a doctor (/lawyer/businessman) in this city.

s. niederschlagen in + D ⟨**sich in etw n.**⟩   to result in (sth); to be reflected in (sth)

- Die Untersuchung der Polizei schlug sich in fünf Verhaftungen nieder.
  The police investigation resulted in five arrests.

- Die Steuerreform wird sich in einer ungerechten Einkommensverteilung niederschlagen.
  The tax reform will result in an unjust distribution of income.

nörgeln an + D ⟨**an jdm/etw n.**⟩   to grumble *or* moan *or* nag about (sb/sth)

- Er muß stets an allem nörgeln.
  He always has to moan about everything.

nörgeln über + A ⟨**über jdn/etw n.**⟩   to crab *or* moan about (sb/sth)

- Viele Lehrer tendieren dazu, über den Schulleiter zu nörgeln.
  Many teachers have a tendency to crab about their principal.

■ Hör auf, immer über das Essen zu nörgeln!
Stop moaning about the food!

notieren (+ prep)   to note down; to make a note of; to jot down; to book

■ Ich notiere den Termin (/die Verabredung/die Addresse) im Kalender.
I'll jot down the date (/appointment/address) in the calendar.

■ Ich habe deinen Namen auf einem Zettel notiert.
I wrote down your name on a piece of paper.

■ Wir haben Sie für den Lehrgang (/die Fahrstunden) notiert.
We have registered (or enrolled) you for the course (/driving lessons).

nutzen *or* nützen (+ prep)   to be of use; to be useful

■ Das Medikament nutzt gegen (*or* bei) Kopfschmerzen.
The medicine is useful against/for headaches.

■ Ich will die Zeit nutzen, um noch etwas zu erledigen.
I want to use the time to get something done.

nutzen zu + D ⟨jdn/etw zu etw n.⟩   to be useful to (sb) for (sth)

■ Ich muß diese Gelegenheit zu meinem Vorteil (/zum Studieren/zu körperlichen Übungen/zum Training/dazu) nutzen.
I must use this opportunity for my advantage (/studying/exercise/training/that).

■ Ich nutze mein Auto nur zu dem Zweck, zur Arbeit zu fahren.
I only use my car to drive to work.

O

ordnen (+ prep)   to order; to organize

- Wir ordnen diese Akten (/Verben) nach dem Alphabet.
  We're alphabetizing these files (/verbs).
- Die Menschenmenge ordnete sich zu einem Festzug.
  The crowd organized itself into a procession.
- Die Frau hat die Blumen zu einem Strauß geordnet.
  The woman arranged the flowers in a bouquet.

s. organisieren zu/als + D/N ⟨(sich) zu/als etw o.⟩   to organize into (sth)

- Die Bürger haben sich zu einer Partei (*or* als Partei) organisiert.
  The citizens have organized themselves into a party.
- Die Soldaten organisierten sich zu einer Marschkolonne (*or* als Marschkolonne).
  The soldiers organized themselves into a column.

(s.) orientieren (+ prep)   to orientate, to orient; to find one's way

- Kannst du dich von diesem Ort (nach Hause) orientieren?
  Can you find your way (home) from this place?
- Es ist unmöglich, sich in dieser Gegend zu orientieren.
  It is impossible to find your way in this neighborhood.

s. orientieren an + D ⟨sich an jdm/etw o.⟩   to orientate oneself with/towards (sb/sth);
to model oneself after (sb/sth)

- Der Vertreter hat sich an den Wünschen der Kunden orientiert.
  The salesman adapted his actions to meet the wishes of his customers.
- Jugendliche neigen dazu, sich mit ihrem Lebensstil an Popstars zu orientieren.
  Teenagers tend to model their lifestyles after (those of) popstars.

orientieren auf + A ⟨jdn/etw auf etw o.⟩   to orientate *or* orient to (sb/sth) with/for
(sth)

- Wir müssen die Tätigkeiten auf bestimmte Ziele orientieren.
  We must direct the activities towards certain aims.

■ Man muß Kinder auf Werte wie Ehrlichkeit (/Bescheidenheit/Fleiß) orientieren.
Children must be instructed about values like honesty (/modesty/hard work).

■ Er ist ganz auf die Werte seiner Gesellschaftsschicht (/italienische Mode) orientiert.
He is thoroughly oriented towards the values of his social class (/Italian fashion).

s. orientieren über + A ⟨jdn über etw o.⟩   to put (sb) in the picture about (sth); to be informed

■ Dieser Reiseprospekt orientiert (Sie) über verschiedene Reiseziele.
This travel brochure gives (you) information about various travel destinations.

■ Sie werden morgen eine Party geben? Darüber war ich nicht orientiert.
They are giving a party tomorrow? I didn't know about that.

■ Er ist über die Ereignisse in Arabien bestens orientiert.
He is well-informed about the events in Arabia.

■ Der Junge hat den Vater darüber nicht orientert, daß er bei der Prüfung durchgefallen ist.
The boy didn't inform his father of having failed the test.

s. orientieren über + A ⟨sich über etw o.⟩   to collect *or* obtain information about (sth)

■ Ich habe mich bereits über die Preise für Videorekorder informiert.
I have already obtained information about the prices of VCRs.

■ Hast du dich über den Vorfall orientiert?
Have you collected information about the incident?

■ Als neuer Personalchef sollte er sich über die Arbeitsbedingungen seiner Angestellten orientieren.
As the new personnel manager he should obtain information about the working conditions of his employees.

P

packen (+ prep)   to pack

- Sie packte die Kleider (/Bücher) in den Koffer (/die Tasche).
  She packed (or put) the dresses (/books) into the suitcase (/bag).

- Packen Sie bitte das Geschenk in Papier (/Watte).
  Please pack (up) (or wrap) the gift in paper (/in cotton).

- Wir müssen das Gepäck auf (/in) den Wagen packen.
  We have to put the luggage on (/in) the car.

- Er hat alle Koffer (/das Zelt) oben auf das Auto gepackt.
  He packed all the suitcases (/the tent) on top of the car.

- Ich muß jetzt das Kind ins Bett (/in eine Decke) packen. *(inf)*
  I have to tuck the child in (/wrap the child in a blanket).

packen (+ prep)   to grab (hold of); to seize

- Er hat ihn am (*or* beim) Kragen (/Mantel/am Arm/am Hals) gepackt.
  He grabbed (or seized) him by his collar (/coat/arm/neck).

- Der Hund hat ihn an der Hose (/am Bein) gepackt.
  The dog grabbed him by his pants (/his leg).

- Die Leidenschaft für Mozart (/Liebe zu van Gogh) hat ihn gepackt.
  Passion for Mozart (/Love for van Gogh) has taken hold of him.

passen (+ prep)   to fit; to suit

- Dieser Deckel paßt nicht auf die Dose (/das Gefäß/die Flasche).
  This lid doesn't fit the can (/jar/bottle).

- Was der Zeuge beschrieb, paßte haargenau auf Herrn Tilgner.
  What the witness described fit Mr. Tilgner exactly (or to a T).

- Der Nachttisch paßt nicht neben (/unter) die Lampe.
  The nightstand doesn't look good (or go) next to (/under) the light fixture.

- Diese Schraube paßt nicht in die Mutter.
  This screw doesn't fit into the nut.

- Das paßt gut unter das Bett (/in den Schrank/in meinen Plan).
  That fits well under the bed (/in the closet/in my plan).

- Dieser Schraubenzieher paßt nicht für diese Schraube.
  This isn't the right screwdriver for this screw.

- Mein Schlüssel paßt nicht (ins Schloß).
  My key doesn't fit (the lock).
- Das Bild paßt besser in das andere Zimmer.
  The picture looks (or goes) better in the other room.

passen zu + D ⟨**zu jdm/etw p.**⟩   to go *or* match with (sth); to be suited to (sb); to suit (sb)

- Das gute Hemd paßt nicht zu seinen Jeans.
  The formal shirt doesn't go with (or match) his jeans.
- Der Lippenstift paßt nicht zu ihrem Gesicht (/blonden Haar).
  The lipstick isn't suited to (or doesn't match) her face (/blond hair).
- Der Teppich paßt gut zur Couch (/zu den Möbeln/zu den Vorhängen).
  The rug matches (or goes well with) the couch (/furniture/curtains).
- Das junge Ehepaar paßt (/Diese Zutaten passen) gut zueinander.
  The new married couple is (/These ingredients are) well-matched (or well-suited for each other).
- Diese bittere Bemerkung paßt nicht zu dir.
  This bitter remark is not your style (or like you).

passen (without prep)   to fit

- Das Hemd paßt mir nicht.
  The shirt doesn't fit me.
- Wann paßt es Ihnen? Paßt es Ihnen morgen (/am Freitag)?
  What time suits you? Would tomorrow (/Friday) be okay?
- Wenn es dem Lehrer paßt, können wir den Aufsatz verschieben.
  If it suits the teacher, we can postpone the essay.
- Das paßt mir gar nicht, daß du immer zu spät kommst.
  I don't like the fact that you always come late.
- Dein neuer Haarschnitt (/Der neue Ansager) paßt ihr überhaupt nicht.
  She doesn't like your new haircut (/the new announcer).

pfeifen (+ prep)   to whistle

- Das Kind kann gut auf den Fingern (/durch die Zähne/mit der Pfeife) pfeifen.
  The child can whistle well with his fingers (/through his teeth/with the whistle).
- Ich frage mich, warum er immer vor sich hin pfeift.
  I wonder why he always whistles to (or by) himself.
- Eine Kugel pfiff ihm um die Ohren.
  A bullet whistled by his ears.

pfeifen (without prep)   to whistle

- Bärbel pfiff ihrem Hund (/ihrem Pferd/dem Tier).
  Bärbel whistled for her dog (/her horse/the animal).
- Herr Bandorf pfeift dieses Spiel.
  Mr. Bandorf is going to referee this match.

pflegen zu (+ infinitive)   to be in the habit of; to be accustomed to

- Er pflegte mit dem Fahrrad nach Hause (/zur Schule) zu fahren.
  He used to ride his bike home (/to school).
- Zum Frühstück pflegte ich ein weichgekochtes Ei zu essen.
  I was in the habit of eating one soft boiled egg for breakfast.
- Wie mein Großvater zu sagen pflegte, „Wer den Pfennig nicht ehrt, ist des Talers nicht wert."
  As my grandfather used to say, "A penny saved, is a penny earned."

(s.) plagen (+ prep)   to bother; to plague; to torment; to pester

- Ich wurde von Kopfschmerzen (/einer Krankheit/ihm) geplagt.
  I was plagued by a headache (/an illness/I was pestered by him).
- Die Kinder haben die Mutter den ganzen Tage mit Wünschen (/Fragen) geplagt.
  The children pestered their mother with requests (/questions) all day.
- Ich habe mich mit dieser Arbeit (/einer Erkältung) geplagt.
  I was plagued by this work (/a cold).

plagen (without prep)   to plague, to torment; to pester, to harass, to bother

- Die Kälte (/Der Hunger/Sein Freund) plagt mich nicht.
  Cold (/Hunger/His friend) doesn't bother me.

prahlen mit + D ⟨mit etw p.⟩   to boast *or* brag about (sth)

- Er prahlt mit seiner Bildung (/seinem Können/seinem Geld/seinem Aussehen).
  He boasts about his education (/ability/money/looks).

(s.) präparieren (+ prep)   to prepare

- Ich muß mich für das Spiel (/die Schule/auf den Unterricht/für eine Herausforderung) präparieren.
  I must prepare myself for the match (/school/class/a challenge).

■ Ich präpariere meinen Sohn für den entscheidenden Test.
I am preparing my son for the test which will decide the matter.

protestieren gegen + A ⟨gegen jdn/etw p.⟩   to protest about/against (sb/sth)

■ Sie protestieren gegen ihn (/seine Programme/die niedrigen Löhne).
They're protesting against him (/his programs/the low wages).

■ Ich protestiere dagegen, daß die Stadt nichts gegen den Smog tut.
I protest the city's stand of not doing anything about the smog.

protzen mit + D ⟨mit jdm/etw p.⟩   to show (sb/sth) off, to brag about (sb/sth)

■ Er protzt immer mit seinem Reichtum (/seiner Kraft/seinen Erfolgen).
He always brags about his wealth (/power/successes).

■ Die Familie protzte mit ihren klugen Kindern (/ihren adligen Vorfahren).
The family bragged about their intelligent children (/their aristocratic ancestors).

prüfen auf + A ⟨jdn/etw auf etw p.⟩   to check (sb/sth) for (sth)

■ Sie haben das Bier auf seine Reinheit (/Beschaffenheit) geprüft.
They checked the beer for its purity (/composition).

■ Man prüft jetzt die Sportler auf Drogen (/Anabolika).
They are checking the athletes now for drugs (/steroids).

■ Der Politiker ist schon auf seine Ehrlichkeit geprüft worden.
The politician has already been checked (or screened) for his honesty.

prüfen in + D ⟨jdn in etw p.⟩   to examine (sb) in (sth)

■ Der Lehrer wird die Schüler in Biologie prüfen.
The teacher will test the students in biology.

■ Wann wird in Französisch geprüft?
When is the French exam?

s. prügeln mit + D ⟨sich mit jdm p.⟩   to fight (sb)

■ Bernd hat sich mit Jürgen wegen Monika geprügelt.
Bernd had a (fist) fight with Jürgen because of Monika.

■ Willst du dich wieder mit mir prügeln?
Do you want to fight (with) me again?

s. prügeln um + A ⟨**sich um jdn/etw p.**⟩   to fight over *or* for (sth)

- Sie haben sich um die besten Plätze (/Spieler) mit mir im Stadion geprügelt.
  They fought with me for the best seats in the stadium (/over who the best players are).

- Er prügelte sich mit ihm um das Geld.
  He fought with him over the money.

Q

(s.) quälen (+ prep)   to bother; to torment; to be bothered *or* pestered; to struggle

- Er wurde von Schmerzen (/Hunger/Reue) gequält.
  He was tormented by (or tortured with) pain (/hunger/remorse).

- Der Patient wird von starkem Husten (/Kopfschmerzen) gequält.
  The patient is troubled by a bad cough (/headache).

- Der Bohrer quält sich in (/durch) dieses dicke Metal.
  The drill has a hard time (drilling) in (/through) this thick metal.

- Ich habe mich durch den tiefen Schnee (/dieses Buch/meine Kindheit) gequält.
  I struggled through the deep snow (/this book/my childhood).

- Meine Oma quält sich morgens nur mühsam aus dem Bett.
  My grandma really struggles to get out of bed in the mornings.

- Ich mußte mich immer quälen, um eine gute Note in Mathe zu kriegen.
  I always had to struggle to get a good grade in math.

quälen mit + D ⟨jdn mit etw q.⟩   to pester (sb) by/with (sth)

- Der Autor quält seine Leser gern mit den grausigsten Horrorgeschichten.
  The author likes to torment his readers with the most grisly horror stories.

- Das Kind quält mich schon seit Tagen mit dem Wunsch (/der Bitte), in den Zirkus (/Vergnügungspark) gehen zu dürfen.
  The child has been pestering me for days with his desire (/request) to be allowed to go to the circus (/amusement park).

   ⟨sich quälen mit etw⟩   to be bothered *or* pestered by/with (sth)

   - Diese Gedanken quälen mich. Quäl dich nicht mit diesen deprimierenden Gedan ken (/Entwicklungen/Problemen)!
     These thoughts torment me. Don't think about (or torment yourself with) these depressing thoughts (/developments/problems).

   - Er quält sich mit der Entscheidung zwischen zwei Frauen (herum).
     He is troubled by having to choose between two women.

(s.) qualifizieren für + A ⟨sich für etw q.⟩   to qualify for (sth)

- Konntest du dich für die Olympischen Spiele (/das Halbfinale) qualifizieren?
  Were you able to qualify for the Olympic games (/the semifinals)?

■ Kann man sich für diesen Job (/Posten) qualifizieren, wenn man einen Kurs besucht?
Can a person qualify for this job (position) by taking a course?

■ Durch Fleiß (/Unterricht/Übung) qualifizierte er sich dafür.
He qualified for it through diligence (/instruction/practice).

■ Ihre Ausbildung qualifiziert sie für den Posten einer Chefsekretärin.
Her education qualifies her for the position of an executive secretary.

(s.) qualifizieren zu + D ⟨(sich) zu etw q.⟩   to qualify to be (sth)

■ Ich habe mich zum Facharbeiter (/Vorarbeiter/Lehrer) qualifiziert.
I'm qualified to be a skilled worker (/foreman/teacher).

■ Der Kurs qualifiziert alle Teilnehmer zu Kaufleuten.
The course qualifies all members to be merchants.

quatschen (+ prep)   to gab (away), to chat (*inf*)

■ Die Schüler (in der letzten Reihe) haben während des Englischunterrichts lange (miteinander) gequatscht.
The students (in the last row) gabbed (with each other) a long time during English class.

■ Meine Tochter quatscht stundenlang am Telefon mit ihrer Freundin.
My daughter chats on the phone for hours with her friend.

quellen (+ prep)   to pour; to stream; to well; to swell

■ Der Brei quillt über den Rand des Topfes.
The porridge is boiling over the rim of the pot.

■ Die Tür ist durch die Feuchtigkeit gequollen.
The door has swollen from the humidity.

quellen aus + D ⟨aus etw q.⟩   to pour *or* gush from (sth)

■ Sein Bauch quillt ihm aus der Hose. (*inf*)
His stomach hangs out (or bulges out) over his pants.

■ Vor Entsetzen quollen ihm die Augen aus den Höhlen.
His eyes bulged from their sockets from horror.

■ Die Menschenmenge quoll aus dem Stadion (/Theater). (*fig*)
The crowd poured out of the stadium (/theater).

■ Der Rauch ist aus dem Auspuffrohr (/brennenden Haus) gequollen.
The smoke billowed out of the exhaust pipe (/burning house).

quittieren mit + D ⟨**etw mit etw q.**⟩   to answer with (sth); to receive with (sth); to take with (sth)

- Die Zuschauer quittierten die Inszenierung mit großem Beifall.
  The audience received the production with a lot of applause.
- Sie hat die Beleidigung mit einem Lächeln (/Achselzucken) quittiert.
  She met (answered) the insult with a smile (/shrug).

R

s. rächen an + D ⟨sich an jdm (für/wegen etw) r.⟩   to take revenge *or* vengeance on (sb) for (sth)

- Ich habe mich an meinem ärgsten Feind gerächt.
  I took revenge on my worst enemy.
- Er will sich an dem Mann für das Verbrechen (*or* wegen des Verbrechens) rächen.
  He wants to take revenge on the man for the crime.
- Amerika wird sich an diesem Feind (/Land) bestimmt rächen.
  America will certainly take revenge on this enemy (/country).
- Es rächte sich (an mir).
  I suffered or had to pay for it.
- Es rächte sich (an ihr), daß sie in den ersten Semestern nicht genug gearbeitet hatte.
  She had to pay for not having worked hard enough in her first semesters.

rasen (+ prep)   to race; to tear

- Ich bin gerast, um rechtzeitig zum Theater zu kommen.
  I hurried in order to get to the theater on time.
- Der Tornado raste durch den Campingplatz (/das Dorf).
  The tornado tore through the campground (/village).
- Der Junge raste mit seinem Motorrad vor meinem Haus auf und ab (/durch die Straßen).
  The boy raced in front of my house (/through the streets) on his motorcycle.
- Der Rennwagen (/Fahrer) raste in die Menge (/gegen eine Mauer).
  The racing car (/driver) crashed (or smashed) into the crowd (/a wall).

rasen vor (+ noun without article) ⟨vor etw r.⟩   to rave with (sth)

- Er raste vor Wahnsinn (/Schmerz/Zorn).
  He was raving with madness (/wild with pain/wild with anger).
- Casanova raste vor Leidenschaft (/Eifersucht).
  Casanova was half-crazed with passion (/jealousy).

raten zu + D ⟨jdm zu jdm/etw r.⟩   to recommend (sb/sth) to (sb); to advise (sb) to do/take/buy, *etc.* (sth)

- Wen raten Sie mir?—Ich rate Ihnen zu diesem Arzt (*or* Ich rate Ihnen diesen Arzt).
  Whom do you recommend?—I recommend this doctor to you.

■ Was (*or* Wozu) raten Sie mir?—Ich rate Ihnen zu diesem Gericht (*or* Ich rate Ihnen dieses Gericht).
What do you recommend to me?—I recommend this dish to you.

■ Ich riet ihr, sofort zum Krankenhaus (/nach Hause/zum Arzt) zu gehen.
I advised her to go to the hospital (/home/to see a doctor) right away.

■ Ich habe ihr zur Sparsamkeit (/Geduld/Toleranz) geraten.
I advised her to be economical (/patient/tolerant).

■ Meinem Mann (/Ihr) ist nicht zu raten.
My husband (/She) does not accept any advice.

■ Wem nicht zu raten ist, dem ist auch nicht zu helfen. (*prov*)
A bit of advice never hurt anybody.

räumen (+ prep)   to clear, to put things away

■ Ich räumte meine Sachen aus der Schublade (/vom Tisch/in die Ecke/zur Seite/in die Schublade).
I cleared my things out of the drawer (/from the table/I put my things into the corner/to the side/I put my things in the drawer).

■ Sie räumte die Gläser vom Tisch (/aus der Geschirrspülmaschine/an eine andere Stelle/in die Küche).
She cleared the glasses from the table (/out of the dishwasher/to another place/in the kitchen).

■ Der Hauswirt sagt, sie müsse bis zum Wochenende die Wohnung räumen.
The landlord says that she has to vacate the apartment by the weekend.

■ Die Polizei räumte den Bahnhof von Betrunkenen und Pennern.
The police cleared the train station of drunks and bums.

■ Die Arbeiter räumen den Bürgersteig vom Schnee.
The workers are clearing the sidewalk of snow.

reagieren auf + A ⟨auf jdn/etw r.⟩   to react to (sb/sth)

■ Der Verletzte hat auf seine Zeichen (/Fragen) überhaupt nicht reagiert.
The injured man didn't react to his signs (/questions) at all.

■ Er reagierte verärgert (/freundlich) auf meinen Vorschlag (/mein Wort).
He reacted angrily (/in a friendly way) to my proposal (/remark).

■ Das Kind reagierte positiv auf das Medikament (/die neue Umgebung).
The child reacted positively to the medicine (/new environment).

rechnen (+ prep)   to calculate; to estimate; to reckon; to do arithmetic; to work out; to count

■ Er rechnet schnell (/schriftlich/mit Zahlen).
He calculates quickly (/He's calculating on paper/with numbers or reckoning in figures).

- Wir rechnen gerade Additionsaufgaben (mit dem Rechner/im Kopf).
  We're doing addition problems at the moment (with the calculator/in our heads).

- Die Lehrerin rechnet (mit den Kindern). Sie haben heute Rechnen. Sie sind gut im Rechnen.
  The teacher is doing arithmetic (with the children). They have arithmetic today. They are good at arithmetic (or good at figures).

- Ich rechne 70 Dollar pro Tag für das Hotelzimmer.
  I estimate (or reckon) it will be $70 a day for the hotel room.

- Die Kinder können schon bis 50 rechnen.
  The children can already do arithmetic with numbers up to 50.

rechnen auf + A ⟨auf jdn/etw r.⟩   to reckon *or* count on (sb/sth)

- Ich kann auf ihre (*or* mit ihrer) Diskretion (/Zuneigung/Liebe) rechnen.
  I can count on her discretion (/affection/love).

- Man kann auf diesen Klempner rechnen. Seine Arbeit ist gut und preiswert.
  You can count on this plumber. His work is good, and it's reasonable.

- Von wem kannst du Hilfe erwarten? Kannst du auf (*or* mit) Markus rechnen?
  From whom can you expect help? Can you count on Mark?

rechnen mit + D ⟨mit jdm/etw r.⟩   to reckon on *or* with (sb/sth)

- Du mußt nicht damit rechnen, daß er pünktlich kommt.
  You shouldn't figure on his coming on time.

- Wir haben nicht mehr mit seinem Kommen rechnen können.
  We couldn't count on his coming any more.

- Ich rechne nächste Woche mit den Munderlohs.
  I'm expecting the Munderlohs next week.

- Meine Eltern rechnen immer mit allem (/dem Schlimmsten).
  My parents are always prepared for everything (/the worst).

- Dieser Politiker ist jemand, mit dem man rechnen muß.
  This politician is someone who must be reckoned with.

- Mit deiner Hilfe (/Ablehnung) hatte ich nicht gerechnet.
  I hadn't figured (or counted) on your help (/refusal).

- Rockefeller ist Milliardär. Er rechnet nicht mit Pfennigen.
  Rockefeller is a billionaire. He doesn't count his pennies.

- Wir müssen morgen mit Regen (/Schnee) rechnen.
  We must figure on rain (/snow) (for) tomorrow.

rechnen zu + D ⟨jdn/etw zu etw r.⟩   to count (sb) among (sth); to class (sb/sth) as (sth)

- Beethoven wird zu den größten Musikern aller Zeiten gerechnet.
  Beethoven is rated as one of the greatest musicians of all time.
- Man rechnete Einstein zu den besten Physikern.
  Einstein ranked among the best physicists.
- Die Schildkröten rechnen zu den Reptilien.
  Turtles are classified as reptiles.
- Die Ausgaben für Miete und Ernährung rechnen zu unseren festen monatlichen Kosten.
  The expenses for rent and food figure among our fixed monthly costs.

reden (+ prep)   to talk, to speak

- Der Bürgermeister redete in einer Universität (/im Fernsehen/zum Volk/am Telefon/vor der Presse/über das Radio).
  The mayor spoke at a university (/on television/to the people/on the phone/before the press/over the radio).

reden mit + D ⟨mit jdm r.⟩   to speak with (sb)

- Ich muß direkt (/offen) mit dem Chef über die Sache reden. Ich weiß, mit dem kann man nicht (leicht) reden.
  I must talk directly (/openly) with the boss about the matter. I know it isn't easy to talk to him.
- Warum redest du mit dir selbst?
  Why are you talking to yourself?
- Reden sie noch miteinander?
  Are they still on speaking terms?
- Ich habe ein Wörtchen mit dir zu reden.
  I want to have a word with you.
- Ich lasse dich nicht in diesem Ton mit deiner Mutter reden.
  I won't let you talk to your mother in that tone.

reden über + A ⟨über jdn/etw r.⟩   to talk *or* speak about (sb/sth)

- Worüber reden sie?—Sie reden immer über Politik.
  What are they talking about?—They always talk about politics.
- Reden wir über etwas anderes!
  Let's change the subject!

- Wir haben über dieses und jenes geredet.
  We talked about this and that.

- Der Junge redet mit seinem Freund über das Mädchen.
  The boy is talking about the girl with his friend.

- Der Angeber redet immer nur über sich.
  The show-off always talks about nobody but himself.

reden von + D ⟨**von jdm/etw r.**⟩   to talk of (sb/sth)

- Er redet immer von seinen Erfolgen (/spannenden Erlebnissen/seinem neuen Sportwagen), aber gesehen habe ich davon noch nichts.
  He keeps talking of his successes (/exciting adventures/new sports car), but I have never seen them/it.

- Sie redet von ihrem Traummann wie von einer Mischung aus Arnold Schwarzenegger und Albert Einstein.
  She talks of her dream man as being a mixture of Arnold Schwarzenegger and Albert Einstein.

reflektieren auf + A ⟨**auf etw r.**⟩   to be interested in (sth); to have one's eye on (sth)

- Die Verwandten reflektierten auf das Erbe ihres Großonkels.
  The relatives had an eye on their great-uncle's inheritance.

- Reflektieren Sie noch auf die Möbel (/den Posten/die Stelle der Sekretärin/die Wohnung)?
  Are you still interested in the furniture (/in the post or position/in the position of secretary/in the apartment)?

- Ich reflektiere nicht darauf, Schulleiter zu werden.
  I'm not interested in becoming a principal.

reflektieren über + A ⟨**über etw r.**⟩   to reflect *or* ponder (up)on (sth)

- Ich habe tief über deinen Plan (/seinen Vorschlag) reflektiert.
  I seriously reflected upon your plan (/his proposal).

- Er reflektierte lange darüber, was er sagen sollte.
  He reflected a long time on what he should say.

- Er reflektierte über seine Scheidung und wurde sehr traurig.
  He reflected on his divorce and became very sad.

reiben (+ prep)   to rub

- Ich habe den Schmutz vom Kühlschrank gerieben.
  I rubbed the dirt from the refrigerator.

- Wie kann ich diesen Tomatenfleck aus dem Hemd reiben?
  How can I rub this tomato stain out of my shirt?

- Das Kind reibt eine schmerzende Stelle am Körper.
  The child is rubbing a painful spot on his body.

s. reiben an + D ⟨sich an jdm/etw r.⟩   to rub (*the wrong way*) against (sb/sth)

- Die beiden haben sich ständig aneinander gerieben.
  Those two were constantly rubbing each other the wrong way.

- Wenn er auch in dieser Firma arbeitete, würde ich mich dauernd an ihm reiben.
  If he worked for this company, too, there would always be friction between him and me.

reichen (+ prep)   to stretch, to extend, to reach; to be enough

- Mein Sohn (/Das Wasser) reicht mir jetzt bis zum Hals (/zur Schulter /zur Stirn).
  My son (/The water) comes up to my neck (/shoulder/forehead) now.

- Unser Grundstück reicht bis an den Fluß (/ihres).
  Our property extends right up to the river (/theirs).

- Das Stadion reicht nicht für die Olympiade.
  The stadium isn't big enough (or *won't suffice) for the Olympic games.*

- Reicht unser Geld (/Brot) nicht bis zum Montag?
  Won't our money (/bread) last until Monday?

- Hoffentlich reicht die Schlagsahne für eine Torte.
  Hopefully, there is enough whipped cream for a cake.

reichen mit + D ⟨mit etw r.⟩   to make do with (sth)

- Ich hoffe, wir reichen mit dem Brot bis Montag.
  I hope the bread will last us until Monday.

reichen (without prep)   to stretch, to reach; to pass (over); to serve; to be enough, to suffice

- Reich mir bitte das Salz! Reicht dein Arm so weit?
  Pass me the salt, please. Does your arm reach that far?

- Er reichte den Gästen Erfrischungen (/Bier/Getränke).
  He served refreshments (/beer/drinks) to the guests.

- Der Zucker hat nicht gereicht.
  There wasn't enough sugar.

reifen zu + D ⟨**zu jdm/etw r.**⟩   to ripen into (sb/sth); to mature

- Peter ist schon zum Manne gereift.
  Peter has already grown into a man.
- Seine kleine Tochter ist in kürzester Zeit zur Frau gereift.
  His young daughter became a woman in no time.
- Im Laufe seines Lebens reiften seine Gedanken zu einer umfassenden Theorie.
  In the course of his life, his thoughts matured into a comprehensive theory.

s. reihen an + A ⟨**sich an etw r.**⟩   to follow (after) (sth)

- Eine Katastrophe reihte sich an die andere.
  One catastrophe followed another.
- Mehrere Todesfälle (/Geburten/Hochzeiten) haben sich aneinander gereiht.
  Several deaths (/births/weddings) followed one another.

reihen auf + A ⟨**etw auf etw r.**⟩   to string (sth) on (sth)

- Wieviele Perlen haben Sie auf die Schnur gereiht?
  How many beads have you strung (on the thread)?

(s.) reimen auf/mit + A/D ⟨**auf/mit etw r.**⟩   to rhyme with (sth)

- Kannst du „Sympathie" auf ein anderes (*or* mit einem anderen) Wort reimen?
  Can you rhyme "sympathy" with another word?
- Das Wort „Sack" reimt sich auf (*or* mit) „Pack."
  The word "sack" rhymes with "pack."

s. reinigen von + D ⟨**sich/jdn/etw von etw r.**⟩   to clean (o.s./sb/sth); to cleanse oneself of (sth)

- Nicole reinigte heute ihr Zimmer (/den Boden/die Wände/die Bücher) vom Staub.
  Nicole dusted her room (/the floor/the walls/the books) today.
- Zuerst muß ich mir die Hände (mit Seife) von dem Schmutz (/dem Öl/der Schmiere) reinigen.
  First I have to clean the dirt (/oil/grease) off my hands (with soap).
- Ich habe meine Füße vom Teer gereinigt.
  I cleaned the tar off my feet.
- Dieser See reinigt sich nicht von selbst. Andere Mittel müssen erwogen werden.
  This lake isn't going to clean itself. Other means must be considered.

■ Sie versuchte, sich von der Schuld (/der Verantwortung/dem Verdacht) zu reinigen.
She tried to cleanse herself of the guilt (/to clear herself of responsibility /to clear herself of suspicion).

reisen (+ prep)   to travel

■ Er ist ins Ausland (/nach London/durch Spanien/im Auto/mit dem Auto/mit dem Schiff/mit dem Wohnwagen/zu Disney World) gereist.
He traveled abroad (/to London/through Spain/in the car/by car/by ship/by motor home/to Disney World).

■ Er reiste in den Urlaub (*or* in die Ferien)(/in die See/aufs Land).
He went away on vacation (/to the ocean/to the country).

reißen an + D ⟨an etw r.⟩   to pull *or* tug on (sth)

■ Der Hund riß heftig an der Leine.
The dog pulled hard on the leash.

⟨**etw an sich reißen**⟩   to seize (sth); to usurp (sth)

■ Der General riß die Macht (/Führung) an sich.
The general seized power (/the leadership).

■ Der Torwart hat den Ball an sich gerissen.
The goalie seized the ball.

■ Du willst immer das Gespräch an dich reißen!
You always want to direct the conversation towards yourself!

reißen aus/von + D ⟨jdm/etw aus/von etw r.⟩   to snatch *or* wrest (sb/sth) out of (sth)

■ Der Junge riß ihr (/mir) den Bleistift (/das Zeug) aus der Hand.
The boy snatched the pencil (/thing) from her (/me).

■ Er riß sich die Kleider vom Leib.
He ripped the clothes off his body.

reißen in + A ⟨in etw r.⟩   to tear *or* rip in(to) (sth)

■ Ich (/Die Säure) riß ein Loch in mein Kleid (/in die Tasche).
I (/The acid) made a hole in my dress (/in my pocket).

■ Er riß das Papier in schmale Streifen (/in fünf Stücke).
He tore the paper into narrow strips (/five pieces).

- Die Katze hat zufällig ein Loch in mein Hemd gerissen.
  The cat accidentally tore a hole in my shirt.
- Die Säge riß einen Schnitt in das Holz.
  The saw made a cut into the wood.
- Die zwei Tiere haben einander in Stücke gerissen.
  The two animals tore each other to pieces.

s. reißen um ⟨sich um jdn/etw r.⟩   to scramble to get (sb/sth)

- Sie rissen sich alle um die Eintrittskarten (/billigen Kleider).
  They all scrambled to get the tickets (/cheap dresses).
- Die Agenturen (/Groupies) reißen sich um diesen Rocksänger.
  The agencies (/groupies) are scrambling to get this rock singer.

reiten (+ prep)   to ride

- Er ritt auf die Jagd (/nach Hause/den Weg entlang/übers Feld/durch die Felder).
  He rode out to hunt (/home/along the road/across the field/through the fields).
- Er ist im Schritt (/Trab/Galopp) geritten.
  He rode at a walk (/trot/gallop).

reiten auf + D ⟨auf etw r.⟩   to ride on (sth)

- Ali Baba ritt auf einem Teppich.
  Ali Baba rode on a carpet.
- Ich habe einmal auf einem Pferd ohne Sattel (/auf einem Kamel/auf einem Elefanten) geritten.
  I once rode a horse without a saddle (/rode a camel/rode an elephant).

reizen zu + D ⟨jdn zu etw r.⟩   to provoke (sb) to (sth) *or* to irritate

- Er reizte sie bis aufs Blut (*or* zur Weißglut) (/bis zu Tränen).
  He made her blood boil (/He provoked her to tears).
- Die Rechtsanwältin reizte ihn (/mich) zum Widerspruch.
  The lawyer provoked him (/me) into contradicting himself (/myself).
- Der Rauch reizt (/mich) zum Husten.
  The smoke makes one cough (/makes me cough).

rennen (+ prep)   to run

- Er rennt nach Hause (/zum Spielplatz/zum Strand/über die Brücke/auf der Straße entlang/über die Straße/um die Ecke).
  He's running home (/to the playground/to the beach/over the bridge/along the street/across the street/around the corner).

- Er rennt wegen jeder Kleinigkeit zum Arzt (/zu seiner Mutter).
  He runs to the doctor (/his mother) for every little thing.

- Sie rennt zu jedem Rockkonzert (/jeder Ausstellung).
  She goes to every rock concert (/exhibiton).

- Ich muß aufs Klo rennen. (*inf*)
  I have to run to the john.

rennen an/gegen + A ⟨an/gegen jdn/etw r.⟩   to run, bump, bang into/against (sb/sth)

- Karl ist mit dem Kopf gegen den Baum (/die Mauer) gerannt.
  Karl bumped (or banged) his head against the tree (/wall).

- Er war so betrunken, daß er gegen einen Laternenpfahl (/einen Passanten) rannte.
  He was so drunk that he ran into a lamp post (/passerby).

retten aus/vor + D ⟨jdn aus/vor jdm/etw r.⟩   to save *or* rescue (sb) from (sb/sth)

- Sie haben ihn aus dem Feuer (/der Gefahr/den Händen der Entführer/einer Verlegenheit) gerettet.
  They rescued him from the fire (/danger/hands of the kidnappers/an embarrassment).

- Sie hat ihn vor dem Ertrinken (/einer drohenden Schande) gerettet.
  She saved him from drowning (/an impending disgrace).

s. retten auf/unter + A ⟨sich auf/unter etw r.⟩   to escape onto/under (sth)

- Ich habe mich (vor dem Feuer) aufs Dach (/unter eine Brücke) gerettet.
  I escaped (from the fire) onto the roof (/under a bridge).

- Er hat sich (vor dem Verbrecher) hinter eine schützende Mauer gerettet.
  He escaped (from the criminal) (by going) behind a protective wall.

richten an + A ⟨etw an jdn/etw r.⟩   to address (sth) to (sb/sth)

- Der Rektor hat seine Mahnungen (/Lobreden) an mich gerichtet.
  The principal directed (or addressed) his exhortations (/praise) to me.

■ Ich möchte nun diese Frage (/Beschwerde/Bitte/Bemerkung) an dich richten.
I would now like to address (or put) this question (/complaint/request/remark) to you.

■ An wen (/An welches Büro) soll ich den Brief richten?
To whom (/To which office) should I address (or direct) the letter?

richten auf + A ⟨etw auf jdn/etw r.⟩   to direct *or* turn *or* point (sth) at/toward(s)
(sb/sth)

■ Er richtete die Waffe (/das Gewehr/die Kamera) auf ihn.
He pointed (or aimed) the weapon (/rifle/camera) at him.

■ Er hat all seine Energie (/Aufmerksamkeit/Bemühungen) auf die Fertigstellung
des Buches gerichtet.
He directed all of his energy (/attention/efforts) towards the completion of the book.

■ Richte bitte das Licht auf mein Buch (/mich).
Please turn the light towards my book (/me).

■ Er richtete den Blick auf das Mädchen (/Gebäude).
He directed his gaze toward the girl (/building).

s. richten gegen + A ⟨sich gegen jdn/etw r.⟩   to be directed *or* aimed at/against
(sb/sth)

■ Meine Kritik richtet sich gegen die Politik der Regierung.
My criticism is directed at the government's policies.

■ Ohne Zweifel richtet sich der Verdacht gegen ihn.
Without a doubt the suspicion is directed towards him.

richten nach + D ⟨etw nach etw r.⟩   to set *or* steer (sth) to (sth)

■ Der Kapitän hat den Kurs nach Süden gerichtet.
The captain set a southerly course.

■ Wir wollen die Segel nach dem Wind richten.
We want to set our sails according to the wind (to sail with the wind).

s. richten nach + D ⟨sich nach jdm/etw r.⟩   to comply with (sb/sth); to conform to
(sb/sth); to act in accordance with (sb/sth)

■ Ich richte mich immer nach den Wünschen (/dem Urteil/den Vorstellungen)
meiner Kirche.
I always conform to the wishes (/the judgment/ideas) of my church.

- Sie richtet sich immer nach der Pariser Mode.
  She always conforms to (or *follows*) *the Paris fashions.*

- Sie richten sich immer nach den Wünschen ihrer Kunden.
  They always comply with their customers' wishes.

- Er richtet sich ganz nach seiner Frau (/Ich richte mich ganz nach Ihnen).
  He'll do whatever his wife wants (/I'll leave it to you or *I'll do what pleases you).*

- Er richtet sich nach den Sternen (/der Wettervorhersage/dem, was sein Vater sagt).
  He goes by the stars (/the weather forecast/what his father says).

- Ich richte mich ganz nach dir (/Ihnen).
  I'll do what you suggest (/I leave it to you).

- Und richte dich danach! (*inf*)
  (Kindly) do as you're told!

riechen an + D ⟨**an jdm/etw r.**⟩   to smell (sb/sth); to sniff (at) (sb/sth)

- Diese Blumen riechen nicht. Ich will an diesen anderen schönen Blumen riechen.
  These flowers don't smell. I want to smell these other beautiful flowers.

- Monika roch an der Milch (/der Rose/der Parfümflasche).
  Monika sniffed (at) the milk (/rose/bottle of perfume).

riechen aus + D ⟨**aus etw r.**⟩   to smell (of) (sth)

- Er hat übel aus dem Mund gerochen.
  He had awfully bad breath.

- Er ißt so viel Knoblauch, daß er aus allen Poren riecht.
  He eats so much garlic that he reeks from every pore.

- Es riecht übel aus dieser Wohnung.
  There is a bad smell coming from this apartment.

riechen nach + D ⟨**nach etw r.**⟩   to smell (of/from) (sth)

- Es riecht nach Fisch (/Minze/faulen Eiern/Gas).
  It smells of (or like) fish (/mint/rotten eggs/gas).

- Er riecht nach Weinbrand (/Schweiß).
  He smells of brandy (/of sweat or *smells sweaty).*

rinnen (+ prep)   to run *or* flow

- Das Wasser (/Der Regen) ist vom Dach geronnen.
  The water (/rain) ran down from the roof.

- Tränen rannen über ihre Wangen (/ihr Gesicht).
  Tears were running down her cheeks (/her face).
- Nach dem Unfall rann ihm das Blut in Strömen aus der Wunde (/der Brust).
  After the accident blood streamed from his wound (/chest).
- Der Schweiß rann ihm vom Rücken (/Gesicht).
  Sweat was running down his back (/face).

rufen (+ prep)   to call; to shout; to sound

- Ich habe ihn vom Fenster aus (/von ferne) gerufen.
  I called him from the window (/a distance).
- Die Geschäfte rufen mich nach Japan (/ins Ausland).
  Business affairs call me to Japan (/abroad).
- Sie riefen den Arzt zu dem kranken Mann.
  They called the doctor to come to attend to the sick man.
- Sie rief um Hilfe (/nach einem Medikament).
  She called (or cried) for help (/a medicine).
- Es fiel mir nicht leicht, mir die Ereignisse wieder ins Gedächtnis zu rufen.
  I had a hard time recalling the events.

rufen nach + D ⟨nach jdm/etw r.⟩   to call for (sb/sth)

- Jens, ruf nach dem Kellner (/einem Glas Wasser)!
  Jens, call for the waiter (/ask for a glass of water).
- Der Patient rief nach der Krankenschwester (/seiner Schwester).
  The patient called or asked for the nurse (/his sister).
- Wir mußten nach dem Arzt rufen (, weil die Lena krank war).
  We had to call for the doctor (because Lena was sick).
- Deine Mutter ruft nach dir (/einer Tasse Kaffee).
  Your mother is calling you (/calling for a cup of coffee).

ruhen auf + D ⟨auf jdm/etw r.⟩   to lie on (sb/sth)

- Möge Gottes Segen auf euch ruhen.
  May God's blessing be with you.
- Auf ihm ruht ein Verdacht (/eine große Verantwortung).
  A suspicion hangs over him (/He bears a lot of responsibility).

S

sagen (+ prep) to say

- Er sagte etwas im Ernst (/im Scherz/aus Bosheit).
  He said something seriously (/jokingly/out of malice).

- Margaret sagte mir etwas ins Ohr (/ins Gesicht/auf den Kopf zu).
  Margaret said something in my ear (/to my face/directly or *frankly* or *without reservation).*

- Wie sagt man „insult" auf Deutsch?
  What is the German word for "insult"? or *How do you say "insult" in German?*

- Er sagte etwas vor sich hin.
  *He said (*or *muttered* or *mumbled) something to himself.*

sagen mit + D ⟨mit etw s.⟩ to say *or* mean by (sth)

- Damit ist noch nicht unbedingt gesagt, daß er gelogen hat.
  This does not necessarily mean that he lied.

- Was willst du damit sagen? —Ich will damit sagen, daß...
  What do you mean (to say) by that? —I'm saying that....

- Mit dieser Bemerkung (/Aussage) sage ich, daß....
  By this remark (/statement) I mean that....

sagen über/von + A/D ⟨etw über jdn/etw, von jdm/etw s.⟩ to say (sth) tell about (sb/sth); to tell (sb) off

- Armut ist keine Schande. Das kann man auch vom (*or* über den) Reichtum sagen.
  Poverty is no shame. One can say the same thing about wealth.

- Karl sagte nur Negatives über den Lehrer (/die Reise/das Stück).
  Karl said only negative things about the teacher (/trip/play).

- Man sagt von dieser (*or* über diese) Firma nur Gutes.
  People say only good things about this company.

- Es sagt doch niemand von ihm (*or* über ihn), daß er nicht für seine Kinder sorgt.
  No one says that he doesn't take good care of his children.

- Was konnte der Zeuge über das Unglück (/Verbrechen) sagen?
  What could the witness say about the accident (/crime)?

- Ich kann darüber nicht viel sagen, außer daß unser Team bei der Meisterschaft einfach Pech hatte.
  I can't say much about it except that our team simply had bad luck at the championship.

- Dieser Brief von deinen Vewandten sagt nichts darüber (/davon).
  This letter from your relatives doesn't mention anything about that (/mention it).

- Das laß ich mir von dir nicht sagen!
  I won't have that from you!
- Laß dir von mir sagen, daß. . . .
  (You can) take it from me that. . . ./Let me tell you that. . . .

sagen zu + D ⟨zu jdm s.⟩   to tell (sb)

- Ich habe zu Peter gesagt, daß Sonia um drei Uhr von Zuhause kommt.
  I said to Peter that Sonia would come from home at three.
- Diese Bemerkung hat sie doch nur so vor sich hin gesagt und nicht zu dir.
  She just muttered this remark to herself and not to you.
- Was sagst du zu meinem Vorschlag (/dazu)?
  What do you think of my suggestion (/about that)?
- Wie sagen Sie zueinander?—Ich sage „du" (/„Sie") zu ihm.
  How (i.e., by what form of "you") do you address each other?—I address him by "du" (/"Sie").

schaffen (+ prep)   to manage; to bring; to put; to cause; to do

- Ich werde den Koffer zur Gepäckausgabe (/zum Bahnhof/nach Hause) schaffen.
  I'll take the suitcase to the luggage claim area (/to the train station/home).
- Ich habe damit (/mit dem Projekt) nichts zu schaffen.
  I have nothing to do with it (/the project).
- Der Krankenwagen schaffte den Verletzten gleich zum Krankenhaus.
  The ambulance managed to take the injured person quickly to the hospital.
- Ich schaffe die alten Spielzeuge in den Keller (/auf den Boden/in den Schrank/in den Kasten).
  I'll put the old toys in the basement (/in the attic/in the closet/into the box).

schalten (+ prep)   to switch; to turn; to operate; to shift

- Schalte den Kühlschrank auf „sehr kalt" („4"/die höchste Stufe)!
  Turn the refrigerator to "very cold" (/"4"/turn the heat up or all the way).
- Bei 30 Kilometern muß man in den dritten Gang schalten.
  At thirty kilometers you have to shift into third gear.
- Er schaltet mit meinen Geräten, als ob sie ihm gehörten.
  He handles my tools as if they belonged to him.
- Du kannst mit deinem Geld (/deiner Zeit/deinem Leben) frei schalten und walten.
  You can do what you like with your money (/time/life).

s. schämen für/wegen + A/G ⟨sich für jdn/etw, wegen jds/etw s.⟩   to be ashamed of (sb/sth)

- Schämst du dich für ihn (/mich/für deinen Bruder) (*or* seinetwegen/meinetwegen/deines Bruders wegen)?
  Are you ashamed of him (/me/your brother)?

- Die Mutter schämte sich für das Verhalten (*or* wegen des Verhaltens) ihres Sohnes.
  The mother was ashamed of her son's behavior.

- Du brauchst dich dessen (*or* dafür) nicht zu schämen.
  You don't need to be ashamed of it.

- Ich schäme mich (wegen) ihrer Handlung (/ihrer Worte) (*or* für ihre Haltung/ihr Wort).
  I'm ashamed (because) of her behavior (/her words).

- Er schämte sich (wegen) seines Betragens (/seiner Feigheit/seines Neides/seiner Unbeherrschtheit) (*or* für sein Betragen/seine Feigheit/seinen Neid/seine Unbeherrschtheit).
  He was ashamed (because) of his conduct (/cowardliness/jealousy/unruliness).

s. schämen vor + D ⟨sich vor jdm s.⟩   to be *or* feel ashamed (in front) of (sb)

- Das Kind schämte sich vor seinen Eltern, weil sie betrunken zum Elternabend erschienen waren.
  The child felt ashamed of his parents because they showed up inebriated at parents' night.

- Für die schlechte Leistung hat sich die Mannschft vor dem Trainer geschämt.
  The team was (or felt) ashamed in front of the coach because of their bad performance.

- Der Autor schämte sich vor dem Verleger, weil er nicht rechtzeitig fertig geworden war.
  The author was ashamed in front of the publisher because he hadn't finished in time.

schätzen auf + A ⟨jdn/etw auf etw s.⟩   to estimate (sb/sth) at (sth)

- Ich schätze den Wert (von) dieser Sache auf tausend Mark.
  I estimate the value of this thing at a thousand marks.

- Worauf (*or* Wie hoch) schätzen Sie die Unkosten für dieses Projekt?
  At what amount do you estimate the expenses for this project?

- Auf wieviel Jahre schätzt du mich?—Ich schätze dich auf vierzig Jahre (*or* Ich schätze, daß du vierzig Jahre alt bist). Monika hat dich für jünger geschäzt.
  How old do you think I am?—I estimate you're forty years old. Monica estimated that you are younger.

schauen (+ prep)   to look

- Fritz schaute zur Erde (/nach unten/nach allen Seiten/zu meiner Seite/um sich/ins Loch/zu Boden/in die Zukunft/).
  Fritz looked to the ground (/down/in all directions/in my direction/around himself/into the hole/at the floor/to the future).
- Ich schaute nach dem (/auf den) Fahrplan.
  I looked for the schedule (/at the schedule).
- Die Sonne schaut durch die Wolken.
  The sun is peeping (or shining) through the clouds.
- Seine Unterhose schaute aus der Hose.
  His underpants were sticking out of his pants.
- Sie schaute ihm (fest/haßerfüllt/verliebt) in die Augen.
  She looked him (straight/at him with hatred/adoringly at him) in the eyes.
- Wut (/Ärger/Verständnis) schaute ihr aus den Augen.
  Rage (/Annoyance/Understanding) was written all over her face.

schauen auf + A ⟨auf jdn/etw s.⟩   to look at (sb/sth)

- Sie hat wieder besorgt auf die Uhr (/sie) geschaut.
  She looked at her watch (/her) with concern again.
- Er schaute auf das Thermometer und sah, daß er Fieber hatte.
  He looked at the thermometer and saw that he had a fever.
- Die Männer da am Strand schauen interessiert auf die Mädchen.
  Those men at the beach are looking interestedly at the girls.

schauen nach + D ⟨nach jdm/etw s.⟩   to look for/after (sb/sth)

- Die Krankenschwester schaut nach dem Patienten.
  The nurse is looking after the patient.
- Meine Mutter schaute nach den Kindern, um sich zu vergewissern, daß sie schliefen.
  My mother looked in on the children to make sure they were sleeping.
- Meine Freundin schaute nach den Blumen (/Hamstern/dem Hund), als wir nicht zu Hause waren.
  My friend looked after the flowers (/hamsters/dog) while we were away.

scheiden (+ prep)   to separate, to part

- Sie schieden die Bewerber nach ihrer Erziehung (/ihrer Rasse/ihrem Geschlecht /ihrem Alter/ihren Ansichten).
  They separated the applicants according to their education (/race/sex/age/views).

- Die Mutter und ihre Tochter sind voneinander in Trauer geschieden.
  The mother and her daughter separated from each other sadly.

- Er ist aus der Firma (/dem Amt) geschieden.
  He left the firm (/resigned from the office).

- Er schied aus dem Leben (/von seiner Heimatstadt).
  He departed this life (/left his home town).

s. scheiden lassen von + D 〈sich von jdm s. lassen〉   to get divorced from (sb); to get a divorce from (sb)

- Ich will mich von ihm scheiden lassen (*or* Ich will die Scheidung beantragen).
  I want to get a divorce (from him) or *divorce him* (or *I want to petition for a divorce).*

- Warum läßt du dich (/nicht) von ihm scheiden?
  Why are (/aren't) you getting a divorce from him?

- Der Filmstar hat sich von seinem fünften Mann scheiden lassen.
  The film star got a divorce from her fifth husband.

- Er ließ sich nicht von seiner Frau scheiden.
  He didn't give his wife a divorce.

- Wir wollten uns (*rarely* voneinander) scheiden lassen, aber der Richter hat uns nicht geschieden. Er sagte, wir müßten länger warten.
  We wanted to get a divorce, but the judge didn't allow it. He said we had to wait longer.

scheitern (+ prep)   to fail; to break down; to fall through

- Das Unternehmen scheiterte am Widerstand einzelner.
  The undertaking fell through because of the opposition of a few.

- Der Plan (/Ihre Ehe) war von vornherein zum Scheitern verurteilt.
  The plan (/Their marriage) was doomed to failure from its inception.

- Ich bin mit meinem Vorhaben (/Projekt) gescheitert.
  My plan (/project) came to nothing/I failed in my plan (/project).

- Unsere Mannschaft scheiterte im Halbfinale an Brasilien (/anden Gegnern).
  Our team was eliminated by Brazil (/the opponents) in the semifinals.

schicken (+ prep)   to send

- Ich schickte die Kiste nach London (/in die Schweiz/meinem Freund ins Haus).
  I sent the box to London (/to Switzerland/to my friend's house).

■ Die Mutter schickte ihn zum Laden (/zum Bäcker/zum Arzt/zum Einkaufen/nach Hause/in den Kindergarten/in die *or* zur Schule/ins *or* zu Bett).
The mother sent him to the store (/the bakery/the doctor/shopping/home/the kindergarten/school/bed).

■ Wir haben unsere Töchter auf die Universität (/in die höhere Schule) geschickt.
We sent our daughters to the university (/to a "Gymnasium").

s. schicken (+ prep)   to be fitting *or* proper

■ Das schickt sich nicht, in deiner Nase zu bohren.
Picking your nose is not proper (or becoming to you).

■ Das schickt sich nicht in der Schule (/in Gesellschaft/für dich/für eine Dame).
That is not proper in school (/in society/for you/for a lady).

schicken an + A ⟨jdm etw, an jdn etw s.⟩   to send (sth) to (sb/sth)

■ Er schickte mir die Bücher (*or* Er schickte die Bücher an mich).
He sent me the books.

■ Ich schicke dir heute diesen Brief (*or* Ich schicke heute diesen Brief an dich).
I'm sending you this letter today.

■ Wann schickst du mir die Sachen (*or* die Sachen an mich)?
When are you going to send the things to me?

■ Er hat die Waren an unser Büro (/unsere Adresse/uns) geschickt.
He sent the goods to our office (/address/us).

s. schicken in + A ⟨sich in etw s.⟩   to resign oneself to (sth)

■ Er schickte sich in sein Los (/in die Umstände/seinen Job).
He resigned himself to his fate (/the circumstances/his job).

schicken nach + D ⟨nach jdm/etw s.⟩   to send for (sb)

■ Sie schickten nach dem Arzt (/Priester/der Polizei/seinem Vater/einem Krankenwagen/Hilfe).
They sent for the doctor (/the priest/the police/his father/an ambulance/help).

(s.) schieben (+ prep)   to push, to shove

■ Gerhard schiebt die Lampe in die Mitte (/zur Seite/nach vorn/in das Auto/an die Wand/vor die Couch).
Gerhard is pushing the lamp to the middle (/to the side/to the front/into the car/to the wall/in front of the couch).

■ Ich habe mich durch die Menge (/an die Spitze der Läufer) geschoben.
I pushed my way through the crowd (/in front (or ahead) of the runners).

■ Er schob den Hut aus der Stirn.
He pushed the hat back from his forehead.

■ Die Mutter schob dem Kind einen Schnuller in den Mund.
The mother shoved a pacifier into the child's mouth.

schieben auf + A ⟨etw auf jdn/etw s.⟩   to blame (sth) on (sb/sth)

■ Sie schoben die Schuld (/die Verantwortung/den Verdacht) auf ihn.
They put the guilt (/responsibility/suspicion) on him.

■ Du schiebst immer alles auf mich (/auf einen Mangel an Zeit/auf die Umstände).
You always blame everything on me (/on a lack of time/on the circumstances).

s. schieben von + D ⟨etw von sich s.⟩   to put (sth) aside

■ Er hat das Glas (/die Zigaretten) von sich weggeschoben.
He pushed the glass (/cigarettes) away.

■ Er wollte die Schuld (/Verantwortung) von sich schieben.
He wanted to avert the guilt (/responsibility).

schießen (+ prep)   to shoot; to fire; to kick; to score

■ Er schoß zu niedrig (/zu weit/in die Luft/mit einer Pistole).
He shot too low (/too far/in the air/with a pistol).

■ Er schießt eine Kugel auf das Tier (/auf den Hasen/auf ihn/auf die Wand).
He's shooting (a bullet) at the animal (/the hare/him/the wall).

■ Der Stürmer hat aufs Tor (/ins Netz/nach vorn) geschossen.
The forward shot (or kicked) at the goal (/into the net/forward).

■ Die Blumen (/Meine Kinder) sind in die Höhe geschossen.
The flowers have sprouted up (/My children have shot up).

■ Er hat ihn in den Fuß (/in den Kopf) geschossen.
He shot him in the foot (/head).

■ Das Blut schoß aus dem Schnitt im Finger.
The blood shot out of the cut in his finger.

schimpfen auf/über + A ⟨auf/über jdn/etw s.⟩   to bitch about (sb/sth) (inf); to curse
(about *or* at) (sb/sth)

■ Er schimpft ständig über seinen Manager (/das neue Büro/alles).
He constantly bitches about his manager (/the new office/everything).

- Er wurde sehr ärgerlich und schimpfte auf uns alle (/auf meinen Bruder/alles).
  He became very angry and swore at all of us (/my brother/everything).

schimpfen mit + D ⟨mit jdm s.⟩   to scold (sb); to tell (sb) off

- Während der Arbeit hat der Lehrer mit mir geschimpft, weil ich aus dem Buch abguckte.
  The teacher scolded me during the exam because I was cheating from the book.
- Wegen der schlechten Noten schimpfte die Mutter mit dem Kind.
  The mother scolded the child because of his bad grades.
- Der Boß schimpfte mit der Sekretärin, weil sie so viele Grammatikfehler machte.
  The boss bawled out the secretary because she made so many grammatical mistakes.

(s.) schlagen (+ prep)   to hit; to beat; to strike; to slap

- Er schlägt mit dem Hammer auf den Nagel (/den Gegenstand).
  He's hitting the nail (/object) with the hammer.
- Der Zimmermann hat einen Nagel in die Wand (/durch das Brett) geschlagen.
  The carpenter drove a nail in the wall (/through the board).
- Sie schlägt mit der Faust auf den Tisch (an die Tür).
  She's beating (or thumping) on the table (/on the door).
- Er hat ihn mit der flachen Hand ins Gesicht (/auf das Ohr) geschlagen.
  He slapped him in the face (/on the ear).
- Er hat ihm auf den Rücken (/auf den Kopf/in den Bauch/in die Eier *sl*) geschlagen.
  He hit him on the back (/on the head/in the stomach/in the balls sl).*
- Er schlägt das Geschirr in Stücke (*or* kurz und klein).
  He's smashing the dishes to pieces.
- Ich schlug mir an die Stirn.
  I slapped my forehead.
- Sein Herz (/Puls) schlug schnell vor Angst (/Erregung).
  His heart (/pulse) was beating fast out of fear (/excitement).
- Der Blitz hat in den Baum geschlagen.
  The lightning struck the tree.
- Beim Tischtennis schlug ich meinen Gegner (mit) 3:1.
  I beat my opponent at ping-pong (by) 3:1.

s. schlagen mit + D ⟨sich mit jdm s.⟩   to fight (with) (sb); to have a fight with (sb)

- Die Jungen haben sich miteinander geschlagen.
  The boys had a fight with each other.

■ Du darfst dich nicht mit deinem Freund (/Bruder) schlagen.
You are not allowed to fight with your friend (/brother).

---

schlagen nach + D ⟨nach jdm s.⟩   to take after (sb); to resemble (sb)

■ Sie schlägt sehr nach ihrem Vater.
She really takes after her father or She greatly resembles her father.

(s.) schleichen (+ prep)   to creep; to sneak, to steal

■ Sie schlich auf Zehenspitzen die Treppe herauf, weil die Eltern schliefen.
She tip-toed upstairs because her parents were sleeping.

■ Ich schlich mich auf leisen Sohlen (/durch die Tür) aus dem Haus.
I sneaked on soft soles (/through the door) (and) out of the house.

■ Der Teenager schlich sich spät in der Nacht durchs Fenster ins Haus und ging leise ins Bett.
Late at night the teenager sneaked into the house through the window and went quietly to bed.

■ Die Muschi ist unter das Bett (/in die Kommode) geschlichen.
The pussycat crept under the bed (/sneaked into the chest of drawers).

(s.) schleppen (+ prep)   to lug; to drag; to haul

■ Ich schleppte die Kiste nach Hause (/in den Bahnhof/in den Zug/in den Keller/auf den Boden/zur Post).
I dragged the box home (/to the train station/into the train/ into the basement/to the attic/to the post office).

■ Er hat (/Ich habe) mich durchs Museum (/durch die ganze Stadt) geschleppt.
He dragged me (I dragged myself) through the museum (/the whole city).

■ Er hat ihn (/seinen Gast) ins Kino (/zu Freunden) geschleppt.
He dragged him (/his guest) to the cinema (/to his friends).

■ Sie schleppten ihn vor den Richter (/zur Polizei).
They hauled him (up) before the judge (/to the police).

■ Sie schleppt sich mit einer Erkältung (/Grippe) herum.
She's dragging (around) with a cold (/the flu).

(s.) schließen an + A ⟨etw an etw s.⟩   to fasten (sth) to (sth)

■ Ich möchte daran die Bedingung schließen, daß . . . .
I would like to add the condition that . . . .

- Kann ich mein Fahrrad an das Geländer schießen?
  Can I fasten my bike to the railings?
- An das Konzert schloß sich eine Party (an).
  There was a dance following the concert.

schließen aus + D ⟨etw aus etw s.⟩   to infer (sth) from (sth)

- Aus seinem Aussehen konnte man nichts über sein Wesen schließen.
  One could not infer anything about his character from his looks.
- Ich schließe aus seinem Brief (/seinem Verhalten/daraus), daß. . . .
  I conclude from his letter (/behavior/that) that. . .

schließen in + A ⟨jdn/etw in etw s.⟩   to contain (sb/sth) in (sth); to include (sb/sth) in (sth)

- Sie haben den Hund in ein Zimmer (/in den Zwinger) geschlossen.
  They locked the dog up in a room (/in its doghouse).
- Diese Aussage schließt einen Widerspruch in sich.
  This statement contains a contradiction.
- Er schloß das Geld (/das Dokument/den Brief/die Akten) in seinen Schreibtisch.
  He locked the money (/document/letter/files) in his desk.

schließen mit + D ⟨mit etw s.⟩   to conclude with (sth)

- Ich möchte meinen Brief mit einem freundlichen Gruß (/einem Gedicht) an Ihre Familie (/dich) schließen.
  I would like to conclude this letter with my best regards (/a poem) to your family (/to you).

  ⟨etw mit jdm s.⟩   to conclude (sth) with (sb)

  - Sie haben einen Vertrag (/Freundschaft/Frieden) mit ihnen geschlossen.
    They concluded a contract (/formed a friendship/arrived at a peaceful conclusion) with them.

schmachten nach + D ⟨nach jdm/etw s.⟩   to yearn for (sb/sth)

- Er schmachtet nach einer Zigarette (/einem Glas Bier).
  He is yearning for a cigarette (/a glass of beer).

- Sie schmachtete nach ihm. *(liter)*
  She was pining for him.

schmecken nach + D ⟨nach etw s.⟩   to taste of (sth); *(fig)* to smack of (sth)

- Das schmeckt nach Fisch (/Minze/ranziger Butter/zu viel Vanille).
  That tastes like fish (/mint/rancid butter/(there is) too much vanilla).
- Die Wurst schmeckt nach dem Grill.
  The sausage tastes like the grill.
- Diese Speise schmeckt nach nichts (/nach mehr).
  This food is tasteless (/It tastes so good; i.e., one would like to eat more).
- Das schmeckt nach Korruption!
  That smacks of corruption!

schmeißen (+ prep)   to throw; to sling; to chuck

- Er hat das Buch in die Ecke (/an die Tafel/in den Schrank/aufs Dach/nach mir) geschmissen.
  He chucked the book in the corner (/at the board/into the closet/on the roof/at me).
- Ich weiß, daß Ingrid sich meinem Sohn an den Hals zu schmeißen versucht.
  I know that Ingrid is trying to throw herself at my son.
- Ich war todmüde und schmiß mich sofort aufs Bett.
  I was dead-tired and threw myself on the bed right away.
- Er schmiß mit Kieselsteinen auf einen Laternenpfahl (/nach dem Kind).
  He threw (or chucked) stones at a lamppost (/the child).

s. schmeißen auf + A ⟨sich auf jdn/etw s.⟩   to throw oneself to/at (sb/sth) *(inf)*

- Ich schmiß mich auf den fliehenden Dieb und hielt ihn fest.
  I threw myself on the fleeing thief and held onto him.
- Du sollst dich nicht auf ihn schmeißen. Er ist schon verheiratet.
  You shouldn't throw yourself at him. He's already married.
- Ich habe mich auf die Decke geschmissen und geschlafen.
  I threw myself on the blanket and slept.

schnappen nach + D ⟨nach jdm/etw s.⟩   to snap *or* take a snap at (sb/sth)

- Das Tier schnappte nach dem Fleisch (/der Karotte/meiner Hand/mir).
  The animal snapped at the meat (/carrot/my hand/me).

- Der Taschendieb schnappte nach ihrer Tasche und rannte weg.
  The pickpocket snatched her purse and ran away.
- Als das Mädchen wieder (aus dem Wasser) auftauchte, schnappte es nach Luft.
  When the girl resurfaced (from the water), she gasped for breath.

schneiden (+ prep)   to cut

- Ich habe mich an der Rasierklinge (/mit dem Messer/an der Säge/am Glas) geschnitten.
  I cut myself on the razor blade (/with the knife/saw/glass).
- Ich habe mich (/mir in den Finger/mir in die Haut) geschnitten.
  I cut myself (/my finger/my skin).
- Er schnitt das Brot (/Fleisch/die Tomaten) mit einem scharfen Messer (in Scheiben).
  He cut (sliced) the bread (/meat/tomatoes) with a sharp knife.
- Der Schüler schnitt seinen Namen in den Tisch (/in das Holz).
  The student cut (or engraved) his name into the table (/wood).
- Die Mutter hat sich beim Gemüseschneiden geschnitten.
  The mother cut herself while cutting vegetables.

schreiben (+ prep)   to write; to spell

- Er schrieb damit auf das Blatt Papier (/an die Tafel/ins Gästebuch).
  He used it to write on the sheet of paper (/on the board/in the guestbook).
- Sie hat für die Zeitung geschrieben.
  She wrote for the newspaper.
- Er schrieb seinen Namen (mit einem Füller) unter den Antrag.
  He put his signature on the petition (with a pen).
- Wie schreibt man das Wort „Cool"?—Das Wort „Cool" schreibt man mit „C".
  How do you write or spell the word "cool"?—The word "cool" is spelled with a "c."

schreiben an + A ⟨**jdm** *or* **an jdn s.**⟩   to write to (sb)

- Ich schreibe bald meinen (*or* an meine) Eltern (/Ihnen *or* an Sie).
  I'll write to my parents (/to you) soon.
- Jetzt bist du an der Reihe, an mich (*or* mir) einen Brief zu schreiben.
  Now it's your turn to write me a letter.

schreiben an + D ⟨**an etw s.**⟩   to write on (sth); to be writing (sth)

- Der Autor schrieb an seinem Roman (/seinen Memoiren) von 1878–81.
  The author was writing his novel (/memoirs) from 1878–81.

■ Der Lehrer schrieb ein Gedicht an die Tafel, das er mit den Schülern besprechen wollte.
The teacher wrote a poem on the blackboard that he wanted to discuss with the students.

schreiben über/von + A/D ⟨über jdn/etw, von jdm/etw s.⟩   to write about (sb/sth)

■ Er schreibt einen Bericht über Friedrich den Großen (/Kuwait).
He's writing a report about Fredrick the Great (/Kuwait).

■ Er schrieb von seinen großen Taten (/Eroberungen).
He wrote about his great deeds (/conquests).

schreien (+ prep)   to shout; to cry out

■ Sie hat um Hilfe geschrien, aber niemand konnte sie hören.
She cried out for help but nobody could hear her.

■ Sie schrie vor Zorn (/Schmerz/Lachen).
She shouted out of anger (/out of pain/roared with laughter).

schreien nach + D ⟨nach jdm/etw s.⟩   to shout for (sb); to cry out for (sth)

■ Das Kind schrie nach seinem Vater (/Milch/dem Spielzeug).
The child shouted for his father (/milk/the toy).

■ Das Baby schreit nach dem Schnuller.
The baby is crying (out) for the pacifier.

■ Die Bürger schrieen nach Vergeltung (/Rache/Krieg/Frieden/Versöhnung).
The citizens cried out for retaliation (/revenge/war/peace/reconciliation).

schreiten zu + D ⟨zu etw s.⟩   to get down to (sth)

■ Die Regierung mußte zum Äußersten (/zur Tat) schreiten.
The government had to take extreme measures (/had to get down to work).

■ Wir müssen jetzt zur Abstimmung (/Wahl) schreiten.
We must now have the vote.

■ Die Familie und die Verwandten schritten hinter dem Sarg her.
The family and the relatives followed behind the casket.

(s.) schützen gegen/vor + A/D ⟨sich/jdn/etw gegen/vor etw s.⟩   to protect (o.s./sb /sth) against/from (sth)

■ Vor Hitze (/Sonnenlicht) schützen! Den Film vor Licht schützen!
Keep away from heat (/sunlight)! Protect the film from light!

- Er schützte seinen Sohn (/sich) vor Ansteckung (/Gefahr).
  He protected his son (/himself) from infection (/danger).

- Das Medikament schützt vor Kopfschmerzen (/der Grippe).
  The medicine protects (one) against headaches (/the flu).

- Du mußt dich gegen ungerechtfertigte Mieterhöhungen Schützen.
  You must protect yourself against unjustifiable rent increases.

- Diese Jacke wird dich gegen den Wind (/den Regen) schützen.
  This jacket will protect you from the wind (/rain).

schwärmen für + A ⟨für jdn/etw s.⟩   to be mad *or* wild *or* crazy about (sb/sth)

- Er schwärmt für schnelle Autos (/für das Windsurfen/blonde Mädchen/sie/diese Art von Filmen).
  He's crazy about fast cars (/wind surfing/blond girls/her/this kind of film).

- Ich schwärme nicht gerade fürs Sticken. (*ironic*)
  I'm not exactly crazy about embroidery.

schwärmen von + D ⟨von jdm/etw s.⟩   (*to relate enthusiastically*) to be enthused about /over (sth); to rave or gush about (sth)

- Sie schwärmte den ganzen Abend von ihrer Türkei-Reise (/von dem guten Essen bei uns/ihrem neuen Mann/der Qualität der Produkte).
  She raved the whole evening about her trip to Turkey (/the good food at our place/her new husband/the quality of the products).

- Sonia schwärmt noch immer davon, wie ihr Vater Brot gebacken hat.
  Sonia still raves about how her father made bread.

schwarzsehen für + A ⟨für jdn/etw s.⟩   to be pessimistic about (sb/sth)

- Bei dem Wetter sehe ich für unsere Wanderung schwarz. Siehst du (die Lage) nicht schwarz?
  With this weather I'm pessimistic about our hiking. Aren't you pessimistic (about the situation)?

- Ich sehe für den Kandidaten (/die Wahl) sehr schwarz.
  I'm very pessimistic for the candidate (/about the election).

schwimmen (+ prep)   to swim

- Er schwamm auf dem Rücken (/im Kraulstil/auf der Seite).
  He swam the backstroke (/Australian crawl/on his side).

- Sie ist zweimal durch das Becken geschwommen.
  She swam twice (across) the swimming pool.

- Einige der Schiffbrüchigen konnten ans Ufer (*or* an Land/zur Insel) schwimmen.
  Some of the shipwrecked people were able to swim ashore (or to the shore/to the island).

- Das Schiffchen des Kindes schwimmt auf dem Teich (/im Wasser).
  The child's little ship is afloat on the pond (/the water).

schwitzen (+ prep)   to sweat

- Er schwitzte vor Hitze (/Aufregung/Anstrengung).
  He sweated from the heat (/the excitement/hard work).

- Er schwitzt am ganzen Körper (/am Kopf/im Gesicht/ an den Händen/unter den Armen/auf dem Rücken/in der Sauna).
  He is sweating all over his body (/on his head/on his face/on his hands/under his arms/on his back/in the sauna).

- Sie schwitzt schnell beim Arbeiten (/beim Spielen/bei der Arbeit).
  She sweats easily while working (/playing/at work).

- Alle Leute schwitzen bei 36 Grad (/bei körperlicher Bewegung/beim Training/bei Sportübungen/beim Bodybuilding).
  All people sweat at 36°C (/during physical exercises/during (athletic) practice/during (athletic) exercises/while body building).

schwören auf + A ⟨auf jdn/etw s.⟩   to swear by (sb/sth)

- Er hat auf die Bibel (/die Verfassung) geschworen.
  He swore on the Bible (/constitution).

- Sie schwört auf die Rezepte von Betty Crocker.
  She swears by the recipes of Betty Crocker.

- Der Trainer schwörte auf seinen Mittelstürmer. Er hatte in jedem Spiel ein Tor geschossen.
  The coach swore by his center forward. He had scored a goal in each game.

- Ich schwöre (darauf), daß ich diesen Mann beim Stehlen gesehen habe.
  I swear I have seen this man stealing.

schwören bei + D ⟨bei jdm s.⟩   to swear by (sb)

- Ich schwöre bei Gott (/allen Heiligen/meiner Ehre/meiner Mutter), daß....
  I swear by God (/all the saints/my honor/my mother) that....

schwören (without prep)   to swear

- Die Soldaten schwören den Fahneneid.
  The soldiers are pledging their allegiance to the flag.
- Ich schwöre (dir), daß seine Anschuldigungen falsch sind.
  I swear (to you) that his accusations are false.
- Schwören Sie (vor diesem Gericht, mit erhobener Hand), daß...?
  Do you swear (before this court, with your hand raised) that...?

(s.) sehen (+ prep)   to see, to look

- Eva sah zu Boden (/nach oben/nach allen Seiten/nach rechts/auf den Bild-schirm/durch die Sonnenbrille/durch das Fenster nach draußen/nach vorn/zum Himmel).
  Eva looked down (/up/in all directions/to the right/at the screen/through the sunglasses/through the window to the outside/ahead/to the sky).
- Der Detektiv sah auf den Verbrecher und....
  The detective looked at the criminal and....
- Ich sah ihr in die Augen (/ins Gesicht).
  I looked her right in the eyes (/face).
- Ich sah ihn (auf der Straße) kommen (/gehen/sprechen/fahren).
  I saw him (on the street) coming (/going/talking/driving).
- Davon (/Von ihr) ist nichts mehr zu sehen.
  There is no sign left of it (/her).
- Ich sehe ihn nicht so talentiert (/erfolgreich/stur) wie du.
  I don't consider (or see) him as gifted (/successful/stubborn) as you do.
- Ich sehe mich (/ihn) in der Zukunft als Anwalt (/Filmstar).
  I see myself (/him) in the future as being a lawyer (/movie star).

sehen an + D ⟨an etw s.⟩   to see from/on (sth)

- Ich sah an seinem Gesicht (/seinen Augen), daß er zornig war.
  I saw in his face (/eyes) that he was angry.
- Woran sehen Sie, daß der Schüler gestern schwänzte?—Ich sehe das an seinem schuldbewußten Gesicht.
  How do you know that the student cut class yesterday?—I can see that from the guilty expression on his face.
- An der Art, wie die Dame lief und sprach (/angezogen war), sah ich, daß sie eine Prostituierte war.
  From the way she was walking and talking (/dressed), I knew she was a prostitute.

sehen auf + A ⟨**auf etw s.**⟩   to be particular about (sth); to pay attention to (sth); to care about (sth)

■ Sie sieht sehr auf Sauberkeit (/Pünktlichkeit).
She is very particular about cleanliness (/punctuality).

■ Sie sieht sehr aufs Geld.
She is very careful with her money.

■ Warum siehst du nur auf deinen Vorteil?
Why are you only considering your own advantage?

■ Ich sehe darauf, daß meine Tochter immer ein Frühstücksbrot mit zur Schule nimmt.
I see to it that my daughter always takes a sandwich to school.

sehen auf/nach + A/D ⟨**auf/nach etw s.**⟩   to look on to (sth)

■ Unser Hotelzimmer sah auf den (*or* nach dem) Berg (/Wald/Garten).
Our hotel room looked out onto the mountain (/forest/garden).

■ Ich sah auf meine Uhr und es war 11.
I looked at my watch, and it was eleven o'clock.

■ Sie hat auf das (*or* nach dem) Thermometer gesehen und die genaue Temperatur notiert.
She looked at the thermometer and noted the exact temperature.

sehen aus + D ⟨**aus etw s.**⟩   to see from (sth); to infer from (sth)

■ Ich sehe aus deinem Brief (/deiner Bemerkung/deinem Akzent/deiner Erscheinung), daß. . . .
I see from your letter (/remark/accent/appearance) that. . . .

■ Aus dem, was sie gesagt hat, kann man sehen, daß sie sehr empfindlich ist.
From what she said one can tell she's very sensitive.

s. sehen lassen (bei + D) ⟨**sich (bei jdm) s. lassen**⟩   to let oneself be seen; to show oneself; to put in an appearance; to drop in on (sb)

■ Er hat sich bei uns (/hier) lange nicht mehr sehen lassen.
He hasn't shown up at our house (/here) for a long time.

■ Der neue Chef ließ sich bei unserer Betriebsfeier sehen.
The new boss put in an appearance at our business party.

■ Wenn du mich wegschickst, werde ich mich nie wieder hier (/bei dir) sehen lassen.
If you send me away, I'll never show my face here again.

- Warum läßt du dich nicht bei mir (/bei mir zu Hause) sehen?
  Why don't you drop in (/drop by at my house)?
- Manche Schauspieler lassen sich bei jedem großen Festival sehen.
  Some actors put in an appearance at every great film festival.
- Laß dich mal (bald) (bei mir) wieder sehen!
  Do come again (soon)!
- Ich lasse mich hier (/in der Schule) nie wieder sehen!
  I will not show my face here (/at this school) again!

sehen in + D ⟨in jdm/etw etw sehen⟩　to look *or* see (sth) in (sb/sth)

- Die Ehefrau sieht in ihrer Nachbarin ihre schlimmste Feindin.
  The wife sees her neighbor as her worst enemy.
- Die USA sahen in der Raketenstationierung in Kuba eine Bedrohung ihrer Sicherheit.
  The USA saw the stationing of the rockets in Cuba as a threat to its security.
- Ich sehe in den Äußerungen des Präsidenten keine Provokation.
  I see no provocation in what the president said.
- Ich sehe in seinen Plänen eine schlimme Bedrohung für die Nachbarländer.
  I see in his plans a serious threat to the neighboring countries.

sehen nach + D ⟨nach jdm s.⟩　to look after *or* take care of (sb)

- Die Krankenschwester sieht nach meinem kranken Bruder.
  The nurse is looking after my sick brother.
- Ich sehe immer wieder einmal nach den Kindern im Garten.
  I'll keep an eye on the children in the backyard.
- Bitte sieh nach der Suppe (/nach dem Kuchen im Backofen), wenn ich beim Einkaufen bin.
  Please have a look at the soup (/the cake in the oven) when I'm gone shopping.
- Unsere Stadt sieht nach anderen Wegen der Abfallbeseitigung.
  Our city is looking into other ways to dispose of garbage.
- Karl, hast du schon nach der Post gesehen?—Nein, aber ich sehe gleich danach.
  Have you checked the mail yet, Karl?—No, but I'll check right away.

s. sehnen nach + D ⟨sich nach jdm/etw s.⟩　to long for (sb/sth)

- Du mußt dich bestimmt nach deinen Kindern (/ihm/Ruhe/zu Hause) sehnen.
  You must certainly be longing for your children (/him/peace and quiet/home).
- Mein Freund sehnt sich nach seiner Heimat (/nach Polen/nach der Schweiz).
  My friend longs for his homeland (/Poland/Switzerland).

- Ich sehne mich danach, dich bald zu sehen (/küssen).
  I long to see (/kiss) you soon.

sein (+ prep)　to be

- Peter ist nach unten (/nach Hause/in die Stadt/an den Strand). (*inf*)
  Peter has gone downstairs (/home/downtown/to the beach).
- Daniel ist nach New York (/auf Urlaub *or* im Urlaub/am Strand/zu Hause/in der Stadt).
  Daniel has gone to New York (/on vacation/to the beach/home/to the city).
- Was ist mit dem Mädchen (/dir)? Ist was?
  What's the matter with the girl (/you)? Is something the matter?
- Wie wäre es mit einer Partie Schach (/einem Glas Wein/diesem Witz)?
  How (or What) about a game of chess (/a glass of wine/How is that for a joke)?
- Der Student (/Professor) ist jetzt auf der Universität Köln.
  The student (/professor) is now (studying) at the University of Cologne.
- Der Schnee ist geschmolzen. Es ist nichts mehr mit (dem) Skifahren. (*fig*)
  The snow has melted. Skiing is out (or over) now.
- Er ist gut zu Tieren (/kleinen Kindern).
  He is good to animals (/little children).
- Sie ist durch und durch New Yorker (/Münchnerin).
  She's a New Yorker (/a person from Munich) through and through.
- Mir ist, als wäre ich da gewesen (/als hätte ich das schon einmal gesehen).
  I feel as though I have been there (/I had seen it once already).
- Er ist aus Deutschland (/der Schweiz/dem Iran/den USA/Amerika).
  He's from Germany (/Switzerland/Iran/the USA/America).
- Er ist gern für sich. Ich bin gern für mich.
  He likes to be alone. I like to be alone.
- Ich bin zu allem (/diesem Plan/dieser Arbeit) fähig.
  I'm capable of doing everything (/this plan/this work).

sein (with infinitive + zu)　to be

- Das ist nicht mit Geld zu bezahlen.
  Money can't buy that.
- Dieses Dokument ist persönlich (/von dir) bei der Bank abzugeben.
  The document is to be delivered by hand (/by you) at the bank.
- Wie ist diese Bemerkung (/dieser Brief) zu verstehen?
  How should this remark (/letter) be understood?

- Er ist nicht zu sehen (/ersetzen/verstehen).
  He cannot be seen (/replaced/understood).
- Mit ihr ist ja nicht zu reden!
  You can't talk to her!
- Es ist zu hoffen (/erwarten), daß Michael das Examen schafft.
  It is to be hoped (/expected) that Michael will pass the exam.

senden (+ prep)   to send; to broadcast

- Er hat den Brief per (*or* durch) Eilboten (/mit der Luftpost) gesandt.
  He sent the letter express (/by air).
- Das Fernsehen (/Der Rundfunk) sandte Aufnahmen von der Fußballweltmeisterschaft nach Amerika.
  The television (/radio) broadcast the World Cup to America.

setzen (+ prep)   to put, to set, to place

- Er setzte den Stuhl (/das Baby) an den Tisch.
  He set the chair (/baby) at the table.
- Er setzte das Kind auf den Stuhl (/den Schoß/auf die Schultern).
  He put the child on the chair (/on his lap/on his shoulders).
- Ich möchte Sie darüber in Kenntnis setzen, daß....
  I would like to inform you that....
- Er hat das in Musik (/in Klammern/in die Zeitung) gesetzt.
  He put that to music (/in parentheses/in the paper).
- Sie setzte den Schnuller (/das Glas) an den Mund (/die Lippen) des Babys.
  She put the pacifier (/glass) to the baby's mouth (/lips).

s. setzen (+ prep)   to sit down

- Ich setze mich ans Fenster (/in einen Sessel/auf den Vordersitz/ nach vorne im Zug/neben ihn/auf ihren Platz/an die Arbeit).
  I'll sit down at the window (/in the armchair/in the front seat/in the front of the train/next to him/at her place/I will get down to work).
- Er setzte sich ins Gras (/ins Licht/in den Schatten/in die Sonne/unter die Eiche/zu uns).
  He sat down in the grass (/in the light/in the shade/in the sun/under the oak tree/ and joined us).

setzen auf + A ⟨etw auf etw s.⟩   to put (sth) on (sth)

- Setzen Sie bitte die Ausgaben auf meine Rechnung.
  Please put the expenditures on my bill.

- Das Theater hat „Faust" auf den Spielplan gesetzt.
  The theater put "Faust" on their program.

- Was setzen wir auf die Tagesordnung (/Speisekarte)?
  What are we going to put on the agenda (/menu)?

- Er setzte sehr viel Geld auf das Pferd (/schwarz/die Nummer 24). (*fig*)
  He bet (or put) a lot of money on the horse (/black/the number 24).

- Die Mutter hat ihr Vertrauen (/ihre Hoffnung) auf mich gesetzt.
  My mother put her trust (/hope) in me.

setzen über + A ⟨**über etw s.**⟩   to jump over (sth); to cross (sth)

- Das Kind (/Pferd) ist über eine Pfütze (/einen Zaun/ein Hindernis) gesetzt.
  The child (/horse) jumped over (or cleared) a puddle (/fence/ hurdle).

- Sie setzten über den Fluß (/den Rhein).
  They crossed the river (/the Rhine).

setzen unter + A ⟨**etw unter etw s.**⟩   to put *or* write down (sth) to (sth)

- Er setzte seinen Namen (*or* seine Unterschrift) unter das Dokument (/ein Komma dahinter/einen Punkt dahinter).
  He put his signature on the document (/a comma after that/a period after that).

s. setzen zu + D ⟨**sich zu jdm s.**⟩   to sit with (sb)

- Ich möchte mich zu Ihnen setzen. Darf ich?
  I would like to join you. May I?

- Willst du dich zu mir (/den Schmidts/uns/dem Mädchen) setzen?
  Do you want to join me (/the Schmidts/us/the girl)?

- Die Familie setzte sich zu Tisch.
  The family sat down at the table to eat.

s. sichern gegen/vor + A/D ⟨**sich gegen/vor etw s.**⟩   to protect oneself against (sth)

- Der Akrobat hat sich durch ein Netz gegen die (*or* vor der) Gefahr gesichert.
  The acrobat protected himself (against the danger of falling) with a net.

- Wir sicherten das Auto mit einem Brett gegen das (*or* vor dem) Wegrollen.
  We prevented the car from rolling by putting a board (behind the tire).

- Es stürmt mächtig. Wir müssen die Fenster vor dem Zuschlagen sichern.
  There's a powerful storm. We must secure the windows from slamming shut.

- Man kann sich einfach nicht gegen alle Gefahren sichern.
  You simply cannot protect yourself against all possible dangers.

siegen über/gegen + A ⟨über/gegen jdn/etw s.⟩   to triumph over (sb/sth)

- Unsere Mannschaft hat wieder (gegen sie) gesiegt (*or* gewonnen).
  Our team won (triumphed over them) again.
- Er hat zehn Kilo abgenommen. Er hat über seine Freßsucht gesiegt.
  He has lost ten kilos. He has triumphed over his gluttony.

sinken (+ prep)   to sink; to go down

- Das Schiff (/Er) ist auf den Grund (des Meeres) gesunken.
  The ship (/He) sank to the bottom (of the ocean).
- Ich bin todmüde auf meinen Stuhl (/zu Boden) gesunken.
  I sank dead-tired into my chair (/to the ground).
- Vor Peinlichkeit wünschte ich, in den Boden zu sinken.
  I was so embarassed that I wished I could have disappeared (into the floor).
- Er sank auf die Knie (/auf die *or* zur Erde).
  He sank to his knees (/to the ground)

sinnen auf + A ⟨auf etw s.⟩   to devise (sth); to think (sth) up; to think of *or* scheme *or* plot (sth)

- Er sann auf allerlei Mittel und Wege, den einflußreichen Posten zu bekommen.
  He devised all kinds of schemes to get the influential position.
- Jahrelang hat er auf Rache gesonnen.
  For years he plotted his revenge.

sinnen über + A ⟨über etw s.⟩   to reflect on *or* brood over (sth)

- Ich sinne darüber, ob dieser Satz richtiges Deutsch ist.
  I have been thinking about whether this sentence is correct German.

sinnen (without prep)   to feel inclined; to ponder

- Ich bin nicht gesonnen, mich mit ihm zu unterhalten.
  I do not feel inclined to have a conversation with him.

sitzen (+ prep)   to sit

- Er saß auf dem Stuhl (/in dem Sessel/auf der Couch/auf dem Boden/vor dem Fernseher/im Gras/am Tisch/zu meinen Füßen/mitten unter den Schülern).
  He was sitting on the chair (/in the armchair/on the couch/on the floor/in front of the TV/on the grass/at the table/at my feet/in the middle of the students).

- Wir saßen beim Essen (/beim Frühstück/beim Mittagessen/beim Kaffee/beim Tee/beim Eis/beim Nachtisch/beim Kartenspiel/beim Schach).
  We were sitting (in order) to eat (/to eat breakfast/to eat lunch/to drink coffee/to drink tea/to have ice cream/to eat dessert/to play cards/to play chess).

- Sie hat fast vier Stunden bei der Friseuse gesessen.
  She sat at the beauty salon almost four hours.

- Er sitzt in der Regierung (/im Vorstand/im Parlament/im Gefängnis/an einer Aufgabe/über seinen Büchern/für ein Porträt).
  He's in the government (/on the board/in Parliament/in jail/sitting over a task/sitting or poring over his books/sitting for a portrait).

- Der Nagel (/Haken) sitzt locker in der Wand.
  The nail (/hook) is loose in the wall.

- Robert sitzt auf der Toilette (*or* auf dem Klo *(sl)*).
  Robert is sitting on the toilet (or in the john (sl)).

sorgen für + A ⟨für jdn/etw s.⟩   to take care of (sb), to look after (sb), to care for (sth); to provide for (sb/sth)

- Sie sorgt für ihre kranke Großmutter (/für die Kleidung der Kinder).
  She is taking care of her sick grandmother (/her children's clothing).

- Die Mutter wird für gutes Essen und kalte Getränke sorgen.
  Mother will supply good food and cold drinks.

- Ich sorge für Bier, Musik und Proviant für die Party.
  I'll take care of (or provide) the beer, music and the supplies for the party.

- Er sorgt immer für seine Familie (/für sich selbst).
  He always provides for his family (/fends for himself).

- Ich muß bald für ein Zimmer (/eine Wohnung/ein Taxi) sorgen.
  I have to find a room (/an apartment/a taxi) soon.

- Ich sorge dafür, daß die Kinder ihre Schularbeiten machen.
  I'll see to it that the children do their homework.

s. sorgen um + A ⟨sich um jdn/etw s.⟩   to be worried about (sb/sth)

- Die Mutter sorgt sich um ihre Kinder, weil sie auf der Straße spielen.
  The mother is worried about her children because they're playing in the street.

- Sie sorgt sich um ihren alkoholkranken Mann (/ihre gemeinsame Zukunft/die Erziehung ihrer Kinder).
  She is concerned about her alcoholic husband (/their future together/the education of her children).

- Ich sorge mich um die Gesundheit meiner Eltern.
  I'm worried about my parents' health.

- Wir sorgen uns um unser Leben (/unsere Zukunft).
  We are worried about our lives (/future).

s. Sorgen machen um + A ⟨sich um jdn/etw Sorgen machen⟩   to worry about (sb/sth)

- Ich mache mir Sorgen um mein Kind bei dem vielen Verkehr heutzutage.
  I worry about my child with all the traffic nowadays.

- Der Vater hat sich um seine an Schule uninteressierte Tochter Sorgen gemacht.
  The father was worried about his daughter who was uninterested in school.

sparen an/mit + D ⟨an/mit etw s.⟩   to be sparing with (sth)

- Wenn man langsamer fährt, spart man (an) Benzin (/Energie).
  If you drive slower, you'll save (on) gas (/energy).

- Spar nicht an (*or* mit der) Sonnencreme. Ein Sonnenbrand ist viel schlimmer.
  Don't be stingy with the suntan lotion; a sunburn is much worse.

- Sie spart am falschen Ende (*or* Platz *or* Ort *or* an der falschen Stelle). Sie spart an Lebensmitteln anstatt an Kosmetik.
  She economizes in the wrong place. She economizes on food instead of cosmetics.

- Der gute Lehrer hat gewöhnlich nicht mit (*or* an) Lob gespart.
  The good teacher was usually lavish in his praise.

- Spar nicht so mit (*or* an) der Butter (/der Sahne/den Rosinen)! Der Kuchen schmeckt sonst nicht.
  Don't skimp on the butter (/cream/raisins)! The cake won't taste good otherwise.

sparen auf/für etw + A ⟨auf/für etw s.⟩   to save up for (sth)

- Nicole spart (bei einer Bank) für (*or* auf) ein Fahrrad (/eine Goldkette).
  Nicole is saving at a bank for a bicycle (/a gold chain).

- Sie spart für ein Haus (/eine Waschmaschine/Menschen in der Dritten Welt/die Ausbildung der Kinder).
  She's saving up for a house (/a washing machine/people in the Third World/the education of her children).

spekulieren auf + A ⟨auf etw s.⟩   to have hopes for/of (sth)

- Der Vorsitzende hat lange auf diese Entwicklung (/diese Entscheidung/diesen Posten) spekuliert.
  The chairman has had hopes for (or *of*) *this development (/decision/ position) for a long time. /The chairman had his eye on this development (/decision/ position).*

- Der Sohn spekuliert schon lange auf den Nachlaß (*or* das Erbe) seines Vaters.
  The son has had an eye on his father's inheritance for a long time.

sperren für + A ⟨etw für jdn/etw s.⟩   to close (sth) to (sb/sth)

- Die Polizei hat den Eingang (/die Brücke/die Straße) für den Verkehr gesperrt.
  The police closed (off) the entrance (/bridge/the street) to traffic.

- Die Regierung hat die Grenzen für die Einfuhr von Waren aus China gesperrt.
  The government has closed the borders to the import of goods from China.

- Das Schloß (/Der Turm) ist für Touristen gesperrt.
  The castle (/tower) is closed (off) to tourists.

s. sperren gegen + A ⟨sich gegen etw s.⟩   to balk (at sth)

- Ich sperrte mich gegen seinen Entschluß, das zu tun.
  I balked at his decision to do that.

- Warum mußt du dich gegen alles sperren? Du sperrst dich sogar dagegen, einen längeren Urlaub zu nehmen.
  Why do you balk at everything? You even balk at taking a longer vacation.

sperren in + A ⟨jdn in etw s.⟩   to shut *or* lock (sb) in (sth)

- Man soll Tiere nicht in einen Käfig sperren.
  People should not keep animals in a cage.

- Der Verbrecher sollte ins Gefängnis gesperrt werden.
  The criminal should be locked (up) in (the) prison.

s. spezialisieren auf + A ⟨sich auf etw s.⟩   to specialize in (sth)

- Die meisten Ärzte spezialisieren sich auf ein bestimmtes Gebiet (/Kinderheilkunde).
  Most doctors specialize in a certain area (/pediatric medicine).

- Ich würde mich gern auf Soziolinguistik spezialisieren.
  I would like to specialize in sociolinguistics.

spielen (+ prep)   to play

■   Sie spielte mit dem Spielzeug (/der Puppe/den Karten/dem Ball/ihm).
She played with the toy (/doll/cards/ball/him).

■   Wir spielen heute gegen sie (/ihre Mannschaft).
We're playing against them today (/their team).

■   Er spielt etwas auf dem Klavier (/auf der Orgel/auf der Geige/auf der Gitarre/auf der Trommel).
He's playing something on the piano (/organ/violin/guitar/drum).

■   Die Band spielt zur Unterhaltung (/zur Hochzeit/zum Vergnügen/zum Tanz).
The band's playing for entertainment (/a wedding/fun/a dance).

■   Was wird hier gespielt?—Man spielt heute in diesem Kino einen alten Film.
What is playing here or What's going on here?—They're showing an old film in this theater today.

■   Sie spielt in der Lotterie (/um den ersten Preis/im Ernst/nur zum Spaß).
She plays in the lottery (/for first prize/seriously/just for fun).

■   Er spielte (Roulette und Backgammon) um Geld (/50 Mark).
He gambled for money (/50 marks) (on roulette and in backgammon).

■   Spielt er lieber seine Stereoanlage oder das Radio?—Bei ihm spielt immer die Stereoanlage.
Does he prefer to have the stereo or the radio on?—He always has his stereo on.

■   Im Auto spielt bei mir immer das Radio (/Country-Musik).
I always have the radio (/country music) on in the car.

■   Die Farbe deines Kleides spielt ins Bräunliche (/Gelbliche).
The color of your dress has a brownish (/yellowish) tinge.

■   Michael Jordan spielt in der Mannschaft der Chicago Bulls.
Michael Jordan plays for the Chicago Bulls.

spielen mit + D ⟨mit jdm/etw s.⟩   to play (around) with (sb/sth); to toy with (sb/sth)

■   Ich will nicht mit ihm (/seinen Gefühlen/seinem Gewissen) spielen.
I don't want to toy with him (/his feelings/his conscience).

■   Ich spielte mit der Idee (/Erwägung), den teuren Mantel zu kaufen.
I played around with the idea (/notion) of buying the expensive coat.

■   Die Kinder dürfen nicht mit Feuer spielen.
The children are not allowed to play with fire.

spotten über + A ⟨über jdn/etw s.⟩   to mock (sb/sth); to poke fun at (sb/sth); to ridicule (sb/sth)

■   Peter spottet über seine Schwester, weil sie einen eigenartigen Haarschnitt hat.
Peter is poking fun at his sister because she has a peculiar haircut.

■ Über ernste Angelegenheiten soll man nicht spotten.
One shouldn't make light of serious matters.

■ Mußt du immer über mich spotten?
Do you always have to ridicule me?

sprechen (+ prep)   to speak, to talk

■ Er sprach im Rundfunk (/im Fernsehen/im Traum/mit sich selbst/vor einer großen Menschenmenge/zu den Zuschauern/mit Akzent).
He spoke (or was speaking) on the radio (/on television/in his sleep/to himself/in front of a large crowd/to the spectators/with an accent).

■ Der Präsident hat über den Rundfunk (*or* das Radio) an das Volk gesprochen.
The president spoke to the people over the radio.

■ Ich spreche aus Erfahrung (/dem Gedächtnis/einer Telefonzelle).
I'm speaking from experience (/memory/a telephone booth).

■ Hermann konnte vor Wut (/Schreck/Erregung) kaum sprechen.
Hermann could hardly speak from rage (/fright/excitement).

■ Kann ich bitte den Manager (/ihn/Frau Schmidt) sprechen?—Er ist für Sie (/niemanden) zu sprechen.
May I speak to the manager (/him/Mrs. Schmidt)?—He's available for you (/not available for anyone).

■ Er war nicht zum Sprechen zu bringen.
You couldn't make him speak.

sprechen für + A ⟨für jdn/etw s.⟩   to speak in place of *or* speak for (sb); to speak on behalf of (sb/sth)

■ Ich spreche für meine Frau, die heute nicht hier sein kann.
I'm speaking on behalf of my wife who cannot be here today.

■ Martin Luther King sprach für alle, die nicht für sich selbst sprechen konnten.
Martin Luther King spoke on behalf of all the people who could not speak for themselves.

sprechen für/gegen + A ⟨für/gegen jdn/etw s.⟩   to speak for/against (sb/sth)

■ Was spricht dafür (/dagegen)?—Vieles spricht dafür (/dagegen).
What is there to be said for (/against) that?—There is much to be said for it (/against it).

■ Der Staatsmann sprach engagiert für den Frieden (/für die Befreiung der Unterdrückten).
The statesman spoke committedly in support of peace (/the oppressed people).

- Das spricht nicht für den neuen Trainer (/die Gesellschaft), daß . . . .
  It doesn't say much for the new coach (/company) that . . . .
- Die Beweise (/Alle Anzeichen) sprechen dafür, daß . . . .
  The evidence (/Everything) points to the fact that . . . .
- Das Ergebnis (/Die Tatsache) spricht für sich (selbst).
  The result (/fact) speaks for itself.
- Peter sprach für (/gegen) die Grünen (/die Erhöhung der Steuern).
  Peter spoke for (/against) the Greens (/a tax increase).

sprechen mit + D ⟨mit jdm s.⟩   to talk to (sb); to have a word with (sb)

- Ich muß mit dem Chef sprechen, um ihn darüber zu informieren.
  I must talk to (or have a word with) the boss to inform him about it.
- Ich habe mit dir zu sprechen. Es ist wichtig, daß ich mit dir bald spreche.
  I have to talk to you. It is important that I talk to you soon.
- (Am Telefon) Ich möchte mit Ihrer Tochter Eva sprechen. Mit wem spreche ich?
  (On the phone) I would like to speak to your daughter, Eva. With whom am I speaking, please?
- Jetzt will ich nicht darüber sprechen. Ich muß erst mit meinem Anwalt sprechen.
  I don't want to talk about it now; I must speak to my lawyer first.
- Sprechen Sie bitte mit lauter (/leiser) Stimme!
  Please speak with a loud (/soft) voice!
- Ich will nicht mit jedem sprechen, der hierherkommt.
  I don't want to talk to everyone who walks in here.
- Die Mitschüler (/Wir) sprechen nicht mehr miteinander.
  The schoolmates (/We) are no longer on speaking terms.
- So mußt du nicht mit mir (/deiner Großmutter) sprechen!
  You mustn't talk (or speak) that way to me (/your grandmother)!

sprechen über/von + A/D ⟨über jdn/etw, von jdm/etw s.⟩   to speak about (sb/sth)

- Worüber spricht der Mann?—Über den Gebrauch der deutschen Tempora (/über die Außenpolitik).
  What is the man speaking about?—He's speaking about German (verb) tenses (/foreign policy).
- Wovon spricht der Mann eigentlich?—Ich habe keine Ahnung, wovon er spricht.
  What (in heaven's name) is the man talking about?—I have no idea what he's talking about.
- Richard Nixon hat mehrmals vor großem Publikum über Recht und Ordnung gesprochen.
  Richard Nixon spoke on several occasions about law and order before a large public.

- Wir sprachen gerade über dich (*or* von dir), als du ankamst.
  We were just talking about you when you arrived.

- Im Seminar sprach der Professor über „Die Verwandlung" von Kafka. Danach sprachen wir weiter darüber. Wir haben auch über den (*or* von dem) gutaussehenden Professor gesprochen.
  The professor talked about "The Metamorphosis" by Kafka in the seminar. Afterwards we talked further about it. We also talked about the good-looking professor.

- Er hat von seiner (*or* über seine) Reise (und über sein neues Buch) gesprochen.
  He talked about his trip (and about his new book).

- Darüber soll man unter keinen Unständen sprechen.
  One should not talk (or speak) of such things under any circumstances.

sprechen vor + D ⟨vor jdm/etw s.⟩   to speak in front of (sb/sth)

- Vor dem Kind solltest du nicht über solche Sachen sprechen.
  You shouldn't speak about such things in front of the child.

- Der Ministerpräsident sprach vor (/zu) dem Parlament.
  The prime minister spoke before (/to) Parliament.

sprechen zu + D ⟨zu jdm s.⟩   to speak *or* address (sb)

- Der Kanzler sprach zu (/vor) Vertretern der Wirtschaft.
  The Chancellor addressed (/spoke in front of) representatives of the economy.

- Der Präsident sprach über den Rundfunk zu den Soldaten am Persischen Golf (/über das Fernsehen an das Volk).
  The President addressed the soldiers in the Persian Gulf over the radio (/the people over the television).

springen (+ prep)   to spring; to leap; to jump

- Paul sprang über den Zaun (/in die Höhe/nach unten/zur Seite/aufs Pferd/über Bord/ins Wasser/auf den Boden/auf seine Schultern).
  Paul jumped over the fence (/up/down/aside/onto the horse/overboard/into the water/on the floor/onto his shoulders).

- Franz, spring schnell zum Nachbarn (/zum Bäcker/zum Geschäft)! *(inf)*
  Franz, run to the neighbor (/to the bakery/to the store) quickly!

springen aus + D ⟨etw springt aus etw⟩   to jump out of (sth)

- Der Zug ist aus den Schienen (/aus dem Gleis) gesprungen.
  The train jumped (or ran off) the rails (/track).

- Das Blut sprang ihm aus der Nase.
  The blood ran (or gushed) (out) from his nose.
- Aus dem Vulkan springen Staub, Lava und Asche.
  Dust, lava, and ashes are gushing out of the volcano.

spritzen (+ prep)   to spray; to squirt; to splash

- Er spritzt (Wasser) auf das Feuer (/auf den Rasen/auf die Wäsche).
  He's spraying (or splashing) water over the fire (/on the lawn/on the clothes).
- Das Kind spritzte mir (mit seiner Wasserpistole) Wasser ins Gesicht (/auf die Kleidung/über meine Jacke).
  The child squirted water on my face (/on my clothes/over my jacket)(with his water gun).
- Man spritzt Pflanzen immer noch mit Chemikalien.
  They still spray plants with chemicals.
- Bitte spritze ein bißchen Schlagsahne (/Ketchup) darauf!
  Please squirt a little whipped cream (/ketchup) on it!
- Sei vorsichtig, daß das heiße Fett nicht aus der Pfanne spritzt.
  Be careful that the hot oil doesn't splatter out of the pan.
- Er hat sein Auto mit einer roten Farbe gespritzt.
  He sprayed (or painted) his car red.
- Ich spritze schnell zur Post (/zum Fleischer). *(fig)*
  I'll dash to the post office (/butcher shop).

spucken (+ prep)   *(inf)* to spit; to spew (out)

- Er spuckte auf den Boden (/ihm ins Gesicht).
  He spat on the ground (/in his face).
- Die Lava (/Das Feuer/Das Blut) spuckte daraus.
  The lava (/fire/blood) spewed from it.
- Der Drache spuckte Feuer aus Maul und Nasenlöchern.
  The dragon spit fire from its mouth and nostrils.

stammen aus/von + D ⟨aus etw, von jdm s.⟩   to date from (sb/sth); to be *or* come from (sb/sth)

- Sie stammt aus gutem Haus (/einer guten Familie/Hamburg).
  She comes from a good home (/a good family/Hamburg).
- Der Ring (/Die alte Bibel) stammt von meiner Großmutter.
  The ring (/old Bible) is from (or belonged to) my grandmother.
- Die Nachricht stammt aus zuverlässiger Quelle.
  The news comes from a reliable source.

- Der Ausspruch (/Die Bemerkung) stammt von ihm (/Oscar Wilde).
  The word (/remark) is from (or was coined by) him (/Oscar Wilde).

- Das Wort „Barbier" stammt aus dem Lateinischen (/von dem lateinischen Wort „barba").
  The word "barber" is derived from Latin (/the Latin word "barba").

starren auf + A ⟨auf jdn/etw s.⟩   to stare at (sb/sth)

- Der Tourist starrte gebannt auf die schöne Aussicht (/den schönen See/auf die hübsche Führerin).
  The tourist gazed at the beautiful view (/lake/pretty guide) with awe.

- Warum starrst du so auf mich (/mein neues Auto)?
  Why are you staring at me (/my new car) like that?

starren in + A ⟨in jdn/etw s.⟩   to stare *or* gaze in(to) (sb/sth)

- Er hat ins Leere (/ins Dunkel/in den Himmel/ins Loch) gestarrt.
  He stared (or gazed) into space (/the darkness/the sky/the hole).

- Die Lehrerin starrte mir (/meinem Bruder) ins Gesicht.
  The teacher stared me in the face (/stared into my brother's face).

starren von/vor + D ⟨von/vor etw s.⟩   to be covered with (sth); to bristle with (sth)

- Der Hinterhof (/Die Küche) hat vor (*or* von) Schmutz gestarrt.
  The back courtyard (/kitchen) was covered with dirt (or was awfully filthy).

- Die Soldaten (/Gladiatoren) starrten von Waffen.
  The soldiers (/gladiators) were laden with weapons.

staunen über + A ⟨über jdn/etw s.⟩   to be astonished *or* amazed at (sb/sth)

- Ich staune über dich (/deine Geschicklichkeit/darüber, wie du den Rekord brachst).
  I am amazed at you (/your cleverness/how you broke the record).

- Die Zuschauer staunten über das Wunderkind.
  The spectators were amazed at the child prodigy.

(s.) stechen (+ prep)   to prick; to sting

- Eine Wespe hat ihn auf dem Kopf (/in den Fuß) gestochen.
  A wasp stung him on the head (/stung his foot).

■   Ich stach mich mit der Nadel (/an den Dornen/an der Rose/in den Finger).
    I pricked myself with the needle (/on the thorns/on the rose/in the finger).

■   Das (/Das Pulver/Der Gestank) sticht in die Augen (/in die Nase).
    That (/The powder/The stench) stings one's eyes (/nose).

■   Die Krankenschwester hat ihr durch die Ohrläppchen gestochen.
    The nurse pierced her ears.

■   Er sticht mit dem Trumpfas.
    He is taking the trick with the ace of trump.

■   Er stach mit einem Schraubenzieher in den Getreidesack.
    He poked (or stabbed) into the grain sack with a screwdriver.

stechen nach + D ⟨nach jdm s.⟩   to stab at (sb)

■   Er stach nach ihm.
    He stabbed at him.

(1) stecken (+ prep)   to put, to place

■   Das Kind steckte den Pfennig in die Flasche (/in den Spartopf).
    The child put (or inserted) the penny into the bottle (/piggy bank).

■   Du mußt den Stecker in die Steckdose stecken, bevor du das Radio anmachst.
    You must put the plug in the outlet before you turn on the radio.

■   Ich habe es in den Umschlag (/in den Briefkasten/in den Koffer/in seine Tasche/mir in den Mund) gesteckt.
    I put it into the envelope (/the mailbox/the suitcase/in his pocket/in my mouth).

■   Sie steckten ihn ins Gefängnis (/ins Bett/in Uniform).
    They put him in jail (/tucked him in bed/put him in uniform).

■   Steck das Hemd in die Hose (/den Rock)!
    Tuck your shirt into your pants (/skirt)!

stecken an + A ⟨etw an etw s.⟩   to put *or* pin (sth) on (sth)

■   Ich habe (mir) den Ehrenpreis (/die Brosche/die Blume) an den Mantel gesteckt.
    I put (or pinned) the prize (/brooch/flower) on the coat.

(2) stecken (+ prep)   to be stuck; to be

■   Die Räder steckten (*or* staken) im Schnee (/Schlamm/Graben).
    The wheels were stuck in the snow (/mud/ditch).

■   Weißt du, ob der Stecker in der Steckdose steckt?
    Do you know if the plug is in the outlet?

■   Der Schlüssel steckt in der Tür (/in dem Schlüsselloch).
    The key is in the door (/keyhole).

■   Die Schraube steckt fest in der Mutter (/im Metall)
    The nut is stuck to the screw (/metal).

■   Er steckt mitten in der Arbeit.
    He is right in the middle of his work.

stehen (+ prep)   to stand; to be; to remain

■   Hans stand auf dem Boden (/an der Tafel/auf Zehenspitzen/an der Bushaltestelle/mitten auf der Straße/im 30. Lebensjahr).
    Hans stood on the floor (/at the blackboard/on his toes/at (or waited at) the bus stop/in the middle of the street/was 30 years old).

■   Der Schauspieler stand vor zehn Jahren auf der Höhe seines Ruhms (/dem Höhepunkt seiner Karriere).
    The actor stood at the height of his fame (/career) ten years ago.

■   Das steht auf dem Tisch (/auf Seite 25/im Buch/unter Druck).
    That is on the table (/on page 25/in the book/under pressure).

■   Wir haben eine Menge Geld auf unserem Konto (/auf der Bank) stehen.
    We have a lot of money in our account (/in the bank).

■   Was steht in dem Magazin (/auf dem Tagesplan/auf der ersten Seite)?
    What is in the magazine (/on the day's schedule/on the first page)?

■   Was steht auf dem Schild (/im letzten Absatz der Geschichte)?
    What does the sign (/the last paragraph of the story) say?

■   Wo steht der Zeiger?—Er steht auf 10 Uhr.
    What does the clock say?—It is 10 o'clock.

■   Wir standen lange miteinander in Briefwechsel (/Kontakt).
    For a long time we corresponded with one another (by letter) (/kept in contact).

■   Er steht immer noch unter dem Schutz des FBI (/seinem Einfluß/dem Einfluß von Drogen).
    He is still under the protection of the FBI (/his influence/the influence of drugs).

■   Dieses Zitat (/Wort/Der Satz/Es) steht bei John Steinbeck.
    This quotation (/word/The sentence/It) is from John Steinbeck.

stehen auf + A ⟨auf etw s.⟩   to be punished with (sth); to be rewarded with (sth)

■   Auf Abtreibung steht in vielen Ländern eine hohe Strafe.
    There is a high penalty for abortion in many countries.

- Auf Vergewaltigung (/Mord) steht lebenslängliches Gefängnis in diesem Land.
  The punishment for rape (/murder) is life imprisonment in this country.
- Auf die Ergreifung des Verbrechers (/Mörders) steht eine Belohnung von 10.000 Mark.
  There is a 10,000 mark reward for the apprehension of the criminal (/murderer).

stehen auf + A ⟨**auf jdn/etw s.**⟩   to be crazy about (sb/sth); (*inf*) to go for (sb/sth)

- Ich stehe sehr auf Schach (/Tennis/schnelle Musik/den Rocksänger)
  I'm crazy about chess (/tennis/fast music/the rock singer).
- Er steht besonders auf Blauäugige (/auf schlanke Brünette).
  He goes for blue eyes (/slim brunettes).

stehen für + A ⟨**für etw s.**⟩   to symbolize (sth); to represent *or* stand for (sth)

- Der Name Albert Einstein steht für Intelligenz und Scharfsinn.
  The name Albert Einstein represents intelligence and wit.
- In diesem Gedicht steht der Falke für Freiheit und Unabhängigkeit.
  In this poem the falcon symbolizes freedom and independence.
- Diese Produkte stehen für Qualität.
  These products stand for quality.

s. stehen mit + D ⟨**sich mit jdm s.**⟩   to fare with (sb)

- Ich stehe mich zur Zeit nicht besonders gut mit meiner Freundin.
  At this time I'm not on particularly good terms with my girlfriend.
- Dieser Student steht sich sehr gut mit seinem Professor.
  This student is on very good terms with his professor.

stehen mit/um + D/A ⟨**mit jdm/etw, um jdn/etw s.**⟩   to be *or* feel well with (sb/sth)

- Alles steht sehr gut mit meiner Oma (/mit dem Unternehmen). *or* Alles steht gut um meine Oma (/um das Unternehmen).
  All is well with my grandmother (/the business).

stehen vor + D ⟨**vor etw s.**⟩   to be stiff with (sth)

- Die Jacke steht vor Schmutz (/Dreck).
  The jacket is stiff with dirt (/from filth).

stehen zu + D ⟨**zu jdm/etw s.**⟩   to stand by (sb/sth); to think about (sb/sth)

- Wie stehen Sie denn zu meinem Vorschlag (/Angebot)?
  What do you think about my proposal (/offer)?
- Wirst du zu deinem Wort (/deiner Aussage/mir in Notzeiten) stehen?
  Will you stand by your word (/statement/me in times of need)?
- Ich finde es anerkennenswert, daß du zu deinen Fehlern stehst.
  I find it commendable (or appreciate) that you admit to your mistakes.
- Ich stehe zu dem, was ich Ihnen versprochen habe.
  I stand by what I've promised you.

steigen (+ prep)   to climb on(to)

- Udo stieg auf die Leiter (/auf einen Stuhl/aufs Podium/über das Hindernis/ins Bett/in die Badewanne/aufs Dach/auf einen hohen Berg/auf einen Baum).
  Udo climbed the ladder (/onto a chair/to the podium/over the obstacle/into bed/into the bathtub/onto the roof/a high mountain/a tree).
- Jens stieg ins Auto (/aufs Fahrrad/vom Fahrrad/in den Zug/in den Bus/in den 2. Stock/vom Baum/aufs Pferd).
  Jens got into the car (/on the bicycle/down from the bicycle/into the train/on the bus/onto the third floor/down from the tree/on the horse).
- Er muß nun aus dem Zug (/Bus/Flugzeug) steigen.
  He must now get off the train (/bus/plane).
- Sein Fieber stieg auf 39 Grad.
  His fever rose to 39 degrees.
- Unsere Miete ist um etwa 10% gestiegen.
  Our rent has increased by about 10%.
- Vor Zorn stieg mir das Blut in den Kopf (/das Gesicht).
  Blood rushed into my head (/face) from anger.

(s.) steigern auf + A ⟨**(sich) auf etw s.**⟩   to intensify to (sth); to increase; to add to (sth)

- Die Geschwindigkeit steigerte sich in 5 Sekunden auf 70 kmh.
  The speed increased to 70 km/h in 5 seconds.
- Der Juwelier steigerte den Preis des Ringes auf 800 Mark.
  The jeweler increased the price of the ring to 800 marks.

(s.) steigern zu + D ⟨**(sich) zu etw s.**⟩   to increase to (sb/sth)

- Sie hat sich zu einer erstklassigen Weitspringerin gesteigert.
  She improved her performance and became a first-class long jumper.

- Ihre Lügen (/Gleichgültigkeit) steigerten (/steigerte) seinen Zorn.
  Her lies (/indifference) increased his rage.

- Der Regen steigerte sich zum Hagelschauer.
  The rain turned into a hailstorm.

stellen (+ prep)   to put; to place

- Ich stelle die Sache unter das Bett (/neben die Lampe/in die Ecke/hinter die Tür/zwischen die Stühle/an die Wand).
  I'll put (or place) the thing under the bed (/next to the lamp/ in the corner/behind the door/in between the chairs/against the wall).

- Ich will mich (/dich) nicht vor diese Entscheidung (/Wahl) stellen.
  I don't want to put myself (/you) in the position of having to make this decision (/choice).

- Er stellte das Auto in die Garage (/das Pferd in den Stall).
  He put the car into the garage (/the horse into the stable).

- Ich habe mir (/ihr) eine Schüssel Suppe auf den Tisch gestellt.
  I put a bowl of soup on the table for myself (/her).

- Es ist prima, daß du jetzt auf dich selbst gestellt bist.
  It is great that you are on your own now.

- Stell den Schalter (/den Hebel) nach rechts (/auf Null/auf „warm").
  Turn the switch (/lever) to the right (/to zero/to "warm").

- Für morgen früh muß ich den Wecker auf 6 Uhr stellen.
  For tomorrow morning I must set the alarm for 6.

- . Ich muß meine Uhr nach dem Radio (/nach deiner/nach der Bahnhofsuhr) stellen.
  I'll have to set my watch by the radio (/by yours/the train station's clock).

- Ich stellte das Bier für die Feier (/für die Feier kalt).
  I donated the beer (/put the beer in a cool place) for the party.

s. stellen (+ prep)   to (go and) stand; to position oneself; to arise

- Ich stelle mich auf die Leiter (/vor die Klasse/ans Fenster/auf einen Stuhl/dorthin/hinter Franz/auf die Zehenspitzen).
  I'll (go and) stand on the ladder (/in front of the class/at the window/on a chair/over there/behind Franz/on tip-toe).

- Der Eisschrank stellt sich von selbst höher.
  The icebox will turn itself up.

- Ich stelle mich auf den Standpunkt, daß wir alle das tun sollen.
  I take the view that we should all do that.

s. stellen gegen + A ⟨**sich gegen jdn/etw s.**⟩   to oppose (sb/sth)

- Ich stellte mich in der Auseinandersetzung gegen meinen Chef.
  I opposed my boss in the conflict.

- Eine Mehrheit stellte sich gegen die Regierung (/die Pläne der Regierung, immer weiter aufzurüsten).
  A majority opposed the government (/the government's plans to keep up the arms race).

s. stellen hinter + A ⟨**sich hinter jdn/etw s.**⟩   to support *or* back (sb/sth)

- Wir stellen uns voll hinter Sie (/ihn/den Plan/den Vorschlag/den Entschluß).
  We fully stand by (or support) you (/him/the plan/the proposal/the decision).

s. stellen vor + A ⟨**sich vor jdn/etw s.**⟩   to shield *or* protect (sb/sth); to stand up for (sb/sth).

- Der Leibwächter stellte sich vor den Präsidenten, um ihn vor Wurfgeschossen zu schützen.
  The bodyguard placed himself in front of the president to protect him from things that were being thrown.

- Der Kanzler stellte sich vor den Verteidigungsminister, der von der Presse scharf angegriffen worden war.
  The chancellor stood up for his defense secretary, who had been attacked sharply by the press.

s. stellen zu + D ⟨**sich zu jdm/etw s.**⟩   to feel *or* think about (sth); to take a (positive/negative) view of (sb/sth)

- Wie stellen Sie sich zu dem neuen Vorgesetzten (/den neuen Vorschriften)?
  How do you feel about the new boss (/regulations)?

- Ich weiß nicht, wie er sich zu meinem Entschluß (/Plan/dazu) stellt.
  I don't know how he feels (or what he thinks) about my decision (/plan/that).

stemmen (+ prep)   to press; to prop

- Wenn mein Vater zornig wird, stemmt er die Arme in die Hüften (*or* Seiten).
  Whenever my father gets mad, he stands arms akimbo.

- Unglaublich, wie er so viel Gewicht in die Höhe (/über sich) stemmen kann!
  It's amazing how much weight he can lift (/over his head)!

s. stemmen gegen + A ⟨sich gegen etw s.⟩   to brace oneself against (sth); to set oneself against (sth); to oppose (sth)

■ Ich habe mich gegen die Tür (/den Schrank) gestemmt.
   I braced myself against the door (/wardrobe).

■ Sie stemmten sich energisch gegen den Bau eines neuen Flughafens.
   They vigorously opposed the building of a new airport.

sterben (+ prep)   to die

■ Achim starb an einem Herzschlag (/einem Unglück/einer Krankheit/einer Verletzung/Altersschwäche/Lungenentzündung).
   Achim died of a heart attack (/an accident/a sickness/an injury/old age/pneumonia).

■ Die alte Frau starb aus Traurigkeit über den Tod ihres Mannes.
   The old woman died of sorrow over the death of her husband.

■ Sie starb durch einen ärztlichen Kunstfehler (/in Narkose/an der Operation).
   She died due to a doctor's mistake (/under anaesthetic/during the operation).

■ Er starb durch einen einzigen Schuß (/einen gedungenen Mörder).
   He died by a single shot (/He was killed by a hired killer).

■ Leider ist das Kind bei der Geburt gestorben.
   Unfortunately the child died at birth.

■ Er ist mit 75 Jahren (*or* im Alter von 75 Jahren) gestorben.
   He died at the age of 75.

sterben für + A ⟨für jdn/etw s.⟩   to die for (sb/sth)

■ Er starb für seine Überzeugung (/Religion/politischen Neigungen).
   He died for his convictions (/religion/political inclinations).

■ Der Soldat starb für sein Land (/sein Vaterland/seinen Kaiser) auf dem Schlachtfeld.
   The soldier died for his country (/fatherland/emperor) on the battle field.

sterben vor (+ noun without article) ⟨vor etw s.⟩   to die of (sth)

■ Ich sterbe vor Angst (,wenn ich nur daran denke). (*fig*)
   I'm frightened to death (or scared stiff) (when I think of that).

■ Renate ist fast vor Angst (/Kälte/Hunger/Neugierde/Lachen) gestorben.
   Renate almost died of fright (/cold/starvation/curiosity/laughter).

stimmen (+ prep)   to be right; to be correct

- In unserem Verhältnis (/Zwischen uns) stimmt in letzter Zeit etwas nicht.
  There has been something wrong with our relationship (/between us) lately.

stimmen für/gegen + A ⟨für/gegen jdn/etw s.⟩   to vote for/against (sb/sth)

- Er hat für (/gegen) die Vereinigung (/den Golfkrieg) gestimmt.
  He voted for (/against) the unification (/the War in the Gulf).

- Ich weiß nicht, ob ich für oder gegen diesen Vorschlag (/dich/diesen Kandidaten) stimmen soll.
  I don't know if I should vote for or against this proposal (/you/this candidate).

stinken (+ prep)   to stink; to reek

- An der Sache (/dem Wahlkampf/dieser Entscheidung) stinkt etwas. *(inf)*
  There's something fishy about it (/this campaign/this decision).

- Der Schüler (/Mann) stinkt vor Faulheit.
  The student (/man) is a lazybones.

stinken nach + D ⟨nach etw s.⟩   to stink (of) (sth)

- Das Zimmer stinkt nach Knoblauch (/faulen Eier/Mist/Schweiß/Farbe).
  The room smells of garlic (/rotten eggs/manure/sweat/paint).

- Auf dem Bauernhof stinkt es nach Kuhmist (/Tieren/Gas).
  There is a smell of cow manure (/animals/gas) on the farm.

- Die Wohnung (/Er) stinkt nach Kneipe (/nach Knoblauch).
  The apartment smells like a bar (/He smells of drink) (/garlic).

- Das stinkt nach Verschwörung (/Lüge/Betrug/höheren Steuern). *(inf)*
  That smells of conspiracy (/That definitely sounds like a lie/That reeks of fraud /higher taxes).

stoßen (+ prep)   to push, to shove; to poke; to kick; to nudge

- Er hat ihn von der Treppe (/ins Schwimmbad/von der Leiter/aus dem Zug/aus dem Haus) gestoßen.
  He shoved him down the stairs (/into the swimming pool/pushed him from the ladder/out from the train/threw him out of the house).

- Er stieß mit dem Ellenbogen (/dem Fuß/dem Kopf) gegen den Schrank.
  He pushed on the cabinet with his elbow (/foot/head).

- Ich wurde von ihm zur Seite (/in die Seite) gestoßen.
  I was pushed to the side (/nudged) by him.

- Sie stieß ihn mit einem Stock (/von sich).
  She poked him with a stick (/pushed him away).

- David, stoß nicht mit den Füßen nach ihm (/mir)!
  David, don't kick him (/me)!

- Das Auto stieß gegen eine Straßenlaterne (/ein anderes Auto).
  The car crashed into a street light (/another car).

(s.) stoßen an + D ⟨sich an jdm/etw s.⟩   to bump *or* run against/into (sb/sth), to knock against (sb/sth)

- Ich stieß mir den Kopf an der niedrigen Decke. *or* Ich stieß mit dem Kopf an die niedrige Decke.
  I bumped my head against the low ceiling.

- Ich stoße mich daran, wenn man grausame Experimente mit Tieren macht.
  I take exception to people doing cruel experiments on animals.

stoßen auf + A ⟨auf jdn/etw s.⟩   to encounter (sb/sth); to hit upon (sb/sth)

- In diesem Artikel bin ich auf eine interessante Hypothese gestoßen.
  I came across an interesting hypothesis in this article.

- Sie sind unerwartet auf Grundwasser (/Gold) gestoßen.
  They struck water (/gold) unexpectedly.

- Wir sind auf einige schwierige Probleme (/Abneigung/Opposition) gestoßen.
  We ran up against some difficult problems (/rejection/opposition).

- Wenn Sie dieser Straße folgen, stoßen Sie direkt auf den Bahnhof.
  If you follow this road, you will come straight to the station.

- In dem Bahnhof bin ich auf einen alten Mitschüler gestoßen.
  I ran into an old classmate in the train station.

streben nach + D ⟨nach etw s.⟩   to strive for (sth)

- Er strebt nach Erkenntnis (/Gewinn/Macht/Ruhm/Vollkommenheit).
  He strives for knowledge (/profit/power/fame/perfection).

- Ich strebe danach, eine gute Ausbildung zu bekommen.
  I'm striving to get a good education.

streichen (+ prep)   to spread; to apply; to stroke; to rub; to strike; to paint; to waft

- Er streicht Butter (/Marmelade/Käse) auf das Brot.
  He's putting (or spreading) butter (/jam/cheese) on the bread.

- Sie hat dem Kind ein Brötchen mit Erdnußbutter gestrichen.
  She made a peanut butter sandwich for the child.

- Ich will mir Butter und Honig aufs Brot streichen.
  I want to spread butter and honey on my bread.

- Er strich mit der Hand über den Seidenstoff (/die Wand/ihr Gesicht).
  He ran his hand over (or felt or stroked) the silk material (/wall/her face).

- Er streicht das Zimmer (/die Wände) mit Latexfarbe.
  He is painting the room (/walls) with latex paint.

- Der Hund streicht mir um die Füße.
  The dog is rubbing against my feet.

- Sie hat sich das Haar aus der Stirn (/dem Gesicht) gestrichen.
  She pushed her hair back from her forehead (/face).

- Er hat sich nachdenklich über das Kinn (/den Bart) gestrichen.
  He thoughtfully stroked his chin (/beard).

streichen aus + D ⟨etw aus etw s.⟩   to strike (sth) out

- Wir können diesen Paragraphen (/dieses Wort) aus dem Vertrag (/Protokoll) streichen.
  We can strike (or eliminate) this clause (/word) from the contract (/these minutes).

- Sie haben den Artikel aus dem Katalog gestrichen.
  They have struck (or eliminated) the item from the catalogue.

(s.) streichen (mit etw) über + A ⟨sich/jdm (mit etw) über etw s.⟩   to stroke (sb) with (sth)

- Ich strich ihr (mit der Hand) über den Rücken (/die Schultern/den Hals/den Kopf).
  I stroked her back (/shoulders/neck/head) (with my hand).

- Ich habe mir mit den Fingern durchs Haar gestrichen.
  I ran my fingers through my hair.

streifen (+ prep)   to touch, to brush; to scrape

- Er hat ihn am Arm (/an seinem Hemd) gestreift.
  He touched him on the arm (/his shirt).

- Er streifte gegen die Stoßstange (/das Mädchen/die frisch gestrichene Tür).
  He brushed against the bumper (/girl/newly-painted door).

- Die Kugel hat ihn nur ein bißchen an der Stirn (/am Kinn) gestreift.
  The bullet just grazed his forehead (/chin).

- Der Lehrer hat dieses Thema (in seinem Vortrag) nur gestreift.
  The teacher only touched on the topic (in his lecture).

streifen durch + A ⟨**durch etw s.**⟩   to roam or ramble *or* prowl through (sth)

- Inge ist durch die Felder (/den Wald/die Gegend) gestreift.
  Inge was roaming (or wandering) through the fields (/forest/area).

(s.) streifen über + A ⟨**(sich) etw über etw s.**⟩   to slip (sth) over/into (sth)

- Er hat (sich) den Stiefel über den Fuß gestreift.
  He slipped the boot on his foot.
- Ich habe (mir) das Hemd (/das Sweatshirt) über den Kopf gestreift.
  I slipped the shirt (/sweatshirt) over his head.

streifen von + D ⟨**etw von etw s.**⟩   to slip (sth) off (sth)

- Sie streifte den Ring von ihrem Finger (/die Strümpfe von ihren Beinen.)
  She slipped the ring off her finger (/the nylons off her legs).
- Sie streifte die Fliege vom Gesicht (/das Fett vom Löffel).
  She brushed the fly from her face (/scraped the fat off the spoon).
- Du solltest langsam mal die Asche von der Zigarre streifen.
  It's about time you knocked the ash off your cigar.

streiken (+ prep)   to strike; to be on strike

- Wofür streiken die Arbeiter? —Sie streiken für höhere Löhne (/längeren Urlaub
  /bessere Arbeitsbedingungen).
  *Why are the workers on strike? —They are striking (or are on strike) for higher
  wages (/longer vacations/better working conditions).*

streiten für/gegen + A ⟨**für/gegen etw s.**⟩   to fight for/against (sth); to fight *or* stand
  up for (sb/sth), to champion the cause of (sb/sth)

- Sie streitet für ihre Prinzipien (/die Idee der Gleichheit/Gerechtigkeit).
  She is fighting for her principles (/the ideal of equality/justice).
- Sie stritten für ihr Land (/gegen ihre Feinde).
  They fought for their country (/against their enemies).

streiten mit + D ⟨**mit jdm/etw s.**⟩   to fight *or* argue with (sb/sth)

- Er stritt mit Fäusten (/Waffen/einem Gewehr/Worten) für seine Sache.
  He fought for his cause with his fists (/weapons/a gun/words).

■ Er hat wieder mit seinem Bruder gestritten.
He fought (or quarrelled) with his brother again.

streiten über + A ⟨über etw s.⟩   to dispute *or* argue about *or* over (sth); to go to
court over (sth)

■ Die Professoren stritten über ein gelehrtes Thema.
The professors had a dispute about a scholarly subject.

■ Wir haben lange über das Problem (miteinander) gestritten.
We argued about the problem (with each other) a long time.

■ Ich will nicht wieder mit dir darüber streiten, daß du vor 12 zu Hause sein mußt.
*I don't want to argue with you again about your having to be home before 12
o'clock.*

s. streiten über + A ⟨sich über etw s.⟩   to quarrel about (sth)

■ Ich will mich nicht wieder über diese Frage (/dieses Problem/die Qualität unserer
Ehe) mit dir streiten.
*I don't want to quarrel with you again about this question (/this problem/the
quality of our marriage).*

■ Darüber kann man (*or* läßt) sich streiten.
That's a debatable (or moot) point.

■ Sie stritten sich über jede Kleinigkeit.
They quarrelled about every little thing.

(s.) streiten um + A ⟨(sich) um etw s.⟩   to argue about (sth), to quarrel about sth

■ Das Ehepaar streitet (sich) oft um nichts.
The married couple often quarrels about nothing.

■ Die Soldaten (/Sportler) stritten um den Sieg.
The soldiers (/athletes) fought for victory.

■ Sie stritten sich um jede Kleinigkeit.
They fought over every little thing.

■ Er hat sich mit seiner geschiedenen Frau nicht nur um die Kinder, sondern auch
um die Möbel gestritten.
*He fought with his divorced wife not only over the children, but also about the
furniture.*

■ Jens streitet sich immer mit Lauras Schwester um die Spielsachen.
Jens always fights over the toys with Laura's sister.

studieren (+ prep)   to study; to be a student, to be at the university

- Er studiert an der Universität Illinois (/an der Harvard Universität).
  He's (a student) (or He's studying) at the University of Illinois (/at Harvard University).

- Ich studierte bei Doktor Martin. Er ist Professor an der Universität Illinois.
  I studied under Doctor Martin. He's a professor at the University of Illinois.

- Er studierte an der Hochschule für Musik (/für Kunst).
  He studied at (or was a student at) the conservatory (/the art college).

- Sie studiert im dritten Jahr Politologie.
  She's a junior (or is in her third year) in college studying political science.

(s.) stürzen (+ prep)   to fall; to plunge

- Er stürzte in den Fluß (/ins Meer/in den See/ins Wasser).
  He fell into the river (/sea/lake/water).

- Sie stürzte von der Leiter (/vom Fahrrad) und brach sich den Arm.
  She fell from (or off) the ladder (/bicycle) and broke her arm.

- Er stürzte ihn (/sich) aus dem Fenster.
  He hurled him out of the window (/He committed suicide by jumping out of the window).

- Der Betrunkene stürzte auf der Straße (/auf dem Eis/auf der Treppe/beim Laufen/zu Boden).
  The drunk man fell on the street (/ice/steps/while walking/to the ground).

- Er hat sich aus dem Zug (/von der Brücke) in den Fluß gestürzt.
  He threw himself from the train (/the bridge) into the river.

- Dirk stürzte an die Tür (/zum Fenster/ins Zimmer/aus dem Haus).
  Dirk rushed to the door (/to the window/into the room/out of the house).

s. stürzen auf + A ⟨sich auf jdn/etw s.⟩   to pounce *or* throw oneself at (sb/sth)

- Er stürzte sich rasch aufs Essen (/auf seinen Feind/mich).
  He pounced on the food (/attacked his enemy/attacked me).

- Sie stürzte sich auf die Post (/Zeitung).
  She anxiously went for the mail (/grabbed the paper).

(s.) stürzen in + A ⟨sich in etw s.⟩   to throw (oneself) into (sb/sth); to plunge into (sth)

- Hans hat sie in Verlegenheit (/Verzweiflung/Unruhe) gestürzt.
  Hans threw her into a state of embarrassment (/despair/agitation).

- Ich stürzte mich in große Unkosten, als ich mir das Haus kaufte.
  I went to a great deal of expense when I bought the house.

- Ich habe mich in das Studium (/ins Vergnügen) gestürzt.
  I plunged into my studies (/flung myself into a round of pleasure).

(s.) stützen (+ prep)   to support; to shore up; to lean

- Jens, du sollst beim Essen nicht die Ellbogen auf den Tisch stützen.
  Jens, you shouldn't support your elbows on the table while you're eating.

- Verzweifelt stützte er den Kopf in die Hände.
  Despairingly, he supported his head on his hands.

- Er stützte seine Theorie (/diese Annahme) durch Beweise.
  He backed up his theory (/this assumption) with proof.

- Kannst du deine Anschuldigungen auf Tatsachen stützen?
  Can you support your accusations with facts?

s. stützen auf + A ⟨sich auf jdn/etw s.⟩   to be based on (sb/sth); to count on (sb)

- Stütz dich auf meinen Arm!
  Support yourself on my arm.

- Der Kranke mußte sich auf den Stock (/Tisch) stützen.
  The sick man had to support himself on the cane (/table).

- Im Alter konnte sie sich nur auf ihre Kinder stützen.
  When she was old, she could only lean on her children (for support).

- Diese Enttäuschung wird ihn hart treffen. Gut, daß er sich auf viele Freunde stützen kann.
  This disappointment will hit him hard. It's good that he has a lot of friends that he can count on.

suchen (+ prep)   to search for; to look for

- In einem Urlaub suche ich Ruhe und Entspannung.
  In a vacation I look for peace and relaxation.

- Man soll nicht in (*or* hinter) allem etwas Schlimmes suchen.
  One should not always look for something bad in everything.

- Sie suchte Schutz vor der Kälte (/dem Regen/Geborgenheit in der Ehe).
  She sought shelter from the cold (/the rain/sought security in marriage).

- Was sucht Frank in einer Frau? —Er sucht Intelligenz, Vermögen und Schönheit!
  What is Frank looking for in a woman? —He looks for intelligence, wealth, and beauty!

- Hier haben wir nichts zu suchen.
  We have no business being here.

suchen nach + D ⟨nach jdm/etw s.⟩   to look for (sb/sth)

- Entschuldigen Sie! Ich suche nach der Haltestelle.
  Excuse me! I'm looking for the bus stop.
- Ich suchte (vergeblich) nach einem passenden Ausdruck (/nach Worten), um mein Mitgefühl zu zeigen.
  I groped (in vain) for an appropriate expression (/words) to show my sympathy.
- Er suchte nach einem Vorwand (/einer Ausrede), der (/die) ihm ermöglichen würde, die Einladung abzulehnen.
  He tried to find a pretext (/an excuse) that would enable him to decline the invitation.
- Der Mechaniker öffnete die Motorhaube und suchte nach der Ursache des Schadens.
  The mechanic opened the hood and looked for the cause of the malfunction.
- Er suchte den Fehler (*or* nach dem Fehler) in der Rechnung.
  He looked for the mistake in the bill.
- Die Polizei suchte die (*or* nach den) Terroristen.
  The police were looking for the terrorists.
- Die Forscher suchten nach einer Gelegenheit, ihre Theorie zu publizieren.
  The researchers were looking for an opportunity to publicize their theory.

T

tadeln (+ prep)   to criticize; blame; to censure; to reprimand

- An seinem Verhalten finde (*or* habe) ich nichts zu tadeln.
  I find nothing to criticize about his behavior.
- An seinem Leben (/seiner Frau/seinem Plan/seinem Deutsch) gibt es nichts zu tadeln.
  There is nothing to criticize about his life (/wife/plan/German).

tadeln für/wegen + A/G ⟨jdn für/wegen etw t.⟩   to criticize *or* blame *or* reprimand (sb) for (sth)

- Er hat seinen Sohn streng für sein schlechtes Benehmen (/seine gemeinen Bemerkungen) getadelt.
  He strongly criticized his son's dreadful behavior (/his mean remarks).
- Der Schuldirektor hat den Schüler für sein Verhalten (*or* wegen seines Verhaltens) getadelt.
  The principal reprimanded the student for his behavior.
- Der Vater mußte ihn für seine (*or* wegen seiner) Frechheit (/Faulheit/ Nachlässigkeit) tadeln.
  The father had to criticize (or reprimand) him for his impudence (/laziness/ negligence).

tadeln (without prep)   to criticize; to blame

- Ich tadelte den frechen Jungen heute. Normalerweise tad(e)le ich nicht gerne.
  I reprimanded the impudent boy today. Normally, I don't like to criticize (people).
- Die tadelnden Bemerkungen (/Blicke) der Lehrerin störten ihn sehr.
  The reproachful remarks (/looks) of the teacher bothered him a lot.

tanzen (+ prep)   to dance

- Er hat mit diesem Mädchen Tango quer durch den Saal getanzt.
  He danced the tango with this girl across the ballroom.
- Ich kann nach dieser Melodie (/dieser Musik/diesem Lied) nicht tanzen.
  I can't dance to this tune (/music/song).
- Sie tanzte vor Freude den ganzen Tag.
  She danced for joy all day.

tasten nach + D ⟨nach etw t.⟩   to feel *or* grope for (sth)

- Er tastete (im dunklen Keller) nach ihrer Hand.
  He groped for her hand (in the dark basement).
- Der Blinde hat mit dem Stock nach dem Weg getastet.
  The blind man felt about with his cane for the way.
- Die Schimpanse tastete nach den Zitzen seiner Mutter.
  The chimpanzee was groping for his mother's teats.
- Der Zauberer tastete (mit dem Zauberstab) in der Schatulle nach etwas.
  The magician was searching for something (with his wand) in the bag.

tauchen in + A ⟨in etw t.⟩   to dive into (sth); to disappear into (sth); to skin dive

- Die Schwimmer sind ins Wasser (/in die Wellen/in den See) getaucht.
  The swimmers dived into the water (/waves/lake).
- Das Kind hat die Hand (/den Kopf/den Gegenstand/die Gabel) ins Wasser getaucht.
  The child dipped his hand (/head/the object/the fork) into the water.

tauchen nach + D ⟨nach etw t.⟩   to dive for (sth)

- Der Taucher ist (*or* hat) nach dem gesunkenen Schiff getaucht.
  The skin diver dived for the sunken ship.
- Er tauchte nach Muscheln (/seinem ins Wasser gefallenen Ring).
  He dived for mussels (/for his ring that had fallen into the water).

taugen für/zu + A ⟨für jdn/etw, zu etw t.⟩   to be suitable for (sb/sth)

- Taugt er für schwere (*or* zu schwerer) Arbeit?
  Is he capable of (or up to) hard work?
- Eva taugt nicht für diesen (*or* zu diesem) Beruf.
  Eva is not suited for this profession.
- Taugt dieses Buch auch etwas für Kinder? —Nein, es taugt nur für erwachsene Leser.
  Is this book suitable for children? —No, it's suitable only for adult readers.
- Taugt dein neuer Computer etwas?
  Is your new computer any good?
- Diese Batterien taugen nicht für meine Fernsehfernbedienung.
  These batteries aren't suited for my TV remote control.

taugen zu + D ⟨zu etw t.⟩   to be suitable for (sth)

- Er taugt nicht zum Lehrer (/Buchhalter).
  He is not suited (or not cut out) to be a teacher (/an accountant).

- Taugt dieses Buch zur Unterhaltung (*or* zum Vergnügen)? —Nein, aber es taugt zum Nachschlagen (/sich Informieren).
  Is this book suited for entertainment? —No, but it is suitable as a reference book (/a source of information).

- Diese Schere taugt nicht zum Haarschneiden.
  These scissors aren't suited for cutting hair.

tauschen (+ prep)   to exchange; to swap

- Sie haben (miteinander) Briefmarken (/Baseballbilder) getauscht.
  They swapped stamps (/baseball cards) (with each other).

- Das Kind hat sein Spielzeug gegen das seines Spielkameraden getauscht.
  The child exchanged his toy with his playmate's.

- Er tauschte Küsse (/einen Blick/Freundlichkeiten/Geschenke) mit ihr.
  He exchanged kisses (/a glance/pleasantries/gifts) with her.

tauschen mit + D ⟨jdn/etw mit jdm/etw t.⟩   to exchange (sb/sth) with (sb/sth)

- Sie haben mit den Plätzen (/Wohnungen/Pflichten/Rädern) (*or* die Plätze/ Wohnungen/Pflichten/Räder) getauscht.
  They exchanged places (/apartments/duties/bicycles).

- Ein deutscher Schüler hat mit einem Schüler in Chikago getauscht.
  A German student exchanged with a student in Chicago.

- Niemand will mit dir tauschen.
  No one wants to be in your place (I don't envy you).

täuschen (+ prep)   to deceive; to betray

- Du hast mich mit deinem Versprechen (/durch dein Vorgehen) getäuscht.
  You deceived me with your promise (/by your action).

- Laß dich nicht durch seine Liebenswürdigkeit (/sein Aussehen) täuschen.
  Don't be misled by his friendliness (/appearance).

s. täuschen in + D ⟨sich in jdm/etw t.⟩   to be deceived by (sb/sth), to be disappointed in (sb/sth)

- Ich habe mich in ihm getäuscht. Es stellte sich heraus, daß er ganz anders war, als ich angenommen hatte.

I was deceived by him. He turned out to be entirely different from what I had assumed he would be like.

- Ich sehe mich in meiner Vermutung getäuscht.
  I see I was mistaken in my assumption.

- Der Ausschuß täuscht sich in der Annahme (wenn er annimmt), daß alle mit dem Plan einverstanden sind.
  The committee is mistaken if they think that everyone is in agreement with the plan.

(s.) teilen (+ prep)   to divide (up); to divide

- Franz, kannst du 54 durch 7 teilen? —54 läßt sich nicht durch 7 teilen.
  Franz, can you divide 54 by 7? —54 cannot be evenly divided by 7.

- 54 geteilt durch 9 ist 6.
  54 divided by 9 is 6.

- Er teilt den Apfel in fünf Stücke (/in der Mitte/in drei gleiche Teile).
  He's dividing (up) the apple into five pieces (/in the middle/into three equal pieces).

- Das Beil teilte das Holz in der Mitte.
  The ax split the wood down the middle.

- Die Bevölkerung ist in ihrer Meinung über die Abtreibung geteilt.
  The population is divided over the abortion issue.

- In dieser Hinsicht (/Bei diesem Thema) teilen sich die Meinungen der Experten.
  The opinions of the experts are divided in this regard (/on this subject).

- Das Ehepaar hat alles (/seine Interessen/sein Vermögen/seine Sorgen) (miteinander) geteilt.
  The married couple shared everything (/their interests/their wealth/ their worries) (with each other).

s. teilen mit + D ⟨sich etw mit jdm t.⟩   to share with (sb/sth)

- Ich will mir mit ihm die Arbeit (/das Großreinemachen) teilen.
  I want to share the work (/housecleaning) with him.

- Die Müllers teilten sich die Kosten (/den Gewinn) mit den Meiers.
  The Müllers and the Meiers shared the costs (/profit).

- Teilst du dir diese Trauben (/Cola) mit mir?
  Are you going to share these grapes (/this Coke) with me?

teilnehmen an + D ⟨**an etw t.**⟩   to take part *or* participate in (sth)

- Der Schüler hat am Unterricht (/an den Diskussionen in der Klasse) nicht teilgenommen.
  The student didn't attend school (/participate in the class discussions).

- Er nahm an der Party (/der Tagung/den olympischen Spielen) teil.
  He joined the party (/participated in the meeting/took part in the Olympics).

- Ich nehme an einem Kurs (über russische Literatur) teil.
  I'm taking a course (in Russian literature).

- Er hat am Krieg (/am Vietnam-Krieg/an der Wahl) teilgenommen.
  He fought in the war (/in the Vietnam War/participated in the election).

- Vertreter aller Parteien nahmen an der Diskussion teil.
  Representatives of all parties participated in the discussion.

- Ärzte aus aller Welt haben an dem Kongreß (/der Konferenz) teilgenommen.
  Doctors from all over the world took part in the convention (/the conference).

- Willst du wirklich an dem Wettbewerb teilnehmen?
  Are you really considering joining the competition?

telefonieren (+ prep)   to make a (tele)phone call

- Ich habe bei ihm (/im Büro/bei Nelson) telefoniert.
  I used his telephone (/the telephone at the office/the Nelsons' phone).

- Ich will ins Ausland (/nach Bonn/nach Amerika/in die Türkei/nach Hause) telefonieren.
  I want to call outside of the country (/Bonn/America/Turkey/home).

telefonieren mit + D ⟨**mit jdm/etw t.**⟩   to make a (tele)phone call to (sb/sth)

- Ich muß mit der Schule (/dem Büro/meiner Mutter) telefonieren.
  I have to call the school (/the office/my mother).

- Er telefonierte mit mir von Hamburg aus (*or* aus Hamburg).
  He called me from Hamburg.

(s.) tippen an/auf/gegen + A ⟨**an/auf/gegen etw t.**⟩   to tap on (sth)

- Sie hat ihn (*or* ihm) auf die Schulter (/an den Rücken/an den Arm) getippt.
  She tapped him on the shoulder (/back/arm).

- Er hat kurz an diesen Punkt (/dieses Thema/daran) getippt.
  He briefly touched on this point (/issue/that).

- Ich tippe darauf, daß der Aktienkurs bald steigt.
  I'll bet that the stocks are going up soon.

- Ich tippe mir an die Stirn zum Zeichen, daß ich etwas dumm finde.
  I tap my forehead to show that I find something dumb.

- Ich habe gegen das Fenster getippt, um ihre Aufmerksamkeit zu erregen.
  I tapped against the window to get her attention.

töten (+ prep)   to kill

- Sie hat das Tier mit einem Stock (/mit einem Beil/mit einer Pistole/durch einen *or* mit einem Schuß) getötet.
  She killed the animal with a stick (/an ax/a pistol/with one shot).

tragen (+ prep)   to carry

- Er trägt den Gegenstand bei sich (/mit sich nach Hause/auf der Handfläche/in der Hand).
  He's carrying the object (/home with him/in the palm of his hand/in his hand).

- Ich muß das Paket zur (*or* auf die) Post (/zum Bahnhof) tragen.
  I have to take the package to the post office (/train station).

- Ich trage das Baby auf dem Rücken (/in einem Korb/auf dem Arm/ins Bett).
  I'm carrying the baby on my back (/in a basket/on my arm/to bed).

- Er trug die Verantwortung (/Schuld) für den Fehler (/Plan).
  He bore the responsibility (/blame) for the mistake (/plan).

- Der Wind trug den Staub (/Rauch) zu mir.
  The wind carried the dust (/smoke) toward(s) me.

- Meine Frau trägt ein Kind unter dem Herzen. *(liter)*
  My wife is with child (or pregnant).

(s.) tragen (+ prep)   to wear

- Sie trägt einen schönen Ring am Finger (/eine Halskette um den Hals).
  She's wearing a beautiful ring on her finger (/a necklace around her neck).

- Sie trug eine Blume im Haar (/an ihrer Jacke).
  She wore a flower in her hair (/on her jacket).

- Die Dame trägt immer Kleidung nach der letzten Mode.
  The lady always dresses according to the latest fashion.

tragen an + D ⟨(schwer) an etw t.⟩   to suffer from (sth); (*fig*) to carry a heavy load

- Er trägt schwer an der Verantwortung für das ganze Unternehmen.
  Being responsible for the entire company is a very heavy load for him.

■   Sie trug schwer an dem Verlust ihres Sohnes.
    She suffered a lot from losing her son.

(s.) tragen mit + D ⟨sich mit etw t.⟩   to contemplate (sth)

■   Ich habe mich mit dem Gedanken (/der Überlegung) getragen, mich bei ihm um den Job zu bewerben.
    I've contemplated the idea (/prospect) of applying to him for the job.

■   Ich trage mich mit der Hoffnung, daß ich die schwere Krankheit überwinden kann.
    I live with the hope that I will be able to overcome the serious illness.

■   Ich weiß nicht, ob er sich mit Heiratsabsichten trägt.
    I don't know if he's thinking of getting married.

trauen (+ prep)   to marry; to trust

■   Sind Sie auf dem Standesamt oder in der Kirche getraut worden? —Der Pfarrer traute uns in der Kirche.
    Did you get married by the justice of the peace or at the church? —The minister married us in the church.

■   Als ich das sah (/hörte), traute ich meinen Augen (/Ohren) kaum.
    When I saw (/heard) that, I could hardly believe my eyes (/ears).

s. trauen (without prep)   to dare (to) do (sth)

■   Traust du dich, in das kalte Wasser zu springen (/ins dunkle Haus zu gehen)?
    Do you dare jump into the cold water (/to go into the dark house)?

■   Er hat sich nicht getraut, seinem Chef zu widersprechen.
    He didn't dare contradict his boss.

trauern über/um + A ⟨über/um jdn/etw t.⟩   to mourn for/over (sb/sth)

■   Sie trauerte um die gefallenen Soldaten.
    She mourned (for) the dead soldiers.

■   Er hat über den Tod seiner Tochter (/den Verlust seines Vermögens) tief getrauert.
    He mourned deeply over the death of his daughter (/the loss of his fortune).

■   Wir trauern um die Opfer der Gewaltherrschaft des Rassenwahns.
    We mourn for the victims of the tyranny of racism.

träumen von + D ⟨**von jdm/etw t.**⟩   to dream about/of (sb/sth)

■ Ich träumte von meiner Freundin (/einem Sportwagen/der Schule).
   I dreamed about (or of) my girlfriend (/a sports car/school).

■ Ich träumte davon, eine Villa am See zu haben.
   I dreamed of having a villa at the lake.

(s.) treffen (+ prep)   to hit

■ Der Schlag (/Er) traf ihn ans Kinn (/an die Wange/ins Gesicht).
   The blow (/He) hit him on the chin (/cheek/face).

■ Er hat ihn (mit dem Fuß/mit der Faust) an seiner empfindlichsten Stelle getroffen.
   He hit his sore spot (with his foot/with his fist).

■ Sie hat ihn in den Arm (/in die Brust) getroffen.
   She hit his arm (/his chest). (implies shooting)

(s.) treffen (+ prep)   to meet

■ Ich habe ihn am Flughafen (/auf der Post/bei einem Basketballspiel/beim Tanzen/beim Briefmarkenkaufen/in der Bank) getroffen.
   I met him at the airport (/at the post office/at a basketball game/while danc-ing/when he was buying stamps/at the bank).

■ Sie trafen sich zufällig auf dem Bahnhof (/bei seinen Freunden/auf der Straße/beim Fleischer/am Strand).
   They accidentally met at the train station (/at his friends' house/on the street/at the butcher shop/on the beach).

■ Wir treffen uns heute abend zum Kartenspielen.
   We're meeting this evening to play cards.

treffen auf + A ⟨**auf jdn/etw t.**⟩   to meet (sb/sth); to encounter (sb/sth)

■ Bei Waterloo traf Napoleon auf den Feind (/starken Widerstand).
   At Waterloo Napoleon encountered the enemy (/powerful resistance).

■ In Chikago sind wir auf eine Menge Deutschstämmiger getroffen.
   In Chicago we met a lot of people of German descent.

(s.) treffen mit + D ⟨**sich mit jdm t.**⟩   to meet (sb)

■ Ich traf mich mit ihr im Bahnhof (/auf dem Parkplatz).
   I met her in the train station (/at the parking lot).

- Wann triffst du dich mit dem Professor?
  When are you meeting with the professor?

treiben (+ prep)   to drive; to propel; to bring; to cause

- Sie haben die Pferde zur Tränke (/in den Stall) getrieben.
  They drove the horses to water (/into the stable).

- Die Armee trieb die Feinde in die Flucht (/von ihrem Territorium).
  The army set the enemies to flight (/drove them out of their territory).

- Der Wind treibt den Ballon durch den Schulhof (/nach Norden).
  The wind is blowing the balloon through the school yard (/northward).

- Er hat ein paar Nägel ins Brett getrieben.
  He drove a few nails into the board.

- Diese Entwicklung wird die Preise in die Höhe (/nach unten) treiben.
  This development will drive the prices higher (/lower).

- Das Schiff treibt mit dem Strom (/Wind).
  The ship is propelled (or *is driven*) *by the current (/wind).*

- Der Vorfall hat ihm kalten Schweiß aus den Poren (/das Blut ins Gesicht/Tränen in die Augen) getrieben.
  The incident made him break out in a cold sweat (/made the blood rush to his face/brought tears to his eyes).

treiben mit + D ⟨(etw/es) mit jdm/etw t.⟩   to trade in with (sb/sth); to go *or* carry on with (sb/sth); to have sex with (sb)

- Deutschland treibt intensiv Handel mit den anderen EG-Staaten.
  Germany has an intensive trade exchange with the other EC countries.

- Mit diesem Lehrer kann man gut seinen Spaß (/nicht seine Spielchen) treiben.
  It's easy to make fun of (/You can't play your little games with) this teacher.

- Er treibt es schon länger mit ihr. (*inf*)
  He has been having sex with her for quite a while.

treiben zu + D ⟨jdn zu etw t.⟩   to bring (sb) into (doing) (sth)

- Der Verlust seines ganzen Vermögens (/Er) trieb ihn zum Selbstmord (/zum Verbrechen/zum Diebstahl).
  The loss of his entire fortune (/He) drove him to commit suicide (/a crime/theft).

- Du darfst sie nicht zum Äußersten (/zur Arbeit) treiben.
  You mustn't push her too far (/make her work).

(s.) trennen (+ prep)   to separate; to part

- Er trennt den Stoff (/die Torte/das Holz) in zwei Hälften.
  He is cutting the material (/cake/wood) in(to) two halves (or in two).
- Sie haben sich im guten (/bösen) getrennt.
  They parted on good (/bad) terms.
- Wir trennten uns an der Ecke. Da trennten sich unsere Wege.
  We separated at the corner. Our ways parted there.
- In diesem Land werden die Leute nach Rasse getrennt.
  In this country the people are separated according to their race.

trennen aus/von + D ⟨sich/jdn/etw von jdm/etw, aus etw t.⟩   to separate from (o.s./sb/sth); to take (o.s./sb/sth) away from (sb/sth)

- Die Mutter hat die Tasche aus dem Hemd getrennt.
  The mother took off (or removed) the pocket of the shirt.
- Auf der Flucht wurden Vater und Sohn voneinander getrennt.
  Father and son were separated during the flight (escape).
- Eine Wasserfläche trennt die Insel vom Festland.
  A stretch of water separates the island from the mainland.
- Ich muß das Eiweiß vom Dotter trennen.
  I have to separate the white from the yolk.
- Sie hat sich von uns getrennt.
  She doesn't work for us any more.
- Unterschiedliche Ideologien trennen diese zwei Systeme (voneinander).
  Contrasting ideologies separate these two systems (from one another).

(s.) trennen von + D ⟨sich von jdm/etw t.⟩   to part *or* split (from sb/sth)

- Ich habe mich von der Firma (/meiner Arbeit) getrennt.
  I left the firm (/I left or quit my job).
- Er konnte sich von dem Plan (/seinen Freunden) nicht trennen.
  He couldn't bear to give up the plan (/to leave his friends).

treten (+ prep)   to kick

- Das Kind hat gegen die Tür (/nach ihm/nach seinem Vater) getreten.
  The child kicked (against) the door (/him/his father).
- Er hat mir ans (or gegen das) Schienbein getreten.
  He gave me a kick on the shin (or kicked my shin).

■ Inge hat ihm in den Hintern (/Bauch) getreten.
Inge kicked him in the behind (/stomach).

■ Der Spieler hat den Ball ins Tor (/übers Tor) getreten.
The player kicked the ball into the goal (/above or over the goal).

treten (+ prep)   to step; to walk; to move

■ Ingo ist aus dem Haus (/ins Zimmer/nach vorn/ans Fenster/in den Flur/auf die
Seite *or* zur Seite/in die Tür) getreten.
*Ingo stepped out of the house (/stepped or walked into the room/stepped or
moved forward/went and stood at the window/stepped out into the hall/stepped
aside/stepped inside the door).*

■ Kinder, tretet nicht in die Pfütze (/auf den Rasen)!
Children, don't step in the puddle (/keep off the grass)!

■ Er trat in den Hintergrund (/Vordergrund/aus dem Dunkel).
*He stepped (or receded) into the background (/stepped into the foreground or
came to the fore/stepped out of the darkness or became famous).*

■ Sie trat zu mir (/an meine Seite) heran.
She walked over to me (/stepped to my side).

■ Er trat mir in den Weg.
He (went and) stood in my way.

treten (+ prep)   to move; to come

■ Treten wir vom Schatten in die Sonne (/vom Rasen auf die Erde).
Let's move out of the shadow into the sun (/from the grass to the bare ground).

■ Das Pronomen tritt an den Anfang des Satzes.
The pronoun comes (or is placed) at the beginning of the sentence.

■ Der Regenwasser tritt durchs Dach.
The rainwater is coming through the ceiling.

■ Ihm trat der Schaum vor den Mund (/der Schweiß aufs Gesicht).
He was foaming at the mouth (/Sweat appeared on his face).

■ Mir traten die Tränen (/trat das Blut vor Zorn) in die Augen.
Tears came to my eyes (/I saw red).

treten (+ prep)   to step *or* walk on

■ Er ist (*or* hat) ihm (/mir) auf den Fuß getreten.
He trod (or stepped) on his (/my) foot.

■ Das Kind ist (*or* hat) seinem Hund auf den Schwanz getreten.
The child stepped on his dog's tail.

■ Sie ist (*or* hat) aufs Gas(pedal) (/auf die Bremse) getreten.
She stepped on the gas (or accelerator) (/stepped on the brake or applied the brakes).

treten (+ prep)   to enter

■ Er ist ins Zimmer (/ins Licht) getreten.
He entered the room (/stepped into the light).

■ Nach der Schule treten die jungen Menschen hinaus ins Leben.
After graduation young people enter the real world.

■ Er ist zu ihr (/dem Mädchen/Monika) in Beziehung getreten.
He entered into relations with her (/the girl/Monica).

■ Er wird ins 30. Lebensjahr treten.
He'll turn 30.

■ Sie traten in den Staatsdienst (/den Ruhestand/in Streik).
They entered the civil service (/retired/went on strike).

(s.) trinken (+ prep)   to drink

■ Marie trinkt aus dem Glas (/der Tasse/dem Becher).
Marie is drinking from the glass (/cup/mug).

■ Er trank in (*or* mit) kleinen Schlucken.
He took small sips.

■ Er trank eine Cola (/sein Getränk) in einem Zug.
He drank a (soda) pop (/his drink) in one swig.

■ Die Kinder tranken an (*or* von) der Quelle.
The children drank from the spring.

■ Peter, du darfst dich nicht zu Tode trinken!
Peter, you mustn't drink yourself to death!

■ Aus diesen Tassen trinkt es sich gut (/schlecht).
It is easy (/difficult) to drink from these cups.

trinken auf + A ⟨auf jdn/etw t.⟩   to drink to (sb/sth)

■ Ich trinke auf Ihr Wohl (*or* Ihre Gesundheit) (/unser Geburtstagskind/unser Glück/deinen Erfolg)!
I drink to your health (/the birthday boy or girl/our happiness/your success)!

■ Worauf wollen wir trinken?
What shall we drink to (or toast)?

tun (+ prep)   to do

- Ich habe heute nichts zu tun als (*or* außer) zu lernen.
  I have nothing to do today but study.

- Sie tut nichts als jammern, faulenzen und essen.
  She does nothing but complain, lie around, and eat.

- Ich kann nichts dagegen (/dafür) tun.
  I can't do anything about (/for) it.

- Ich werde etwas für meine Ausbildung (/ihn) tun.
  I will do something about my education (/him).

- Unter 150 Mark tut der Verkäufer es nicht.
  The salesman won't do it for less than 150 marks.

- Ich habe nichts mit ihr zu tun.
  I have nothing to do with her.

- Sie will mit mir nichts mehr zu tun haben.
  She's done (or She's through) with me (or She wants nothing more to do with me).

- Der Junge tut so, als ob er Lehrer sei.
  The boy pretends to be (or acts as though he's) the teacher.

tun (+ prep) (*inf*)   to put

- Er tut das dorthin. Er tut es in einen Koffer.
  He is putting it there. He is putting it in the suitcase.

- Er tut Salz und Pfeffer an die Speisen (/die Suppe).
  He is putting salt and pepper on the food (/in the soup).

- Sie haben ihn auf die Schule (/in eine andere Schule/in ein Heim) getan. (*inf*)
  They sent him to school (/another school/a home).

U

(s.) üben (+ prep)   to practice

- Die Kinder übten heute Rechnen (/ihre Aussprache/ihr Englisch) in der Klasse, und dann gingen sie in die Turnhalle und trainierten (*or* übten) Basketball (/Freiwürfe/Weitsprung/den Salto rückwärts).
  The children practiced arithmetic today in class (/their pronunciation/their English), and then they went to the gymnasium to practice basketball (/free throws/long jumping/the backward summersault).

- Er übt eine Melodie auf der Geige (/Gitarre/Trompete/Trommel/dem Klavier).
  He's practicing a tune on the violin (/guitar/trumpet/drum/piano).

- Der Schüler soll seine Biologie (/das Einparken) mit dem Lehrer üben.
  The student should study biology (/practice parking) with the teacher.

- Ich übte mich am Barren (/auf dem Trampolin/am Reck).
  I practiced on the parallel bars (/trampoline/horizontal bar).

s. üben in + D ⟨sich in etw ü.⟩   to practice (sth)

- Ich habe mich im Gebrauch des Werkzeuges (/dieser Säge) geübt.
  I practiced handling the tool (/this saw).

- Ich muß mich täglich im Lesen (/Schreiben/Schwimmen/Tauchen/Tennis/Debattieren) üben.
  I have to practice reading (/writing/swimming/diving/tennis/debate) daily.

s. überbieten in + D ⟨sich in etw ü.⟩   to outdo one another in (sth); to surpass in (sth)

- Die Supermärkte überbieten sich darin, Kunden durch aggressive Werbung anzuziehen.
  The supermarkets outdo each other in trying to attract customers by means of aggressive advertising.

- Sie überboten sich in Höflichkeiten.
  They outdid each other in civilities.

übereinkommen mit + D ⟨mit jdm ü.⟩   to agree with (sb)

- Sie sind (mit uns) übereingekommen, es so zu machen.
  They agreed (with us) to do it like this.

■ Ich kam mit ihm überein, eine Partnerschaft zu entwickeln.
I agreed with him to develop a partnership.

übereinstimmen mit + D ⟨mit jdm/etw (in etw) ü.⟩   to agree *or* concur with (sb/sth) on (sth)

■ Ich stimme mit dir vollkommen überein.
I totally agree with you.

■ Das stimmt mit den Tatsachen nicht überein.
That does not agree (or concur) with the facts.

■ Stimmst du mit meiner Meinung überein?—Ja, ich stimme darin mit dir überein, daß. . . .
Do you agree with my opinion?—Yes, I agree (or I am in agreement) with you in that. . . .

■ Die Farbe der Krawatte stimmt mit der des Hemdes überein.
The color of the necktie matches that of the shirt.

überfallen (+ prep)   to attack; to fall over; to descend (up)on

■ Man überfiel ihn mit Knüppeln (/hinterrücks/von allen Seiten).
They attacked him with clubs (/from behind/from all sides).

■ Die Presse hat den Präsidenten mit Fragen überfallen.
The press bombarded the president with questions.

■ Ihre Freundin überfiel sie beim Saubermachen (/mitten in der Arbeit/mit ihren Beschwerden/mit ihren Bitten)
Her friend unexpectedly dropped in on her while she was cleaning house (/in the middle of the job/deluged her with her complaints/deluged her with her requests).

übergehen auf + A ⟨auf jdn ü.⟩   to pass to (sb/sth)

■ Nach dem Tod der Mutter ist das Haus (/die Firma) auf die Tochter übergegangen.
After the mother's death, the house (/firm) went to the daughter.

■ Sein Charakter und Wesen sind auf den Sohn übergegangen.
His character and nature were passed on to his son.

■ Als der Prüfling nicht mehr weiter wußte, ging er auf ein anderes Thema über.
When the candidate (for a degree) had exhausted his knowledge, he switched to a different topic.

übergehen in + A ⟨in etw ü.⟩   to turn *or* change into (sth)

■ Das alte Gebäude wird in den Besitz der Staates übergehen.
The old building will become the property of the state.

- Der antike Gegenstand ging in meinen Besitz (/in meine Hände) über.
  The antique object came into my possession (/my hands).
- Er ist von einer Tonart in eine andere übergegangen.
  He changed from one key to another.
- Die Eisdiele ist in andere Hände übergangen.
  The ice cream parlor changed hands (i.e., is now owned by someone else).
- Das Weinen des Babys ging in Wimmern über.
  The baby's crying turned into whimpering.

übergehen zu + D ⟨zu etw ü.⟩   to go over to (sth)

- Er ging zum Feinde (/zur Gegenpartei/zur Defensive) über.
  He went over to the enemy (/to the opposition party/on the defensive).
- Der Lehrer geht jetzt zu einem anderen Thema über.
  The teacher is now switching over to another subject.
- Nach der Pause gehen wir zum zweiten Teil der Tagesordnung über.
  After the break we'll proceed to the second part of our agenda.
- Man ist jetzt dazu übergegangen, Autos mit Robotern herzustellen.
  They have now begun producing cars with robots.

überhäufen mit + D ⟨mit etw ü.; mit etw überhäuft sein⟩   to overwhelm *or* overflow with (sth); to inundate; to be swamped with (sth)

- Der Schreibtisch meines Vaters ist mit Akten (/Büchern) überhäuft.
  My father's desk is overflowing with files (/books).
- Sie haben ihn mit Arbeit (/Aufträgen) überhäuft.
  They overwhelmed (or flooded) him with work (/orders or assignments).
- Der Wissenschaftler wurde mit Ehrungen (/Vorwürfen/Geld) überhäuft.
  The scientist was inundated with honors (/reproaches/ money).
- Der Lehrer ist mit furchtbar viel Arbeit überhäuft worden.
  The teacher has been swamped with a tremendous amount of work.

übernachten (+ prep)   to sleep; to spend *or* stay the night

- Wir haben im Hotel (/im Freien/im Wohnwagen/auf dem Feld/im Wald) übernachtet.
  We stayed (or slept) the night at a hotel (/outside/in the camper/in the field/in the woods).

übernachten bei + D ⟨bei jdm ü.⟩   to stay with (sb), to sleep *or* stay at sb's place

- In Berlin übernachtete ich bei Verwandten (/meinem Freund).
  I spent the night with relatives (/at my friend's) in Berlin.

■ Die drei Austauschschüler können bei mir (/uns) übernachten.
The three exchange students can stay overnight at my (/our) place.

überprüfen auf + A ⟨**jdn/etw auf etw ü.**⟩   to check (sb/sth) for (sth)

■ Die Polizisten überprüften den Verdächtigen auf Waffen.
The policemen checked the suspect for weapons.

■ Die Zollbeamten haben alle Koffer auf Rauschgift überprüft.
The custom officials checked all suitcases for drugs.

überraschen (+ prep)   to surprise

■ Karl überraschte mich mit einem Geschenk (/seiner Ankunft).
Karl surprised me with a gift (/his arrival).

■ Er hat uns mit der (guten) Nachricht überrascht, daß. . . .
He surprised us with the (good) news that. . . .

■ Sie war (angenehm) überrascht über sein gutes Aussehen (/seine Intelligenz).
She was (pleasantly) surprised by his good looks (/intelligence).

überraschen bei + D ⟨**jdn bei etw ü.**⟩   to surprise *or* catch (sb) doing (sth)

■ Sie haben ihn beim Naschen (/Stehlen) überrascht.
They caught him nibbling (/stealing).

■ Die Polizei überraschte die Diebe dabei, als sie die gestohlenen Sachen versteckten.
The police caught the thieves when they were hiding the stolen goods.

überreden zu + D ⟨**jdn zu etw ü.; sich zu etw ü. lassen**⟩   to persuade (sb) to do (sth), to talk (sb) into (sth); to let oneself be persuaded

■ Ich habe meinen Freund zum Mitmachen (/zum Mitspielen) überredet.
I talked my friend into participating (/playing along).

■ Der Verkäufer hat mich zum Kauf (/Verkauf) des Autos nicht überreden können.
The salesman could not talk me into buying (/selling) the car.

■ Er ließ sich dazu überreden (/, nach Deutschland zu fliegen).
He let himself be talked into it (/flying to Germany).

■ Ich habe mich dazu überreden lassen, auf deinen Vorschlag einzugehen.
I was talked into accepting your proposal.

übersetzen (+ prep)   to translate

■ Kannst du mir diesen Brief (Wort für Wort) übersetzen?
Can you translate this letter (word for word) for me?

■ Er übersetzte den Aufsatz aus dem (*or* vom) Deutschen ins Englische (/Französische/Persische/Holländische).
He translated the composition (or essay) from German into English (/French /Persian/Dutch).

■ Der Satz läßt sich schwer (/leicht) (ins Deutsche) übersetzen.
The sentence is hard (/easy) to translate (into German).

■ Ich will meine Gedanken in konkrete Schritte übersetzen.
I want to translate my thoughts into concrete steps.

übertragen (+ prep)   to pass on; to transmit; to communicate

■ Auf welchem Sender wird dieses Ereignis übertragen? Wird es von CBS übertragen?
On which TV station will this event be broadcast? Will it be on CBS?

■ Er übertrug den Artikel (aus dem *or* vom Englischen) ins Deutsche.
He translated the article (from English) to German.

■ Das Theaterstück (/Tennisspiel/Ein Konzert) wurde gestern live im Rundfunk (/im Fernsehen/von 5 Sendern) übertragen.
The play (/tennis match/A concert) was broadcast live on the radio (/on television/by five television channels) yesterday.

■ Er überträgt seine Aufzeichnungen auf ein Blatt Papier (/ins reine).
He is making a copy of his notes on a sheet of paper (/a good copy).

übertragen auf + A ⟨etw auf etw ü.⟩   to transfer (sth) to (sb/sth); to transmit (sth) to (sb/sth)

■ Ich muß eine Summe (von 1.000 Mark) auf ein anderes Konto übertragen.
I'll have to transfer a sum (of 1,000 marks) to another account.

■ Du darfst deine Maßstäbe nicht auf die Leistungen von Kindern übertragen.
You mustn't apply your standards to the achievements of children.

■ Es ist problematisch, Ergebnisse aus der Tierforschung auf Menschen zu übertragen.
Transferring results from animal research to human beings is questionable.

■ Der AIDS-Kranke hat seine Krankheit auf seine Freundin übertragen.
The AIDS victim transmitted his disease to his girlfriend.

s. übertragen auf + A ⟨**sich auf jdn ü.**⟩   to pass (sth) on to (sb)

■ Diese Stimmung (/Krankheit/Panik/Der Fimmel) überträgt sich auf alle Teenager.
This mood (/disease/panic/fad) is catching on (or is spreading) among all teenagers.

■ Ich wünschte, daß sein Glück sich auf mich übertragen könnte.
I wished that his luck could be passed on to me.

übertreffen an + D ⟨**jdn an etw ü.**⟩   to surpass (sb) in (sth)

■ Niemand kann sie an Intelligenz (/Schönheit/an Schläue) übertreffen.
No one can surpass her in intelligence (/beauty/slyness).

■ Manche glauben, daß die Amerikaner die Japaner an Gründlichkeit (/an Gedankenschärfe/an Fleiß) übertreffen.
Some believe that the Americans surpass the Japanese in thoroughness (/innovation/hard work).

■ Ben Johnson übertraf alle anderen Läufer an Schnelligkeit.
Ben Johnson ran faster than all other runners.

übertreffen in + D ⟨**in etw ü.**⟩   to surpass in (sth)

■ Niemand übertrifft Garrison Keillor in der Fähigkeit, das Leben im Mittel-Westen Amerikas zu schildern.
Nobody surpasses Garrison Keillor in his ability to describe life in the Midwest.

■ Er kann mich durch Fleiß in Mathe (/im Tennis) übertreffen.
By working hard he can surpass me in math (/tennis).

überweisen (+ prep)   to transfer; to refer

■ Ich bin von meinem Arzt zu Ihnen (/ins Krankenhaus/zum Facharzt) überwiesen werden.
I've been referred to you (/the hospital/a specialist) by my doctor.

■ Ich will diese Summe direkt auf mein Konto (/Sparkonto) überweisen.
I want to transfer this sum directly into my account (/savings account).

■ Dieser Antrag wird an die entsprechenden Behörden überwiesen werden.
This petition will be transferred to the appropriate authorities.

(s.) überzeugen von + D ⟨**sich/jdn von etw ü.**⟩   to convince (o.s./sb) of (sth)

■ Ich habe ihn von der Richtigkeit meines Entschlusses (/von dem Irrtum/von seiner Schuld) überzeugt.
I convinced him of the validity of my decision (/of the mistake/of his guilt).

■ Ich habe mich selbst (davon) überzeugt, daß nichts mit ihr los war.
   I assured myself that nothing was wrong with her.

■ Sie können sich selbst (davon) überzeugen, daß kein Benzin mehr im Tank ist.
   You can check for yourself that there is no more gas in the tank.

■ Ich will dich davon überzeugen, daß alles in Ordnung ist.
   I want to convince you that everything is okay.

überzeugt sein (von) + D   to be convinced

■ Ich bin (davon) überzeugt , daß ich das schaffen kann.
   I am convinced (or certain) that I can do that.

■ Sie können (davon) überzeugt sein, daß ich mein Versprechen halten werde.
   You can rest assured (or be certain) that I'll keep my promise.

■ Sie dürfen überzeugt sein, daß ich alles Mögliche tun werde.
   You may rest assured that I'll do everything possible.

(s.) umbringen (+ prep)   to murder; to kill oneself *or* commit suicide

■ Er hat sich (/ihn) mit Gift umgebracht.
   He killed himself (/him) with poison.

■ Er brachte sie mit einem Gewehr (/auf grausame Weise/aus Haß/wegen Ehebruchs) um.
   He murdered her with a gun (/in a gruesome way/out of hatred/because she had committed adultery).

■ „Warum willst du dich umbringen?", fragte ihn der Schauspieler.
   "Why do you want to commit suicide?" the actor asked him.

umgeben mit/von + D ⟨jdn mit etw u.; von jdm/etw u. sein⟩   to surround with/by (sb/sth)

■ Sie hat ihn mit Liebe und Zuneigung umgeben.
   She surrounded him with love and affection.

■ Er war von Bewunderern (/Feinden/Künstlern) umgeben.
   He was surrounded by admirers (/enemies/artists).

■ Unser Garten ist von Tannenbäumen umgeben.
   Our backyard is surrounded by evergreen trees.

umgehen mit + D ⟨mit jdm/etw u.⟩   to know how to handle *or* treat (sb/sth)

■ Er ist mit seiner Frau behutsam (/grob) umgegangen.
   He treated his wife gently (/roughly).

- Der Dompteur kann gut mit Hunden (/Tieren/Schülern) umgehen.
  The trainer knows how to handle dogs (/animals/students).

- Kannst du damit (/mit der Maschine) umgehen?
  Can you operate that (/the machine)?

- Anne ging mit ihrem Geld klug (/vorsichtig) um.
  Anne handled her money prudently (/carefully).

umschalten (+ prep)   to switch over; to flick; to turn

- Schalte (den Schalter) auf „kalt" um!
  Turn the switch to "cold."

- (Im Fernsehen:) Wir schalten jetzt nach Hollywood (/ins Ausland/ zum Wetterbericht/zu den Olympischen Spielen/zum Reporter) um.
  (On TV:) Now we are going over or *we're going over to Hollywood (/to foreign countries/to the weather report/to the Olympic games/to the reporter).*

- Ich will das Radio auf einen anderen Sender (/auf 99 FM) umschalten.
  I want to switch the radio over to another station (/99 FM).

s. umsehen nach + D ⟨sich nach jdm/etw u.⟩   to look around for (sb/sth)

- Ich sehe mich nach einem passenden Geschenk für meine Frau um.
  I'm looking for a good gift for my wife.

- Sie hat sich lange nach dem Kind umgesehen, aber sie fand es nicht.
  She looked around for the child a long time but didn't find him.

umsetzen in + A ⟨etw in etw u.⟩   to convert *or* transpose (sth) into (sth)

- Das Kind hat all sein Taschengeld in Eis (/Spielzeuge) umgesetzt.
  The child spent all his pocket money on ice cream (/toys).

- Der Ausschuß setzte seine Diskussionen (/Pläne) in die Tat um.
  The committee put their discussions (/plans) into action.

- Man hat das Buch in ein Drehbuch umgesetzt.
  They converted the book into a film script.

umsteigen (+ prep)   to change (*buses, trains, etc.*)

- Muß ich nach Köln umsteigen, oder gibt es einen Intercity Zug?
  Do I have to transfer for Cologne or is there an intercity train?

■ Sie müssen in einen anderen Zug (/von einem Auto ins andere/von der U-Bahn in einen Bus) umsteigen.
You have to change (or switch) trains (/cars/from the subway to a bus).

■ Ich muß hier nach Blankenese (/in Richtung Reeperbahn) umsteigen.
I must change here for Blankenese (/the Reeperbahn).

umstellen auf + A ⟨auf etw u.⟩   to switch over to (sth)

■ Sie stellten alles auf Computer um.
They computerized everything.

■ Sie haben von Kohle auf Erdgas (/Elektrizität) umgestellt.
They changed from coal to natural gas (/electricity).

■ Wir haben von Butter auf Margarine umgestellt.
We have switched from butter to margarine.

umwandeln in + A ⟨jdn/etw in jdn/etw u.⟩   to change (sb/sth) into (sb/sth)

■ Es ist sinnvoll, Sonnenenergie in Strom umzuwandeln.
It makes sense to transform solar energy into electricity.

■ Heute ist es möglich, einen Mann durch eine Operation in eine Frau umzuwandeln.
It is possible today to change a man into a woman by means of an operation.

■ Sie haben das alte Kaufhaus in ein modernes Einkaufszentrum umgewandelt.
They have turned the old department store into a modern mall.

unterbringen (+ prep)   to put (up); to accommodate

■ Er hat seine Bekannten aus Amerika im Hotel (/bei mir/in seiner eigenen Wohnung) untergebracht.
He put his friends from America up in a hotel (/at my house/in his own apartment).

■ Kannst du noch eine Person in deinem Auto (/bei dir) unterbringen?
Can you manage to put another person (or do you have room for another person) in your car (/at your house)?

■ Wir bringen bald den Opa in einem Altersheim unter.
We're going to put grandpa in an old people's home soon.

■ Wir möchten das Kind während der Ferien bei Verwandten unterbringen.
We would like to leave our child with relatives during the vacation.

■ Ich möchte mein Gedicht (/meinen Essay) in Ihrem Magazin unterbringen.
I would like to publish my poem (/essay) in your magazine.

- Ich kann nicht alles in dem Koffer (/dem Lastwagen/meinem Terminplan) unterbringen.
  I can't put (or fit) everything in the suitcase (/truck/my schedule).

- Wo kann ich den Wagen unterbringen?
  Where can I put the car?

- Niemand war begeistert, als der Manager seinen Bruder in dieser Stellung (/bei dieser Firma) unterbrachte.
  No one was pleased when the manager (used his influence to) put his brother in this position (/in this company).

untergehen (+ prep)   to sink; to go down

- Die Sonne geht hinter den Bergen (/ins Meer) unter.
  The sun is setting behind the mountains (/into the ocean).

- Das Kind (/Ding) fiel ins Wasser und ging unter.
  The child (/thing) fell into the water and went under.

- Sein Weinen ging in dem Lärm im Bahnhof unter.
  His cries were drowned (out) by the noise in the train station.

- Das römische Reich ist im 5. Jahrhundert untergegangen.
  The Roman Empire collapsed (or fell) in the fifth century.

(s.) unterhalten mit + D ⟨sich/jdn mit etw u.⟩   to entertain *or* amuse (o.s./sb) with (sth)

- Jon, bitte unterhalte unseren Freund (mit Musik, usw) bis ich komme.
  Jon, please entertain our guest (with music, etc.) until I come.

- Ich unterhielt das Kind mit den Spielzeugen, als du weg warst.
  I entertained the child with the toys when you were gone.

- Der Junge unterhält sich mit der neuen Schallplatte.
  The boy is entertaining himself with the new record.

s. unterhalten mit + D ⟨sich mit jdm (über etw) u.⟩   to talk to *or* with (sb) (about sth)

- Die Schüler unterhalten sich (miteinader) über ihren Lehrer.
  The students are talking (with each other) about their teacher.

- Ich will mich mit ihm über unsere Verabredung heute abend unterhalten.
  I want to talk to him about our date this evening.

- Ich unterhalte mich gern mit deinem Bruder. Mit ihm kann man sich immer gut unterhalten.
  I like to talk to your brother. He's always easy to talk to.

- Jette, du mußt dich mal direkt mit dem Schulleiter darüber unterhalten.
  Jette, you should talk to the principal directly about that some time.

unterhalten zu + D ⟨etw zu jdm/etw u.⟩   to be in touch *or* contact with (sb/sth)

- Ich unterhalte enge Kontakte zu meinem Freund in Chile.
  I am regularly in touch with my friend in Chile.

- Deutschland hat seit dem zweiten Weltkrieg gute Beziehungen zu den USA unterhalten.
  Germany has had good relations with the U.S. since World War II.

unterkommen bei + D ⟨bei jdm u.⟩   to stay at (sb's place); to find a job

- Ich kam in Berlin bei meinen Freund (/bei meinen Verwandten) unter.
  I stayed at my friend's house (/with my relatives) in Berlin.

- Er hofft, bei unserem Unternehmen unterzukommen.
  He's hoping to get a job at our company.

- Er ist für die Nacht bei ihnen (/in einer Pension) untergekommen.
  He stayed at their place (/in an inexpensive hotel) for the night.

unternehmen gegen + A ⟨etw gegen jdn/etw u.⟩   to do (sth) about (sb/sth)

- Du mußt unbedingt etwas gegen den Dreck in deiner Wohnung (/deine Rückenbeschwerden/deinen schlechten Atem) unternehmen.
  You really have to do something about the dirt in your apartment (/your back pains/your bad breath).

- Die Staatsanwaltschaft hat nichts gegen ihn unternommen, denn es fehlten die klaren Beweise.
  The district attorney did not do anything against him because there was no clear evidence available.

- Ich bin nun mal so langsam. Was kann ich dagegen unternehmen?
  I am so slow (by nature). What can I do about it?

unterrichten (+ prep)   to teach

- Er unterrichtet an dieser Schule (/an einem Gymnasium/an der Universität/in der neuen Oberschule/auf einer Technischen Schule).
  He teaches at this school (/at a Gymnasium/at the university/in the upper level school/at a technical school).

- Er unterrichtet Deutsch an der neuen Gesamtschule.
  He teaches German at the new comprehensive school.

- Sie unterrichtet einen Leistungskurs (/diese Klasse/diese Schüler) in Chemie.
  He teaches an advanced course (/this class/these students) in chemistry.
- Der Lehrer unterrichtete die Schüler in Gesang (/Musik/Deutsch).
  The teacher taught the students how to sing (/music/German).
- Er hat sie in einer technischen Fertigkeit unterrichtet.
  He taught them (or trained them in) a technical skill.

unterrichten über/(von) + A/D ⟨**jdn über** (*rarely* **von etw u**).⟩   to inform about *or* acquaint (sb) with (sth)

- Diese Sendung unterrichtet die Zuhörer über die Ereignisse (*or* von den Ereignissen) des Tages.
  This radio program informs its listeners about the events of the day.
- Das Büro hat mich darüber (*or* davon) (/über meinen Termin) unterrichtet.
  The office notified me about it (/my appointment).
- Ich unterrichtete ihn über das Ereignis (/unsere Besprechung).
  I informed him about the incident (/our meeting).
- Dieses Reisebuch unterrichtet einen über das Klima (/die Sehenswürdigkeiten/günstige Unterkünfte) in Italien.
  This traveller's guide acquaints you with the climate (/sights/reasonable accommodations) in Italy.

s. unterrichten über + A ⟨**sich über jdn/etw u**.⟩   to inform oneself on/about (sth)

- Der Außenminister ließ sich von seinem Referenten über die Lage im Nahen Osten unterrichten.
  The foreign secretary had his assistant fill him in on the situation in the Middle East.
- Ich unterrichte mich immer über die neuesten Entwicklungen im Bereich der Psychologie (/über die Lage der Nation).
  I keep up with the latest developments in psychology (/the state of the nation).

unterscheiden (+ prep)   to distinguish; to differentiate

- Man muß genau zwischen seinen Versprechen und seinem Handeln unterscheiden.
  One must distinguish clearly between his promises and his actions.
- Aus dieser Entfernung kann ich die Fußballer (/Sachen) nicht mehr unterscheiden.
  From this distance I can't tell the soccer players (/things) apart.
- Diese Bäume (/Vorschläge) sind leicht (/schwer) zu unterscheiden.
  It's easy (/difficult) to distinguish beween these trees (/suggestions).

unterscheiden nach + D ⟨nach etw u.⟩   to distinguish *or* differentiate according to (sth)

- Die Eier werden nach Größe (/Gewicht) unterschieden.
  The eggs are distinguished (or separated) on the basis of size (/weight).
- Man hat die Tiere nach verschiedenen Merkmalen unterschieden.
  They classified the animals according to various characteristics.

unterscheiden von + D ⟨jdn/etw von jdm/etw u.⟩   to differentiate *or* distinguish (sb/sth) from (sb/sth)

- Kannst du diese Zwillinge (voneinader) unterscheiden?
  Can you tell these twins apart?
- Man muß das Wesentliche vom Unwesentlichen unterscheiden lernen.
  One has to learn to distinguish between the essential and the nonessential.
- Seine rote Mütze unterscheidet ihn von den anderen Jungen.
  His red cap distinguishes him from the other boys.

s. unterscheiden von + D ⟨sich von etw u.⟩   to differ (from) (sth)

- Worin unterscheidet sich ein Esel von einem Maultier?
  What is the difference between a donkey and a mule?
- Ich glaube, ich unterscheide mich klar von meinem Bruder durch größere Zielstrebigkeit (/größeren Fleiß).
  I think I'm clearly different from my brother because I'm more single-minded (/hard-working).
- Wodurch unterscheiden sich die beiden Zeitungen (voneinander)?
  How are these two papers different (from one another)?

untersuchen (+ prep)   to examine; to look into; to investigate; to search

- Die Polizei untersuchte ihn nach Waffen (/Drogen).
  The police searched him for weapons (/drugs).
- Die Biologin untersucht etwas unter dem Mikroskop.
  The biologist is examining something under the microscope.
- Wir haben den Opa vom Arzt untersuchen lassen.
  We had our grandfather examined by the doctor.

untersuchen auf + A ⟨jdn/etw auf etw u.⟩   to examine for (sth)

- Der Arzt wird mich (/das Blut) auf Zucker (/auf Infekte) untersuchen.
  The doctor will examine me (/my blood) for my blood sugar level (/infection).

■ Diese Techniker untersuchen Milch auf ihren Fettgehalt (hin).
These technicians are investigating the milk for the fat content.

■ Der Psychologe will ihn auf seinen Geisteszustand (hin) untersuchen.
The psychologist wants to examine his mental state.

■ Das Labor untersucht die Gewebeprobe auf Krebszellen (hin).
The laboratory is examining the tissue sample for cancerous cells.

urteilen nach + D ⟨nach etw u.⟩   to judge by/from (sth)

■ Du mußt nicht nach dem äußeren Schein urteilen.
You shouldn't judge by outward appearances.

■ Seinem Erfolg (/Aussehen) nach zu urteilen, hat er viel im Leben geschafft.
Judging by his success (/appearance), he's accomplished a lot in his life.

■ Nach seinem Reden (/Benehmen/Erfolg) zu urteilen, scheint er viel Erfahrung zu haben.
Judging from his speech (/behavior/success), he seems to be very experienced.

urteilen über + A ⟨über jdn/etw u.⟩   to judge (sb/sth)

■ Der Richter (/Deine Frau) hat ganz richtig über ihn geurteilt.
The judge (/Your wife) judged him perfectly.

■ Dieser Richter kann nicht darüber (*or* über diesen Fall) urteilen (,weil er ein eigenes Interesse an dem Fall hat).
This judge is not qualified to rule on that (or in this case) (because he's got his own interest in the case).

■ Der Richter urteilte sehr mild (/streng) über den Verbrecher.
The judge pronounced a mild (/severe) punishment (or sentence) for the criminal.

V

verabreden mit + D ⟨etw mit jdm v.⟩   to arrange a meeting with (sb/sth); to have an arrangement with (sb/sth)

■ Sie haben eine Konferenz (/einen Termin/einen Treffpunkt/ein Rendezvous/einen Mord/eine Meuterei) miteinander verabredet.
 They have arranged a conference (/an appointment/a place to meet/a rendezvous/a murder or conspired to murder/conspiracy).

■ Frankreich hat mit Deutschland verabredet, keine Grenzkontrollen mehr durchzuführen.
 France has an arrangement with Germany not to check people at the border any more.

s. verabreden mit + D ⟨sich mit jdm v.⟩   to arrange to meet (sb); to meet (sb)

■ Ich habe mich mit ihr um 8 Uhr vor der Universität verabredet.
 I have arranged to meet her in front of the university at 8 o'clock.

■ Mit wem hattest du dich verabredet?
 Who did you have a date with?/With whom did you have an appointment?

(s.) verabreden (without prep)   to arrange

■ Wir haben verabredet, daß wir in der Turnhalle spielen werden.
 We have arranged (for us) to play in the gymnasium.

■ Ich bin leider schon verabredet.
 Unfortunately, I already have a previous (or prior) engagement.

■ Sie verabreden sich für heute abend (in der Mensa).
 They're arranging a date for this evening (at the cafeteria).

verabredet sein mit + D ⟨mit jdm v. sein⟩   to have a date *or* an engagement *or* a (*business*) appointment with (sb)

■ Ich bin für morgen mit ihm verabredet.
 I have arranged (or I am) to meet him tomorrow (or I have a date/an appointment with him tomorrow).

■ Mit wem bist du verabredet?
 Whom are you meeting/Who is your date?

verabschieden (+ prep)   to say goodbye to; to hold a farewell ceremony for

■ Ich bin vom Büro (/von dem Boß) wunderschön verabschiedet worden.
I was given a wonderful farewell by (the people working in) my office (/by the boss).

■ Die Familie verabschiedete ihren Gast herzlich am Flughafen (/am Bahnhof/an der Bushaltestelle).
The family gave their guest a cordial farewell at the airport (/train station/bus stop).

s. verabschieden von + D ⟨sich von jdm v.⟩   to say goodbye to (sb)

■ Ich verabschiedete mich von Paul (/ihm/allen).
I said goodbye to Paul (/him/everyone).

■ Er verließ die Party, ohne sich (vom Gastgeber) zu verabschieden.
He left the party without saying goodbye (to the host).

■ Ich habe mich von ihr mit einem Küßchen auf die Lippen verabschiedet.
I said goodbye to her with a little kiss on the lips.

(s.) verändern (+ prep)   to change

■ Du hast dich zu deinem Vorteil (/Nachteil/deinen Ungunsten) verändert.
You've changed for the better (/the worse/unfavorably).

■ Er hat sich (/Ick habe mich) in den lezten Jahren gar nicht verändert.
He hasn't (I haven't) changed at all in recent years.

■ Dieses Unglück hat ihn vollkommen verändert.
This accident has changed him completely.

■ An dem neuen Modell von Mercedes haben sie das Design stark gegenüber den alten Modellen verändert.
They have really changed the design of the new Mercedes models compared to previous models.

veranlassen zu   + D ⟨jdn zu etw v.⟩   to lead (sb) to (sth); to make (sb) do (sth); to induce (sb) to do (sth)

■ Sie veranlaßte mich durch ihre ständigen Einwände, meine Meinung zu ändern.
Her constant objections led me to change my opinion.

■ Was hat den Präsidenten zu dieser Erklärung veranlaßt?
What led the president to make this statement (or explanation)?

■ Die Regierungskrise veranlaßte den Pressesprecher zu einer Erklärung.
The governmental crisis caused the spokesman to make a statement (or *give an explanation*).

■ Geldsorgen haben ihn dazu veranlaßt, Überstunden zu machen.
Financial worries caused him to work overtime (or put in extra hours).

■ Seine Freunde veranlaßten ihn dazu, Drogen zu nehmen.
His friends induced him to take drugs.

■ Das veranlaßt mich zu dem Entschluß, allein nach Chikago zu fliegen.
That leads me to my decision to fly to Chicago alone.

■ Ich fühlte mich (dazu) veranlaßt, ihn zu ermahnen.
I felt compelled (or *obliged*) *to tell him off.*

s. verantworten für/wegen + A/G ⟨**sich für/wegen etw v.**⟩   to justify (sth)

■ Wer solche Verbrechen begeht, wird sich auch für sein Verhalten (*or* wegen seines Verhaltens) vor dem Gesetz (/vor Gott/vor Gericht) zu verantworten haben.
Whoever commits such crimes will also have to answer to the law (/God/the court) for his actions.

■ Du wirst dich für deine böse (*or* wegen deiner bösen) Tat vor einem Richter (/vor deinem Vater/dem Priester/deinem Gott) verantworten müssen.
You will have to justify your evil act before the judge (/your father/the priest/your God).

verantwortlich sein für + A ⟨**für jdn/etw v. sein**⟩   to be responsible for (sb/sth)

■ Er ist für seine Tat (/sein Verhalten/seine Kinder) verantwortlich.
He's responsible for his deed (/behavior/children).

■ Ich bin dafür verantwortlich, daß alle ihre Arbeiten erledigen.
I am responsible for everyone doing their jobs.

■ Die Firma ist für die Schäden (/den Bau) voll verantwortlich.
The company is fully responsible for the damages (/construction).

verbannen (+ prep)   to exile

■ Napoleon wurde auf die Insel St. Helena verbannt.
Napoleon was banished to St. Helen's island.

■ Der Dissident wurde nach Siberien (/ins Exil/auf eine einsame Insel) verbannt.
The dissident was banished to Siberia (/into exile/to a desert island).

verbannen aus + D ⟨**aus etw v.**⟩   to exile from (sth)

■ Man hat den Diktator aus seinem Vaterland verbannt.
They exiled the dictator from his fatherland.

■ Immer wieder versuchte er vergeblich, das Bild seiner Geliebten aus seiner Erinnerung (/seinen Gedanken) zu verbannen.
In vain, he kept trying to banish the image of his lover from his memory (/his thoughts) again.

verbieten (+ prep)   to forbid; to prohibit

■ Der Arzt hat ihm das Rauchen (/den Genuß von Alkohol) verboten.
The doctor forbade him to smoke (/to use alcohol).

■ Die Mutter verbot dem Kind, auf der Straße zu spielen.
The mother forbade the child to play on the street.

■ Diese Wahl (/Dieser Plan/Sein Vorschlag) verbietet sich von selbst.
This option (/This plan/His suggestion) has to be ruled out.

■ Es ist bei Strafe (/vom Gesetz/von der Polizei) verboten,. ... .
It is forbidden (and punishable) by a fine (/law/the police). . . .

verbinden mit + D ⟨jdn mit etw v.⟩   to bandage (sb)

■ Die Schwester verband den Patienten mit frischen Kompressen.
The nurse dressed the patient's wounds with fresh compresses.

⟨**etw mit etw verbinden**⟩   to connect to (sth); to combine (sth) with (sth); to link (sth)

■ Der Fluß verbindet das Dorf mit der Stadt.
The river connects the village to the city.

■ Er will den Urlaub mit einer Geschäftsreise verbinden.
He wants to combine his holiday with a business trip.

■ Der Lehrer verbindet Phantasie mit Gelehrsamkeit.
The teacher combines imagination with scholarliness.

■ Seine Frau verbindet Klugheit mit Schönheit.
His wife is intelligent as well as beautiful.

⟨**jdn mit jdm/etw verbinden**⟩   to be attached to (sb/sth) by (sb/sth); to have (sth) in common with (sb/sth)

■ Die Erinnerung an unsere gemeinsame Vergangenheit verbindet mich mit meinem Freund.
The memory of our common past ties me to my friend.

■ Die Liebe zur Musik Beethovens verbindet mich mit vielen Menschen.
I share a love of Beethoven's music with a lot of people.

⟨**jdn mit jdm/etw verbinden**⟩   to connect (sb) to (sb)

- (Am Telefon:) Könnten Sie mich bitte mit dem Abteilungsleiter (/der Damenabteilung) verbinden?
  (On the telephone:) Could you please connect me to the department manager (/women's department)?

- (Am Telefon:) Mit wem bin ich verbunden?
  (On the telephone:) With whom am I speaking?

s. verbinden mit + D ⟨**sich mit jdm/etw v.**⟩   to unite with (sb/sth)

- Die Gemäßigten wollten sich nicht mit der Likudpartei verbinden.
  The moderates did not want to unite with the Likud party.

- Wenn sich die Iraker mit den Iranern verbinden, wird die Lage für die USA noch schwieriger.
  If the Iraqis unite with the Iranians, the situation will become even more difficult for the U.S.A.

- Herr Müller will sich mit Fräulein Meier verbinden.
  Mr. Müller wants to get married to Miss Meier.

⟨**sich mit etwverbinden**⟩   to combine with (sth)

- Wasser verbindet sich nicht mit Öl.
  Water doesn't mix with oil.

- Gin verbindet sich mit Tonic (*or* Gin und Tonic verbinden sich) zu einem köstlichen Getränk.
  Gin and tonic combine to make a delicious drink.

verbrauchen (+ prep)   to use

- Mein Auto verbraucht zu viel Benzin (/12 Liter Benzin auf 100 kilometer).
  My car uses too much gas (/gets 21 miles to the gallon).

- Der Schneider verbrauchte vier Meter Stoff für den Anzug.
  The tailor used four meters of cloth for the suit.

(s.) verbreiten (+ prep)   to spread; to disseminate

- Der Sprecher des Weißen Hauses hat die Rede (/Meinung) des Präsidenten in den Zeitungen (/über Rundfunk und Fernsehen) verbreitet.
  The White House press secretary circulated the President's speech (/opinion) to the newspapers (/over the radio and television).

■   Das Gerücht verbreitete sich im ganzen Land (/über die Grenze).
The gossip spread throughout the country (/across the border).

s. verbreiten über + A ⟨**sich über etw v.**⟩   to expound on (sth)

■   In meinem Vortrag mußte ich mich über dieses kritische Thema verbreiten.
I had to expound on this critical subject in my lecture.

verbringen (+ prep)   to spend

■   Wir verbrachten unseren Urlaub in den Bergen (/an der See/im Ausland/in der Türkei/auf den Autobahnen).
We spent our vacation in the mountains (/at the seaside/abroad/in Turkey/on the expressways).

■   Ich habe den ganzen Nachmittag in der Stadt (/im Zug/in einem Kino/bei meiner Freundin) verbracht.
I spent the whole afternoon in the city (/on the train/in a movie theater/at my friend's house).

s. verbünden mit/gegen + D/A ⟨**sich mit jdm/etw, gegen jdn/etw v.**⟩   to ally oneself with/against (sb/sth)

■   Alle Länder haben sich gegen den Irak verbündet.
All the countries united against Iraq.

■   Ich habe mich mit ihm verbündet.
I allied myself with him./I sided with him.

■   Die chinesische Armee verbündetete sich mit der Regierung gegen die aufständischen Studenten.
The Chinese army sided with the government against the revolutionary students.

verdienen (+ prep)   to earn; to make

■   Wieviel verdienen Sie am Tag (/in der Woche/im Monat /in der *or* pro Stunde/an dieser Sache/am Kauf dieses Autos)?
How much do you make a day (/a week/a month/in an or *per hour/on this item/on the sale of this car)?*

■   Womit hast du das verdienst?
What have you done to deserve (or *earn*) *that?*

■   Ich habe das nicht von dir verdient.
I didn't deserve that from you!

■ Im Supermarkt (/Bei der Arbeit im Imbiß) verdienst du nur den Mindestlohn.
You earn no more than minimum wage in the supermarket (/working in a fast food place).

■ Bei dem Geschäft (/Verkauf dieser Sache/Dabei) ist nicht viel zu verdienen.
You can't make a lot of money with this deal (/with the sale of this item/There's not much money in that).

vereinbaren mit + D ⟨etw mit etw v.⟩   to reconcile (sth) with (sth)

■ Das (/Dieses Benehmen) kann ich mit meinem Gewissen nicht vereinbaren.
I cannot reconcile that (/this behavior) with my conscience.

■ Max konnte den Dienst in der Armee nicht mit seinen pazifistischen Überzeugungen vereinbaren.
Max couldn't reconcile service in the army with his pacifistic convictions.

vereinbaren mit + D ⟨etw mit jdm v.⟩   to arrange (sth) with (sb); to agree on

■ Ich muß für heute eine Besprechung mit ihnen vereinbaren.
I have to arrange a meeting with them for today.

■ Wir müssen noch einen Treffpunkt (/einen Zeitpunkt für unser Treffen/einen Preis für die Waren) vereinbaren.
We still have to arrange a place for our meeting (/a time for our meeting/agree on a price for the goods).

⟨**mit etw zu vereinbaren sein**⟩   to be compatible with (sth)

■ Das ist mit meiner Zeit nicht zu vereinbaren (*or* Das läßt sich mit meiner Zeit nicht vereinbaren).
I cannot find the time for it.

■ Das Essen von Sahnetorten ist wohl kaum mit deiner Diät (/deinen guten Vorsätzen) zu vereinbaren. (*or* Das Essen von Sahnetorten läßt sich wohl kaum mit deiner Diät (/deinen guten Vorsätzen) vereinbaren.)
Eating cream cakes is hardly compatible with your diet (/your good intentions).

(s.) vereinigen (+ prep)   to unite; to join; gather

■ An seinem 75. Geburtstag hat er alle seine Freunde um sich vereinigt.
On his 75th birthday he gathered all his friends around him.

■ Der Vorsitzende hat alle Stimmen auf sich vereinigt.
The chairman gathered all the votes.

■ Hier vereinigen sich die zwei Autobahnen.
The two expressways merge together here.

(s.) vereinigen mit + D ⟨**(sich) mit jdm/etw v.**⟩   to unite *or* to join with (sb/sth)

■ Hans, warum hast du dich mit allen anderen gegen mich vereinigt?
Hans, why have you united with everyone against me?

■ Die Studenten wollen sich mit den Arbeitern vereinigen.
The students want to unite with the workers.

■ Unsere Ansichten (/Absichten) lassen sich nicht miteinander vereinigen.
Our views (/intentions) are not compatible.

s. vereinigen zu + D ⟨**sich zu etw v.**⟩   to merge *or* unite into (sth)

■ Die Sozialdemokraten in Ost- und Westdeutschland vereinigten sich zu einer großen Partei.
The social democrats in East and West Germany combined to form one big party.

■ Möbel, Teppiche, Tapete und Bilder haben sich zu einem harmonischen Ganzen vereinigt.
Furniture, carpets, wallpaper, and paintings merged into a harmonious whole.

■ Ost- und Westdeutschland haben sich zu einem Land vereinigt.
East and West Germany united to become one country.

verfallen (+ prep)   to decay; to fall into disrepair

■ Über die Jahrhunderte verfielen viele Bauwerke zu Staub.
Over the centuries lots of buildings decayed into dust.

■ In der Zeit der Kriege verfielen die Sitten auf ein beklagenswertes Niveau.
During the wars the moral standard deteriorated to a deplorable level.

verfallen in + A ⟨**in etw v.**⟩   to sink into (sth)

■ Er ist in Schweigen verfallen.
He fell into silence.

■ Nach seinem Tod verfiel seine Frau in eine traurige Stimmung (/in Depressionen).
After his death his wife sank into a melancholy mood (/depression).

verfolgen (+ prep)   to persecute; to pursue

■ Man hat sie aus politischen (/rassischen/religiösen) Gründen verfolgt.
They persecuted them for political (/racial/religious) reasons.

- Sie ist sehr sorgfältig. Sie verfolgt jeden Gedanken bis ins Detail.
  She is really meticulous. She pursues each thought in detail.
- Die Spur (/Der Verbrecher) wurde vom Detektiv verfolgt.
  The trail (/criminal) was pursued by the detective.

verfolgen mit + D ⟨jdn mit etw v.⟩   to pursue (sb) with (sth); to badger (sb) with (sth)

- Er hat sie mit Bitten (/mit Haß/mit den Augen) verfolgt.
  He badgered her with requests (/pursued her with hatred/followed her with his eyes).
- Was für einen Zweck verfolgen Sie damit?
  What are you aiming at?

verfügen über + A ⟨über jdn/etw v.⟩   to have (sth) at one's disposal; to have (sth); to be in charge of (sb/sth)

- Er verfügt über 5.000 Mark im Monat (/über eine beachtliche Summe/über ein großes Wissen/über sein Taschengeld).
  He has 5,000 marks a month (to live on) (/a considerable sum/great knowledge/He can do what he pleases with his pocket money).
- Ich verfüge über genügend Einfluß, so daß ich. . . .
  I have enough influence so that I. . . .
- Er kann über seine Zeit frei (/mich nicht/seine Schwester nicht/sein Geld frei) verfügen.
  He can do with his time as he pleases (/He can't tell me what to do/He can't tell his sister what to do/He can do with his money as he pleases).
- Verfügen Sie über mich (/unsere Wohnung, wenn wir in Urlaub sind)!
  I am at your service (/You can use our apartment when we are on vacation).
- Als Junge verfügte er über außerordentliche Körperkräfte.
  When he was a boy, he had extraordinary physical strength.

verführen zu + D ⟨jdn zu etw v.⟩   to encourage (sb) to do (sth); to seduce

- Diese offenen Kisten verführen ja direkt zum Diebstahl.
  These open boxes are an encouragement (or invitation) to steal.
- Darf ich Sie zu einem Eis (/zu Kaffee und Kuchen) verführen?
  May I talk you into having ice cream (/coffee and cake)?
- Er hat mich zum Spielen (/Trinken/Essen) verführt.
  He talked me into playing (/drinking/eating).
- Er verführte sie dazu, mit ihm ins Bett zu gehen.
  He seduced her into going to bed with him.

vergehen (+ prep)   to go by; to pass (by)

- Darüber (/Über das Lesen der Sonntagszeitung) verging ein voller Tag.
  It (/Reading the Sunday paper) took a whole day.

- Dabei (/Bei dieser langweiligen Arbeit) vergeht einem das Lachen.
  This (/This boring work) is enough to make you stop laughing.

- Mir ist die Lust (/der Appetit auf das *or* an dem Brot) vergangen, als ich den Schimmel sah.
  I was put off (/I lost my appetite for the bread) when I saw the mold.

- Wie die Zeit vergeht.
  How time flies.

s. vergewissern über + A ⟨**sich über etw v.**⟩   to make sure of (sth)

- Der Kinobesitzer vergewisserte sich (darüber), daß der junge Mann wirklich 18 war.
  The owner of the movie theater made sure that the young man was really 18.

- Ich habe mich (darüber) vergewissert, daß die Tür abgeschloßen war.
  I made sure the door was locked.

(s.) vergiften (+ prep)   to poison

- Ich habe mich an Pilzen (/am Restaurantessen/durch verdorbene Milch/an der giftigen Pflanze/durch schlechtes Fleisch) vergiftet.
  I got food poisoning from mushrooms (/the restaurant food/spoiled milk/the poisonous plant/bad meat).

- Er vergiftete seine Frau mit Tabletten.
  He poisoned his wife with pills.

(s.) vergleichen mit   + D ⟨**sich/jdn/etw mit jdm/etw v.**⟩   to compare (o.s./sb/sth) with (sb/sth)

- Man kann Los Angeles nicht mit New York vergleichen.
  You can't compare Los Angeles with New York.

- Man sollte ihn mit seinem älteren Bruder nicht vergleichen.
  You shouldn't compare him with his older brother.

- Wie könntest du dich wohl mit mir vergleichen?
  How could you compare yourself with me?

- Man vergleicht den klugen Jungen mit einem Computer.
  People compare the smart boy to a computer.

s. vergnügen mit + D ⟨sich mit jdm/etw v.⟩   to amuse oneself with (sb/sth)

■ Ich könnte mich immer mit Lesen (/Schach/Haustieren/Kochen/Basketballspielen) vergnügen.
I could always amuse (or entertain) myself by reading (/by playing chess/with pets/by cooking/by playing basketball).

■ Das Kind vergnügte sich mit Spielen (/Basteln).
The child amused himself by playing games (/making things).

■ Ich vernügte mich damit, eine halbe Stunde Gymnastik zu machen.
I had fun exercising for half an hour.

s. verhalten (+ prep)   to behave; to react

■ Ich weiß nicht, wie ich mich als Direktor verhalten sollte.
I don't know how I ought to behave (or react) as director.

■ Mir gegenüber verhält er sich immer herablassend (/anständig/ gemein).
He always behaves condescendingly (/pleasantly/meanly) towards me.

■ Wie verhältst du dich in solcher Situation (/bei einem Erdbeben)?
How do you react in such a situation (/during an earthquake)?

   ⟨es/eine Sache verhält sich⟩   to be

   ■ Wie verhält es sich damit? —Die Sache verhält sich folgender-maßen: . . . .
   How do things stand? —The thing stands as follows: . . . .

   ■ Die Sache (/Es) verhältes sich ganz anders (/genau umgekehrt).
   The thing (/It) is entirely different (/exactly the other way around).

   ■ Mit den anderen Teenagern (/Ehen) verhält sich genauso.
   It's the same thing with the other teenagers (/marriages).

s. verhalten zu + D ⟨sich zu etw v.⟩   to behave towards (sth); to react

■ A verhält sich zu B wie X zu Z.
A is to B as X is to Z.

■ Wie wirst du dich zu seiner Initiative (/zudiesem Angebot/dazu) verhalten?
How will you respond to his initiative (/his offer/that)?

verhandeln mit + D ⟨mit jdm v.⟩   to negotiate with (sb)

■ In Amerika muß man immer über den Preis des Wagens mit dem Autohändler verhandeln.
In America you always have to negotiate the price of a car with the dealer.

■ Wie ist es mit dem Preis? Gibt es da noch etwas zu verhandeln? —Ja, wir können über den Preis (/darüber) noch verhandeln.
How about the price? Is there any room to negotiate? —Yes, we can still discuss the price (/it).

■ Die Supermächte verhandeln (miteinander) über die Abrüstung.
The superpowers are negotiating (with each other) over the disarmament.

verharren auf/bei/in + D 〈 **auf/bei/in etw v.**〉   to maintain *or* adhere to (sth) (*liter*)

■ Er verharrte auf seinem Standpunkt (/in *or* bei seinem Entschluß/ in *or* bei seiner Meinung).
He adhered to his viewpoint (/decision/opinion).

■ Sie hat (*or* ist) in ihrem Stillschweigen verharrt.
She maintained her silence.

■ Karl verharrt noch in seinem Irrtum (/seiner Stellung).
Karl still persists in his error (/maintains his position).

■ Die Soldaten präsentierten das Gewehr. Sie verharrten in der Stellung, bis der Hauptmann sagte: „Rührt Euch!"
The soldiers presented arms. They remained in that position until the captain said, "Stand at ease!"

s. verheiraten mit + D 〈**sich mit jdm v.**〉   to marry (sb); to get married to (sb)

■ Er hat sich mit einer reichen Frau verheiratet.
He married a rich woman. (or He got married to a rich woman.)

■ Willst du dich mit ihm verheiraten? —Ja, wir heiraten bald.
Do you want to marry him? —Yes, we're getting married soon.

■ Ich habe mich letzten Monat verheiratet. —Mit wem?
I got married last month. —To whom?

verheiratet sein mit + D 〈**mit jdm/etw v. sein**〉   to be married *or* wedded to (sb/sth)

■ Sie ist (glücklich) mit ihm verheiratet.
She is (happily) married to him.

■ Er ist mit seiner Firma (/seinem Auto) verheiratet. (*fig, inf*)
He's married to his company (/car).

verhelfen zu + D 〈**jdm zu jdm/etw v.**〉   to help (sb) to get (sth); to help (sb) to do (sth)

■ Er hat mir zu einer guten Stellung verholfen.
He helped me to get a good job.

■ Ich verhalf ihm zu seinem Glück (/zum Sieg/zu seinem Eigentum/zu seinem Recht).
I helped make him happy (/him to victory/him to obtain his property/him to come into his own).

■ Ich habe ihr zu einer Wohnung (/einem Auto/einem Mann) verholfen.
I helped her find an apartment (/car/husband).

verkaufen (+ prep)   to sell

■ Sie verkaufen die Sache unter (/über) ihrem Wert.
They're selling the thing under (/above) its value.

■ Sie verkaufen das für zehn Mark (/für zu viel/unter Wert).
They're selling that for ten marks (/for too much/for less than it's really worth).

■ Man verkauft Eis (/Wurst) an einem Stand (/über den Tresen).
They are selling ice cream (/sausage) at a stand (/over the counter).

verkaufen an + A ⟨jdm *or* an jdn etw v.⟩   to sell (sb) (sth)

■ Er hat mir sein Auto (*or* Er hat sein Auto an mich) verkauft.
He sold me his car.

■ Das Gebäude wurde an die Gemeinde verkauft.
The building was sold to the community.

(s.) verkaufen an + A ⟨sich/etw jdm *or* an jdn v.⟩   to sell (o.s./sth) to (sb)

■ Ich habe mich ganz und gar der Firma (*or* an die Firma) verkauft. (*fig*)
I'm committed body and soul to the company.

■ Die Prostituierte verkauft ihren Körper an ihre Freier.
The prostitute sells her body to her clients.

■ Es fällt der neuen Lehrerin schwer, sich gut an die Schüler zu verkaufen.
The new teacher has a hard time selling herself to the students.

s. verkaufen (without prep)   to sell

■ Diese Zeitung (/Dieses Auto) verkauft sich gut (/schlecht).
This newspaper (/car) is a good (/bad) seller.

verkehren (+ prep)   to run; to fly

■ Der Zug (/Bus/Das Flugzeug) verkehrt (alle Stunde) zwischen hier und da.
The train (/bus/plane) runs (or operates) (every hour) between here and there.

verkehren in + D ⟨**in etw v.**⟩   to frequent (sth); to mix in (sth)

- Er verkehrt in guten Familien (/in Wissenschaftlerkreisen).
  He socializes in a circle of good families (/mixes with scientists).

verkehren in + A ⟨**etw ins Gegenteil v.**⟩   to reverse (sth)

- Sie verkehrte die Tatsachen (/die Worte/den Sachverhalt/den Sinn der Sache/ihre gute Absicht) ins Gegenteil.
  She reversed the facts (/words/content/meaning of the matter/her good intention).

verkehren mit + D ⟨**mit jdm v.**⟩   to associate with (sb)

- Er hat oft mit ihr schriftlich (/telefonisch) verkehrt.
  He often corresponded with her (/by phone).
- Er hat mit ihr (geschlechtlich) verkehrt.
  He had (sexual) intercourse with her.
- Sie verkehren miteinander freundschaftlich.
  They're on friendly terms.

verlangen (+ prep)   to demand; to want

- Wieviel verlangen Sie für diesen Artikel (/die Ware/dafür)?
  How much are you asking for (or do you want for) this article (/these goods/that)?
- Wer verlangt mich am Telefon?
  Who wants me on the telephone?
- Der Lehrer verlangt (von den Schülern nichts als) Fleiß und Pünktlichkeit.
  The teacher demands (nothing less than) diligence and punctuality (from the students).
- Es verlangt mich danach, mehr über deine Reise (/deinen Plan) zu hören.
  I am anxious (or eager) to hear more about your trip (/your plan).
- Es wird von jedem verlangt, rechtzeitig hier zu sein.
  Everyone is expected to be here on time.

verlangen nach + D ⟨**nach jdm/etw v.**⟩   to ask (for) (sb/sth); to long for (sb/sth); to crave for (sb/sth)

- Dein Bruder ist am Telefon und verlangt nach dir.
  Your brother is on the phone and is asking for you.
- Ihm wurde schwindlig und er mußte nach Wasser (/einem Medikament/dem Arzt) verlangen.
  He got dizzy and had to ask for water (/medicine/the doctor).

- Der Mann verlangte (heiß) nach seiner Frau.
  The man longed (or yearned) (passionately) for his wife.
- Mein Magen verlangt nach deutschen Brötchen (/Schwarzbrot/mexikanischem Essen).
  My stomach craves German rolls (/black bread/Mexican food).

s. verlassen auf + A ⟨sich auf jdn/etw v.⟩   to rely *or* depend on (sb/sth)

- Sie verläßt sich ganz auf ihn (/seine Empfehlung/das Auto/sein Versprechen).
  She totally relies (or depends) on him (/his recommendation/the car/his promise).
- Dieser Plan geht bestimmt schief, verlaß dich drauf!
  This plan will fail; count on it.
- Kann ich mich auf diesen Jungen (/Angestellten) verlassen? Ist er fleißig?
  Can I depend on this boy (/employee)? Is he hard-working?
- Ich verlasse mich darauf, daß du die Arbeit rechtzeitig fertig machst.
  I'm relying on you to finish the job on time.

(s.) verlaufen (+ prep)   to go off; to get lost

- Die Kinder haben sich (im Park/in der Stadt/am Strand) verlaufen.
  The children got lost (in the park/in the town/at the beach).
- Seine Schritte hatten sich im Schnee (/auf dem matschigen Weg) verlaufen.
  His footsteps had disappeared in the snow (/on the muddy pathway).
- Dieser Weg verläuft nach Osten (/Süden) durch den Wald.
  This path runs east (/south) through the forest.
- Ich habe mich im Wald (/in der Stadt) verlaufen.
  I got lost in the woods (/city).

verlegen (+ prep)   to transfer; to move; to mislay; to misplace; to lay

- Sie hat ihr Portemonnaie irgendwo im Restaurant verlegt.
  She misplaced her purse somewhere in the restaurant.
- Die Deutschen haben den Sitz der Regierung nach Berlin verlegt.
  The Germans have moved the seat of government to Berlin.
- Wohin verlegte er seine Praxis (/seinen Betrieb)? Nach Hamburg?
  Where did he move his practice (/business)? To Hamburg?
- Man hat den Fußboden mit Mosaik (/Parkett/Fliesen) verlegt.
  They laid mosaic (/parquet/tiles) on the floor.
- Man verlegte Kabel (/Leitungen) im Haus (/unterm Bürgersteig/unter der Straße).
  They laid cables (/pipes) in the house (/under the sidewalk/under the road).

verlegen auf + A ⟨**etw auf etw v.**⟩ to postpone until (sth)

- Wir müssen die Besprechung (/den Termin) auf morgen verlegen.
  We must postpone the meeting (/appointment) until tomorrow.

- Das Treffen ist auf morgen (/April/kurz vor Weihnachten) verlegt worden.
  The meeting has been postponed until tomorrow (/April/shortly before Christmas).

s. verlegen auf + A ⟨**sich auf etw v.**⟩ to resort to (sth); to take (sth) up

- Ich habe mich in der letzten Zeit auf Computer (/ein neues Hobby) verlegt.
  I have taken to computers (/a new hobby) lately.

- Er verlegte sich aufs Unterrichten (/Schachspielen/Gärtnern).
  He took up teaching (/playing chess/gardening).

- Als Schmeicheleien nichts nützten, verlegte er sich aufs Bitten.
  When flattery didn't work, he resorted to pleading.

- Als der Handel mit Schreibmaschinen nicht mehr profitabel war, verlegte er sich auf den Verkauf von Computern.
  When the market for typewriters stopped being profitable, he turned to selling computers.

verleiten zu + D ⟨**jdn zu etw v.**⟩ to lead *or* encourage or induce (sb) to (sth)

- Er hat ihn zum Betrügen(/zum Lügen/zu einem Verbrechen) verleitet.
  He induced (or encouraged) him to cheat (/lie/commit a crime).

- Er verleitete sie zur Sünde (/zum Ehebruch/zur Völlerei).
  He led her into sin (/He encouraged her to commit adultery/gluttony).

- Er verleitete mich dazu, nicht die Wahrheit zu sagen.
  He encouraged me not to tell the truth.

(s.) verletzen (+ prep) to injure

- Er hat mich (/sich) mit diesem Gerät verletzt.
  He injured me (/himself) with this tool.

- Ich verletzte mich an dem Messer (/an dem rostigen Nagel/an dem Schraubenzieher/an der Rasierklinge).
  I injured myself on the knife (/rusty nail/screwdriver/razor blade).

- Ich verletzte mich am Finger (/auf der Stirn/unterm Knie).
  I injured myself on my finger (/on my forehead/below the knee).

- Nichts verletzt mich mehr als Ablehnung.
  Nothing hurts me more than rejection.

s. verlieben in + A ⟨**sich in jdn/etw v.**⟩   to fall in love with (sb/sth)

- Ich verliebte mich in das Mädchen (/Auto/die Idee).
  I fell in love with the girl (/car/idea).

verliebt sein in + A ⟨**in jdn/etw v. sein**⟩   to be in love with (sb/sth)

- Sie ist in dieses Haus (/diese Speise/deinen Vorschlag) ganz verliebt.
  She has completely fallen in love with this house (/this food/your suggestion).
- Sie war in ihn hoffnungslos verliebt.
  She was hopelessly in love with him.

verlieren (+ prep)   to lose

- Ich verlor das Geld im Zug (/im Bus/im Bahnhof/auf der Straße).
  I lost the money in the train (/bus/train station/on the street).
- Sie haben einander im Gedränge verloren.
  They lost each other in the crowd.
- In (*or* Mit) ihm verlieren wir einen wahren Freund.
  In him we lose a true friend.
- Du verlierst nicht viel an diesem Fernsehprogramm (/ihm).
  You're not missing much in this TV show (/him).
- Er verlor kein Wort darüber. Man soll kein Wort darüber verlieren.
  He didn't say a word about it. You shouldn't waste any words on it.
- Er verlor das Spiel (/die Wette/das Geld/den Fall) gegen ihn.
  He lost the game against (/bet with/money to/the case against) him.
- Er hat bei ihm an Achtung verloren.
  He went down in his eyes (or estimation).
- Vor lauter Alkohol verlor er seine Hemmungen (/sein Gedächtnis).
  Because of a lot of alcohol, he lost his inhibitions (/memory).

verlieren an (+ noun without article) ⟨**an etw v.**⟩   to lose (sth)

- Bei genauerem Hinsehen verlor sie an Reiz (/Schönheit/Charme/Aussehen).
  On closer inspection she lost (some of) her appeal (/beauty/charm/looks).
- Die Regierung hat an Einfluß (/Kraft/Kredit) verloren.
  The government has lost (some of) its influence (/power/credit).
- Das Haus hat durch das Feuer an Wert verloren.
  Because of the fire, the house has lost (some of) its value.

verlieren durch + A ⟨durch etw v.⟩   to lose through/by (sth)

■ Der lustige Film verliert erheblich durch die Synchronisation.
The funny film loses a lot by being dubbed.

■ Das wunderschöne Bild verliert (an Schönheit) durch den häßlichen Rahmen.
The magnificent painting looks less beautiful in that ugly frame.

s. verlieren in + D ⟨sich in etw v.⟩   to get lost in (sth)

■ Ich habe mich in der großen Stadt (/in Einzelheiten) verloren.
I got lost in the big city (/details).

■ Er verliert sich leicht in Gedanken (/in guten Büchern).
He easily gets (or becomes) lost in thought (/good books).

■ Die 3.000 Zuschauer verloren sich förmlich in dem riesigen Stadion.
The 3,000 spectators virtually disappeared in the huge stadium.

s. verloben mit + D ⟨sich mit jdm v.⟩   to become *or* get engaged to (sb)

■ Ich habe mich mit Jennifer (/dem Mädchen) verlobt.
I got engaged to Jennifer (/the girl).

■ Er verlobte sich gestern offiziell mit ihr.
He got officially engaged to her yesterday.

verlobt sein mit + D ⟨mit jdm v. sein⟩   to be engaged to (sb)

■ Sie ist seit einem halben Jahr (mit ihm) verlobt.
She has been engaged (to him) for half a year.

verlocken zu + D ⟨jdn zu etw v.⟩   to entice *or* tempt (sb) to (sth)

■ Das blaue Wasser verlockt (einen) zum Schwimmen (*or* Baden).
The blue water entices one to go swimming.

■ Der herrliche Schnee verlockte uns zum Skifahren (/zu einer Schneeball-schlacht/zu einer Schlittenfahrt).
The beautiful snow enticed us to go skiing (/to have a snowball fight/to take a sleigh ride).

■ Dieser Reiseprospekt verlockt mich dazu, eine Reise zu machen.
This travel brochure tempts me to take a trip.

vermieten an + A ⟨jdm *or* an jdn etw v.⟩   to rent *or* lease (sth) to (sb)

- Sie hat dem (*or* an den) Studenten ein Zimmer vermietet.
  She rented a room to the student.

- Er vermietete mir (*or* an mich) ein Auto (/eine Wohnung/ein Klavier).
  He rented (or leased) a car (/an apartment/a piano) to me.

s. vernarren in + A ⟨sich in jdn/etw v.⟩   to fall for (sb/sth) (*inf*)

- Ich habe mich in die Frau (/das Spiel/Laura/den Jungen) vernarrt.
  I'm crazy about the woman (/the game/Laura/the boy).

vernarrt sein in + A ⟨in jdn/etw v. sein⟩   to be crazy *or* nuts about (sb/sth); to be infatuated with (sb)

- Ich bin in diesen Sport (/Disney World/die Schauspielerin/dieses Haus) ganz vernarrt.
  I'm totally crazy about this game (/Disney World/the actress/this house).

verpacken in + A ⟨etw in etw v.⟩   to wrap (sth) in (sth); to pack (sth) in (sth)

- Verpacken Sie bitte die Waren (/die Blumen/das Geschenk) in Papier!
  Please wrap the goods (/flowers/gift) in paper.

- Er verpackte die Flaschen in Kisten.
  He packed the bottles in boxes.

- Die Mutter hat die Sachen gut in den Koffer verpackt.
  The mother packed the things well in the suitcase.

(s.) verpflichten (+ prep)   to oblige; to place under an obligation

- Der Präsident wird auf die Bibel (/Verfassung) verpflichtet.
  The president is sworn in on the Bible (/constitution).

- Der Fußballspieler hat sich für fünf Jahre (/beim HSV/in Italien) verpflichtet.
  The soccer player is under contract to play (/for the HSV (Hamburg soccer club)/in Italy) for five years.

- Ich habe mich verpflichtet, für (/gegen) ihn zu stimmen.
  I am obliged to vote for (/against) him.

verpflichten zu + D ⟨jdn zu etw v.⟩   to make (sb) do (sth)

- Er kann mich nicht dazu verpflichten, das zu tun.
  He cannot make me do that.

- Die Gemeinde (/Ich) verpflichtete mich zur Übernahme der Kosten für den Fußweg.
  The community forced me (/I was obliged) to take care of the expenses for the sidewalk.
- Das verpflichtet Sie zu nichts (/nicht zum Kauf des Autos).
  There is no obligation involved (or No strings are attached) (/That does not oblige you to buy the car).
- Der Richter hat die Geschworenen zum Schweigen verpflichtet.
  The judge bound the jury to silence.

s. verpflichtet fühlen zu + D ⟨sich zu etw. v. fühlen⟩   to feel obligated to do (sth)

- Ich fühle mich verpflichtet, ihm zu helfen (/zur Hilfeleistung).
  I feel obligated to help him (/to help).
- Ich fühle mich dazu verpflichtet, meinen betrunkenen Freund nach Hause zu fahren.
  I feel obligated to drive my drunk friend home.

verpflichtet sein zu + D ⟨zu etw. v. sein⟩   to be obliged to do (sth)

- Der Zeuge ist nicht zum Schweigen (/Sprechen/Kommen) verpflichtet.
  The witness is not obliged to remain silent (/speak out/to come).
- Mein Sohn ist Ihnen (für Ihre Unterstützung) sehr zu Dank verpflichtet.
  My son is deeply obliged to you (for your support).

(s.) verraten (+ prep)   to betray; to give away

- Du hast dich mit deiner Lüge (/durch deinen Blick) verraten.
  You gave yourself away by your lie (/look).
- Sein Akzent verrät ihn leicht. Durch seinen Akzent verriet er sich.
  His accent easily gives him away. He was betrayed by his accent.
- Durch das Lächeln hat das Kind sich (/seine Absicht) verraten.
  The child's smirk betrayed him (/his intention).

verreisen (+ prep)   to go away (on a trip *or* journey)

- Wir sind mit dem Auto (/der Bahn) verreist.
  We went on vacation by car (/train).
- Verreisen Sie wieder nach London?
  Are you going away again to London?

verrückt sein auf/nach + A/D ⟨auf jdn/etw *or* nach jdm/etw v. sein⟩   to be crazy
about (sb/sth)

- Ich bin verrückt auf (*or* nach) Dillgurken (/indisches (*or* indischem) Essen/Bob-Dylan-Platten).
  I'm crazy about dill pickles (/Indian food/Bob Dylan records).

- In den 60er Jahren waren viele Jugendliche verrückt auf die (*or* nach den) Beatles und die (den) Stones.
  In the 60's many young people were crazy about the Beatles and the Stones.

(s.) verschieben auf + A ⟨etw auf etw v.; etw vershiebt sich⟩   to postpone (sth) to
(sth)

- Er verschob die Aufgabe (/Reise) auf einen späteren Zeitpunkt.
  He postponed the task (/trip) to a later date.

- Er hat seinen Flug (/die Abreise) auf nächsten Monat verschoben.
  He postponed his flight (/departure) to next month.

- Die Beseitigung der Umweltschäden läßt sich nicht auf die nächste Generation verschieben.
  The eradication of environmental damage cannot be left for the next generation.

verschwenden an/auf + A ⟨etw an/auf jdn/etw v.⟩   to waste (sth) on (sb/sth)

- Er hat so viel Arbeit (/Mühe) daran (*or* darauf) verschwendet.
  He wasted so much work (/effort) on it.

- Darauf (*or* Daran) brauchen wir keine Mühe zu verschwenden.
  We don't need to waste any effort on that.

- Ich würde keinen Gedanken (/kein Geld) an den Plan verschwenden.
  I wouldn't waste much thought (/money) on the plan.

verschwenden für + A ⟨etw für jdn/etw v.⟩   to waste (sth) on (sb/sth)

- Er verschwendete viel Geld (/Zeit) für dieses Projekt (/Mädchen).
  He wasted (or squandered) a lot of money on this project (/girl).

- Er verschwendet seine Energie (/sein Leben/seinen Geist) für (*or* an *or* auf) diese Sache.
  He is wasting his energy (/life/intellect) on this matter.

verschwinden (+ prep)   disappear

- Er verschwand hinter der Tür (/durch die Tür/im Keller).
  He disappeared behind the door (/through the door/in the basement).

- Das Auto ist im Tunnel (/Nebel) verschwunden.
  The car disappeared into the tunnel (/fog).
- Er verschwand aus meinem Blickfeld (/der Politik).
  He disappeared from my sight (/politics).

versehen mit + D 〈etw mit etw v.〉   to put (sth) on/in (sth)

- Wir haben das Zimmer mit Teppichen (/Tapeten/Vorhängen/einem Schloß) versehen.
  We furnished the room with carpets (/wallpapered the room/decorated the room with curtains/put a lock on the door).
- Ich will mein Wörterbuch mit einem Umschlag versehen.
  I want to put a dust-jacket on my dictionary.
- Er versah das Schriftstück mit einem Stempel (/seiner Unterschrift).
  He put a stamp on the document (/signed the document).
- Die Eltern versahen die Kinder mit Geld (/Essen/Kleidung).
  The parents furnished money (/food/clothing) for the children.

versehen sein mit + D 〈mit etw v. sein〉   to have (sth)

- Sind Sie mit allem versehen?
  Do you have everything you need?
- Dieses Auto ist mit Nebelscheinwerfern versehen.
  This car has (or comes with) fog lights.

versessen sein auf + A 〈auf etw v. sein〉   to be very keen on (sth); to be mad *or* crazy about (sth)

- Er ist auf Kriminalfilme (/Schokolade) ganz versessen.
  He's crazy about mysteries (/chocolates).
- Sie ist versessen darauf, in Rockkonzerte zu gehen.
  She is mad about going to rock concerts.
- Vor ein paar Jahren war sie noch auf Michael Jackson versessen, aber heute findet sie ihn langweilig.
  A few years ago she was mad about Michael Jackson, but these days she finds him boring.

versetzen (+ prep)   to transfer

- Er wurde nach Frankreich (/in die USA/an die Elfenbeinküste/in eine andere Stadt/zu einer anderen Filiale) versetzt.
  He was transferred to France (/the U.S./the Ivory Coast/another city/a different branch).

- Der Beamte wird nächstes Jahr in den Ruhestand versetzt.
  The official will retire next year.
- Der Schüler wurde (/nicht) in die 8. Klasse versetzt.
  The student was (/not) moved (or *promoted*) *to the 8th grade.*

versetzen in + A ⟨jdn in etw v.⟩   to bring (sb) into a certain state

- Die Musik hat uns in Bewegung (/in eine frohe Stimmung/in Begeisterung) versetzt.
  The music made us move (/put us in a good mood/filled us with enthusiasm).
- Das Buch versetzte ihn in seine Jugend (/in frühere Zeiten) zurück.
  The book took him back to his youth (/times gone by).
- Er versetzte mich in Raserei (/einen Freudentaumel/Angst).
  He sent me into a frenzy (/ecstacy or *made me joyous/made me afraid).*

(s.) versetzen in + A ⟨sich/jdn in etw v.⟩   to put (sb/o.s.) in (sth)

- Ich würde ihn (/mich) nicht gerne in die Lage versetzen, das tun zu müssen.
  I wouldn't like to put him (/myself) in a positon to have to do that.
- Bei ihren Treffen versetzen sich die alten Männer immer in eine frühere Zeit (/ihre Jugend).
  At their meetings the old men always relive an earlier period (/their youth).

(s.) versichern gegen + A ⟨sich/jdn gegen etw v.⟩   to insure (o.s./sb) against (sth)

- Ich habe mich (/meine Familie) gegen Krankheit versichert.
  I have insured myself (/my family) against illness.
- Er versicherte sich (/sein Haus) ausreichend gegen Diebstahl (/Feuer).
  He insured himself (/his house) adequately against theft (/fire).
- Der Fahrer versicherte mir, daß er das Auto gegen Unfall versichert hatte.
  The driver assured me that he had insured the car against accidents.

(s.) versöhnen mit + D ⟨sich/jdn mit jdm/etw v.⟩   to reconcile (o.s./sb) with (sb/sth); to become reconciled with (sb/sth)

- Die UNO will diese zwei Völker (miteinander) versöhnen.
  The U.N. wants to reconcile these two nations.
- Nach der Auseinandersetzung hat sie sich mit ihm (/ihrer Mutter) versöhnt.
  After the argument she made up with him (/her mother).
- Du mußt dich mit Gott (/deinem Schicksal) versöhnen.
  You must make peace with God (/reconcile yourself with your fate).

■ Du kannst so nicht weiterleben. Du mußt dich mit deiner Frau (/deinen Freunden) versöhnen.
You can't go on living like this; you must reconcile (or make peace) with your wife (/friends).

versorgen mit + D ⟨jdn mit etw v.⟩   to provide (sb) with (sth)

■ Er versorgte seine Familie mit allem, was nötig ist.
He provided his family with everything that is necessary.

■ Die Versorgungsunternehmen versorgen die Stadt mit Strom (/Gas/Wasser/ Wärme).
The public utility companies provide the city with electricity (/gas/water/heat).

s. verständigen mit + D ⟨sich mit jdm v.⟩   to communicate with (sb)

■ Ich konnte mich nur schwer mit dem schwerhörigen Mann verständigen.
I couldn't communicate well with the man who was hard of hearing.

■ Wegen der Störgeräusche haben wir uns am Telefon kaum miteinander verständigen können.
Due to disturbing noises, we could scarcely communicate with each other on the telephone.

■ Es war schwierig, sich mit dem Ausländer zu verständigen.
It was difficult to communicate with the foreigner.

(s.) verständigen über + A ⟨sich über etw v.⟩   to reach agreement on (sth)

■ Sie verständigten sich schnell über den Preis (/die Bedingungen/das Wesentliche).
They quickly reached agreement concerning the price (/the conditions/the essentials).

■ Deutschland und Polen haben sich endlich über den Verlauf der Grenze verständigt.
Germany and Poland finally agreed on the exact position of their common border.

(s.) verstecken (+ prep)   to hide; to conceal

■ Die Mutter mußte die Süßigkeiten vor dem Kind verstecken.
The mother had to hide the sweets from the child.

■ Das Kind (/Kaninchen) hat sich hinter dem Busch versteckt.
The child (/rabbit) hid behind the bush.

■ Ich habe mich (/meinen Zorn) vor den Gästen versteckt.
I hid (myself) (/I hid my anger) from the guests.

■ Der Vater versteckt immer seine Brieftasche und seine Schlüssel in der Schublade (/auf dem Regal).
The father always hides his wallet and keys in the drawer (/on the shelf).

s. verstehen auf + A ⟨sich auf etw v.⟩   to be (an) expert at *or* on *or* in (sth); to be very good at (sth)

■ Erika, ist dir klar, daß Bernd sich gut auf Mathematik versteht?
Erika, are you aware that Bernd is an expert in math?

■ Ich verstehe mich auf Briefmarken (/aufs Basteln/auf Hunde).
I'm an expert on stamps (/at making things/with dogs).

■ Ich verstehe mich gut darauf, mit Haustieren (/Jugendlichen) umzugehen.
I really know how to handle pets (/youth).

s. verstehen mit + D ⟨sich mit jdm v.⟩   to get along with (sb)

■ Ich verstehe mich mit unserer Schuldirektorin wirklich gut. Verstehst du dich mit ihr?
I get along real well with our new principal. Do you get along with her?

■ Er versteht sich sehr gut mit mir.
He gets along very well with me.

■ In dieser Hinsicht verstehe ich mich mit dem Kollegen.
I get along with my co-worker in this respect.

verstehen unter + D ⟨etw unter etw v.⟩   to understand (sth) by (sth)

■ Ich verstehe unter „Sozialismus" ein System, daß . . . .
My understanding of "socialism" is that it is a system which . . . .

■ Was verstehst du unter „Freier Wille?"
What is your understanding of "free will?"

■ Ich verstehe nicht darunter (/unter Freiheit), daß du tun kannst, was du willst.
I don't understand by that (/freedom) that you can do whatever you want.

verstehen von + D ⟨etw von etw v.⟩   to know (sth) about (sth)

■ Paul redet viel über klassische Bücher, aber ich glaube nicht, daß er viel davon (/von Literatur) versteht.
Paul talks a lot about the classics, but I don't think he knows much about them (/about literature).

■ Was verstehst du von Kunst (/Fußball)?
What do you know about art (/soccer)?

■ Von Linguistik versteht Sonia mindestens ebensoviel wie Sabine.
Sonia knows at least as much about linguistics as Sabine.

■ Daß er einige dumme Bemerkungen gemacht hat, versteht sich von selbst.
It goes without saying that he made some stupid remarks.

verstoßen gegen + A ⟨gegen etw v.⟩   to offend against (sth)

■ Dein Beharren auf deiner Position verstößt gegen den gesunden Menschenverstand (/jede Vernunft).
Your persistence in your position goes against common sense (/all reason).

■ Die für die Exxon Valdez Verantwortlichen haben gegen viele Gesetze (/Regeln/Vorschriften) verstoßen.
Those in charge of the Exxon Valdez violated many laws (/rules /regulations).

versuchen mit + D ⟨es mit jdm/etw v.⟩   to give (sb) a try; to try (sth)

■ Der Lehrer hat es mit Güte und mit Strenge versucht.
The teacher tried both leniency and severity.

■ Der Vorarbeiter will es noch einmal mit dem neuen Arbeiter versuchen.
The foreman wants to give the new worker another chance.

■ Ich versuchte es noch einmal mit den Tabletten, aber sie hatten keine Wirkung.
I gave these pills another try, but they didn't have any effect.

versuchen zu (+ infin) ⟨v. etw zu tun⟩   to try to (do)

■ Er versuchte, es ihr zu erklären.
He tried to explain it to her.

■ Ich will versuchen, ob ich es schaffen kann.
I want to see if I can do it.

■ Versuche nicht, dich schnell zu entscheiden!
Don't try to decide quickly.

(s.) vertagen auf + A ⟨sich/etw auf etw v.⟩   to adjourn until (sth)

■ Wir vertagen die Sitzung auf morgen (/Montag/August).
We'll adjourn the meeting until tomorrow (/Monday/August).

■ Der Bundestag hat sich auf nächste Woche vertagt.
The Bundestag (i.e., German parliament) adjourned until next week.

vertauschen mit + D ⟨etw mit etw v.⟩ to exchange (sth) for (sth) (by mistake)

- Der Schüler hat den Bleistift mit einem Kuli vertauscht.
  The student confused the pencil with a ballpoint pen.

- Die Dame hat ihren Platz (/Sitz/Hut) vertauscht. Sie hat ihren mit meinem vertauscht.
  The lady took the wrong place (/seat/hat). She had hers confused with mine.

(s.) verteidigen gegen + A ⟨sich/jdn/etw gegen jdn/etw v.⟩ to defend (o.s./sb/sth) against (sb/sth)

- Er hat sich (/mich) gegen den Angreifer verteidigt.
  He defended himself (/me) against the attacker.

- Das Land (/Das Militär/Der Soldat) verteidigte sich gegen den Feind.
  The country (/military/soldier) defended itself (/himself) against the enemy.

- Der Rechsanwalt verteidigte den Angeklagten gegen die Angriffe des Staatsanwaltes.
  The defense attorney defended the accused against the district attorney's attacks.

- Ich muß mich gegen dieses Unrecht verteidigen.
  I must defend myself against this injustice.

s. vertiefen in + A ⟨sich in etw v.⟩ to become absorbed in (sth)

- Ich habe mich ganz in den Roman vertieft.
  I was really engrossed in the novel.

- Er vertieft sich in seine Arbeit (/das Spiel/die Zeitung).
  He becomes absorbed in his work (/the game/the newspaper).

vertieft sein in + A ⟨in etw v. sein⟩ to be engrossed in (sth)

- Ich war ganz vertieft in mein Spiel (/in das Schachspiel).
  I was engrossed in my game (/the chess game).

- Stör sie nicht! Sie ist ins Gespräch (/in Gedanken/in ihre Arbeit) vertieft.
  Don't disturb her! She is absorbed in the conversation (/deep in thought/ deep into her work).

s. vertragen mit + D ⟨sich mit jdm v.⟩ to get on *or* along with (sb)

- Unsere Kinder vertragen sich gut mit den Kindern unserer Nachbarn.
  Our children get along well with the neighbors' children.

- Ich vertrage mich immer schlecht (/gut) mit meiner älteren Schwester.
  I always get on badly (/fine) with my older sister.

■ Der Physiklehrer verträgt sich nicht mit den Schülern.
The physics teacher doesn't get along with his students.

s. vertragen mit + D ⟨sich mit etw v.⟩   to go with (sth); to be consistent with (sth)

■ Das Rot der Bluse verträgt sich nicht mit dem Grün des Rockes.
The (shade of) red in the blouse doesn't go with the green in the skirt.

■ Das Blumenmuster auf diesem Hemd verträgt sich (nicht) gut mit den Streifen auf dieser Hose.
The flower pattern on this shirt goes (does not go) well with the stripes on this pair of trousers.

■ Was er sagte, vertrug sich nicht mit seinen sonstigen Ansichten.
What he said was inconsistent with his other views.

■ Deine Diskussionsbeiträge vertragen sich nicht damit, daß du jetzt gegen den Antrag bist.
Your contributions to the discussion are not conistent with your current opposition to the motion.

vertrauen auf + A ⟨jdm/einer Sache *or* auf jdn/etw v.⟩   to trust (sb/sth); to have trust in (sb/sth)

■ Du kannst ihm (*or* auf ihn) unbedingt vertrauen.
You can trust him fully (or have complete trust in him).

■ Ich habe leider seiner (*or* auf seine) Ehrlichkeit vertraut.
Unfortunately, I trusted his honesty.

■ Ich vertraue auf mein Glück (/mein Urteil/meine Ansicht).
I trust my luck (/judgement/opinion).

■ Ich vertraue auf Gott (/Gerechtigkeit/Menschlichkeit).
I put my trust in God (/justice/humanity).

■ Ich vertraue darauf, daß er sein Wort hält.
I trust that he'll keep his word.

vertreten (+ prep)   to stand in for; to represent

■ Ich wurde durch meinen Anwalt (vor einem Richter) vertreten.
I was represented (or My case was pleaded) by my attorney (before a judge).

■ Es wäre schwierig, solche Handlungsweise vor deinen Eltern (/deinem Lehrer) zu vertreten.
It would be difficult to justify your behavior to your parents (/teacher).

■ Herr Rühe vertritt die konservative Partei in dieser Diskussionsrunde.
Mr. Rühe represents the conservative party on this panel.

- Kannst du mich (/meine Interessen) bei der Sitzung vertreten?
  Can you represent me (/my interests) at the meeting?

verursachen (+ prep)   to cause

- Er hat durch seine Behauptung viel Schaden (/Elend) verursacht.
  He caused a lot of damage (/hardship) by his assertion.
- Was hat die Entwicklungen in Osteuropa verursacht?
  What was it that caused the developments in Eastern Europe?

verurteilen zu + D ⟨jdn zu etw v.⟩   to condemn (sb) to (sth); to sentence (sb) to (sth)

- Der Richter verurteilte ihn zu vier Jahren Gefängnis (/zum Tode/zu einer Gefängnisstrafe/zum Tode durch den Strang).
  The judge sentenced him to four years in prison (/death/a prison term/death by hanging).
- Er wurde zu einer Geldstrafe von 8.000 Mark verurteilt.
  A fine of 8,000 marks was imposed on him.

verurteilt sein zu + D ⟨zu etw v. sein⟩   to be condemned *or* sentenced to (sth)

- Er ist zum Tode (wegen Mordes/wegen Totschlags) verurteilt.
  He is condemned to death (because of murder/because of manslaughter).
- Ihr Plan war von vornherein zum Scheitern verurteilt.
  Their plan was doomed to fail from the outset.
- Er ist dazu verurteilt, einen Monat Gemeinschaftsarbeit zu machen.
  He is sentenced to doing a month of community work.

verwandeln in + A ⟨jdn/etw in jdn/etw v.⟩   to turn (sb/sth) into (sb/sth)

- Wir haben die Garage in ein Schlafzimmer verwandelt.
  We changed the garage into a bedroom.
- Die Hexe hat den Prinzen in einen Bettler (/Hund) verwandelt.
  The witch turned the prince into a beggar (/dog).

s. verwandeln in/zu + A/D ⟨sich in *or* zu etw v.⟩   to change *or* turn into (sth)

- In dem Roman hat der Mann sich in einen Käfer verwandelt.
  In the novel the man turned into a bug.

- Nach dieser (geistigen) Erfahrung habe ich mich zu einer anderen Person (*or* in einen anderen Menschen) verwandelt.
  After this (spiritual) experience I have become a different person.

verwechseln (+ prep) to mix up; to get muddled *or* mixed up

- Ich habe ihn mit seinem Bruder (/seinem Freund) verwechselt.
  I got him mixed up with his brother (/friend).
- Die zwei Männer sehen sich zum Verwechseln ähnlich.
  The two men are the spitting image of each other.
- Ich verwechselte meinen Schirm (vielleicht mit Peters).
  Perhaps I mistook my umbrella for Peter's.
- Er verwechselt immer den Dativ mit dem Akkusativ.
  He always gets the dative mixed up with the accusative.

verweisen an + A ⟨jdn an jdn/etw v.⟩ to refer (sb) to (sb/sth)

- Ich bin von Herrn Schmidt an Sie (/diese Abteilung) verwiesen worden.
  I've been referred to you (/your department) by Mr. Schmidt.
- Man hat den Arbeitslosen an den Inhaber des Ladens verwiesen.
  They referred the unemployed man to the store owner.

verweisen auf + A ⟨(jdn) auf etw v.⟩ to refer (sb) to (sth)

- Auf ihre Anfrage hin verwies man sie auf die amtlichen Vorschriften.
  They referred her to the official regulations based on her petition.
- Der Autor verwies auf eine Textstelle (/ein Bild/ein Gedicht).
  The author referred to a passage in the text (/picture/poem).

verweisen aus/von + D ⟨jdn aus etw v.⟩ to expel (sb) from (sth)

- Großbritannien verwies den Botschafter aus dem Land (*or* des Landes.)
  Great Britain expelled the ambassador from the country.
- Peter ist schon zweimal von einer Schule verwiesen worden.
  Peter has already been expelled from a school twice.

verwenden (+ prep) to use; to employ

- Die Schüler verwenden dieses Buch im Unterricht.
  The students use this book in class.

■ Sie hat Zucker und Rosinen (/diese Zutaten) für den Kuchen verwendet.
   She used sugar and raisins (/these ingredients) in the cake.

■ Man verwendet dieses Pulver nur zum Geschirrwaschen.
   This soap powder is used only for dishwashing.

verwenden auf + A ⟨etw auf etw v.⟩   to spend (sth) on (sth)

■ Er verwandte zu viel Zeit (/Mühe/Energie) auf das Projekt.
   He spent too much time (/effort/energy) on the project.

s. verwenden für + A ⟨sich (bei jdm) für jdn/etw v.⟩   to intercede with (sb/sth); to approach (sb) on (sb's) behalf

■ Er verwandte sich beim Direktor für sie.
   He approached the director on her behalf.

■ Ich habe mich schon sehr häufig für dich beim Chef verwandt, aber jetzt mußt du dir selbst helfen.
   I have interceded for you several times with the boss, but now you will have to help yourself.

(s.) verwickeln in + A ⟨sich in etw v.⟩   to become entangled in (sth); to get caught up in (sth)

■ Sie verwickelten ihre Nachbarn in ein längeres Gespräch.
   They involved their neighbors in a rather long conversation.

■ Je mehr er aussagt, desto mehr verwickelt er sich in Widersprüche.
   The more he testifies, the deeper he gets entangled in contradictions.

■ Brich den Kontakt mit den Leuten da ab! Du verwickelst dich da immer mehr in eine unerfreuliche Geschichte.
   Break off contact with those people! You are getting more and more involved in a very unpleasant affair.

verwundert sein über + A ⟨über jdn/etw v. sein⟩   to be amazed *or* astonished at (sb/sth)

■ Ich war sehr über seine Bemerkung (/darüber/sie) verwundert.
   I was really amazed at his remark (/or surprised at that/her).

■ Ich bin sehr über das (schlimme) Benehmen eures Kindes verwundert.
   I am very astonished at the (bad) behavior of your child.

verzichten auf + A ⟨auf jdn/etw v.⟩   to do without (sb/sth)

- Er hat auf Alkohol (/Süßigkeiten/sein Vergnügen/sein Vorhaben) verzichtet.
  He gave up alcohol (/sweets/his pleasures/his plan).

- Obwohl er nicht besonders reich ist, verzichtet er auf sein Erbteil.
  Although he isn't particularly rich, he's giving up his inheritance.

- Möchten Sie eine Zigarette? Danke, aber ich verzichte darauf.
  Would you like a cigarette? Thank you, but I'll do without.

- Ich würde eher aufs Essen verzichten als auf meinen Computer (/Wagen).
  I'd rather do without food than my computer (/car).

- Er verzichtete auf seinen Anspruch (/seine Forderung/sein Recht).
  He abandoned his claim (/demand/right).

- Auf deine Hilfe könnte ich verzichten.
  I could do without your help.

- Er verzichtete auf den Thron (/zu Gunsten seiner Schwester).
  He renounced his throne (/in favor of his sister).

(s.) verziehen (+ prep)   to twist; to shape; to bend; to get out of shape; to stretch

- Das Fenster (/Das Brett) ist schon seit Jahren verzogen.
  The window (/board) has been warped for years.

- Meine Hose hat sich (beim Waschen) leider verzogen.
  Unfortunately, my pants got out of shape (during washing).

- Der Clown verzog den Mund zu einer Grimasse (/einem Grinsen).
  The clown screwed his mouth into a grimace (/a grin).

- Die Firma (/Er) ist nach Hamburg (/ins Ausland) verzogen.
  The company (/He) moved to Hamburg (/out of the country).

- Falls verzogen, bitte zurück an den Absender.
  If the addressee has moved, return to sender.

- Ich verziehe mich (nach Hause/in die Stadt/auf die Toilette/ins Bett). (*inf*)
  I'm going (home/to the city/to the bathroom/to bed).

verzweifeln (+ prep)   to despair

- Sie verzweifelte am Leben (/an den Menschen/an ihrem betrunkenen Mann).
  She despaired of life (/human beings/her drunk husband).

- Es gibt keinen Grund zu verzweifeln. Verzweifle nicht!
  There is no reason to despair. Don't despair!

vorbeifahren an + D ⟨**jdn an etw v.**⟩   to drive (sb) past (sth)

■ Ich fahre ihn am Bahnhof (/am Kino/an der Haltestelle) vorbei.
I'll drive him to the train station (/movies/bus stop).

■ Auf dem Weg zur Arbeit sind wir an der Kirche (/dem Supermarkt/der Sporthalle) vorbeigefahren.
On our way to work we passed the church (/supermarket/gymnasium).

vorbeifahren bei + D ⟨**bei jdm v.**⟩   to drop *or* call in on (sb); to stop *or* drop by (sb's house)

■ Kannst du mich bei ihr (/zur Party) vorbeifahren.
Can you run (or drive) me to her place (/the party).

■ Ich fahre heute bei ihm (/deiner Tante) vorbei.
I'll stop at his house (/your aunt's house) today.

■ Wann fährst du bei mir vorbei?
When will you drop by my house/When will you call on me?

■ Ich bin bei euch vorbeigefahren, aber ihr wart nicht zu Hause.
I stopped at your place but you weren't home.

vorbeigehen an + D ⟨**an jdm/etw v.**⟩   to go past *or* by (sb/sth); to overlook (sth)

■ Ich bin an deinem Haus (/dem Theater/den Demonstranten) vorbeigegangen.
I went past your house (/the theater/the demonstrators).

■ Die schönsten Tage unseres Lebens gehen am schnellsten vorbei.
The most beautiful days of our lives go by the fastest.

■ Er ging an der Wirklichkeit (/Gelegenheit/Chance) vorbei.
He missed the truth (/opportunity/chance).

■ An Herrn Müller werden wir bei der nächsten Beförderung nicht vorbeigehen können.
We will not be able to overlook (or pass over) Mr. Müller for the next promotion.

vorbeigehen bei + D ⟨**bei jdm v.**⟩   to drop *or* call in on (sb); to stop *or* drop by (sb's house)

■ Bitte geh doch bei der Bibliothek vorbei und bring (mir) das Buch zurück!
Please stop by the library and return the book (for me).

■ Ich ging bei ihm (/der Apotheke) vorbei und holte die Arznei ab.
I stopped at his house (/the pharmacy) and picked up the medicine.

vorbeikommen an + D ⟨**an jdm/etw v.**⟩   to pass (by) (sb/sth); to get around (sth)

- Wenn du an dem Bahnhof vorbeikommst, kauf mir bitte zwei Fahrkarten nach Bremen.
  If you pass by the train station, would you please buy me two tickets to Bremen.

- Ich bin an drei Tankstellen (/einigen Touristen) vorbeigekommen.
  I passed by three gas stations (/some tourists).

- Ich komme an seiner Bitte (/seiner Frage/seiner Forderung/seinem Blick) nicht vorbei.
  I am unable to avoid his request (/question/demand/glance).

- Es wäre wohl schwierig, an ihm (/daran) vorbeizukommen.
  It would probably be difficult to avoid him (/that).

- Ich komme nicht daran (/an der Beobachtung/an der Tatsache) vorbei, daß er besser ist als ich.
  There is no getting around it (/the observation/the fact) that he is better than I.

- Der Stürmer kam im ganzen Spiel nicht an seinem Gegenspieler (/dem Verteidiger) vorbei.
  The forward didn't manage to get past his opponent (/defender) during the whole game.

vorbeikommen bei + D ⟨**bei jdm v.**⟩   to drop *or* call in on (sb); to stop *or* drop by (sb's house)

- Ich möchte morgen bei dir vorbeikommen und mir das Geld abholen.
  I would like to stop at your place tomorrow and pick up my money.

- Kommen Sie doch einmal am Wochenende bei uns vorbei!
  Come by our place some time on the weekend.

vorbeireden an + D ⟨**an jdm/etw v.**⟩   to talk around (sb/sth); to skirt (sb/sth)

- Sie haben aneinander vorbeigeredet.
  They talked at cross purposes.

- Sie redeten am Thema vorbei und trafen den Kern der Sache nicht.
  They talked around the problem and didn't get to the heart of the matter.

- Du redest kosequent am Punkt (/am Problem/an mir) vorbei!
  You're consistently missing the point (/not addressing the problem/what I say or *You don't respond to my words).*

(s.) vorbereiten auf/für + A ⟨**sich/jdn/etw auf/für etw v.**⟩   to prepare (o.s./sb/sth) for (sth)

- Ich bereitete mich auf (*rare* für) die Prüfung (/den Unterricht) vor.
  I prepared for the test (/for class).

■ Der Lehrer hat die Schüler auf (*or* für) einen Test vorbereitet.
  The teacher prepared the students for a test.

■ Ich habe mich in Gedanken auf (*or* für) meinen Vortrag (/meine Herzoperation) vorbereitet.
  I have gathered my thoughts for my lecture (/I mentally prepared for my heart operation).

■ Ich muß dich darauf (/auf die schlimme Nachricht) vorbereiten, daß. . . .
  I must prepare you for the fact (/for the bad news) that. . . .

■ Ich bereite mich (/die Mannschaft) auf (*or* für) den Wettbewerb vor.
  I'm preparing myself (/the team) for the match.

vorbereitet sein auf/für   **+ A** ⟨**auf/für etw v. sein**⟩   to be prepared for (sth)

■ Darauf (*or* Dafür) war sie nicht vorbereitet.
  She wasn't prepared for that.

■ Bist du auf (*or* für) das Examen (/die Reise/die Party) vorbereitet?
  Are you prepared for the exam (/trip/party)?

vorbringen (+ prep)   to say; to state; to allege; to claim

■ Was haben Sie gegen den Angeklagten (/die Klage/den Plan/die Entscheidung/die Forderung) vorzubringen?
  What do you have to say about the defendant (/complaint/plan/decision/demand)?

■ Ich brachte dagegen vor, daß er alles monopolisieren wollte.
  I objected to the fact that he wanted to monopolize everything.

■ Der Richter fragte den Angeklagten: „Was haben Sie zu Ihrer Entschuldigung vorzubringen?"
  The judge asked the defendant, "What have you to say in your defense?"

■ Als Entschudigung brachte er vor, daß er nie da gewesen wäre.
  He alleged (or said) that he had never been there as an excuse.

■ Er hat zu seiner Verteidigung vorgebracht, daß. . . .
  He said in his defense that. . . .

vorkommen (+ prep)   to occur

■ Diese Elefanten (/Tiere/Pflanzen) kommen nur in Indien vor.
  These elephants (/animals/plants) are found only in India.

■ In dem Brief kommen viele grammatische Fehler vor.
  There are many grammatical mistakes in the letter.

■ Dieses Wort kommt bei Kafka (/im Englischen) oft vor.
This word occurs often in Kafka's work (/in English).

■ Das kommt in den besten Familien vor.
Things like that can happen in the best of families.

vorkommen (without prep) to occur; to seem, to appear

■ Diese Frau (/Dieses Bild/Diese Melodie) kommt mir bekannt vor.
This lady (/picture/melody) seems familiar to me.

■ Es kommt mir vor, als ob. . . .
It seems to me as if. . . .

vorsehen für + A ⟨jdn/etw für etw v.⟩ to have (sb) in mind for (sth); to intend (sth)
for (sth)

■ Er ist für die Position des Vorsitzenden (/dieses Amt) vorgesehen.
He's being considered for the chairmanship (/for this office).

■ Meine Party ist für den 18.7. vorgesehen.
My party is planned for the 18th of July.

■ Die Vorführung ist für nächsten Monat vorgesehen.
The performance is planned for next month.

■ Sie haben das Geld für einen Teppich (/die Krebsforschung) vorgesehen.
They have earmarked the money for a rug (/cancer research).

■ Sehen Sie bitte einen Platz (/einen Stuhl/eine Karte) für mich vor!
Please reserve a seat (/chair/ticket) for me.

■ Was hast du für diesen Sommer vorgesehen?
What is your schedule for this summer?

vorsehen hinter/unter + D ⟨hinter/unter etw v.⟩ to appear *or* peep (sth) out from
behind/under (sth)

■ Bei ihr sieht der Büstenhalter unter der Bluse vor.
Her bra is showing through her blouse.

s. vorstellen bei + D ⟨sich bei jdm/etw v.⟩ to have *or* go for an interview with
(sb/sth)

■ Ich habe mich bei dieser Firma (/bei Siemens) vorgestellt.
I went for an interview with this company (/Siemens).

- Du mußt dich beim Chef der Firma vorstellen. Vielleicht bekommst du die Stelle dann.
  You must go for an interview with the boss. Maybe then you'll get the job.

s. vorstellen unter + D ⟨**sich etw unter etw v.**⟩   to understand (sth) by (sth)

- Was stellst du dir darunter vor?
  What do you understand by that?

- Darunter kann ich mir nichts vorstellen.
  It doesn't mean anything to me.

- Unter „Great America" stelle ich mir einen großen Vergnügungspark vor.
  I picture "Great America" as a large amusement park.

- Das stelle ich mir unter guter Musik (/einem vergnüglichen Abend) vor.
  That's my idea of good music (/a pleasant evening).

s. vorstellen (without prep)   to imagine; to introduce

- Stell dir mal vor, was mir passiert ist!
  Just imagine what happened to me!

- Ich möchte mich Ihnen vorstellen.
  I would like to introduce myself.

vorübergehen an + D ⟨**an jdm/etw v.**⟩   to ignore (sb/sth); to pass (sb) by

- Daran (/An diesem Vorschlag/An dieser Bemerkung/An diesem Bewerber/An ihm) kann man nicht vorübergehen.
  You can't ignore that (/this proposal/this remark/this applicant/We can't pass him by or overlook him).

- Ich hoffe, diese Krankheit (/dieses Unglück) wird an mir vorübergehen.
  I hope this illness (/bad luck) will bypass me.

W

wachen bei + D ⟨bei jdm w.⟩   to sit up with (sb); to keep watch by (sb's bedside)

- Wir wachten die ganze Nacht bei meiner kranken Großmutter.
  We sat up the whole night with my sick grandmother.
- Die Krankenschwester hat die ganze Nacht hindurch bei ihm (/an seinem Bett) gewacht.
  The nurse sat up with him through the night (/at his bed).

wachen über + A ⟨über jdn/etw w.⟩   to (keep) watch over (sb/sth); to supervise (sb/sth)

- Der Direktor wachte über die Einhaltung der Vorschriften.
  The director saw to it that the directions were observed.
- Der Nachtwächter (/Der Polizist) wachte darüber, daß niemand. . . .
  The night watchman (/The policeman) watched that no one. . . .
- Die Krankenschwester wacht darüber, daß der Kranke die Pillen einnimmt.
  The nurse will see to it that the sick man takes the pills.
- Ich wachte darüber, daß die Kinder nicht mit dem Feuer spielten.
  I watched (or saw to it) that the children didn't play with fire.

wachsen (+ prep)   to grow

- Solche Pflanzen wachsen in diesen Gegenden (/auf diesem Boden) nicht.
  Such plants don't grow in these areas (/in this soil).
- Diese Bäume (/Pflanzen) sind in die Breite und Höhe gewachsen.
  These trees (/plants) have grown broader and taller.
- Das Kind ist ihm ans Herz gewachsen.
  The child has grown dear to him (or to his heart).
- Er (/Seine Energie) wächst mit seinen Aufgaben.
  He (/His energy) grows with (the corresponding rise in) his duties.
- Das Kind ist in die Höhe gewachsen.
  The child has gotten taller (or shot up).
- Mein Junge ist mir über den Kopf gewachsen.
  My boy has grown taller than me.

(s.) wagen (+ prep)   to venture; to risk; to dare

- Er hat für ihn (/die Sache) sein Leben gewagt.
  He risked his life for him (/the cause).

- Bei diesem kalten Wetter wage ich mich nicht aus dem Haus (/ins Wasser/ins Freie/zur Schule).
  I don't dare to leave the house (/go into the water/go outside/go to school) in this cold weather.

- Der Alte wagt sich nicht mehr aus dem Haus (/auf die Straße in der Nacht/durch den Park/durch den Wald/auf das Gebiet).
  The old man doesn't venture out of the house any more (/onto the street at night/through the park/through the woods/into that area).

s. wagen an + A ⟨sich an etw w.⟩   to venture to do (sth)

- Ich wage mich nicht an Elektronik (/ans Autoreparieren/daran).
  I dare not work on electronics (/on cars/dare not do it).

- Wagst du dich an diese komplizierte Aufgabe (/die Lösung des Problems/unseren schwierigen Mitarbeiter) heran?
  Do you dare to face this complicated assignment (/face the solution of the problem/approach our difficult co-worker)?

(s.) wagen zu (+ infinitive) ⟨es w., etw zu tun⟩   to venture to do (sth); to dare (to) do (sth)

- Wage nicht, das ohne mein Erlaubnis zu tun!
  Don't you dare do that without my permission!

- Das Kind wagte nicht, ihn anzublicken.
  The child didn't dare to look at him.

- Ich wage nicht zu hoffen, daß. . . .
  I don't dare to hope that. . . .

- Ich wage es nicht, ihn darum zu bitten (/das zu tun).
  I don't dare to ask him about that (/to do that).

- Kannst du es wagen, deinen ehemaligen Freund anzurufen?
  Can you risk calling your former boyfriend?

- Wie können Sie es wagen, das zu sagen? Ich wagte kein Wort zu sagen.
  How can you dare to say that? I did not dare (to) say a word.

wählen (+ prep)   to choose; to select; to pick; to elect

- Man hat ihn ins Parlament (/in den Ausschuß/in die Handelskammer) gewählt.
  They elected him to Parliament (/elected or voted him to be a member of the committee/to the Board of Trade).

- Sie wählten ihn zum Präsidenten (/zum König or zum Kaiser/zum Kanzler/zum Vorsitzenden/zur Bürgermeisterin).
  They elected him president (/chose him as their king or emperor/chancellor /president or chairman/chose her for mayor).

■ Der Vorsitzende wurde durch Handaufheben gewählt.
  The chairman was elected by a show of hands.

■ Von welchem Alter an darf man wählen?—Mit 18 (*or* Ab 18) kann man wählen.
  At what age can you vote?—You can vote at 18.

■ Ich kann mich nicht entschließen, welches Geschenk ich für ihn wählen soll.
  I can't decide which gift I should choose for him.

■ Ihn würde ich mir nicht zum Freund (/zum Vorbild) wählen.
  I wouldn't pick (or choose) him as my friend (/model).

■ Ich wähle meine Worte (/meine Freunde) vorsichtig und mit Bedacht.
  I choose my words (/friends) carefully and prudently.

■ Wir können zwischen diesen zwei Restaurants (/Speisen/Möglichkeiten) wählen.
  We can choose between these two restaurants (/foods/possibilities).

■ Hast du etwas aus der Speisekarte gewählt?
  Have you picked something from the menu?

wahrnehmen (+ prep)   to perceive; to be aware of; to distinguish

■ Kannst du den Geruch im Haus (/in der Küche) wahrnehmen?
  Are you aware of (or Can you smell) the odor in the house (/kitchen)?

■ Ich nehme alles um mich herum (sehr bewußt) wahr (/Ich nehme nichts mehr wahr).
  I'm aware of everything around me (/I'm no longer aware of anything).

■ Das Geräusch ist so leise, man kann es kaum mit den Ohren wahrnehmen.
  The sound is so soft, you can hardly hear it.

■ Er hat von den Vorfällen (/dem Termin/der Frist/der Angelegenheit/allem) nichts mehr wahrgenommen.
  He wasn't aware of the events (/appointment/deadline/matter/anything).

■ Der Rechtsanwalt nahm meine Interessen (/Rechte) meinem Nachbarn gegenüber wahr.
  The attorney looked after my interests (/rights) where my neighbor was concerned.

(s.) wälzen (+ prep)   to roll; to surge

■ Ich habe mich die ganze Nacht im Bett (/im Schlaf) gewälzt.
  I tossed and turned in my bed (/sleep) all night.

■ Die Kinder haben sich auf dem Boden (/im Gras/im Schmutz) gewälzt.
  The children rolled on the ground (/on the grass/in the dirt).

■ Sie wälzte den Teig in Mehl (/Ei).
  She coated the dough with flour (/egg).

- Der Komiker erzählte so gute Witze, daß das Publikum sich vor Lachen wälzte. *(fig)*
  The comedian told jokes that were so funny that the audience cracked up with laughter (or split their sides with laughter). (fig)

- Die Fans wälzten sich zum Ausgang.
  The fans surged along to the exit.

wälzen auf + A ⟨etw auf jdn w.⟩   to shift (sth) to (sb)

- Er hat die Schuld (/Verantwortung) auf seinen Bruder gewälzt.
  He shifted (or shoved) the blame (/responsibility) on his brother.

- Ich will die Probleme nicht auf dich (/andere) wälzen.
  I don't want to dump the problems on you (/others).

wandern (+ prep)   to wander; to roam; to hike; to travel; to go; to walk

- Ich bin mit meiner Frau durch den Bayerischen Wald gewandert.
  My wife and I hiked through the Bavarian forest.

- Ich bin gestern gemütlich durch die Innenstadt (/mehrere Kaufhäuser/den Park) gewandert.
  Yesterday I strolled leisurely through the downtown area (/several department stores/the park).

- Meine Gedanken wanderten in die Heimat (/Ferne/Vergangenheit).
  My thoughts wandered off to my homeland (/far away/into the past).

- Sie ließ ihre Blicke über die Menschenmenge (/von mir zu ihm) wandern.
  Her gaze wandered over the crowd (/from me to him).

- Die Wolken wandern am Himmel.
  The clouds are drifting in the sky.

- Der Brief ist durch die ganze Gruppe (/ins Feuer/in den Papierkorb/durch viele Hände/ins Leihhaus) gewandert.
  The letter was passed though the whole group (/went into the fire/went into the wastepaper basket/went through a lot of hands/ended up at the pawnbroker).

warnen vor + D ⟨jdn vor jdm/etw w.⟩   to warn (sb) of (sth)

- Er hat ihn vor Taschendieben (/der Gefahr/dem bösen Hund) gewarnt.
  He warned him of pickpockets (/danger/the mean dog).

- Sie warnte mich davor, den Wagen offen zulassen.
  She warned me against leaving the car unlocked.

■ Ich habe die Kinder davor gewarnt, in dem Fluß zu schwimmen.
   I warned the kids about swimming in the river.

warten auf + A ⟨auf jdn/etw w.⟩   to wait for (sb/sth)

■ Wir warten jetzt schon eine Stunde auf den Zug (/unseren Opa/den Abflug).
   We have already been waiting for the train (/our grandpa/the plane's departure)
   for one hour.

■ Ich habe auf Einlaß (/Antwort/solch ein Programm) gewartet.
   I waited to be let in (/for an answer/for such a program).

■ Ich habe lange darauf gewartet, daß du dich entschuldigst.
   I've waited a long time for your apology.

■ Zu Hause wartet eine Überraschung auf dich.
   There is a surprise waiting for you at home.

warten mit + D ⟨mit etw w.⟩   to wait with (sth)

■ Wir mußten mit der Abfahrt warten. Meine Schwester war noch nicht fertig.
   We had to wait with (or delay) the departure. My sister wasn't yet ready.

■ Wir warten mit dem Essen, bis Vater kommt.
   We are holding lunch until father arrives.

■ Der Spezialist will noch mit der Röntgenbehandlung warten.
   The specialist wants to wait with (or delay) the X-ray treatment.

■ Ich habe lange mit der Heirat (/auf das richtige Mädchen) gewartet.
   I waited a long time for marriage (/for the right girl).

(s.) waschen (+ prep)   to wash

■ Wäschst du die Wäsche in (*or* mit) der Waschmaschine oder noch mit der Hand?
   Do you wash your laundry in (or with) a washing machine or by hand?

■ Ich wusch mich (/das Kind/ihn) von oben bis unten.
   I washed myself (/the child/him) from top to bottom.

■ Ich wusch mir den ganzen Körper von Kopf bis Fuß.
   I washed my entire body from head to toe.

■ Nachdem du die Hemden mit Waschpulver gewaschen hast, mußt du sie gut
   ausspülen.
   After washing the shirts with detergent, you will have to rinse them properly.

■ Man benutzt das Verb „waschen" mit Wäsche; bei Geschirr sagt man „abwaschen."
   One uses the verb "waschen" with laundry; with dishes one uses "abwaschen."

wechseln (+ prep)   to change; to exchange

■ Ich möchte Deutsche Mark in (*or* gegen) Dollar wechseln.
I'd like to change German marks for dollars.

■ Beim Auto muß man das Öl (/die Reifen) regelmäßig wechseln.
You have to change the oil in (/tires on) a car regularly.

■ Du willst bei Kathrin schlafen? Gut, aber nimm Wäsche zum Wechseln mit.
You want to sleep over at Kathryn's? Okay, but take along clean clothes.

wechseln mit + D ⟨**etw mit jdm w.**⟩   to exchange (sth) with (sb)

■ Könnte ich den Platz mit Ihnen wechseln?
Could I change seats with you?

■ Sie wechselten Briefe (/ein paar Worte/einen Händedruck/Blicke/die Ringe
/Komplimente) (miteinander).
*They exchanged letters (/a few words/a handshake/glances/rings/compliments)
with one another).*

wechseln (without prep)   to change

■ Ich will meine Stellung (/mein Auto/meine Schule/meine Kleidung) wechseln.
I want to change jobs (/cars/schools/my clothing).

wegkommen über + A ⟨**über etw w.**⟩   to get over (sth)

■ Ich komme nicht darüber weg, daß du das tatsächlich geschafft hast.
I can't get over the fact that you actually accomplished that.

■ Sie konnte schließlich über den Verlust ihres Sohnes wegkommen.
She was finally able to get over the loss of her son.

s. wehren gegen + A ⟨**sich gegen jdn/etw w.**⟩ to defend oneself against
(sb/sth)

■ Ich habe mich gegen seinen Plan (/ihn/seinen Vorschlag/seine Ideologie) gewehrt.
I fought (against) his plan (/him/his proposal/his ideology).

■ Der kontroverse Kolumnist mußte sich oft gegen Angriffe (/Anschuldigun-
gen/Vorwürfe/Verleumdungen/Kritik) wehren.
*The controversial columnist often had to defend himself against attack (/accusa-
tions/reproaches/slander/criticism).*

weichen von + D ⟨von jdm/etw w.⟩ to yield *or* give way to (sb/sth)

- Der Feind wich (von seiner Stellung/vor der Übermacht).
  The enemy backed out (from its position/yielded to a superior power).
- Meine Absicht (/Meine Meinung/Mein Entschluß) ist ganz klar. Ich werde davon absolut nicht weichen.
  My intention (/opinion/decision) is very clear. I will not budge from it.
- Sein Anspruch war überzogen. Ich bin nicht von der Stelle gewichen.
  His demand was unreasonable. I refused to budge (give an inch).
- Die Mutter ist nicht vom Bett meines kranken Vaters gewichen.
  My mother didn't leave my father's sickbed.

(s.) weinen (+ prep) to cry; to weep

- Was er vorschlug, war zum Weinen.
  What he suggested was enough to make you cry.
- Es ist zum Weinen mit deiner Unpünktlichkeit (/Faulheit).
  Your tardiness (/laziness) is enough to make me want to weep.
- Er brachte mich (/das Mädchen) zum Weinen.
  He made me (/the girl) cry.
- Sie weinte sich (/Ich weinte mich) in den Schlaf.
  She cried herself (/I cried myself) to sleep.
- Sie weinte sich (/Ich weinte mir) die Augen rot (*or* aus dem Kopf).
  She cried her (/I cried my) eyes out (or head off).

weinen nach + D ⟨nach jdm/etw w.⟩ to cry for (sb/sth)

- Das Baby weinte nach seinem Schnuller (/dem Busen seiner Mutter/seinem Vater/dem Essen).
  The baby cried for his pacifier (/mother's breast/father/food).

weinen über + A ⟨über etw w.⟩ to cry *or* weep over (sth)

- Die Frau weinte über das Gerücht, daß ihr Mann sich in eine andere Frau verliebt hätte.
  The woman wept over the rumor that her husband had fallen for another woman.
- Sie weinte über jede Kleinigkeit (/ihr Pech/ihr Mißgeschick).
  She wept over every little thing (/her bad luck/misfortune).
- Die alte Dame hat bitterlich über den Tod ihres Sohnes geweint.
  The old lady wept bitterly over the death of her son.
- Die Schauspielerin weinte vor Freude über den Gewinn des Oscars.
  The actress cried for joy over winning the Oscar.

weinen um + A ⟨**um jdn/etw w.**⟩   to cry for (sb/sth)

- Sie weinte bittere Tränen um ihren Sohn, der sich umgebracht hatte.
  She wept (bitter tears) for her son who had committed suicide.
- Um den Ajatollah haben im Westen sicher nicht viele geweint.
  Certainly not many people in the West cried over (the death of) the Ayatollah.
- Es ist sinnlos, um Verlorenes zu weinen.
  It makes no sense to cry over what's been lost.
- Es ist normal, daß man um die Verstorbenen weint.
  It is normal that people cry over the dead.

weinen vor + D ⟨**vor etw w.**⟩   to cry with (sth)

- Er weinte vor Schmerz (/Zorn/Glück).
  He cried with pain (/anger/happiness).
- Der Alte weinte leise vor sich hin.
  The old man quietly cried to himself.
- Man wußte nicht, ob er vor Schreck oder vor Freude weinte.
  You didn't know if he was crying from fear or from joy.

weisen (+ prep)   to show, to point

- Der Zeiger wies auf die 12.
  The hand of the clock pointed to the 12.
- Der Pfeil weist nach Süden (/oben/unten).
  The arrow is pointing south (/up/down).
- Er wies auf einen Stern (/ein Auto/mich).
  He pointed to a star (/a car/me).
- Das Kind wies auf den Rollstuhlfahrer (/zum Himmel).
  The child pointed at the wheelchair driver (/sky).
- Der Lehrer wies die Schüler zur Ruhe (/Ordnung). (*fig*)
  The teacher ordered the students to be quiet (/behave themselves).

weisen aus/von + D ⟨**jdn aus/von etw w.**⟩   to expel (sb) from (sth)

- Sie haben ihn aus dem Lande (/aus dem Hause/von der Schule) gewiesen.
  They expelled him from the country (/threw him out of their house/expelled him from the school).
- Der Schiedsrichter wies ihn vom Feld (*or* Platz).
  The referee ordered or *sent him off the field.*
- Ich muß diese Anschuldigungen (/den Verdacht) energisch von mir weisen.
  I must reject these accusations (/the suspicion) forcefully.

(s.) wenden (+ prep)   to turn

- Sie hat den Kopf (/das Gesicht) zu ihm gewandt.
  She turned her head (/face) towards him.

- Meine Gedanken wandten sich auf das Mädchen (/darauf).
  My thoughts turned to the girl. (liter)

- Er hat sich zur Seite (/nach Norden/nach links/nach ihm) gewandt.
  He turned to the side (/north/left/towards him).

- Bitte wende die Würste (auf dem Grill).
  Please turn the sausages (on the grill).

- Auf dieser engen Straße kann man schlecht (mit dem Auto) wenden.
  It's hard to turn (your car) on this narrow street.

- Der Bauer wendet das Heu auf der Wiese.
  The farmer is turning over the hay on the meadow.

s. wenden an + A ⟨sich an jdn w.⟩   to consult (sb); to turn to (sb/sth)

- Ich wandte (*less common:* wendete) mich an einen Polizisten (/den Rechtsanwalt) um Rat (/Hilfe).
  I turned to (or consulted) a policeman (/an attorney) for advice (/help).

- Das Magazin wendet sich vor allem an die Jugend (/Erwachsene/Kinder/Elektriker).
  The magazine targets primarily youth (/adults/children/electricians).

- Der Kurs wendet sich an diejenigen, die über geringe Kenntnisse der deutschen Sprache verfügen.
  The course is aimed at those who have little knowledge of German.

s. wenden gegen + A ⟨sich gegen jdn/etw w.⟩   to come out against (sb/sth); to oppose (sb/sth)

- Der Präsident wandte sich in seiner Rede gegen höhere Steuern (/einige Journalisten/die Aufrüstung).
  In his speech, the president opposed an increase in taxes (/some journalists /armaments).

- Ich weiß nicht, warum du dich gegen mich (/meinen Plan) gewandt hast.
  I don't know why you have turned against me (/my plan).

wenden in + A ⟨etw in etw w.⟩   to turn (sth) over in (sth)

- Ich wende jetzt das Kotelett (/den Fisch/das Fleisch) in Mehl.
  I'm now rolling the cutlet (/fish/meat) in flour.

■ Nach ein paar Minuten mußt du den Pfannkuchen in der Pfanne wenden.
After a few minutes you have to turn the pancake over in the frying pan.

(s.) wenden von + D ⟨**sich/etw von jdm/etw w.**⟩   to turn away from (sb/sth)

■ Er konnte kein Auge von dem Mädchen wenden.
He couldn't take his eyes off the girl.

■ Ich wandte mich absichtlich von ihr ab und ging davon.
I purposely turned away from her and left.

■ Nach Jahren der Treue wandte er sich von seinem Freund (/seiner Partei).
After years of loyal support, he turned away from his friend (/party).

s. wenden zu + D ⟨**sich zu jdm/etw w.**⟩   to turn to face (sb/sth); to turn towards
(sb/sth)

■ Seine Gesundheit hat sich zum Besseren (/Schlimmeren) gewendet.
His health took a turn for the better (/worse).

■ Er hat sich zum Gehen (/zur Tür/zum Ausgang/zur Flucht) gewendet.
He turned to go (/toward the door/toward the exit/He took flight).

■ Es hat sich alles noch zum Guten (*or* Besten) gewendet.
It still all turned out for the best.

■ Sie hat sich mit Abscheu von ihm gewendet.
She turned away from him in disgust.

werben für + A ⟨**für jdn/etw w.**⟩   to advertise (sth); to promote (sb/sth)

■ Sie werben im Fernsehen für diese Waren (/diesen Apparat/Colgate).
They are advertising this merchandise (/this appliance/Colgate) on television.

■ Der Politiker warb intensiv für seine Partei (/Kollegen).
The politician tried hard to get support for his party (/colleagues).

■ Sie haben für den SPD-Kandidaten mit Fernsehspots (/Plakaten/Flugblättern) geworben.
They supported the SPD candidate with TV spots (/posters/leaflets).

werben um + A ⟨**um jdn/etw w.**⟩   to solicit (sb/sth); to court (sb/sth); to try to attract
or woo (sb/sth)

■ Sie warben um die Unterstützung der Arbeiter (/um neue Kunden).
They solicited the support of the workers (/new customers).

■ Diese Partei wirbt intensiv um junge Wähler (/Stimmen)
This party is trying hard to attract young voters (/votes).

- Die Zeitung wirbt um neue Abonnenten (/Leser).
  The newspaper is trying to attract new subscribers (/readers).

- Er hat um ihre Liebe (/Freundschaft/Gunst) geworben.
  He courted her for her love (/friendship/favor).

- Jahrelang hat er um das Mädchen geworben. Nun ist sie seine Frau.
  He wooed the girl for years. Now she is his wife.

werden aus + D ⟨aus jdm/etw w.⟩   to become of (sb/sth)

- Was ist aus deinem alten Freund geworden?—Aus ihm ist ein Herzspezialist (/nichts) geworden.
  What has become of your old friend?—He has become a heart specialist (/He's gotten nowhere in life).

- Was soll aus dem Jungen noch werden?
  What is going to become of the boy?

- Aus dem Geschäft ist nichts geworden.
  The deal came to nothing/The deal fell through.

- Aus Öl und Sand (/diesen Bestandenteilen) wird Asphalt.
  Asphalt comes from (or is made out of) oil and sand (/these elements).

werden zu + D ⟨zu etw w.⟩   to turn to (sth); to become (sth)

- Die Leiche wurde zu Staub (/Die Sphinx wurde zu Stein).
  The corpse turned to dust (/The Sphinx turned into stone).

- Er ist zum Mann (/Verräter/Alkoholiker) geworden.
  He has become a man (/a traitor/an alcoholic).

- Der Junge ist ihnen zur Last geworden.
  The boy became a burden to them.

- Wasser wird bei 0° Celsius zu Eis.
  Water turns into ice at 0° Celsius.

- Zuerst war die Arbeit neu für ihn, aber schon nach kurzer Zeit wurde sie ihm zum Alltag.
  At first the job was new to him, but after only a short while, it became routine to him.

- Sie ist zum Gespött (/zum Spielball) ihrer Vorgesetzten geworden.
  She has become the laughingstock (/plaything) of her superiors.

- Nach anfänglicher Unsicherheit ist es nun (zu einer) Gewißheit geworden: Wir gehen nach Chikago.
  After initial uncertainty, we now know for sure: We are going to Chicago.

(s.) werfen (+ prep)   to throw

- Er warf den Ball ins Tor (/in den Korb/in die Höhe/gegen die Wand/zu seinem Mitspieler).
  He threw the ball in the goal (/in the basketball hoop/in the air/against the wall/to his teammate).

- Er hat ihn ins Schwimmbad (/ins Gras/aufs Bett) geworfen.
  He threw him into the pool (/onto the grass/onto the bed).

- Laß mich meine Einwände (/Sorgen) in diese Diskussion werfen.
  Let me throw my objections (/concerns) into this discussion.

- Man hat ihn aus der Firma (/dem Haus) geworfen.
  They threw (or kicked) him out of the firm (/house).

- Ich will nur einen Blick ins Zimmer (/auf die Landkarte/in den Spiegel) werfen.
  I only want to have a glance into the room (/at the map/in the mirror).

- Ich war sehr müde und mußte mich sofort aufs Bett (/in einen Sessel/aufs Sofa/auf eine Bank) werfen. (*inf*)
  I was very tired and had to throw myself onto the bed (/in an armchair/onto the sofa/onto a bench).

- Er warf sich auf die Knie (/zu Boden).
  He threw himself to his knees (/to the floor).

- Ich habe mich schnell in die Kleider geworfen und bin gegangen. (*inf*)
  I quickly threw on my clothes and left.

- Das Modell warf die Kleider von sich.
  The model undressed quickly.

werfen auf + A ⟨etw auf jdn/etw w.⟩   to throw (sth) at (sb/sth)

- Er hat etwas auf den Boden (/Teppich) geworfen.
  He threw something on the floor (/rug).

- Die Scheinwerfer haben ihr Licht auf die ganze Straße (/übers Feld/auf mich) geworfen.
  The headlights lit up the whole street (/shone across the field/shone on me).

- Die Demonstranten haben Eier auf den Politiker geworfen.
  The demonstrators threw eggs at the politician.

- Zu Weihnachten werfen sie alle billigen Waren auf den Markt.
  At Christmas they dump all the cheap goods on the market.

- Er warf vorwurfsvolle (/leidenschaftliche) Blicke auf sie.
  He cast reproachful (/passionate) glances at her.

s. werfen auf + A ⟨sich auf jdn/etw w.⟩   to throw oneself into (sth)/onto (sb)

- Nach den Ferien warf sie sich voller Energie auf ihre Arbeit (/die Vorbereitung des Kongresses).
  She energetically threw herself into her work (/the preparation for the convention) after the vacation.

- Bei der Party hast du dich ja förmlich auf sie geworfen.
  You really (or literally) threw yourself at her at the party.

werfen mit + D ⟨mit etw nach jdm/etw w.⟩   to throw (sth) at (sb/sth)

- Sie hat mit einem faulen Ei nach dem Politiker (/Polizeiwagen) geworfen.
  She threw a rotten egg at the politician (/police car).

- Er warf mit Steinen (/Bleistiften/Kissen) nach meinem Freund.
  He threw stones (/pencils/pillows) at my friend.

- Die Kinder warfen mit Kissen nacheinander.
  The children threw pillows at each other.

werfen mit + D ⟨mit etw um sich w.⟩   to throw about (sth)

- Nach ihrem Lottogewinn hat sie mit Geld (/Geschenken) nur so um sich geworfen.
  After winning in the lottery, she really threw a lot of money (/presents) around.

- Er wirft mit seinen Kenntnissen (/großen Worten) nur so um sich.
  He is showing off his knowledge (/bandies about big words).

wetten auf + A ⟨auf jdn/etw w.⟩   to bet on (sb/sth)

- Ich habe mit meinem Freund (um 5 Dollar) auf (/gegen) den Sieg dieses Teams gewettet.
  I bet my friend (5 dollars) that this team would (/wouldn't) win.

- Ich wette (10 Dollar) darauf, daß er nicht gewinnt.—Ich wette dagegen.
  I'll bet you (ten dollars) that he won't win.—I'll bet against it.

- Wieviel wettest du auf dieses Pferd?—Ich wette drei zu eins (/10 Mark).
  How much are you betting on this horse?—I'll bet three to one (/ten marks).

wetten (mit) um + A ⟨(mit jdm) um etw w.⟩   to bet (sb) (sth)

- Ich wette mit dir um 20 Mark (/um eine Opern Karte).
  I'll bet you 20 marks (/a ticket to the opera).

- Wir wetteten (miteinander) um ein Stück Torte (/um ein Glas Bier).
  We bet each other a piece of cake (/a glass of beer).

wetten (without prep)   to bet

- Ich wette, daß er rechtzeitig ankommt.
  I bet that he'll come on time.

- So haben wir nicht gewettet!
  That wasn't our bet!

(s.) wickeln in + A ⟨sich/jdn/etw in etw w.⟩   to wrap (o.s./sb/sth) in (sth)

- Die Eltern hatten das Baby (i.e., in Windeln) gewickelt.
  The parent had changed the baby's diapers.

- Ich wickelte mich in eine dicke Decke.
  I wrapped myself in a thick blanket.

- Bitte wickeln Sie dieses Geschenk (/diese Blumen) in Papier!
  Please wrap this gift (/these flowers) in paper!

(s.) wickeln um/auf + A ⟨sich/etw um/auf etw w.⟩   to wind (o.s./sth) around/onto (sth)

- Die alte Frau wickelt das Garn auf eine Rolle.
  The old woman is winding her yarn onto a roll.

- Die Schlange (/Pflanze) wickelte sich um den Zweig.
  The snake (/plant) wrapped itself around the branch.

- Du solltest einen Bindfaden um das Paket wickeln.
  You ought to wrap a string around the package.

s. wickeln um + A ⟨sich etw um etw w.⟩   to wrap (sth) around (sth)

- Ich habe mir eine Mullbinde um den verletzten Finger gewickelt.
  I wrapped a bandage around my injured finger.

- Ich sollte mir einen Schal um den Kopf (/Hals) wickeln.
  I should wrap a scarf around my head (/neck).

s. widerspiegeln in + D ⟨sich in etw w.⟩   to be reflected in (sth)

- Diese Erfahrung (/Diese Bitterkeit/Diese Einstellung/Dieser Haß) spiegelt sich in seinen Romanen (/ihm/seiner Persönlichkeit) wider.
  This experience (/bitterness/attitude/hatred) is reflected in his novels (/him/his personality).

- Ihre Silhouette (/Der schöne Mond) hat sich im Wasser widergespiegelt.
  Her silhouette (/The beautiful moon) was reflected in the water.

winken (+ prep)   to wave

- Ich winkte mit der Hand (/einem Fähnchen/dem Taschentuch).
  I waved my hand (/a little flag/my handkerchief).
- Er winkte das Taxi (/den Kellner) zu sich.
  He called (or signaled) the taxi (/waiter) to come over to him.
- Winken Sie bitte den Kellner an den Tisch!
  Please signal to the waiter (to come to the table)!
- Sie stand an der Tür und winkte (zum Abschied).
  She stood at the door and waved (to say good-bye).

winken (without prep)   to wave

- Er hat einem Taxi (/dem Kellner) gewinkt.
  He hailed a taxi (/signaled the waiter to come over).
- Seine Eltern standen am Bahnsteig und winkten.
  His parents stood at the train station platform and waved.
- Wenn dir diese Aufgabe gelingt, winkt dir eine Belohnung.
  If you succeed in this task, you can expect a reward.

wirken auf + A ⟨auf jdn/etw w.⟩   to have an effect on (sb/sth)

- Dieser Raum (/Mann) wirkt auf mich bedrückend.
  This room (/man) has a gloomy (or depressing) effect on me.
- Diese Arznei wirkt auf die Nerven (/den Magen).
  This medicine affects the nerves (/stomach).
- Dieses Erlebnis (/Buch) hat nachhaltig auf ihn gewirkt.
  This event (/book) made a lasting impression on him.
- Sein Sinn für Humor wirkt sehr stark auf Frauen.
  His sense of humor greatly impresses women.

wirken für + A ⟨für etw w.⟩   to work *or* be active for (sth)

- Unser Freund wirkte sein Leben lang für die Obdachlosen in unserer Stadt (/für das Rote Kreuz).
  Our friend actively supported the homeless in our city (/worked for the Red Cross) all his life.
- Der tägliche Spaziergang wirkt Wunder für Omas Gesundheit.
  The daily walk works wonders for grandma's health.

wirken gegen + A ⟨gegen etw w.⟩   to work against/for (sth)

- Die Tabletten wirken gut gegen Kopfschmerzen.
  The pills are good for a headache.
- Ein langer Urlaub wirkt wunderbar gegen Streß.
  A long vacation works wonders for stress.

wirken (without prep)   to work

- Tee oder Kaffee wirkt anregend.
  Tea or coffee has a stimulating effect.
- Dein Verhalten wirkte peinlich.
  Your behavior was embarrassing.
- Er wirkte als Rektor der Schule. (*liter*)
  He worked as the principal of the school.
- Er hat zehn Jahre in Afrika als Missionar gewirkt.
  He worked in Africa for ten years as a missionary.

wissen über + A ⟨über jdn/etw etw w.⟩   to know (sth) about (sb/sth)

- Ich habe gar nichts über die Geschichte Spaniens (/Alexander den Großen) (in der Prüfung) gewußt.
  I didn't know anything about Spanish history (/Alexander the Great) (on the exam).
- Weißt du etwas Genaueres (/Zuverlässiges) über seinen Unfall?
  Do you know something more specific (/reliable) about his accident?
- Wir wissen wenig über das Leben nach dem Tod.
  We know very little about life after death.
- Was willst du über das Leben Arnold Schwarzeneggers wissen?
  What do you want to know about the life of Arnold Schwarzenegger?

wissen über/von + A/D ⟨über *or* von etw w.⟩   to know about/of (sth)

- Weißt du von der (*or* über die) Angelegenheit, die...?
  Do you know about the affair or *business that...?*
- Ich möchte gern mehr über das (*or* von dem) Mittelalter wissen.
  I would like to know more about the Middle Ages.
- Mein Freund aus Kanada weiß viel von (*or* über) Deutschland.
  My friend from Canada knows a lot about Germany.
- Ein Blinder weiß nicht viel von Schönheit, aber er weiß (theoretisch) etwas darüber.
  A blind man doesn't know much about (physical) beauty but (theoretically) he knows something of it.

wissen um + A ⟨um jdn/etw w.⟩   to know about/of (sb/sth)

- Meine Frau weiß um ihre Schwäche: Sie liebt Schokolade.
  My wife knows her weakness: She loves chocolate.

- Erika weiß um ihre Schönheit (/Intelligenz) und zeigt das auch.
  Erika knows she is beautiful (/intelligent) and shows it off.

- Meine Mutter wußte um ihren Tod. Sie muß das gefühlt haben.
  My mother knew she was about to die. She must have felt that.

wissen von + D ⟨von etw w.⟩   to know about/of (sth)

- Er wußte von dem Mädchen (nur den Namen).
  He knew about the girl (He only knew her by name).

- Ich weiß schon von dem Ausverkauf durch meine Nachbarin.
  I already know about the sale from my neighbor.

- Der alte Fleischer ist gestorben. Wußtest du davon?
  The old butcher died. Did you know about that?

- Ich wußte schon von dem (*or* um den) Verkauf deines Hauses.
  I already knew about the sale of your house.

- Du verhieltst dich, als ob du von nichts wüßtest.
  You behaved as if you didn't know a thing.

wissen zu (+ infinitive)   to know

- Er hat gewußt, das Leben zu genießen.
  He knew how to enjoy life.

- Paul, du müßtest dich eigentlich zu benehmen wissen.
  Paul, you ought to know how to behave yourself.

wohnen (+ prep)   to live

- Er wohnt (in der) Fischers Allee 89.
  He lives at (number) 89 Fischers Allee.

- Er wohnt bei seinem Bruder (/den Eltern).
  He lives at his brother's (/parents') (house).

- Er wohnt (als Mieter) im dritten Stock.
  He lives (as a tenant) on the fourth floor.

- Er wohnte zur Miete (/zur Untermiete).
  He lived in a rented apartment (/was a subletter).

■ Sie wohnten in dem Vorort (/Tür an Tür/fünf Minuten von der Schule entfernt/über ihren Freunden/zwei Jahre dort/auf dem Lande).
They lived in the suburb (/next door/five minutes from the school/above their friends/there for two years/in the country).

s. wundern über + A ⟨sich über jdn/etw w.⟩   to be surprised at/about (sb/sth)

■ Ich wunderte mich über seine Kraft (/seine Dummheit/sein Wissen).
I was surprised at (or about) his power (/stupidity/knowledge).

■ Ich wundere mich sehr (darüber), daß du das tatsächlich gesagt hast.
I am very surprised that you actually said that.

■ Er hat sich sehr über das gemeine Verhalten des Kindes gewundert.
He was really surprised at (or about) the child's mean behavior.

■ Ich wundere mich über die Größe des Grand Canons.
I am amazed at the size of the Grand Canyon.

(s.) wünschen (+ prep)   to wish

■ Ich wünsche mir eine Flasche Kölnischwasser von dir.
I'd like a bottle of cologne from you.

■ Ich wünsche dir herzlich alles Gute zum Geburtstag. (*or* Herzlichen Glückwunsch zum Geburtstag).
I wish you a happy birthday. (Happy birthday!)

■ Was wünschst du dir zum Geburtstag (/zu Weihnachten/für deine guten Noten)?
What do you wish (to get) for your birthday (/for Christmas/for getting good grades)?

■ Ich wünsche mir ein gesundes Leben für meine Frau und mich.
I would like my wife and me to have a healthy life.

■ Ich wünschte, ich hätte mehr Ferien (/,daß ich bei euch sein könnte).
I wished I had more vacation (/that I was at your place).

s. wünschen als/zu + N/D ⟨sich jdn als jd/zu jdm w.⟩   to wish (sb) to be (sb/sth); to wish (sb) as (sb/sth)

■ Ich wünsche mir meine Frau als Vanderbilt (/Reiche/Schauspielerin/Königin).
I wish my wife were (or was) a Vanderbilt (/a rich woman/a movie actress /a queen).

■ Wen wünschst du dir als Freund (*or* zum Freund/als *or* zum Lehrer)?
Whom do you wish to be your friend (/teacher)?

■ Wir wünschten uns diesen Kandidaten als Kanzler (/Parteichef).
We wished this candidate was the chancellor (/the leader of the party).

s. wünschen zu (+ infinitive)   to wish

- Ich wünsche mir, dich bald wiederzusehen.
  I wish I could see you again soon.
- Sie wünschte sich, diesen Mann zu heiraten.
  She wished to marry this man.

wurzeln in + D ⟨**in etw w.**⟩   to be rooted in (sth)

- Diese Pflanze wurzelt tief in der Erde (/im Boden).
  This plant is rooted deep into the earth (/ground).
- Vertrauen auf andere Menschen wurzelt fest in ihr. (*fig*)
  Trust in other people is rooted deeply in her.
- Seine Werke wurzeln in der Philosophie des Rationalismus.
  His works are rooted in the rationalistic philosophy.

wüten gegen + A ⟨**gegen jdn/etw w.**⟩   to storm *or* rage at (sb/sth)

- Er wütete (wie ein Tier) gegen den Angreifer (/einen angreifenden Panzer).
  He charged (like an animal) at the attacker (oncoming or *attacking tank).*
- Der Mann wütete vor Zorn (gegen seine Gegner/gegen seine Widersacher).
  The man was wild with rage (against his opponents/against his adversaries).

Z

zahlen (+ prep) to pay

- Ich zahlte ihm 10 Dollar für das Buch (/mit einem 10 Dollar Schein).
  I paid him ten dollars for the book (/with a ten dollar bill).
- Ich zahle für das Hotelzimmer (/mein Bier).
  I'll pay for the hotel room (/for my beer).
- Meine Eltern zahlen dir (*or* für dich) das Abendessen (/die Karten/das Taxi).
  My parents will pay for your supper (/ticket/taxi)
- Ich habe einen hohen Preis dafür gezahlt.
  I paid a high price for that.
- Du mußt das Geld an mich (*or* Du mußt mir das Geld) zahlen.
  You must pay the money to me.
- Du mußt das Geld direkt an die Bank (/an ihn/ans Geschäft) zahlen.
  You must pay the money directly to the bank (/to him/to the store).
- Man kann den Betrag mit einem Scheck (/durch Überweisung/im voraus/auf einmal/(in) bar/in Raten) zahlen.
  You can pay the amount by (or with a) check (/with a transfer/in advance/at once/(in) cash/in installments).
- Sie müssen dafür in (*or* mit) Schweizer Franken (/kanadischen Dollars /Italienischen Lire/Deutscher Mark) zahlen.
  You must pay for that in Swiss francs (/Canadian dollars/Italian lire/German marks).
- Wir zahlen immer noch an dem Auto (/der Spülmaschine).
  We are still paying for (or making payments on) the car (/the dishwasher).

zählen (+ prep) to count

- Das Kind kann schon bis hundert zählen.
  The child can already count to a hundred.
- Zähl von 10 bis 1 rückwärts (und dann vorwärts), Stefan!
  Stefan, count from 10 to 1 backwards (and then forwards)!
- Wir zählen die Tage und die Stunden bis zum Ende der Schule.
  We're counting the days and the hours until the end of school.
- Sie zählt um die (/nicht mehr als/etwa/gerade) 32 Jahre.
  She is about (/no more than/approximately/just) 32 years old.
- Wieviele Punkte zählt diese Karte bei diesem Spiel?
  How many points does this card count in this game?

zählen auf + A ⟨**auf jdn/etw z.**⟩   to count *or* rely on (sb/sth)

- Frank zählt auf dich (/auf deine Hilfe).
  Frank counts on you (/on your help).
- Du kannst darauf zählen, daß ich komme.
  You can count on it that I'll come.
- Peter veranstaltet morgen eine Party. Er zählt auf Sie.
  Peter is having a party tomorrow. He's depending on you.

zählen nach + D ⟨**nach etw z.**⟩   to count (in)to (sth)

- Sein Vermögen zählt nach Millionen (/Tausenden).
  His fortune runs into the millions (/thousands).
- Die Anzahl der Toten infolge des Vulkanausbruchs hat nach Hunderten gezählt.
  The number of deaths from the volcano eruption ran in the hundreds.

(s.) zählen zu + D ⟨**sich/jdn/etw zu jdm/etw z.**⟩   to regard (o.s. (s.)/sb/sth) as being among (sb/sth)

- Er hat mich zu seinen Freunden (/Feinden) gezählt.
  He counted me (or regarded me as being) among his friends (/enemies).
- Ich zähle mich zu den gescheitesten Schülern unserer Schule.
  I regard myself as one of the smartest students of our school.
- Ich zähle diese Zeit in Hamburg zu den besten in meinem Leben.
  I regard this period in Hamburg as being among the best periods in my life.

zählen zu + D ⟨**zu jdm/etw z.**⟩   to belong to *or* count as (sb/sth)

- Churchill zählt zu den besten Politikern dieses Jahrhunderts.
  Churchill ranks as one of the best politicians of this century.
- Zu welchem Land zählt dieser Fluß?
  To which country does this river belong?
- Armenisch zählt zur Indo-Europäischen Sprachgruppe.
  Armenian belongs to the Indo-European group of languages.

zählen (without prep)   to count

- Dieses Büro zählt 34 Angestellte.
  This office numbers (or has) 34 employees.
- Wieviele Einwohner zählt diese Stadt?
  How many people live in this city?

s. zanken mit + D ⟨sich mit jdm z.⟩ to quarrel *or* squabble with (sb)

■ Ich habe mich mit ihm (über sein schlechtes Benehmen) gezankt.
I quarrelled (or had a quarrel) with him (about his bad behavior).

■ Die Kinder zanken sich (miteinander) um ein Spielzeug.
The children are quarrelling (with one another) over a toy.

■ Sie zanken sich (/miteinander) immer ums Geld (/um jede Kleinigkeit/ darum, wer heute das Auto nehmen darf).
They always squabble (with one another) about money (/every little thing/who gets to take the car today).

zehren an + D ⟨an jdm/etw z.⟩ to wear (sb/sth) out

■ Der Streß der letzten Wochen hat sehr an meiner Gesundheit (/anmir) gezehrt.
The stress of the last few weeks has really put a strain on my health (/worn me out).

zehren von + D ⟨von etw z.⟩ to live off/on (sth)

■ Seit Jahren zehrt sie nur noch von den Erfolgen ihrer ersten Romane.
For years now she has been living off the success of her first novels.

■ Wir zehrten noch wochenlang von unserem tollen Urlaub (/den Erinnerungen/Gedanken an die schöne Zeit in Frankreich).
We lived on the memories of our great vacation for weeks (/off our memories/on our recollections of the wonderful time in France).

zeichnen (+ prep) to draw

■ Er zeichnet mit dem Bleistift (/mit dem Farbstift/mit Tusche/auf dem Papier/nach einem Muster).
He's drawing with a pencil (/with a colored pen/with ink/on the paper/according to a pattern).

■ Ich habe an der Landschaft (/an dem Plan/an dem Bild/an dem Muster/an dem Entwurf/an der Wiese/nach der Natur) lange gezeichnet.
I spent a long time drawing the landscape (/plan/picture/model/ blueprint/meadow /from nature).

■ Ich zeichnete das Porträt (/die Brücke) aus dem Gedächtnis.
I drew the portrait (/bridge) from memory.

■ Die Polizei zeichnet ein sehr negatives Bild von diesem Verbrecher.
The police draw a very vicious picture (portrait) of this criminal.

■ Er zeichnet die Frau (/das Pferd) nach dem Leben (/nach einer Photographie).
He drew the posing woman (/standing horse) (/from a picture).

(s.) zeigen (+ prep)   to point; to show; to appear

- Er zeigte in diese Richtung (/nach Norden/zur Seite/zum Horizont /zum Himmel).
  He pointed in this direction (/north/to the side/to the horizon/to the sky).
- Er zeigte große Lust zum Tennisspielen (/Wandern/Segeln).
  He really felt like playing tennis (/hiking/sailing).
- Sie zeigt keinerlei Lust zur Hausarbeit (/dazu, das Bad sauberzumachen/, sich zur Vorsitzenden wählen zu lassen).
  She doesn't feel at all like doing housework (/cleaning the bathroom/running for chairwoman).
- Er hat Interesse daran (/Verständnis dafür/Angst davor/Freude daran) gezeigt.
  He showed interest in (/understanding for/fear of/joy about) that.
- Ich habe mich ihm gegenüber dankbar (/anerkennend) gezeigt.
  I showed my appreciation to him (/recognition of him).
- Er zeigte sich feindlich gegen mich.
  He behaved in a hostile manner towards me.
- Daran zeigt sich (*or* Das zeigt), daß du nichts davon verstehst.
  That shows that you don't understand that at all.

zeigen auf + A ⟨auf jdn/etw z.⟩   to point at/to (sb/sth)

- Der Zeuge zeigte den Angeklagten.
  The witness pointed to the accused.
- Die Uhr (/Der Uhrzeiger) zeigt auf 12.
  The clock shows 12 (/The clock hand points to 12).
- Die Museumsführerin zeigte auf das Bild und erklärte. . . .
  The museum guide pointed to the picture and explained. . . .

s. zeigen + mit ⟨sich mit jdm z.⟩   to let oneself be seen with (sb)

- Zeigst du dich wirklich so (/in diesem Kostüm) mit ihm bei der Feier?
  Are you really going to be seen like that (/in this costume) with him at the celebration?
- Neuerdings zeigt sich der Filmstar immer häufiger mit der hübschen Tennisspielerin.
  The film star has recently let himself be seen more and more often with the pretty tennis player.

zeigen nach + D ⟨nach etw z.⟩   to point (to) (sth)

- Die Magnetnadel zeigte nach Norden (/Süden).
  The compass needle pointed (to the) north (/south).

■   Der Zeiger zeigt nach Norden (auf warm/auf Null/auf über Null).
The indicator points north (/to warm/to zero/above zero).

zelten (+ prep)   to camp

■   Wir werden auf einem Campingplatz (/im Wald/in den Bergen/in den Alpen/im Lager/im Tal/am Strand) zelten.
We will camp at a camping site (/in the forest/in the mountains/in the Alps/at the camp/in the valley/at the beach).

zerfallen in + A ⟨in etw z.⟩   to fall into (sth)

■   Die Tasse zerfiel in drei Teile.
The cup fell (and broke) into three pieces.

■   Das Reich zerfiel unmittelbar nach dem Tod des Königs in viele Fürstentümer.
The empire fell into many principalities right after the king's death.

■   Er hat die Tablette in Wasser zerfallen lassen.
He dropped the pill into the water (to dissolve it).

■   Das Buch zerfällt in 24 Kapitel.
The book is divided into 24 chapters.

zerlegen in + A ⟨in etw z.⟩   to take (sth) apart; (*math*) to reduce (sth)

■   Er zerlegte den Motor in alle Einzelteile.
He disassembled the motor completely.

■   Die Schüler mußten den Satz in seine Satzteile zerlegen.
The students had to diagram the sentence.

■   Die Zahl 32 läßt sich in 8 mal 4 zerlegen.
The number 32 can be factored into 8 times 4.

zerren (+ prep)   to pull; to strain

■   Ich zerrte einen schweren Koffer hinter mir her über den Hof (/über die Straße/auf der Straße/auf dem Bürgersteig/in den Keller).
I dragged a heavy suitcase behind me across the yard (/across the street/on the street/on the sidewalk/into the cellar).

■   Ich zerrte mein Kind hinter mir her.
I dragged my kid behind me.

■   Er hat ihn aus dem Bett (/dem Wagen) gezerrt.
He dragged him out of the bed (/pulled him out of the car).

- Sie haben ihn vor Gericht (/durch *or* in den Schmutz) gezerrt.
  They took him to court (/They dragged him through the dirt, i.e., smeared him).

- Sie haben die Affäre an die Öffentlichkeit gezerrt.
  They dragged the affair into the limelight.

zerren an + D ⟨an jdm/etw z.⟩   to pull *or* tug at (sb/sth)

- Der Hund zerrt an der Leine (/an der Kette).
  The dog is tugging on the leash (/chain).

- Diese gefährlichen Tests zerren an den Nerven (/meinen Kräften).
  These dangerous tests are nerve-racking (/hard on me).

- Die Presse hat das Privatleben des Politikers rücksichtslos an die Öffentlichkeit gezerrt.
  The press recklessly dragged the politician's private life into the limelight.

zeugen für/gegen + A ⟨für/gegen jdn z.⟩   to testify for/against (sb)

- Er zeugte in dem Prozeß für (/gegen) diesen Mann (/ihn/sie).
  He testified in the trial for (/against) this man (/him/her).

- Sie will nicht vor Gericht gegen (/für) den Verbrecher zeugen.
  She does not want to testify in court against (/for) the criminal.

zeugen für/von + A/D ⟨für/von etw z.⟩   to testify to (sth)

- Seine Tat zeugt von Mut (/Ehrlichkeit/Großzügigkeit).
  His deed is a testament to his courage (/honesty/generosity).

- Seine Rede zeugte von großer Erfahrung.
  His speech showed great experience.

- Das zeugt für seine (*or* von seiner) guten Erziehung.
  That is evidence of his good education (or upbringing).

- Diese Ruinen in Persepolis zeugen von einer großen Vergangenheit.
  These ruins at Persepolis are witness to a great past.

ziehen (+ prep)   to pull; to draw; to tug

- Er zog die Sache aus der Tasche (/in diese Richtung/hinter sich her/aus dem Boden/vom Finger).
  He pulled the thing out of his pocket (/in this direction/behind him/out of the ground/from his finger).

- Er zog das Segelboot (/den ertrinkenden Menschen) aus dem Wasser.
  He pulled the sailboat (/the drowning person) out of the water.

- Er hat etwas (von unten/aus dem Brunnen) nach oben gezogen.
  He pulled something (from the bottom/from the well) up.

- Sie zog ihn auf die Seite. Sie zog ihn auf ihre Seite. (*fig*)
  She drew him aside. She won him over.

- Das Baby weint. Du solltest es an dich (/deine Brust) ziehen.
  The baby's crying. You ought to hold him close (/put him on your breast).

- Der Cowboy zog den Revolver aus seinem Pistolenhalfter.
  The cowboy drew the gun from his holster.

- Ich muß einen Pullover über die Bluse ziehen.
  I must put a sweater on over the blouse.

- Das Kind zieht Linien in sein Heft (/an die Wand).
  The child drew lines in his notebook (/on the wall).

- Man kann keinen Vergleich zwischen diesen zwei Dingen ziehen.
  You can't draw a comparison between these two things.

- Ich zog den Nagel aus dem Holz.
  I pulled the nail out of the wood.

- Sie zieht die Gardine vors Fenster.
  She's drawing (or pulling) the curtain across the window.

- Das Kind zog das Spielzeug neben sich.
  The child pulled the toy next to him.

- Er zog meine Vorschläge (/unsere Einwände) ins Absurde (/ins Lächerliche).
  He turned my suggestions (/our objections) into something absurd (/a joke).

ziehen (+ prep)   to move; to go; to roam

- Die Menschenmenge ist durch die Straßen gezogen.
  The crowd roamed the streets (or marched through the streets).

- Er wollte durch die Welt und in die Fremde ziehen.
  He wanted to go abroad and travel to places he had never been.

- Die Länder (/Sie) zogen in den Krieg.
  The countries (/They) went to war.

- Wir zogen nach München (/nach Japan/an einen anderen Ort/in diesen Vorort/aufs Land/in die Stadt/zu den Eltern).
  We moved to (live in) Munich (/Japan/another place/this suburb/the country/the city/our parents' home)

- Die Vögel ziehen nach Norden.
  The birds are going north.

- Das Gewitter ist nach Westen gezogen.
  The storm moved west.

ziehen an + D ⟨an etw z.⟩   to pull on/at (sth)

- Das Tier zog an dem Seil (/an der Leine).
  The animal pulled at the rope (/tugged on the leash).

- Der Hund hat an der Kette (/dem Herrn) gezogen.
  The dog was tugging on the chain (/pulling his master).

ziehen an + D ⟨an etw z.⟩   to pull *or* have a puff on (sth)

- Er hat so stark an der Pfeife (/Zigarette) gezogen, daß er husten mußte.
  He inhaled on his pipe (/cigarette) so deeply that he had to cough.

ziehen an + D ⟨jdn an etw /sich z.⟩   to pull (sb) by (sth); to attract (sb) to oneself

- Er zog ihn an den Ohren (/am Hemd/am Gürtel/an den Haaren).
  He pulled him by the ears (/shirt/belt/hair).

- Durch ihre Freundlichkeit zieht sie alle Menschen an sich.
  She attracts everyone through her friendliness.

ziehen auf + sich ⟨etw auf sich z.⟩   to draw (sth) to oneself

- Sie hat alle Blicke (/die Aufmerksamkeit) auf sich gezogen.
  She drew the eyes of everyone (/the attention) to her.

- Du darfst ihren Zorn (/Unmut/Haß) nicht auf dich ziehen.
  You mustn't draw her anger (/annoyance/hatred) on yourself.

ziehen aus + D ⟨etw aus etw z.⟩   to pull (sth) out from (sth)

- Er hat die Blumen (/die Pflanzen) aus der Erde gezogen.
  He pulled the flowers (/plants) out of the soil.

- Der Kaufmann zieht großen Gewinn aus seinem Geschäft.
  The businessman makes a lot of profit from his business.

- Ich ziehe keinen Vorteil aus seinem Vorschlag.
  I draw no advantage from his suggestion.

- Was für Nutzen (/Gewinn) kannst du daraus ziehen?
  What use is that to you (/What profit can you gain from it)?

(s.) ziehen durch + A ⟨(sich) durch etw z.⟩   to run through (sth)

- Der Weg zieht sich im Zickzack durch die Berge.
  The pathway zigzags through the mountains.

- Das Motiv des Verlustes zieht sich durch den ganzen Roman.
  The motif of loss runs (is woven) throughout the novel.
- Bevor du den neuen Pullover anziehst, solltest du ihn mal durchs Wasser ziehen.
  Before you wear the new sweater, you should wash it.

ziehen in + A ⟨**in etw z.**⟩   to draw in(to) (sth)

- Der Rauch vom Grill ist in die Wohnung (/ins Zimmer) gezogen.
  The smoke from the barbecue has drifted into the apartment (/room).
- Die Feuchtigkeit ist mir in die Knochen gezogen.
  The dampness has crept into my bones (i.e., I'm beginning to feel ill).

ziehen nach + D ⟨**etw nach sich z.**⟩   to have consequences for (sth)

- Diese Entscheidung (/Dieser Schmuggel) könnte schlimme Folgen nach sich
  Ziehen.
  This decision (/smuggling) could have serious consequences.
- Wenn wir ein neues Schwimmbad bauen, wird das erhebliche Kosten für die
  Gemeinde nach sich ziehen.
  If we build the new pool, it will entail considerable expenses for the community.

zielen auf + A ⟨**auf jdn/etw z.**⟩   to aim at (sb/sth)

- Der Jäger zielte auf den Hasen (/die Scheibe).
  The hunter aimed at the rabbit (/target).
- Er hat die Waffe (/Bemerkung) auf ihn gezielt.
  He aimed the weapon (/remark) at him.
- Diese Maßnahmen (/Pläne) zielen auf die Obdachlosen.
  These measures (/plans) are aimed at the homeless.
- Was er sagte, zielte auf dich (/die Ausländer).
  What he said was aimed at (or meant for) you (/foreigners).

(s.) zieren mit + D ⟨**sich/etw mit etw z.**⟩   to garnish (sth) with (sth); to make a fuss
about (sth); to hesitate

- Die Eltern zieren sich gern mit den Erfolgen ihrer Kinder.
  *The parents like to show off (literally: garnish themselves with) their children's
  accomplishments.*
- Zier dich nicht immer so beim Haarewaschen, Jens!
  Don't make such a fuss about getting your hair washed, Jens!

- Sie zierte sich ein wenig mit ihrer Antwort.
  She needed a bit of coaxing before she answered.

zittern (+ **prep**)   to shake; to tremble

- Das Laub zitterte im leichten Wind.
  The leaves shook in the light wind.
- Als er den Kaffee trank, zitterte seine Hand.
  His hand was shaking as he drank the coffee.
- Er zittert an allen Gliedern (/mit den Händen/am ganzen Körper).
  All of his limbs (/His hands) are shaking (or trembling) (/His body shakes or trembles).
- Während der Prüfung saßen wir im Nebenzimmer und zitterten für ihn.
  While he took the exam, we were sitting nervously in the room next door.

zittern um + A ⟨um jdn z.⟩   to fear for (sb's) life

- Nach dem Unfall zitterten alle um das Leben des Rennfahrers (/um ihn).
  After the accident everybody feared for the race-car driver's life (/for him).

zittern vor + D ⟨vor etw z.⟩   to shake *or* tremble with (sth)

- Er zitterte vor Angst (/Kälte) (an allen Gliedern).
  He was trembling (all over) with fear (/cold).
- Mir zittern die Knie (/die Hände) vor Angst.
  My knees (/hands) are shaking from fear.
- Meine Stimme hat vor Erregung gezittert.
  My voice was trembling with excitement.

zittern vor + D ⟨vor jdm/etw z.⟩   to be terrified of (sb/sth)

- Sie zittert jetzt schon vor dem Horrorfilm (/der Matheprüfung).
  She's already terrified of the horror film (/math exam).
- Ich zittere vor seiner Wut (/meinem zornigen Vater).
  I fear his rage (/my angry father).

zucken (+ **prep**)   to twitch

- Beim Impfen zuckte ich.
  I flinched while being vaccinated.

■ Hartmut zuckte vor Schreck (/Schmerzen).
Hartmut started from fright (/pain).

■ Ein Fisch zuckte an der Angel.
A fish tugged on the line.

■ Als er an den heißen Ofen faßte, zuckte seine Hand zurück.
When he touched the hot oven, his hand jerked back.

■ Der Schmerz zuckte (mir) durch den ganzen Körper (/in die Glieder). Ich leide
an einem nervösen Zucken (des Körpers).
*The pain shot right through my body (or me) (/parts of my body). I'm suffering
from a nervous disorder which makes me tremble.*

■ Wann immer er die Antwort nicht weiß, zuckt er mit den Schultern.
Whenever he doesn't know the answer, he shrugs (his shoulders).

■ Es zuckte ihm in der Hand (/im Bein).
He had a twinge in his hand (/leg).

■ Ein Lächeln zuckte um ihren Mund, als sie die richtigen Karten bekam.
A smile played on her lips when she was dealt the right card.

■ Es zuckte mir in den Fingern, ihm eine Ohrfeige zu geben.
I was itching to box his ears.

zufrieden sein mit + D ⟨mit jdm/etw z. sein⟩   to be happy *or* satisfied with (sb/sth)

■ Ich bin mit ihm (/dem neuen Auto/meiner Sekretärin) zufrieden.
I'm happy (or satisfied) with him (/the new car/my secretary).

■ Er ist mit nichts (/meiner Leistung) zufrieden.
Nothing pleases him (/He's happy with my achievement).

s. zufriedengeben mit + D ⟨sich mit etw z.⟩   to be content *or* satisfied with (sth)

■ Die Arbeiter gaben sich überhaupt nicht mit der geringen Gehaltserhöhung
zufrieden.
The workers were not happy at all with the low salary increase.

■ Ich werde mich nie damit zufriedengeben, bei dieser Arbeit zu bleiben.
I will never be happy staying at this job.

■ Gibst du dich damit (/mit deinem Leben/mit deinen Leistungen/mit deiner bis-
herigen Arbeit) zufrieden?
Are you happy with that (/your life/your achievements/your work up to now)?

zugehen auf + A ⟨auf jdn/etw z.⟩   to approach (sb/sth); to go toward (sb/sth)

■ Er geht auf die Wand (/ihn/das Gebäude/den Wald) zu.
He's walking toward (or approaching) the wall (/him/the building/the forest).

■ Ich gehe langsam auf die Fünfzig zu.
  I'm approaching fifty (or soon going to be fifty).

■ Wir gehen nun dem (*or* auf den) Herbst (/auf deinen Geburtstag) zu.
  Fall (/Your birthday) is drawing near.

■ Er ging geradewegs auf den Ausgang (/sein Studium/das Essen) zu.
  He went straight (or right up) to the exit (/his studies/the food).

■ Es fällt ihr nicht schwer, auf (andere) Menschen zuzugehen. (*fig*)
  Approaching (other) people comes easy to her.

■ Nach ihrem Streit ging er wieder auf sie zu. (*fig*)
  After their quarrel he approached her (i.e., to make an attempt at reconciliation).

zugehen (without prep)   to reach

■ Das Paket (/Die Nachricht) ging mir gestern zu.
  I received the package (/the news) yesterday.

■ Das Paket ist uns (/mir) noch nicht zugegangen.
  The package hasn't reached us (/me) yet.

zukommen auf + A ⟨auf jdn/etw z.⟩   to come towards *or* (directly) up to (sb/sth)

■ Unsere Freunde kommen (direkt) auf uns (/unser Haus) zu.
  Our friends are coming (directly) to us (/our house).

■ Das Gewitter kommt direkt (*or* geradewegs) auf uns zu.
  The storm is coming directly (or straight) towards us.

■ Die Kinder sind mit ausgebreiteten Armen auf mich zugekommen.
  The children came to me with open (or wide-spread) arms.

■ Ich habe es nicht gern, wenn alle diese Arbeit auf einmal auf uns zukommt.
  I don't like it when all of this work comes to us all at once.

zulassen zu + D ⟨jdn zu etw z.⟩   to admit (sb) to (sth)

■ Lassen sie uns zu diesem Film (/dieser Veranstaltung) zu? Oder sind wir noch zu jung dafür?
  Will they admit us to this movie (/event)? Or are we still too young for it?

■ Der Abiturient wurde zum Studium zugelassen.
  The high school graduate was admitted to the university.

■ Man muß viele Bedingungen erfüllt haben, um zur Abiturprüfung (/zum Examen) zugelassen zu werden.
  One has to have fulfilled a lot of conditions to be admitted to the "Abitur" examination (/exam).

- In Deutschland muß jedes Auto vom TÜV zum Verkehr zugelassen werden.
  In Germany every car must have a TÜV license (inspection certificate) before it is cleared for driving.

- Die Aktien der Firma sind zum Handel an der Börse zugelassen worden.
  The shares of the company have been admitted for trade at the stock exchange.

zulaufen auf + A ⟨**auf jdn/etw z.**⟩   to run towards (sb/sth), to come running towards (sb/sth)

- Er lief auf den Abwehrspieler zu, spielte ihn aus und schoß ein Tor.
  He ran towards the defender, outmaneuvered him, and scored (a goal).

- Die Krise im Nahen Osten ist auf den Krieg zugelaufen.
  The Middle East crisis led to the war.

- Er (/Das Kind) kam geradewegs auf uns zugelaufen.
  He (/The child) came running straight towards us.

- Der Weg lief direkt auf den Bauernhof zu.
  The road ran directly to the farm.

zunehmen an + D ⟨**an etw (*Bedeutung, Ansehen, Gewicht, usw*) z.**⟩   to gain (sth) (*importance, respect, weight, etc.*)

- Das vereinte Deutschland wird politisch an Bedeutung (/Einfluß/Gewicht) zunehmen.
  The united Germany will gain political importance (/influence/weight).

- Mist! Ich habe schon wieder an Gewicht zugenommen.
  Shoot! I've gained weight again.

s. zurechtfinden (+ prep)   to find one's way around (sth)

- Sie kann sich in ihrem Studium nicht mehr zurechtfinden.
  She is not able to cope with her studies anymore.

- Wie findest du dich in dieser Tabelle (/Karte/Stadt) zurecht?
  How do you make sense out of this chart (/map/city)?

- Ich kann mich bei Dunkelheit (*or* in der Dunkelheit) hier nicht zurechtfinden.
  I cannot find my way around here in the darkness.

- Ich finde mich (gut) in diesem Nachschlagewerk (/Atlas) zurecht.
  This reference book (/atlas) is easy for me to use.

s. zurechtfinden mit + D ⟨sich mit jdm/etw z.⟩   to get the hang of (sth); to get used to (sb/sth) (*inf*)

■ Jetzt, nach drei Monaten, finde ich mich ganz gut mit dem neuen Computer (/der modernen Schreibmaschine) zurecht.
Now, after three months, I'm starting to get the hang of my new computer (/the modern typewriter).

■ Du hast dich schnell mit der neuen Mitarbeiterin zurechtgefunden, oder?
You have gotten used to (working with) the new co-worker quickly, haven't you?

zurechtkommen (+ prep)   to come in time; to cope

■ Er kam gerade noch zum Theater (/Bus) zurecht.
He just made it to the theater (/bus) in time.

■ Ich komme ohne die Spülmaschine (/das Auto/die neue Sekretärin) zurecht.
I can manage without the dishwasher (/car/new secretary).

■ Niemand weiß, ob er tatsächlich im Leben (*or* in der Welt) zurechtkommen kann.
No one knows if he indeed can cope with life.

zurechtkommen mit + D ⟨mit jdm/etw z.⟩   to manage on (sth); to get along (well) with (sb/sth) (*inf*)

■ Ich kann damit (/mit 30 Mark am Tag) einfach nicht zurechtkommen.
I simply can't manage on that (/30 marks a day).

■ Er kommt mit den Kindern (/den Kollegen/der Maschine) gut zurecht.
He gets along well with the children (/his co-workers/He knows how to operate the machine well).

zurückfallen auf + A ⟨auf jdn z.⟩   to reflect on (sb)

■ Das Benehmen der Schüler fällt oft auf die Lehrer zurück.
The behavior of the students often reflects (badly) on the teachers.

■ Deine Tat wird auf dich zurückfallen.
Your deed will reflect on you.

zurückfallen in + A ⟨in etw z.⟩   to fall *or* lapse back into (sth)

■ Holger ist in seine alte Gewohnheit (/seine alten Tricks) zurückgefallen.
Holger has reverted to his old habit (tricks).

■ Mein kranker Großvater fiel in die Kissen zurück.
My sick grandfather fell back onto the pillows.

■ Gerd ist in diesem Semester (in der Schule) sehr zurückgefallen.
Gerd has fallen behind a lot (in school) this semester.

zurückführen auf + A ⟨**etw auf etw z.**⟩   to lead (sth) back to (sth)

■ Er hat den Unfall auf das Fehlen eines klaren Verkehrsschildes zurückgeführt.
He put the cause of the accident on the lack of a clear traffic sign.

■ Wie könnte man ihn auf den rechten Weg zurückführen?
How could one lead him back on the right track?

■ Das Unglück ist nur auf deine Nachlässigkeit zurückzuführen.
The accident is due to nothing but your carelessness.

■ Dein Einwand führt mich auf das eigentliche Anliegen zurück.
Your objection leads me back to my original concern.

■ Der Mißerfolg dieses Planes ist darauf zurückzuführen, daß. . . .
The failure of this plan is due to the fact that. . . .

zurückgehen auf + A ⟨**auf jdn/etw z.**⟩   to go back to (sb/sth)

■ Seine philosophischen Gedanken gehen auf die Griechen (/Kant) zurück.
His philosophical thoughts go back to the Greeks (/Kant).

■ Diese Wendung geht auf Shakespeare (/das Mittelalter) zurück.
This phrase goes back to Shakespeare (/the Middle Ages).

■ Ist man bei dieser wissenschaftlichen Arbeit auf verläßliche Quellen zurückgegangen?
Did they refer to reliable sources in this scientific work?

(s.) zurückhalten mit + D ⟨**(sich) mit etw z.**⟩   to restrain oneself; to hold (sth) back; to refrain from interfering

■ Ich hielt mich mit meinen Gefühlen (/meinen Tränen/meinem Zorn) zurück.
I kept back my feelings (/tears/anger).

■ Er hält (sich) mit seiner Meinung (/seinen Kenntnissen/seinem Urteil) nicht zurück.
He doesn't refrain from giving his opinion (/showing his knowledge/ passing judgment).

zurückhalten von + D ⟨**jdn von etw z.**⟩   to keep (sb) from (doing) (sth)

■ Ich konnte ihn nicht davon zurückhalten, das zu tun.
I wasn't able to stop him from doing that.

■   Einer von uns sollte sie von (*or* vor) dieser Dummheit zurückhalten.
One of us should keep her from this stupidity.

zurückkehren zu + D ⟨**zu jdm/etw z.**⟩   to return *or* go back to (sb/sth)

■   Diese Leute wollten zur Natur (/zum einfachen Leben/zu Gott) zurückkehren.
These people wanted to go back to nature (/a simple life/return to God).

■   Sie hoffte, daß ihr Mann zu ihr zurückkehren würde.
She hoped that her husband would return to her.

zurückkommen auf + A ⟨**auf jdn/etw z.**⟩   to refer to (sb/sth); to return *or* come back to (sb/sth)

■   Ich möchte auf deinen Einwand (/dein Vorhaben) zurückkommen.
I'd like to come back to your objection (/your plan).

■   Ich werde auf Ihre Bemerkung (/Sie) später wieder zurückkommen.
I will refer to your remark (/get back to you) again later.

zurückschrecken vor + D ⟨**vor etw z.**⟩   to shy away from (sth)

■   Er ist im letzten Moment vor dieser Tat zurückgeschreckt.
He shied away from doing this deed at the last moment.

■   Er ist vor kriminellen Geschäften (/Drogenschmuggel) nicht zurückgeschreckt.
He did not stop at (or shy away from) criminal deals (/drug smuggling).

■   Ich kenne ihn gut. Boris schreckt vor nichts zurück.
I know him well. Boris stops at nothing.

■   Er ist davor (/vor dem Gesetz) zurückgeschreckt.
He shied away from doing that (/avoided the law).

■   Der Gedanke an die Kosten ließ ihn davor (/vor dem Kauf eines Hauses) zurückschrecken.
The thought of the cost (or expense) stopped him from it (/buying a house).

zurückstehen hinter + D ⟨**hinter jdm/etw z.**⟩   to take second place to (sb/sth)

■   Die Qualität dieser Produkte (/Autos) steht hinter der anderer zurück.
The quality of these products (/cars) takes second place to that of the others.

■   Ich versuche sehr, nicht hinter meinem Bruder (/ihr) zurückzustehen.
I'm trying hard not to come off worse than my brother (/her).

■   Deine Leistungen stehen hinter denen des letzten Semesters zurück.
Your achievements aren't quite as good as those of last semester.

zurücktreten von + D ⟨von etw z.⟩   to withdraw *or* back out from (sth); to resign from (sth)

- Er ist von dem Vertrag (/dem Plan/seinem Vorschlag/dem Kauf meines Hauses) zurückgetreten.
  He withdrew from the contract (/plan/proposal/purchase of my house).

- Er trat vom Amt des Außenministers (*or* Er trat als Außenminister) zurück.
  He resigned from his position as foreign secretary.

(s.) zurückziehen (+ prep)   to pull *or* draw back; to retire

- Wegen des Protests haben sie die Werbung (/das Angebot/die Klage/die Truppen/die Bewerbung) zurückgezogen.
  Because of the protest, they withdrew the advertisement (/offer/complaint/troops /application).

- Ich habe mich ins Privatleben (/von meinem Posten/meinem Antrag) zurückgezogen.
  I withdrew into private life (/from my position/my petition).

- Er zog sich von der Welt (/von seinen Geschäften/in die Einsamkeit/in ein Kloster) zurück.
  He withdrew from the world (/from his businesses/went into solitude/ went into a monastery).

- Die Abgeordneten (/Ausschüsse) zogen sich zur Beratung zurück.
  The representatives (/committees) retired (to a different room) to discuss the matter at hand.

zusammenhängen mit + D ⟨mit etw z.⟩   to be joined together, to be connected to (sth)

- Diese Bretter hängen mit Leim (miteinander) zusammen.
  These boards are joined with glue.

- Das hängt damit zusammen, daß du deine Aufgabe nicht gemacht hast.
  That is connected to the fact that you didn't do your task.

- Dieses Stück Land hing einmal mit dem Festland zusammen.
  This stretch of land was once connected to the mainland.

- Meine Kopfschmerzen hängen mit dem feuchten Wetter zusammen.
  My headaches are caused by the humid weather.

- Es wird wohl damit zusammenhängen, daß. . . .
  It is all probably related to the fact that. . . .

zutreffen auf/für + A ⟨für/auf jdn/etw z.⟩   to apply to (sb/sth)

- Das (/Die Regelung) trifft für (*or* auf) alle Studenten zu.
  That (/The regulation) applies to all students.

- Das Gesetz triff für (*or* auf) alle Ausländer (/ihn) zu.
  The law applies to all foreigners (/him).

- Deine Vorschläge treffen nicht für (*or* auf) diese Situation zu.
  Your suggestions don't apply to this situation.

- Diese Beschreibung trifft überhaupt nicht auf Georg (/darauf *or* dafür) zu.
  This description does not apply to George (/it) at all.

zweifeln an + D ⟨**an sich/jdm/etw z.**⟩   to doubt (o.s./sb/sth)

- Ich zweifle nicht an seinem guten Willen, aber Erich wird es sicher nicht schaffen.
  I don't doubt his good intention, but Erich will certainly not accomplish it.

- Ich zweifle an seinem Verstand. Daran ist nicht zu zweifeln.
  I doubt his common sense. There's no question about it.

- Allmählich begann sie, an sich selbst (/an seiner Treue) zu zweifeln.
  Gradually she began to doubt herself (/his fidelity).

- Zuerst schien er der richtige Mann für den Job, aber nach ein paar Monaten begannen seine Mitarbeiter an ihm (/an seinen Fähigkeiten) zu zweifeln.
  At first he seemed to be the right man for the job, but after a few months, his co-workers began to doubt him (/his abilities).

- Ich zweifle daran, ob er richtig gehandelt hat.
  I doubt if he acted appropriately.

zwingen (+ prep)   to force; to compel

- Man hat ihn auf die Knie gezwungen.
  They forced him onto his knees.

- Die politischen Umstände zwangen ihn in den Widerstand.
  The political circumstances forced him to join the resistance.

- Man hat die Firma (/die Arbeiter) an den Verhandlungstisch gezwungen.
  They forced the company (/workers) to the bargaining table.

(s.) zwingen zu + D ⟨**sich/jdn/etw zu etw z.**⟩   to force (o.s./sb/sth) to (do) (sth)

- Ich zwang mich zur Ruhe (/zum Lächeln/zum Arbeiten).
  I forced myself to keep calm (/to smile/to work).

- Seine Intelligenz zwang mich zur Bewunderung.
  His intelligence forced me to admire him.

- Sie haben ihn zum Nachgeben (/Gehorsam/Sprechen/Essen/Handeln) gezwungen.
  They forced him to give in (/obey/speak/eat/act).

- Ich kann ihn nicht dazu (/zum Gehorsam/zum Rücktritt) zwingen.
  I can't force him to do it (/to obey/step down).

- Ich habe mich (dazu) gezwungen, das zu tun.
  I forced myself to do that.

- Diese Probleme zwangen mich dazu, den Plan aufzugeben.
  These problems forced me to give up the plan.

- Ich weiß genau, daß man niemanden zu seinem Glück zwingen kann.
  I know for sure that you can't force people to be happy.

Appendix
Grammatical Tables

PREPOSITIONS

With accusative

bis	to, until, as far as
durch	through
entlang	along
für	for
gegen	against
ohne	without
um	around, about, near
wider	against

With dative

aus	out of, of, from
außer	except, besides
bei	near, with, at, at the house of
entgegen	against, opposite, toward
gegenüber	opposite
mit	with
nach	to, toward, after, according to
seit	since
von	of, from, by

With accusative (motion) or dative (stationary)

an	at, on, to
auf	on, upon, to
hinter	behind
in	in, into, at, to
neben	beside, next to
über	over, about, across, above
unter	under, beneath, below, among
vor	before, in front of, ago
zwischen	between

With genitive

(an)statt	instead of
außerhalb	outside of
diesseits	on this side of
innerhalb	inside of, within
jenseits	on that side of
oberhalb	above
trotz	in spite of
um ... willen	for the sake of
unterhalb	under, beneath below
während	during, while
wegen	because of, owing to

PERSONAL PRONOUNS

Nominative	Accusative	Dative
ich	mich	mir
du	dich	dir
er, sie, es	ihn, sie, es	ihm, ihr, ihm
wir	uns	uns
ihr	euch	euch
sie	sie	ihnen
—	—	—
Sie	Sie	Ihnen

REFLEXIVE PRONOUNS

Accusative	Dative
mich	mir
dich	dir
sich	sich
uns	uns
euch	euch
sich	sich
—	—
sich	sich

INTERROGATIVE PRONOUNS

Nominative	wer	was
Accusative	wen	was
Dative	wem	
Genitive	wessen	

RELATIVE AND DEMONSTRATIVE PRONOUNS

	Singular			
	Masculine	Feminine	Neuter	Plural
Nominative	der	die	das	die
Accusative	den	die	das	die
Dative	dem	der	dem	denen
Genitive	dessen	deren	dessen	deren

DEFINITE ARTICLES

	Singular			Plural
	Masculine	Feminine	Neuter	
Nominative	der	die	das	die
Accusative	den	die	das	die
Dative	dem	der	dem	den
Genitive	des	der	des	der

DIESER-WORDS

	Singular			Plural
	Masculine	Feminine	Neuter	
Nominative	dieser	diese	dieses	diese
Accusative	diesen	diese	dieses	diese
Dative	diesem	dieser	diesem	diesen
Genitive	dieses	dieser	dieses	dieser

The **dieser**-words are **der, dieser, jeder, jener, mancher, solcher,** and **welcher.**

INDEFINITE ARTICLES AND EIN-WORDS

	Singular			Plural
	Masculine	Feminine	Neuter	
Nominative	ein	eine	ein	keine
Accusative	einen	eine	ein	keine
Dative	einem	einer	einem	keinen
Genitive	eines	einer	eines	keiner

The **ein**-words include **kein** and the possessive adjectives: **mein, dein, sein, ihr, unser, euer, ihr,** and **Ihr.**

PRESENT TENSE VERB FORMS

Infinitive	*spiel-en	sammel-n	find-en	tanz-en	ankomm-en
	stem + ending	stem + ending	stem + ending	stem + ending	stem + endin
ich	spiel-e	samml-e	find-e	tanz-e	komm-e . . . ar
du	spiel-st	sammel-st	find-est	tanz-t	komm-st . . . a
er, sie, es	spiel-t	sammel-t	find-et	tanz-t	komm-t . . . an
wir	spiel-en	sammel-n	find-en	tanz-en	komm-en . . . ⸗
ihr	spiel-t	sammel-t	find-et	tanz-t	komm-t . . . an
sie, Sie	spiel-en	sammel-n	find-en	tanz-en	komm-en . . . ⸗

Note the following exceptions in the preceding chart:

*a. These endings are used for all verbs except the modals, **wissen, werden,** and **sein.**

b. Verbs ending in **-eln** drop the "**e**" of the ending-**eln** in the **ich-** form: **ich sammle, ich segle, ich mogle** . . . , and add only **-n** in the **wir-, sie-,** and **Sie-**form. These forms are always identical with the infinitive: **mogeln, wir mogeln, sie mogeln, Sie mogeln.**

c. Verbs with a stem ending in **-d, -t** or **-m, -n** preceded by another consonant (except **-l,** or **-r**) have an **-e-** before the **-st** and **-t** endings: **du findest, er findet, ihr findet; du reitest, er reitet, ihr reitet; du atmest, er atmet, ihr atmet; du rechnest, er rechnet, ihr rechnet.**

d. The **-st** ending of the **du-**form contracts to **-t** when the verb stem ends in a sibilant (**-s, -ss, -ß, -z,** or **-tz**). Thus the **du-, er-,** and the **ihr-**forms are identical.

e. In speaking, the **ich-**form is often used without the ending **-e: ich spiel', ich hab', ich frag'.** The omission of the **-e** is shown in writing by an apostrophe.

f. In present tense, separable prefixes are separated from the verb and are in the last position.

VERBS WITH A
STEM-VOWEL CHANGE**

Infinitive	geben	sehen	fahren	laufen
	e ⟩ i	e ⟩ ie	e ⟩ ä	e ⟩ äu
ich	gebe	sehe	fahre	laufe
du	gibst	siehst	fährst	läufst
er, sie, es	gibt	sieht	fährt	läuft
wir	geben	sehen	fahren	laufen
ihr	gebt	seht	fahrt	lauft
sie, Sie	geben	sehen	fahren	laufen

As the chart above indicates, there are some strong verbs that have a stem-vowel change:

a. Some strong verbs have a stem-vowel change **e ⟩ i** in the **du-** and the **er-**form.

b. Some strong verbs have a stem-vowel change **e ⟩ ie** in the **du-** and the **er-**form.

c. Some strong verbs have a stem-vowel change **e ⟩ ä** in the **du-** and the **er-**form.

d. Some strong verbs have a stem-vowel change **e ⟩ äu** in the **du-** and the **er-**form.

**For a list of strong verbs and their principal parts see pp. 370–371.

SIMPLE PAST TENSE

	Weak verbs			Strong verbs	
	folgen	**arbeiten**	**begegnen**	**tranken**	**raten**
ich	folg-**te**	arbeit-**ete**	begegn-**ete**	trank-	riet-
du	folg-**test**	arbeit-**etest**	begegn-**etest**	trank-**st**	riet-**est**
er, sie, es	folg-**te**	arbeit-**ete**	begegn-**ete**	trank-	riet-
wir	folg-**ten**	arbeit-**eten**	begegn-**eten**	trank-**en**	riet-**en**
ihr	folg-**tet**	arbeit-**etet**	begegn-**etet**	trank-**t**	riet-**et**
sie, Sie	folg-**ten**	arbeit-**eten**	begegn-**eten**	trank-**en**	riet-**en**

a. Weak verbs have the past-tense marker -**te** plus the personal endings.
b. A weak verb with stem endings in -**d**, -**t** or -**m**, -**n** preceded by another consonant (except -**l** or -**r**) has a past-tense marker -**ete** plus personal endings.
c. Strong verbs have a stem-vowel change plus personal endings.

AUXILIARIES: sein, haben, werden

	Present	**Past**	**Present**	**Past**	**Present**	**Past**
ich	bin	war	habe	hatte	werde	wurde
du	bist	warst	hast	hattest	wirst	wurdest
er, sie, es	ist	war	hat	hatte	wird	wurde
wir	sind	waren	haben	hatten	werden	wurden
ihr	seid	wart	habt	hattet	werdet	wurdet
sie, Sie	sind	waren	haben	hatten	werden	wurden

MODAL AUXILARIES: Present, Simple Past, and Past Participle

	dürfen	**können**	**mögen**	**müssen**	**sollen**	**wollen**
Present: ich	darf	kann	mag	muß	soll	will
du	darfst	kannst	magst	mußt	sollst	willst
er, sie, es	darf	kann	mag	muß	soll	will
wir	dürfen	können	mögen	müssen	sollen	wollen
ihr	dürft	könnt	mögt	müßt	sollt	wollt
sie, Sie	dürfen	können	mögen	müssen	sollen	wollen
Simple past	dürfte	konnte	mochte	mußte	sollte	wollte
Past participle	gedurft	gekonnt	gemocht	gemußt	gesollt	gewollt

VERB CONJUGATIONS: STRONG
VERBS: sehen and kommen
A. INDICATIVE

	Present (/I see/come)		Simple past (/I saw/came)	
ich	sehe	komme	sah	kam
du	siehst	kommst	sahst	kamst
er, sie, es	sieht	kommt	sah	kam
wir	sehen	kommen	sahen	kamen
ihr	seht	kommt	saht	kamt
sie, Sie	sehen	kommen	sahen	kamen

	Present perfect (I have seen/come)				Past perfect (I had seen/come)			
ich	habe		bin		hatte		war	
du	hast		bist		hattest		warst	
er, sie, es	hat	gesehen	ist	gekommen	hatte	gesehen	war	gekommen
wir	haben		sind		hatte		waren	
ihr	habt		seid		hattet		wart	
sie, Sie	haben		sind		hatte		waren	

	Future (I will see/come)			
ich	werde		werde	
du	wirst		wirst	
er, sie, es	wird	sehen	wird	kommen
wir	werden		werden	
ihr	werdet		werdet	
sie, Sie	werden		werden	

B. IMPERATIVE

	Imperative (See/Come)	
Familiar singular	Sieh!	Komm(e)!
Familiar plural	Seht!	Kommt!
Formal	Sehen Sie!	Kommen Sie!

C. SUBJUNCTIVE

Present-time subjunctive (I would see/come)

	General subjunctive		Special subjunctive	
ich	sähe	käme	sehe	komme
du	sähest	kämest	sehest	kommest
er, sie, es	sähe	käme	sehe	komme
wir	sähen	kämen	sehen	kommen
ihr	sähet	kämet	sehet	kommet
sie, Sie	sähen	kämen	sehen	kommen

Past-time subjunctive (I would have seen/come)

	General subjunctive				Special subjunctive			
ich	hätte		wäre		habe		sei	
du	hättest		wärest		habest		seiest	
er, sie, es	hätte	gesehen	wäre	gekommen	habe	gesehen	sei	gekommen
wir	hätten		wären		haben		seien	
ihr	hättet		wäret		habet		seiet	
sie, Sie	hätten		wären		haben		seien	

Future-time subjunctive (I would see/come)

	General subjunctive				Special subjunctive			
ich	würde		würde		werde		werde	
du	würdest		würdest		werdest		werdest	
er, sie, es	würde	sehen	würde	kommen	werde	sehen	werde	kommen
wir	würden		würden		werden		werden	
ihr	würdet		würdet		werdet		werdet	
sie, Sie	würden		würden		werden		werden	

D. PASSIVE VOICE

	Present passive (I am seen)		Past passive (I was seen)	
ich	werde		wurde	
du	wirst		wurdest	
er, sie, es	wird	gesehen	wurde	gesehen
wir	werden		wurden	
ihr	werdet		wurdet	
sie, Sie	werden		wurden	

	Present perfect passive *(I have been seen)*	*Past perfect passive* *(I had been seen)*
ich	bin	war
du	bist	warst
er, sie, es	ist	war
wir	sind $\Big\}$ gesehen worden	waren $\Big\}$ gesehen worden
ihr	seid	wart
sie, Sie	sind	waren

	Future passive (I will be seen)
ich	werde
du	wirst
er, sie, es	wird
wir	werden $\Big\}$ geshen werden
ihr	werdet
sie, Sie	werden

DATIVE VERBS

antworten	glauben
befehlen	helfen
begegnen	leid tun
danken	nützen
dienen	passen
erlauben	passieren
fehlen	raten
folgen	schaden
gefallen	schmecken
gehorchen	verzeihen
gehören	weh tun
gelingen	

The verbs **glauben, erlauben,** and **verzeihen** may take an impersonal accusative object: **ich glaube es; ich erlaube es.**

PLURAL OF NOUNS

Group	Singular	Plural	Type	Comments
1	das Zimmer	**die Zimmer**	0 (no change)	Masculine and neuter
	der Mantel	**die Mäntel**	¨ (umlaut)	nouns ending in **-el, -en,**
	der Garten	**die Gärten**	¨ (umlaut)	**-er**
2	der Tisch	**die Tische**	-e	
	der Stuhl	**die Stühle**	¨e	
3	das Bild	**die Bilder**	-er	Stem vowel **e** or **i**
	das Buch	**die Bücher**	¨er	cannot take umlaut
	das Haus	**die Häuser**	¨er	Stem vowel **a,o,u** and
				diphthong **au** take umlaut
4	die Uhr	**die Uhren**	-en	
	die Lampe	**die Lampen**	-n	
	die Freundin	**die Freundinnen**	-nen	
5	das Radio	**die Radios**	-s	Mostly foreign words

Gender of nouns and plural forms are not always predictable. Therefore, one must learn each noun together with its article (**der, die, das**) and its plural form. There are, however, certain patterns within this paradigm of inflections. Although there are always exceptions to these patterns, one may find them helpful in remembering the plural forms of many nouns. Most German nouns form their plurals in one of the five ways shown in the chart above. These are further explained below:

1. Nouns in Group 1 do not have any ending in the plural. Sometimes they take an umlaut.
2. Nouns in Group 2 add the ending **-e** in the plural. Sometimes they take an umlaut. Note: There are many one-syllable words in this group.
3. Nouns in Group 3 add the ending **-er** in the plural. They always take an umlaut wherever possible, that is, when the noun contains the vowels **a, o,** or **u,** or the diphthong **au.** Note: There are no feminine nouns in this group. There are many one-syllable words in this group.
4. Nouns in Group 4 add the ending **-en** or **-n** in the plural. They never add an umlaut. Note: There are many feminine nouns in this group. Feminine nouns ending in **-in** add the ending **-nen** in the plural.
5. Nouns in Group 5 add the ending **-s** in the plural. They never add an umlaut. They also never add the dative plural **-n** ending. Note: There are many words of foreign origin in this group.

MASCULINE NOUNS TAKING -(E)N

	Singular	Plural
Nominative	der Herr	die Herren
	der Student	die Studenten
Accusative	den Herrn	die Herren
	den Studenten	die Studenten
Dative	dem Herrn	den Herren
	dem Studenten	den Studenten
Genitive	des Herrn	der Herren
	des Studenten	der Studenten

Some other masculine nouns that take an **-n** or **-en** in all cases except the nominative case are: **der Automat, der Bauer, der Journalist, der Junge, der Jurist, der Kollege, der Mensch, der Nachbar, der Neffe, der Patient, der Polizist, der Soldat, der Tourist.**

A few masculine nouns of this class add **-ns** in the genitive: **der Name** > **des Namens; der Gedanke** > **des Gedankens; der Glaube** > **des Glaubens.**

ADJECTIVE ENDINGS AFTER DER-WORDS

	Singular			Plural
	Masculine	Feminine	Neuter	
Nominative	-e	-e	-e	-en
Accusative	-en	-e	-e	-en
Dative	-en	-en	-en	-en
Genitive	-en	-en	-en	-en

The following words expressing quantity can be used only in the plural with their corresponding adjective endings for **der**-words: **alle, beide.**

ADJECTIVE ENDINGS AFTER EIN-WORDS

	Singular			Plural
	Masculine	Feminine	Neuter	
Nominative	-er	-e	-es	-en
Accusative	-en	-e	-es	-en
Dative	-en	-en	-en	-en
Genitive	-en	-en	-en	-en

ADJECTIVE ENDINGS FOR ADJECTIVES
NOT PRECEEDED BY ARTICLES

	Singular			
	Masculine	Feminine	Neuter	Plural
Nominative	-er	-e	-es	-e
Accusative	-en	-e	-es	-e
Dative	-em	-er	-em	-en
Genitive	-en	-er	-en	-er

The following words expressing quantity can be used only in the plural with their corresponding endings for adjectives not preceded by articles: **andere, ein paar, einige, mehrere, viele, wenige.**

PRINCIPAL PARTS: The following list contains all the irregular verbs used in this book. Verbs with separable or inseparable prefixes are not included when the basic verb form has been introduced (example *kommen, ankommen*). Verbs with stem vowel change as well as those constructed with a form of *sein* have also been indicated. In most cases only one meaning for each verb is shown. Additional meanings can be found in the main text.

Infinitive	Past (Imperfect)	Past Participle	Present 3rd Person Singular	Meaning
beginnen	begann	begonnen	beginnt	to begin
biegen	bog	gebogen	biegt	to bend
bieten	bot	geboten	bietet	to offer
binden	band	gebunden	bindet	to tie
bitten	bat	gebeten	bittet	to ask
bleiben	blieb	ist geblieben	bleibt	to stay, remain
brechen	brach	gebrochen	bricht	to break
brennen	brannte	gebrannt	brennt	to burn
bringen	brachte	gebracht	bringt	to bring
denken	dachte	gedacht	denkt	to think
dringen	drang	ist gedrungen	dringt	to penetrate
entscheiden	entschied	entschieden	entscheidet	to decide
erschrecken	erschrak	erschrocken	erschrickt	to frighten
fahren	fuhr	ist gefahren	fährt	to drive
fallen	fiel	ist gefallen	fällt	to fall
finden	fand	gefunden	findet	to find
fliegen	flog	ist geflogen	fliegt	to fly
fließen	floß	ist geflossen	fließt	to flow, run
geben	gab	gegeben	gibt	to give
gehen	ging	ist gegangen	geht	to go
geschehen	geschah	ist geschehen	geschieht	to happen
gewinnen	gewann	gewonnen	gewinnt	to win
graben	grub	gegraben	gräbt	to dig
greifen	griff	gegriffen	greift	to grab
haben	hatte	gehabt	hat	to have
halten	hielt	gehalten	hält	to hold
heben	hob	gehoben	hebt	to lift
helfen	half	geholfen	hilft	to help
hängen	hing	gehangen	hängt	to hang
kennen	kannte	gekannt	kennt	to know
kneifen	kniff	gekniffen	kneift	to pinch
kommen	kam	ist gekommen	kommt	to come
laden	lud	geladen	lädt	to load
lassen	ließ	gelassen	läßt	to leave, let
laufen	lief	ist gelaufen	läuft	to run
leiden	litt	gelitten	leidet	to suffer
lesen	las	gelesen	liest	to read
liegen	lag	gelegen	liegt	to lie, be located
messen	maß	gemessen	mißt	to measure
nehmen	nahm	genommen	nimmt	to take
raten	riet	geraten	rät	to guess

reiten	ritt	ist geritten	reitet	to ride (an animal)
reißen	riß	gerissen	reißt	to tear
rennen	rannte	ist gerannt	rennt	to run
riechen	roch	gerochen	riecht	to smell
rinnen	rann	ist geronnen	rinnt	to run (liquids)
rufen	rief	gerufen	ruft	to call
scheiden	schied	geschieden	scheidet	to separate, part
schieben	schob	geschoben	schiebt	to push
schießen	schoß	geschossen	schießt	to shoot
schlagen	schlug	geschlagen	schlägt	to hit, beat
schleichen	schlich	ist geschlichen	schleicht	to creep, sneak
schließen	schloß	geschlossen	schließt	to shut, close
schmeißen	schmiß	geschmissen	schmeißt	to fling, throw
schneiden	schnitt	geschnitten	schneidet	to cut
schreiben	schrieb	geschrieben	schreibt	to write
schreien	schrie	geschrie(e)n	schreit	to shout, cry
schreiten	schritt	ist geschritten	schreitet	to stride, walk
schwimmen	schwamm	ist geschwommen	schwimmt	to swim
sehen	sah	gesehen	sieht	to see
sein	war	ist gewesen	ist	to be
senden	sandte	gesandt	sendet	to send, transmit
sinken	sank	ist gesunken	sinkt	to sink
sitzen	saß	gesessen	sitzt	to sit
sprechen	sprach	gesprochen	spricht	to speak
springen	sprang	ist gesprungen	springt	to jump
stechen	stach	gestochen	sticht	to sting
stehen	stand	gestanden	steht	to stand
steigen	stieg	ist gestiegen	steigt	to climb
sterben	starb	ist gestorben	stirbt	to die
stinken	stank	gestunken	stinkt	to stink
stoßen	stieß	gestoßen	stößt	to push, thrust
streichen	strich	gestrichen	streicht	to strike, cancel,
streiten	stritt	gestritten	streitet	to quarrel, fight
tragen	trug	getragen	trägt	to carry
treffen	traf	getroffen	trifft	to meet
treiben	trieb	getrieben	treibt	to pursue, do
treten	trat	ist getreten	tritt	to step
trinken	trank	getrunken	trinkt	to drink
tun	tat	getan	tut	to do
verlieren	verlor	verloren	verliert	to lose
wachsen	wuchs	ist gewachsen	wächst	to grow
waschen	wusch	gewaschen	wäscht	to wash
weichen	wich	ist gewichen	weicht	to yield, give way
weisen	wies	gewiesen	weist	to point out, show
wenden	wandte	gewandt	wendet	to turn
werben	warb	geworben	wirbt	to woo, recruit
werden	wurde	ist geworden	wird	to become; be
werfen	warf	geworfen	wirft	to throw
wissen	wußte	gewußt	weiß	to know (fact)
ziehen	zog	gezogen	zieht	to pull
zwingen	zwang	gezwungen	zwingt	to force

Glossary

(be) **about**   s. handeln um/von/über

(become) **absorbed in**   s. vertiefen in

accommodate   unterbringen

accuse of   anklagen wegen

accustom to   gewöhnen an

(be) **accustomed to**   pflegen zu

achieve   bringen auf/zu, erreichen

acknowledge   bestätigen in

acquaint

  acquaint with   unterrichten über

  (be) **acquainted with**   bekannt sein mit

act against   handeln gegen

adapt o.s. to   s. einstellen auf

add or attach to   ansetzen an

address

  address to   richten an

  address with   anreden mit

  address *or* speak   sprechen zu

  address with "du"-form   (s.) duzen mit

adhere to   verharren auf/bei/in

adjourn   (s.) vertagen auf

adjust   abstimmen auf

  adjust to   einstellen auf

  adjust *or* conform to   s. anpassen an

admit to   aufnehmen in, zulassen zu

admonish   mahnen zu

adopt   nehmen zu

advertise   werben für

advise to   raten zu

(be) **affected by**   betroffen sein von

(be) **afraid of**   bangen vor, Angst haben vor, s. fürchten vor

agitate against   hetzen gegen

agree   einwilligen

  agree on   vereinbaren mit

  agree to   eingehen auf

agree upon   s. absprechen über

agree with   s. einigen mit, einverstanden sein mit, übereinkommen mit, übereinstimmen mit

find agreement on   (s.)verständigen über

come to an agreement with   s. arrangieren mit

aim at   abzielen auf, zielen auf, anlegen auf

allege or **claim**   vorbringen

allude to   anspielen auf

ally with   s. verbünden mit/gegen

(get) **along**

  get along (well) with   (gut) zurechtkommen mit

  get along with   auskommen mit, s. verstehen mit, s. vertragen mit

(be) **amazed at**   staunen über, verwundert sein über

(be) **amongst**   gehören zu

amount to   hinauslaufen auf

  amount or **come to**   s. belaufen auf

  amount or **be limited to**   s. erschöpfen in

amuse o.s. with   s. amüsieren mit, s. vergnügen mit

anger

  be angered about   s. entrüsten über

answer to   antworten auf

anticipate from   ablesen von

(be) **anxious about**   Angst haben um

(take) **apart**   zerlegen in

apologize to/for   s. entschuldigen bei/für/wegen

appeal to   appellieren an, s. berufen auf

appear   vorkommen

  appear out of   tauchen aus

  appear with   s. zeigen mit

  appear or **peep out from**   vorsehen hinter/unter

  put in an appearance   s. sehen lassen

apply   beantragen

  apply for   s. bewerben um

  apply to   anwenden auf, zutreffen auf/für

appoint   berufen

  appoint as   bestellen als

  have an appointment   bestellen

approach   gehen auf, s. heranmachen an, zugehen auf

  approach or **ask about**   ansprechen auf

argue

argue about   (s.) streiten über/um

argue with   s. auseinandersetzen mit

(do) **arithmetic**   rechnen

(get) **around**   herumkommen um, vorbeikommen an

arrange   ordnen, vereinbaren

  arrange a meeting with   verabreden (mit)

  make an arrangement with   s. absprechen mit

arrive   ankommen

(be) **ashamed of**   s. schämen für/wegen/vor

ask

  ask about   s. erkundigen nach/über, fragen nach

  ask for   bitten um, verlangen nach

  ask to   auffordern zu

  ask (sb) to come   bestellen

  ask or **approach about**   ansprechen auf

assert o.s. against   s. durchsetzen gegen

assess   bewerten mit

associate with   verkehren mit

(be) **astonished at**   staunen über

(go) **astray**   irregehen

attach or **add to**   ansetzen an

attack   s. hermachen über, überfallen

  attack or **go for**   eindringen auf

attain   gelangen zu

(pay) **attention to**   achten auf

attract attention   auffallen

avoid   herumkommen um

(be) **aware**   wahrnehmen

back out from   zurücktreten von

(be) **badly off with**   hapern mit

balk at   s. sperren gegen

bandage   verbinden mit

bang   knallen

bargain over   handeln über/um

base

  base on   basieren auf

  be based on   basieren auf, beruhen auf, s. stützen auf

  base or **found on**   aufbauen auf

be   sein, s. befinden, stecken

  be or **fare (well)**   (gut) stehen mit/um

bear (comparison) with   (den Vergleich) aushalten mit
beat   (s.) schlagen
become of   werden aus
beg (for mercy, etc.)   jammern um
begin   ansetzen zu
  begin with   beginnen mit
behave towards   s. verhalten zu
believe in   glauben an
belong   gehören
bend   (s.) neigen, (s.) verziehen
bet on   wetten auf/um
betake o.s.   s. begeben
betray   täuschen, (s.) verraten
bind into   binden zu/in
blame for   tadeln für/wegen
boast about   prahlen mit
border on   grenzen an
borrow from   s. borgen von/bei
bother   (s.) plagen
  bother by   quälen mit
  bother o.s. with   s. abgeben mit
brace o.s. against   s. stemmen gegen
brag, show off   protzen mit
break
  break down   scheitern
  break into   ausbrechen in, einbrechen bei/in
bring
  bring into (doing)   treiben zu
  bring into (sth)   versetzen
  bring to   bringen auf
broadcast   senden
brush *or* **touch**   streifen
build
  build on   bauen auf
  build up into   aufbauen zu
bum around   bummeln
bump *or* **knock**   anstoßen
bump *or* **run against**   (s.) stoßen an
burn into/onto   brennen in
bury into   graben in

(be) **busy**
   be busy with (s.) beschäftigen mit
   be busy *or* **work** s. betätigen
buy kaufen
calculate rechnen
call
   call for rufen nach
   call *or* **phone** anrufen
   be called for by gehören zu
camp zelten
(be a) **candidate for** kandidieren für
capitulate to kapitulieren vor
care
   care about s. machen aus
   take care sehen nach
   take care of sorgen für, s. kümmern um
carry tragen
   carry with o.s. bei/mit s. führen
   carry on with treiben mit
catch
   catch at ertappen bei
   catch *or* **infect** (s.) anstecken
(get) **caught up in** s. verwickeln in
cause treiben, verursachen
chain to ketten an
change (s.) verändern, wechseln
   change *(buses, etc.)* umsteigen
   change into einwechseln in/gegen, umwandeln in, (s.) verwandeln in/zu
   change *or* **turn into** übergehen in
chase after jagen nach
cheat
   cheat from abgucken bei/von
   cheat *or* **copy from** abschreiben von/bei
check kontrollieren nach/auf
   check for prüfen auf, überprüfen auf
cheer about jubeln über
chew on kauen an/auf
choose wählen
clean from s. reinigen von

clear räumen
climb klettern
  climb in einsteigen in
  climb on/onto steigen
cling to haften an, s. hängen an, s. klammern an
close to sperren für
coincide with s. decken mit
combine with verbinden mit
come
  come from/with/over/to kommen aus/mit/über/zu
  come to/upon/under kommen auf/unter
  come within/under fallen in/unter
  come down herunterkommen
  come in time recht, zeitig kommen
  come off *(a habit, etc.)* herunterkommen von
  come *or* **be from** stammen aus/von
  come out herauskommen mit
  come out of herauskommen aus
  come running towards zulaufen auf
  come to terms with sth s. abfinden (mit)
  come toward/to zukommen auf
command disponieren über
communicate with s. verständigen mit
compare with (s.) messen an/mit, vergleichen mit
(be) **compatible with** vereinbar sein mit
compel to zwingen zu
compensate for (s.) entschädigen für
compete with/for konkurrieren mit/um
complain about s. beklagen über, s. beschweren über, klagen (über)
comply with s. richten nach
(be) **conceited about** s. einbilden auf
concentrate on s. konzentrieren auf
concern
  concern *or* **be concerned with** s. befassen mit
  be concerned about besorgt sein um
  have concern for gehen um
conclude
  conclude from folgern aus
  conclude with schließen mit
condemn to verurteilen zu

condescend to   s. herablassen zu

conduct   leiten

confirm   bestätigen in

conform *or* **adjust to**   s. anpassen an

congratulate on   beglückwünschen zu, gratulieren zu

connect

   connect with   verbinden mit

   be connected together   zusammenhängen mit

(give) consent to   einwilligen in

conserve with   haushalten mit

consider *or* **examine**   s. auseinandersetzen mit

   consider to be   erachten für/als

consist of/in   bestehen aus/in

(be) consistent with   s. vertragen mit

consult   (s.) wenden an

contemplate   s. tragen mit

(be) content with   s. begnügen (mit), s. zufriedengeben mit

contribute to   beitragen zu, mitwirken an/bei

control   (s.) kontrollieren

convert into   umsetzen in

convince of   überzeugen von

coordinate with   s. abstimmen mit

cope with   zurechtkommen mit

copy *or* **cheat from**   abschreiben von/bei

count

   count among   rechnen zu

   count on   rechnen auf

   count on/to/as   zählen auf/nach/zu

cover with   decken mit

crab *or* **moan about**   nörgeln über

crave for   geizen nach, verlangen

(be) crazy   stehen auf

   be crazy about   schwärmen für, vernarrt sein in, verrückt sein auf

creep   (s.) schleichen

criticize for   tadeln für/wegen

cry

   cry for/over/with   weinen nach/über/um/vor

   cry out for   schreien nach

curse   fluchen auf/über

  curse about/at   schimpfen (auf/über)

cut   schneiden

  cut o.s. off from   s. abschließen von

dance   tanzen

dare   (s.) wagen

date

  date from   stammen aus/von

  have a date with   verabredet sein mit

(have a bad) **deal with**   hereinfallen mit

decay   verfallen

(be) **deceived by**   s. täuschen in

decide

  decide about   befinden über

  decide on   bestimmen über, s. entscheiden für/über, s. entschließen zu

declare

  declare as   erklären für

  declare o.s. for/against   s. aussprechen für/gegen

defend

  defend against   (s.) verteidigen gegen

  defend o.s. against   (s.) wehren gegen

deliver   liefern

demand   verlangen

  demand from   fordern von

demarcate against   (s.) abgrenzen gegen

demonstrate for/against   demonstrieren für/gegen

demote to   degradieren zu

depend on   abängen von, ankommen auf, hängen an, liegen an, s. verlassen auf

(be) **dependent on**   abhängig sein von, angewiesen sein auf

(be) **derived from**   ableiten aus/von, s. herleiten von

descend upon   überfallen

describe as   (s.) bezeichnen als

despair   verzweifeln

develop into   (s.) entwickeln zu

deviate from   abweichen von

devise   sinnen auf

die

  die for/of   sterben für/vor

  die *or* **itch for**   brennen auf

differ
> **differ from**   s. unterscheiden von
> **differ from/about**   differieren von

differentiate from   unterscheiden von

dig for   graben nach

direct   lenken
> **direct to/against/toward**   richten auf/gegen/nach

disappear   s. verlieren, verschwinden

(be) **disappointed in**   enttäuscht sein von/über

discuss with   s. auseinandersetzen mit, diskutieren über

(be) **disgusted at**   (s.) ekeln vor

(be) **dismayed at**   betroffen sein über

(have at one's) **disposal**   verfügen über

disregard   s. hinwegsetzen über

dissociate from   (s.) distanzieren von

dissolve in   (s.) auflösen in, (s.) lösen in

dissuade from   abbringen von

distinguish according to   unterscheiden nach

distract from   ablenken von

dive   tauchen
> **dive into/for**   tauchen in/nach

divide up   teilen

(get) **divorced from**   s. scheiden lassen von

do   tun
> **do about**   unternehmen gegen
> **do without**   verzichten auf

dodge   s. herumdrücken um, kneifen vor

(be) **done with**   geschehen mit

doubt   zweifeln an

(get) **down to**   s. heranmachen an

drag   (s.) schleppen, zerren
> **take a drag**   ziehen an

draw   zeichnen
> **draw attention to**   aufmerksam machen auf
> **draw from**   beziehen aus
> **draw near to**   herankommen an
> **draw nearer to**   heranziehen zu
> **draw to/into**   ziehen auf/in

dream about/of   träumen von

drink to   anstoßen auf, trinken auf

drive   treiben, fahren
  drive past   vorbeifahren an
drop *or* **call in**   vorbeifahren bei
  drop *or* **call in on**   vorbeigehen bei, vorbeikommen bei
  drop *or* **stop by**   vorbeigehen bei
duck out   kneifen vor
dwell on   s. aufhalten bei/mit, s. ausbreiten über
earn   verdienen
eat   zu sich nehmen
eavesdrop   lauschen
(be) **economical with**   haushalten mit
educate to   erziehen zu
(have an) **effect on**   einwirken auf, wirken auf
elect   wählen
elevate o.s. above/to   s. erheben über/zu
emerge from   herauskommen bei
emigrate   auswandern
empathize with   s. einfühlen in
(be) **employed**
  be employed at   angestellt sein bei
  be employed by   beschäftigt sein bei
encounter   stoßen auf, treffen auf
encourage
  encourage to   anreizen zu
  encourage to do   verführen zu
  encourage *or* **lead to**   verleiten zu
end
  end with   enden auf/mit
  end *or* **finish**   abschließen mit
endure   aushalten
(get) **engaged to**   s. verloben mit
enjoy   s. erfreuen an
(be) **enough**   reichen
enroll at   (s.) anmelden bei
(become) **entangled in**   s. verwickeln in
enter   (ein)treten
entertain with   (s.) unterhalten mit
enthuse about   schwärmen von
(be) **enthusiastic about**   s. begeistern für, begeistert sein von
entice to   verlocken zu

envy for/because of   beneiden um/wegen

equip

  equip with   ausstatten mit

  be equipped with   ausgestattet sein mit, ausgerüstet sein mit

emerge from   tauchen aus

escape

  escape from   fliehen vor, flüchten vor/aus

  escape onto/under   s. retten auf/under

  escape with   davonkommen mit

estimate at   schätzen auf

(give) **evidence about**   aussagen über

examine

  examine for   untersuchen auf

  examine in   prüfen in

  examine *or* **consider**   s. auseinandersetzen mit

exchange

  exchange for   austauschen gegen, eintauschen für/gegen, vertauschen mit

  exchange with   tauschen mit, wechseln mit

excuse   (s.) entschuldigen

exert

  exert on   ausüben auf

  exert *or* **strain**   s. anstrengen

exile to/from   verbannen auf/aus

exist   bestehen

expect

  expect from   (s.) erwarten von

  expect of   annehmen von

expel from   verweisen aus/von, weisen aus/von

(be) **expert at**   s. verstehen auf

expound on   s. verbreiten über

express *or* **voice about**   s. äußern über

extend   reichen

  extend (over) to   s. erstrecken auf

extract from   (s.) lösen aus

(have an) **eye on**   reflektieren auf

face on   liegen nach

fail   scheitern

fall   (s.) stürzen

  fall into   zerfallen

  fall on/into/in   fallen auf/in/an

fall under/within   fallen in/unter
fall back into   zurückfallen in
fall for   s. vernarren in
fall in love with   s. verlieben in
fare
    fare well/badly   (s.) ergehen
    fare with   s. stehen mit
fasten   anschließen an
    fasten to   heften an, (s.) schließen an
fear for   bangen um, fürchten um, zittern um, tasten nach
feel *or* **think about**   s. stellen zu
fetch   holen
fiddle about   s. zu schaffen machen an
    fiddle around with   herumspielen an/auf/mit
fight
    fight for   s. einsetzen für
    fight for/against/with   streiten für/gegen/mit
    fight through/for/against   (s.) kämpfen durch/für/gegen
    fight with   s. schlagen (mit)
    fight with/for   kämpfen mit/um
    fight with/over   s. prügeln mit/um
    be able to fight   ankommen gegen
fill with   füllen mit
find
    find as   befinden für/als
    find on/with   aussetzen an
    find fault with   herumnörgeln an
    find one's way around   s. zurechtfinden
finish *or* **end**   abschließen mit
fish for/from   fischen auf/aus
fit   passen
    fit *or* **put**   einsetzen
    fit out with   ausrüsten mit
fix up *or* **build**   aufbauen
flee from   flüchten vor/aus
flirt with   kokettieren mit
flow   fließen
    flow in   einmünden in
    flow *or* **run**   rinnen
fly   fliegen

focus on   einstellen auf
follow   s. anlehnen an, folgen auf, s. reihen an
(be) **fond of**   hängen an
forbid   verbieten
force to   zwingen zu
  force one's way into   eindringen in
found *or* **base on**   aufbauen auf
free from   (s.) lösen von
frequent   verkehren
(make) **friends with**   s. anschließen an, s. befreunden mit
fulfill with   erfüllen mit
(make) **fun of**   s. amüsieren über, s. lustig machen über
(make a) **fuss about**   (s.) zieren
gab   quatschen
gain   gewinnen an
  gain *(respect, etc.)*   zunehmen an
garnish with   (s.) zieren mit
get   holen
  get (to sth by chance)   geraten
  get angry with   s. ärgern über
  get down to   schreiten zu
  get down to doing   s. machen an
  get off   aussteigen
  get on/onto   einsteigen in
  get out   aussteigen aus
  get out of   (s.) drücken um
  get over   hinwegkommen über, wegkommen über
give   geben
  give *or* **think of**   geben auf
  give time and attention to   eingehen auf
  give up   kapitulieren vor, lassen von
(be) **glad for**   s. freuen für
glance   blicken
go
  go away (on a trip)   verreisen
  go back to   zurückgehen auf, zurückkehren zu
  go beyond   s. erheben über
  go by/beyond   gehen nach/über
  go by   vergehen
  go down   untergehen

go down well with   ankommen bei

go for/against   gehen auf/gegen

go for *or* **attack**   eindringen auf

go into   eingehen auf

go off   (s.) verlaufen

go on about   s. auslassen über

go out to   ergehen an

go over to   übergehen zu

go past *or* **by**   vorbeigehen an

go steady with   gehen mit

go to   gehen an/auf

go toward *or* **approach**   zugehen auf

go with   s. vertragen mit

be going on   gehen vor

(say) **goodbye to**   s. verabschieden von

gossip over   klatschen über

govern over   herrschen über

grab   packen

grasp   greifen

grasp with   ergreifen bei

greet   s. grüßen mit

grin   grinsen

grope for   tasten nach

grow   wachsen

grumble about   nörgeln an

guard against   s. hüten vor

guide   führen, lenken

be guided by   s. leiten lassen von

gush from   quellen aus

(be in the) **habit of**   pflegen zu

hand *or* **give in**   abgeben

handle   umgehen mit

hang   hängen

get the hang of   s. zurechtfinden mit

hang around   s. herumtreiben

happen   kommen zu

(be) **happy**

be happy for/about   s. freuen für/über

be happy with   zufrieden sein mit, s. zufriedengeben (mit)

harmonize with   harmonieren mit

haul   (s.) schleppen
have   versehen sein mit
head for *or* **aim**   halten auf/nach
hear   hören an
   hear from/about   hören von
   hear from/for   erfahren von
heat   erhitzen auf
   get heated over   s. erhitzen an/über
help
   help with   helfen bei
   help to do   verhelfen zu
hide   (s.) verstecken
hike   wandern
hit   (s.) schlagen, treffen
hold   halten
   hold (on) to   festhalten an
   take hold of   greifen
   hold up against   bestehen gegen/neben
hope
   hope for   hoffen auf
   have hope for/of   spekulieren auf
(be) **horrified at**   entsetzt sein für
hound   hetzen auf
hunt   jagen auf
identify as   identifizieren als
   identify o.s. with   s. identifizieren mit
ignore   vorübergehen an
imagine   s. vorstellen
immigrate to   einwandern in/nach
(be) **impatient with**   brennen vor
(attach) **importance to**   halten auf
impose   erkennen auf
impress   imponieren
include in   aufnehmen in, einbeziehen in, schließen in
increase to   (s.) steigern zu
indicate to   hindeuten auf
(be) **indignant**
   be indignant at   s. entrüsten über
   be indignant at/about   s. aufregen über

induce to   bewegen zu

indulge in   s. ergehen in

infect *or* **catch**   (s.) anstecken

  get infected by   s. infizieren bei/mit

infer   sehen aus

  infer from   schließen aus

(have) **influence on**   eingehen in

inform

  inform about   aufklären über, (s.) informieren über

  inform about/on   unterrichten über/von

ingratiate o.s. with   s. einschmeicheln bei

injure   (s.) verletzen

inquire about   s. erkundigen nach/über, fragen nach

insist on   beharren auf, bestehen auf, dringen auf

inspire to   inspirieren zu

insure against   (s.) versichern gegen

intend for   bestimmen für/zu, vorsehen für

(be) **intent on**   ausgehen auf

intercede with   s. verwenden für

(be) **interested in**   s. interessieren für

interfere

  interfere in   eingreifen in

  interfere with   s. einmischen in

interview

  interview about   interviewen zu

  have an interview with   s. vorstellen bei

introduce   (s.) vorstellen

  introduce to/into   einführen bei/in

invest in   investieren in

investigate   ermitteln gegen, untersuchen

invite   einladen

involve

  involve in   beteiligen an

  get involved in/with   s. einlassen auf/in/mit

  be involved   beteiligt sein

(be) **issued to**   ergehen an

itch *or* **die for**   brennen auf

join

  join in   (s.) einschalten

  join to   eintreten in

join with   (s.) vereinigen mit
be joined together   zusammenhängen mit
judge by/from   urteilen nach/über
juggle with   jonglieren mit
jump
   jump out   springen aus
   jump over   hinwegsetzen über
justify   s. verantworten für/wegen
(be very) **keen on**   versessen sein auf
keep
   keep back from   (s.) zurückhalten mit/von
   keep on at   herumreiten auf
   keep *or* **stick to**   bleiben bei
   keep up with   nachkommen mit
(be) **kept by**   s. aushalten lassen von
kick   eintreten auf, stoßen, treten
   get kicked out of   hinausfliegen aus
kill   töten
   kill o.s.   s. umbringen um
kiss   küssen
knock
   knock at/on   anklopfen an
   knock at/on/in/out   klopfen an/auf/in/von
   knock *or* **bump**   anstoßen
know
   know about/of   wissen über/von/um
   know by   erkennen an
lack   fehlen an
   lack of   mangeln an
lament over/about   jammern über
land   landen
lapse back into   zurückfallen in
laugh at   lachen über, s. lustig machen über
lay
   lay (down)   (s.) legen
   lay (value) upon   geben auf
lead   leiten
   lead to   führen in/zu, veranlassen zu
   lead back to   zurückführen auf
   lead *or* **encourage to**   verleiten zu

leaf through   blättern in
lean   stützen
  lean against/on/over/from   s. lehnen an/gegen/über/aus
  lean *or* **rest against**   (s.) anlehnen an
learn
  learn about   erfahren über
  learn from   lernen von/bei
lease to   vermieten an
let   lassen
(assume) **liability for**   einstehen für
(be) **liable for**   haften für
liberate from   (s.) befreien aus/von
lie
  lie on   ruhen auf
  lie on/with/in   liegen auf/mit/in
limit to   (s.) beschränken auf
link with   s. knüpfen an
listen
  listen for   lauschen
  listen to   hören auf
live   wohnen
  live on   leben von
  live off *or* **on**   zehren von
lock *or* **shut in**   sperren in
long for   s. sehnen nach, verlangen nach
look   blicken, gucken
  look after   s. kümmern um, sorgen für
  look around for   s. umsehen nach
  look at   (s.) ansehen
  look at/after   schauen auf/nach
  look down on   herabblicken auf
  look for   suchen nach
  look forward to   s. freuen auf
  look like   aussehen nach
  look on/onto/after/from/in   sehen an/auf/nach/aus/in
lose
  lose through   verlieren an/durch
  make (sb) lose   bringen um
(get) **lost**
  lost in   s. verlieren in

be lost   geschehen sein um
get lost   (s.) verlaufen
(be in) **love with**   verliebt sein in
lower   herabsetzen
lure   locken
(be) **mad about**   schwärmen für, fliegen auf, versessen sein auf
(be) **made out for**   lauten auf
maintain to   verharren auf/bei/in
make
  make of (sth)   machen aus
  make *or* **do it with**   machen mit
  make (sb) do   verpflichten zu
  make (sb) do   veranlassen zu
manage   schaffen
  manage on   ausreichen mit, zurechtkommen mit
march in   einziehen in
marry   heiraten, trauen, s. verheiraten mit
  get married   heiraten
match   harmonieren mit
  be match for   aufnehmen mit
  be a match for   (s.) messen mit
  be match with   passen zu
mean by   s. denken bei, meinen mit
measure with/in   messen mit/nach
meddle in   s. einmischen
meet   (s.) treffen auf/mit
(become a) **member of**   eintreten in
merge into   s. vereinigen zu
(have in) **mind for**   vorsehen für
mislead   irreführen
misplace   verlegen
(be) **mistaken about**   s. irren um
mix
  mix in   verkehren in
  mix up   verwechseln
  mix with   verkehren mit
moan
  moan over   klagen um
  moan over/about   jammern über
  moan *or* **crab about**   nörgeln über

mock spotten über

(put in the) **mood for** einstimmen auf

mourn for/over trauern über/um

move

    move in einziehen

    move *or* **transfer** verlegen

(get) **muddled up** verwechseln

murder (s.) umbringen

nag about nörgeln an

(make) **nasty remarks** lästern über

need for brauchen für/zu

negotiate

    negotiate over handeln über/um

    negotiate with verhandeln mit

nibble

    nibble at naschen an/von

    nibble on knabbern an

note down notieren

(be) **obedient to** s. fügen in

obey s. fügen

object to einwenden gegen

oblige (s.) verpflichten

(be) **occupied with** (s.) beschäftigen, beschäftigt sein mit

occur kommen zu, vorkommen

offend anstoßen bei

    offend against verstoßen gegen

(take) **office in** einziehen in

(have an) **opinion** halten von

oppose s. stellen gegen, s. wenden gegen

order bestellen, ordnen

organize to (s.) organisieren zu/als

orientate toward/to (s.) orientieren an/auf

outdo one another in s. überbieten in

(be) **outraged** s. entrüsten über

overflow with überhäuft sein mit

overlook vorbeigehen an

overwhelm with überhäufen mit

pack packen

    pack in einpacken, verpacken in

paint streichen

part (s.) trennen

participate in s. beteiligen an, mitmachen bei, teilnehmen an

(be) **particular about** sehen auf

pass

  pass by vergehen, vorübergehen an

  pass by vorbeikommen an

  pass off as s. ausgeben als

  pass on to übertragen auf

  pass over reichen

  pass to übergehen auf

pay bezahlen, zahlen

  pay for aufkommen für

  pay (the penalty) of büßen für

  pay attention to achten auf

  pay for with büßen mit

penetrate dringen

  penetrate into eindringen in

perceive wahrnehmen

persecute verfolgen

persuade to bewegen zu, überreden zu

(be) **pessimistic about** schwarzsehen für

phone *or* **call** anrufen, telefonieren

pick

  pick up abholen

  pick (sb) up s. anlachen

pierce stechen in

pinch kneifen in

place

  place *or* **fit in** einsetzen in

  place *or* **put** stellen

  place *or* **put on** stecken an

  place *or* **set on/down** setzen auf/unter

plague plagen

play machen auf

  play (around) with spielen mit

  play a part in mitwirken an/bei

  play around on herumspielen auf

  play off against ausspielen gegen

plead for/with flehen um/zu

(be) **pleased about** s. freuen über, erfreut sein über

(get) **pleasure from**   s. freuen an

point

   point at/in   deuten auf/in/nach

   point at/to   (s.) zeigen auf/nach

   point out to   hinweisen auf

   point *or* **show**   weisen

poison   (s.) vergiften

poke   stoßen

postpone

   postpone to   verschieben auf

   postpone until   verlegen auf

pounce at   s. stürzen auf

pour *or* **well from**   quellen aus

practice   (s.) üben in

prefer *or* **side with**   halten mit

prepare   (s.) präparieren

   prepare for   (s.) vorbereiten auf/für

press

   press for/to   drängen auf/zu

   press on   drücken auf/an

   press *or* **prop**   stemmen

prevail against   aufkommen gegen, s. durchsetzen gegen

prevent from   bewahren vor, hindern an

prick   (s.) stechen

prohibit   verbieten

promote   werben für

(be) **prone to**   disponiert sein für/zu, neigen zu

protect

   protect o.s. against   s. sichern gegen/vor

   protect against/from   (s.) schützen gegen/vor

protest about/against   protestieren gegen

provide with   versorgen mit

provoke to   reizen zu

pull

   pull (behind) o.s.   herziehen hinter

   pull on   reißen an

   pull on/to/from   ziehen an/auf/aus

pull *or* **draw back**   (s.) zurückziehen

pull *or* **tug at**   zerren an

punish

  punish for/to   bestrafen für/mit

  be punished with   stehen auf

pursue with   verfolgen mit

push   (s.) drängen, drücken, (s.) schieben

  push *or* **shove**   stoßen

put

  put *or* **place**   stellen, setzen, tun

  put (aside)   s. schieben von

  put (sb) in (sth)   s. versetzen in

  put down   herziehen über

  put sb in the picture *or* **orientate about**   orientieren über

  put o.s. in sb's position   s. hineinversetzen in

  put on   versehen mit

  put on   ansetzen auf, auftragen auf

  put *or* **fit**   einsetzen

  put *or* **place on**   stecken an

  put up against   anlegen

  put up *or* **put**   unterbringen

qualify for/to be   (s.) qualifizieren für/zu

quarrel

  quarrel about   (s.) streiten über/von

  quarrel with   s. anlegen mit, s. auseinandersetzen mit, s. zanken mit

quit (doing)   aufhören mit

race   rasen

rage *or* **storm at**   wüten gegen

rail against   s. aufhalten über

rave with   rasen vor

reach   gelangen zu, zugehen

  reach for   greifen zu/nach

react   s. verhalten

  react to   reagieren auf

read   lesen

  read from   ablesen aus

receive with   quittieren mit

reckon on/with   rechnen auf/mit

recommend to   raten zu
reconcile with   aussöhnen mit, vereinbaren mit, (s.) versöhnen mit
reduce   herabsetzen, zerlegen in
refer   überweisen
   refer to   s. beziehen auf, verweisen an/auf, zurückkommen auf
reflect
   reflect in   s. widerspiegeln in
   reflect on   nachdenken über, sinnen über, zurückfallen auf
   reflect on/upon   reflektieren über
   be reflected in   s. niederschlagen in
refrain from   (s.) zurückhalten mit
(take) **refuge in**   s. flüchten in
regard as   zählen zu
rejoice about   jubeln über
rely on   s. verlassen auf, zählen auf
remain   bleiben
remember   s. erinnern an
remind of   erinnern an
rent to   vermieten an
replace with/by   ersetzen durch
reply to   antworten auf, entgegnen auf, erwidern auf
report
   report on   berichten über/von
   report to   (s.) melden bei
represent   stehen für, vertreten
rescue from   retten aus/vor
resemble   schlagen nach
reserve   buchen
resign o.s. to   s. schicken in
resort to   s. flüchten in, greifen zu, s. verlegen auf
respond to   eingehen auf
(be) **responsible for**   haften für, verantwortlich sein für
rest
   rest on   liegen auf
   rest *or* **lean against**   (s.) anlehnen an
restrain   (s.) zurückhalten mit
result
   result from   s. ergeben aus, folgen aus, hervorgehen aus
   result in   s. niederschlagen in

retire   (s.) zurückziehen

return

   return to   zurückkehren zu

   return *or* **come back to**   zurückkommen auf

(take) **revenge on**   s. rächen an

reverse   (s.) verkehren in

revolve (around)   s. drehen um

rhyme with   (s.) reimen auf/mit

(be) **riddled with**   starren von/vor

ride

   ride on   reiten auf

   be taken for a ride by   hereinfallen auf

ridicule   spotten über

(be) **right** *or* **correct**   stimmen

ripen   reifen zu

risk to do   (s.) wagen zu

roam   irren, wandern

   roam (through)   streifen durch

roll   (s.) wälzen

(be) **rooted in**   wurzeln in

rub on/against   (s.) reiben an

rule (over)   herrschen über

run   laufen

   run for/against   kandidieren für/gegen

   run to/against   rennen gegen

   run away from   fliehen vor

   be run down   heruntersein

   run into   stoßen auf

   run *or* **bump against**   (s.) stoßen angegen

   run *or* **flow**   rinnen

   run through   (s.) ziehen durch

   run towards   zulaufen auf

rush   hetzen

(be) **satisfied with**   zufrieden sein mit

save

   save from   retten aus/vor

   save up for   sparen auf/für

say   äußern, sagen, vorbringen

(be) **scared at**   erschrecken über

scold   schimpfen mit

score   schießen

scramble (to get)   s. reißen um

search

   search after   forschen nach

   search for   durchsuchen nach, suchen nach

seduce   verführen

see   (s.) ansehen

   see on/in/from   (s.) sehen an/in/aus

seek   suchen

seem   vorkommen

(be) **seized with**   ergreifen von

select   wählen

sell to   verkaufen an

send   geben, senden

   send to/for   schicken an/nach

(be) **sentenced to**   verurteilt sein zu

separate   scheiden

   separate from   (s.) trennen aus/von

serve as   dienen als/zu

set

   set against   einnehmen gegen

   set for   decken für

   set off for   s. auf den Weg machen

   set up as   s. niederlassen als

settle (down)   s. niederlassen

   settle down in   s. eingewöhnen in, s. einleben

   settle up with   abrechnen mit

sew on   nähen an/auf

shake *or* **tremble with**   zittern vor

share with   s. teilen mit

shield   s. stellen vor

shift to   wälzen auf

shirk   (s.) drücken vor

(be) **shocked**   s. entrüsten über

   be shocked at   (s.) erschrecken bei

shoot   schießen

(there is a) **shortage**   hapern an

shout for   schreien nach

show   (s.) zeigen
   show around   führen durch
   show how to do   bekannt machen mit
   show *or* **point**   weisen
shrug off with   abtun mit
shut *or* **lock in**   sperren in
shy away from   zurückschrecken vor
side with *or* **prefer**   halten mit
sign up for   (s.) melden
signify with   bezeichnen mit
sink   sinken, untergehen
   sink into   s. graben in, verfallen in
sit   sitzen
   sit down   s. niederlassen
   sit down with   s. setzen zu
   sit up with   wachen bei
(be) **situated**   s. befinden
slam   knallen
slap   (s.) klatschen, schlagen
sleep *or* **stay at**   übernachten bei
slip on *or* **over/in/off**   (s.) streifen über/in/von
smack   (s.) klatschen
smell
   smell at/of/from   riechen an/aus/nach
   smell of   duften nach
smile at   anlachen
snap at   schnappen nach
snatch out of   reißen aus/von
sneak   (s.) schleichen
snuggle up to   s. anschmiegen an
solicit   werben um
sound   rufen
(be) **sparing with**   sparen an/mit
speak
   speak for/against/about   sprechen für/gegen/über/von
   speak of   s. aussprechen über
   speak to   ansprechen
   speak with/about/of   reden mit/über/von
specialize in   s. spezialisieren auf

spend

  spend on/for ausgeben für

  spend (time) verbringen, (s.) aufhalten

  spend on verwenden auf

spit spucken

splash spritzen

split from s. trennen von

spray spritzen

spread um sich greifen, streichen, (s.) verbreiten

  spread over s. ausdehnen auf/über, decken über

spring springen

squabble with s. zanken mit

squat (s.) hocken

squeeze herumdrücken an

stab

  stab at stechen nach

  stab in/through (s.) jagen in/durch

stand aushalten

  stand by halten zu, stehen zu

  stand in for vertreten

  stand up for eintreten für

  stand up to bestehen vor

staple to heften an

stare at starren auf

start

  start doing s. begeben

  start out from ausgehen von

state vorbringen

stay bleiben

  stay at unterkommen bei

  stay the night übernachten

steer lenken

step on treten auf

stick

  stick on ankleben an

  stick to haften an, kleben an

  stick *or* **keep to** bleiben bei

  stick *or* **stay with** s. halten an

sting   (s.) stechen

(be) **stingy with**   geizen mit

stink of   stinken nach

stir up against   hetzen gegen

stock up with/on   s. eindecken mit

stop   aufhören mit, halten

   stop or **drop by**   vorbeifahren, vorbeigehen bei

storm or **rage at**   wüten gegen

strain   zerren

   strain or **exert**   s. anstrengen

stretch   s. erstrecken, reichen

strike   streiken

   strike out   streichen aus

string on   reihen auf

strive for   s. bemühen um, streben nach

stroke with   (s.) streichen mit

stroll   bummeln

struggle with   s. herumschlagen mit

(be) **stuck**   stecken

study   studieren

stuff in   füllen in

submit to   s. ergeben in

substitute for   einwechseln für

(be) **successful with**   s. durchsetzen mit

sue   klagen gegen

suffer from   kranken an, leiden an/unter, tragen an

(be) **sufficient**   ausreichen

suit   passen zu

   be suited for   geeignet sein für/zu/als

(be) **suitable for**   s. eignen als/für/zu, taugen für/zu

summon as   bestellen zu

supply   eindecken, liefern

support   (s.) stützen

(make) **sure of**   s. vergewissern über

surpass in   (s.) überbieten in, übertreffen an/in

surprise   überraschen

   be surprised at/about   s. wundern über

surround with/by   (s.) umgeben mit/von

swear
   swear by   schwören auf/bei
   swear to   schwören auf
sweat   schwitzen
swim   schwimmen
switch   schalten
   switch over   umschalten
   switch over to   umstellen auf
tack to   heften an
take
   take upon/out/for   nehmen an/auf/aus/von/für
   take after   geraten nach
   take for   halten für
   take part in   teilnehmen an
   take second place to   zurückstehen hinter
   take turns with   s. abwechseln mit
talk   reden
   talk about   erzählen über/von
   talk to/in front of   sprechen mit/vor
   talk to/with   s. unterhalten mit
   talk around   vorbeireden an
tap on   (s.) tippen an/auf/gegen
taste of   schmecken nach
teach   anleiten zu, unterrichten
tear in   reißen in
tease about   necken mit
(make a) **telephone call to**   telefonieren mit
tell about   erzählen über/von, sagen über/von
tempt to   verlocken zu
tend to   neigen zu
(be) **terrified of**   zittern vor
testify
   testify for/against   aussagen für/gegen
   testify for/against/to   zeugen für/gegen/von
thank for   s. bedanken bei, danken für
think of/in/about   denken an/in/über/von
threaten with   drohen mit
throw out   hinauswerfen
   throw at/about   (s.) werfen auf/mit

throw to/at   (s.) schmeißen auf
   throw o.s. into   stürzen in
tie
   tie (down) to   (s.) festlegen auf
   tie to   knüpfen an
   tie (up) to   s. binden an
   tie o.s. to   s. ketten an
(have a good) **time at**   s. amüsieren bei
torment   (s.) quälen
(be in) **touch with**   unterhalten zu
touch *or* **brush**   streifen
(give a) **tour of**   führen durch
trade
   trade in/with   handeln mit
   trade in with   treiben mit
transfer   überweisen, versetzen
   transfer to   übertragen auf
   transfer *or* **move**   verlegen
translate   übersetzen
transmit   übertragen
travel   reisen
   go travel   fahren
treat   umgehen mit
tremble *or* **shake with**   zittern vor
triumph over   siegen über/gegen
trouble over/about   s. bemühen um
(have) **trust in**   vertrauen auf
try   versuchen mit
   try on   (s.) anpassen
tune to   einstellen auf
turn   abbiegen, (s.) drehen an
   turn into   s. auswachsen zu, machen zu
   turn over/away/to   (s.) wenden in/von/zu
   turn to *or* **ask**   s. halten an
   turn into   verwandeln in
   turn *or* **switch**   schalten
   turn out   geraten
   turn to *or* **become**   werden zu
twist   (s.) verziehen
twitch   zucken

understand   s. einfühlen in
  understand by   s. vorstellen unter
  understand by/about   verstehen unter/von
(be) **uninterested in**   desinteressiert sein an
unite   s. verbinden mit
  unite with   s. vereinigen
(be) **up to**   liegen bei
urge (to do)   drängen zu
(be) **urgent**   eilen mit
use   verbrauchen, verwenden
  use as   benutzen als
  be of use   nutzen or nützen
(be) **used to**   gewöhnt sein an
  get used to   s. eingewöhnen, s. einleben, s. gewöhnen, zurechtfinden mit
(be) **useful for**   zu gebrauchen sein zu/als
  be useful to   nutzen zu
utter *or* **say**   von s. geben
vent out on   auslassen an
venture to do   s. wagen an
visit   kommen zu
voice *or* **express about**   s. äußern über
vomit   von s. geben
vote
  vote for   stimmen für/gegen
  vote on   abstimmen über
vouch for   einstehen für
wait for/with   warten auf/mit
walk on   treten auf
wander   irren, wandern
want   verlangen
warn
  warn against   abraten von
  warn of   warnen vor
  warn on account of   mahnen wegen
wash   waschen
waste on   verschwenden an/auf/für
watch
  watch out for   aufpassen auf
  watch over   wachen über

watch out for   s. hüten vor

wave   winken

wear   tragen

  wear out   zehren an

(be) **wedded to**   verheiratet sein mit

weep   (s.) weinen

weigh heavily on   lasten auf

whine for   jammern nach

whistle   pfeifen

win   gewinnen

  win over to   einnehmen für

wish   (s.) wünschen

withdraw   (s.) zurückziehen

  withdraw from   zurücktreten von

woo *or* **attract**   werben um

work

  work for/against   wirken für/gegen

  work on/for/against/toward   arbeiten an/für/gegen/zu

  work out   klappen

  work o.s. up into   s. hineinsteigern in

  work *or* **busy o.s. with**   s. betätigen mit

  work *or* **research on**   arbeiten über

  be working on   bauen an

worry about   s. machen aus

  be worried about   besorgt sein über, Angst haben um, s. sorgen um

wrap

  wrap in   verpacken

  wrap in/around   (s.) wickeln in/um

  wrap (up) in   (s.) hüllen in

write to/on/about   schreiben an/über/von

(be) **wrong about**   s. irren in

yearn for   schmachten nach, (s.) sehnen nach

yield *or* **give way to**   weichen von/vor